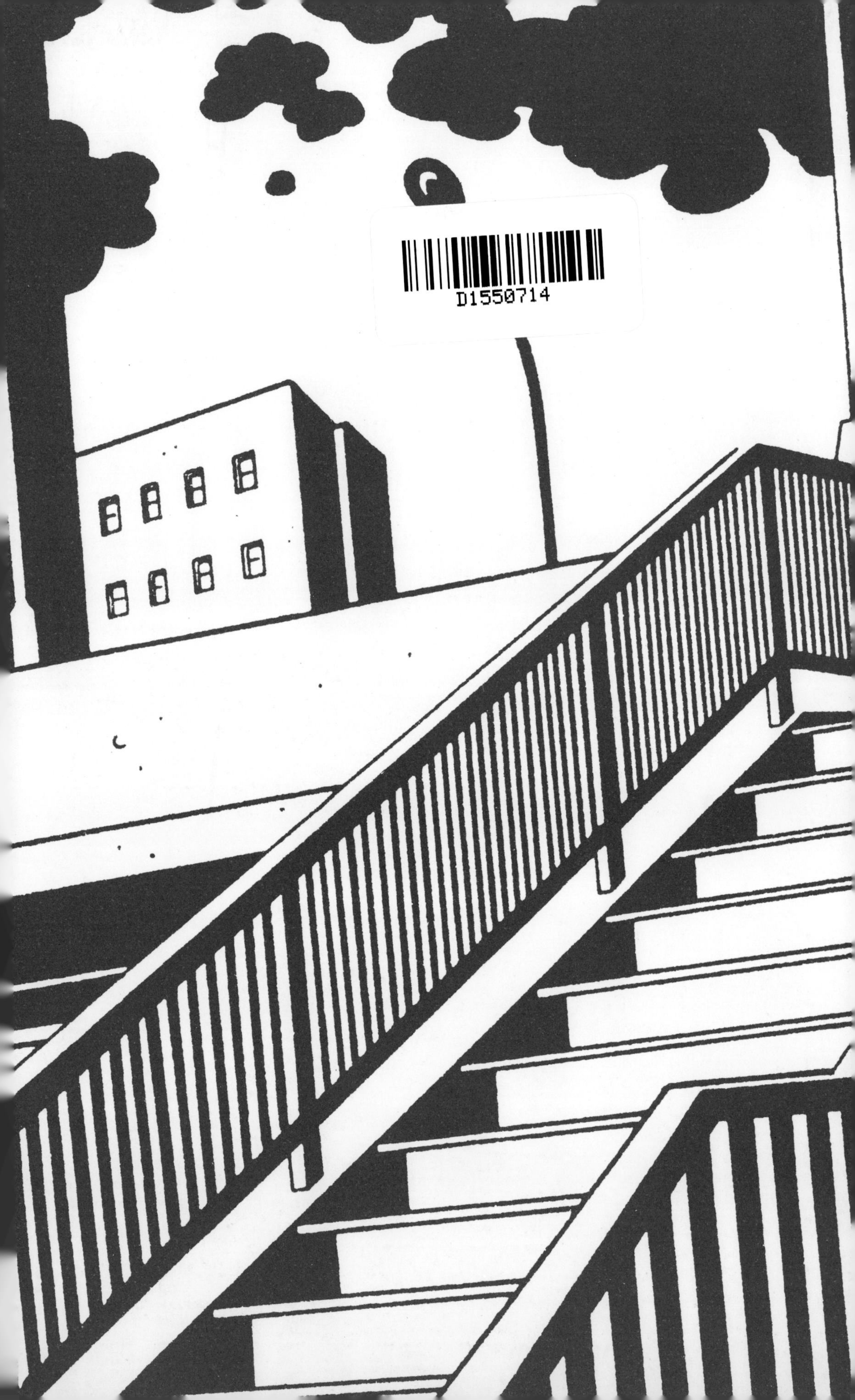

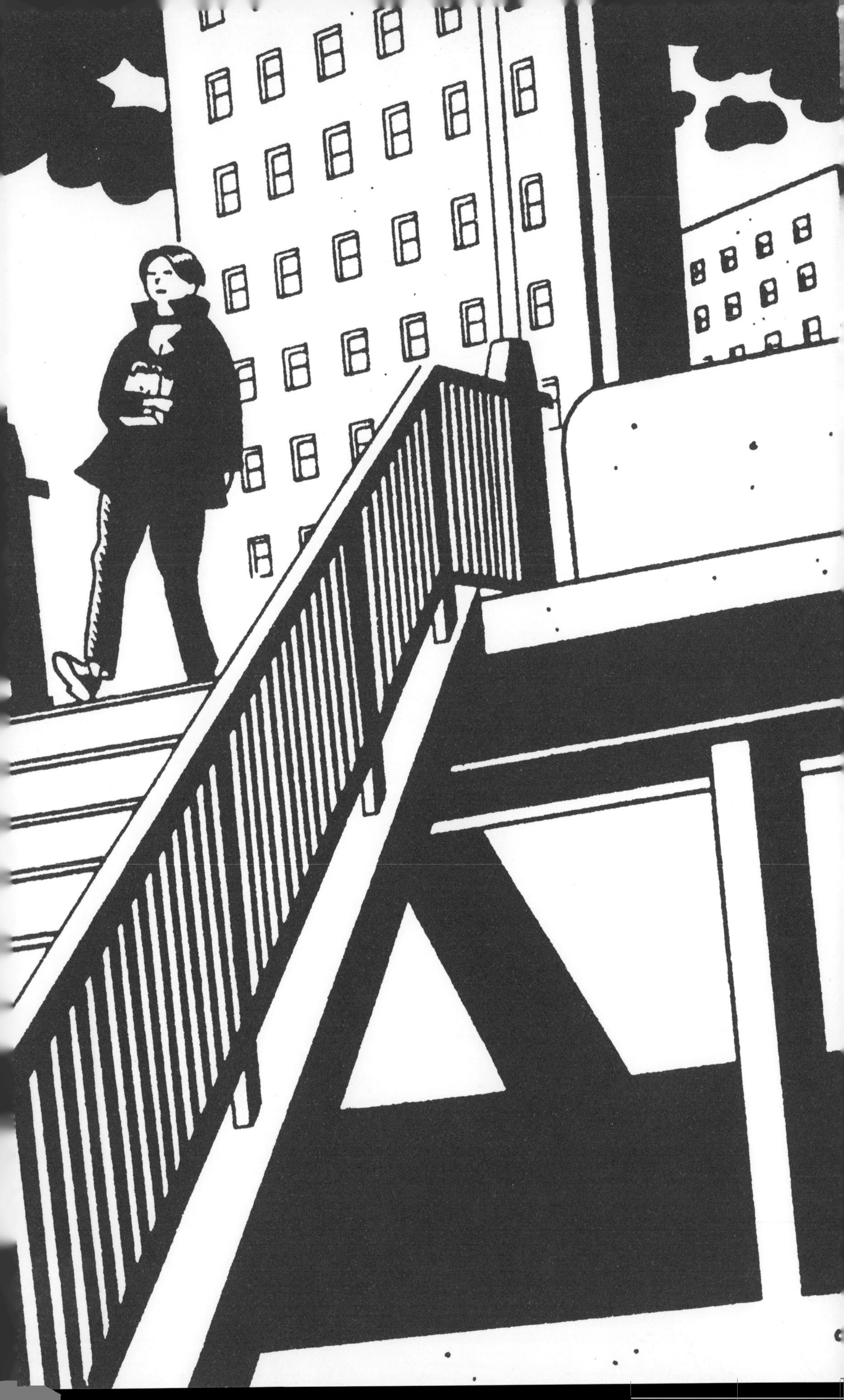

THE HORROR

OF COLLIER COUNTY

PUBLISHER
Mike Richardson

SERIES EDITOR
Diana Schutz

COLLECTION EDITOR
Daniel Chabon

ASSISTANT EDITORS
Brett Israel and Chuck Howitt

DESIGNER
Brennan Thome

DIGITAL ART TECHNICIAN
Adam Pruett

 Facebook.com/DarkHorseComics
 Twitter.com/DarkHorseComics

Advertising Sales: (503) 905-2315

To find a comics shop in your area, visit comicshoplocator.com.

THE HORROR OF COLLIER COUNTY

This volume collects *The Horror of Collier County* #1–#5.

Published by
Dark Horse Books
A division of
Dark Horse Comics LLC
10956 SE Main Street
Milwaukie, OR 97222

DarkHorse.com

First hardcover edition: May 2019
ISBN 978-1-50670-995-6

1 3 5 7 9 10 8 6 4 2
Printed in China

Library of Congress Cataloging-in-Publication Data

Names: Tommaso, Rich, author, illustrator.
Title: The horror of Collier County / written and illustrated by Rich Tommaso.
Description: 20th anniversary edition. | First hardcover edition. |
  Milwaukie, OR : Dark Horse Books, May 2019. | "This volume collects The
  Horror of Collier County #1–#5."--Title page verso.
Identifiers: LCCN 2018057155 | ISBN 9781506709956 (hardback)
Subjects: LCSH: Comic books, strips, etc. | BISAC: COMICS & GRAPHIC NOVELS /
  Horror. | COMICS & GRAPHIC NOVELS / Manga / Science Fiction.
Classification: LCC PN6727.T65 H66 2019 | DDC 741.5/973--dc23
LC record available at https://lccn.loc.gov/2018057155

THE HORROR
OF COLLIER COUNTY

WRITTEN AND ILLUSTRATED BY RICH TOMMASO

DARK HORSE BOOKS

CONTENTS

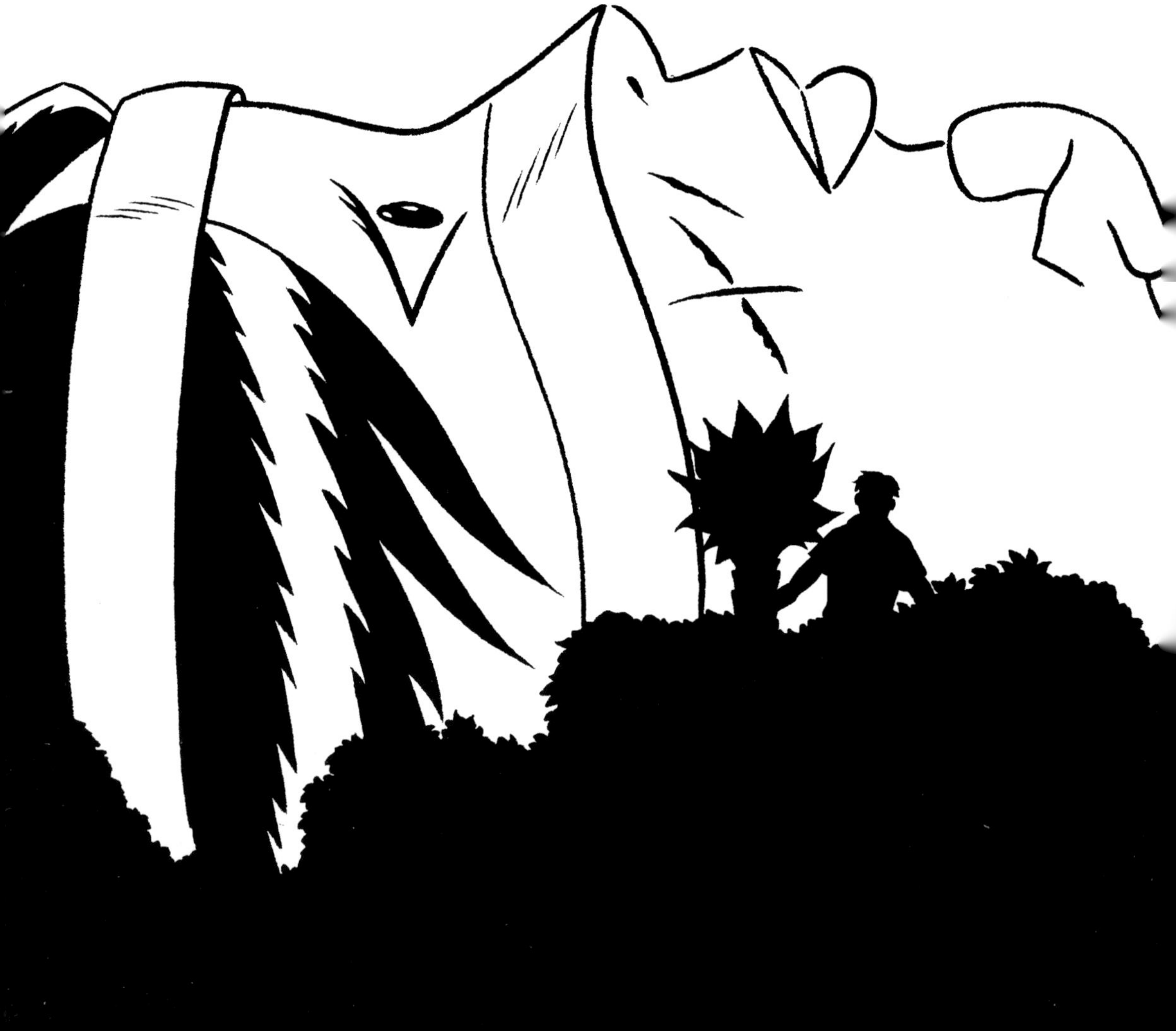

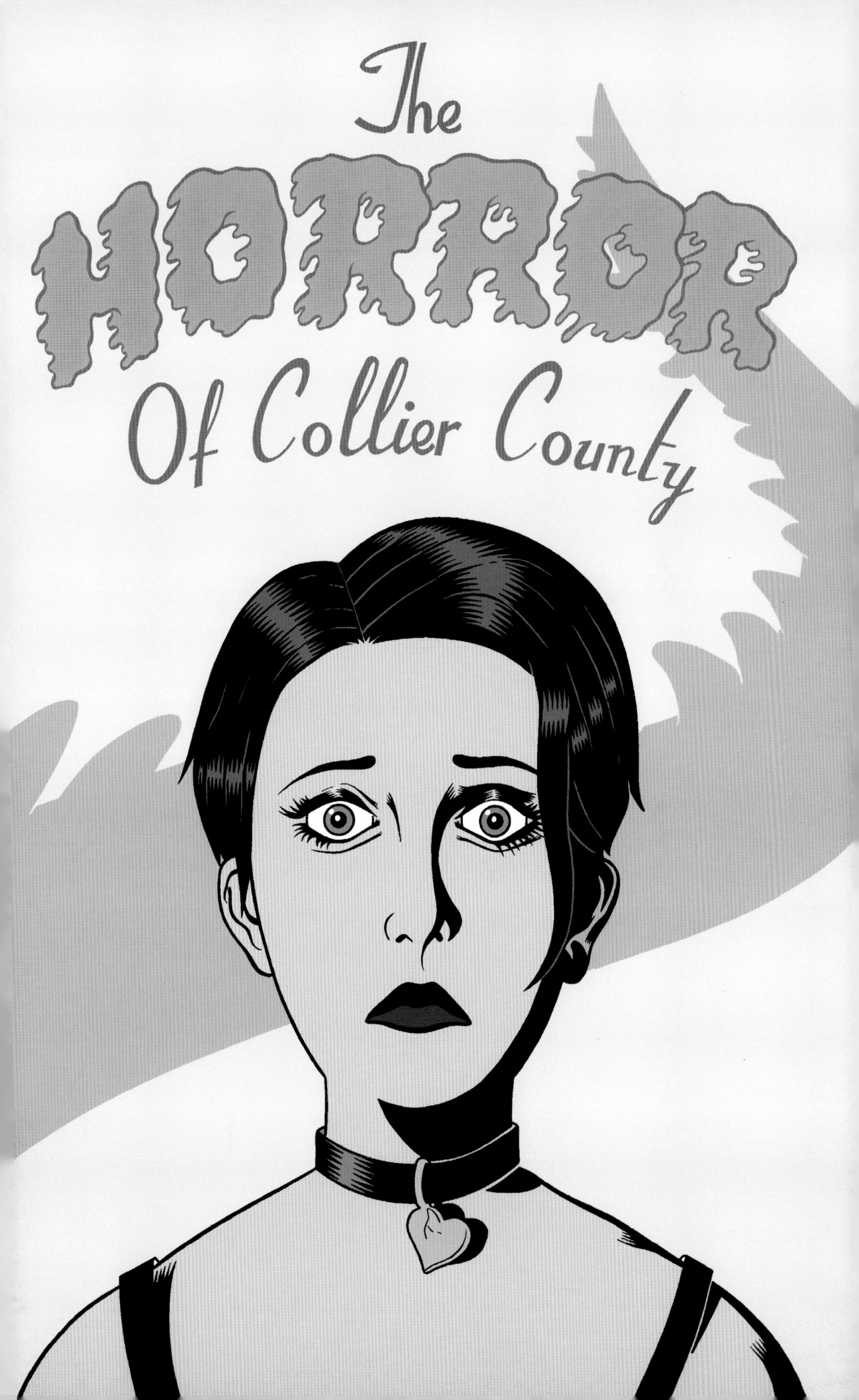
The
HORROR
Of Collier County

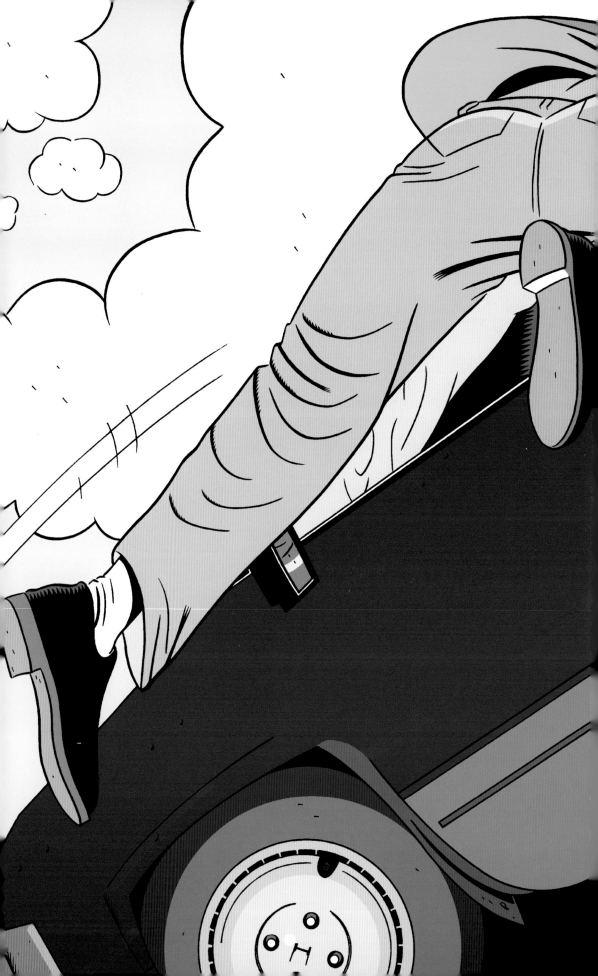

CHAPTER ONE

"THEM"

BY RICH TOMMASO

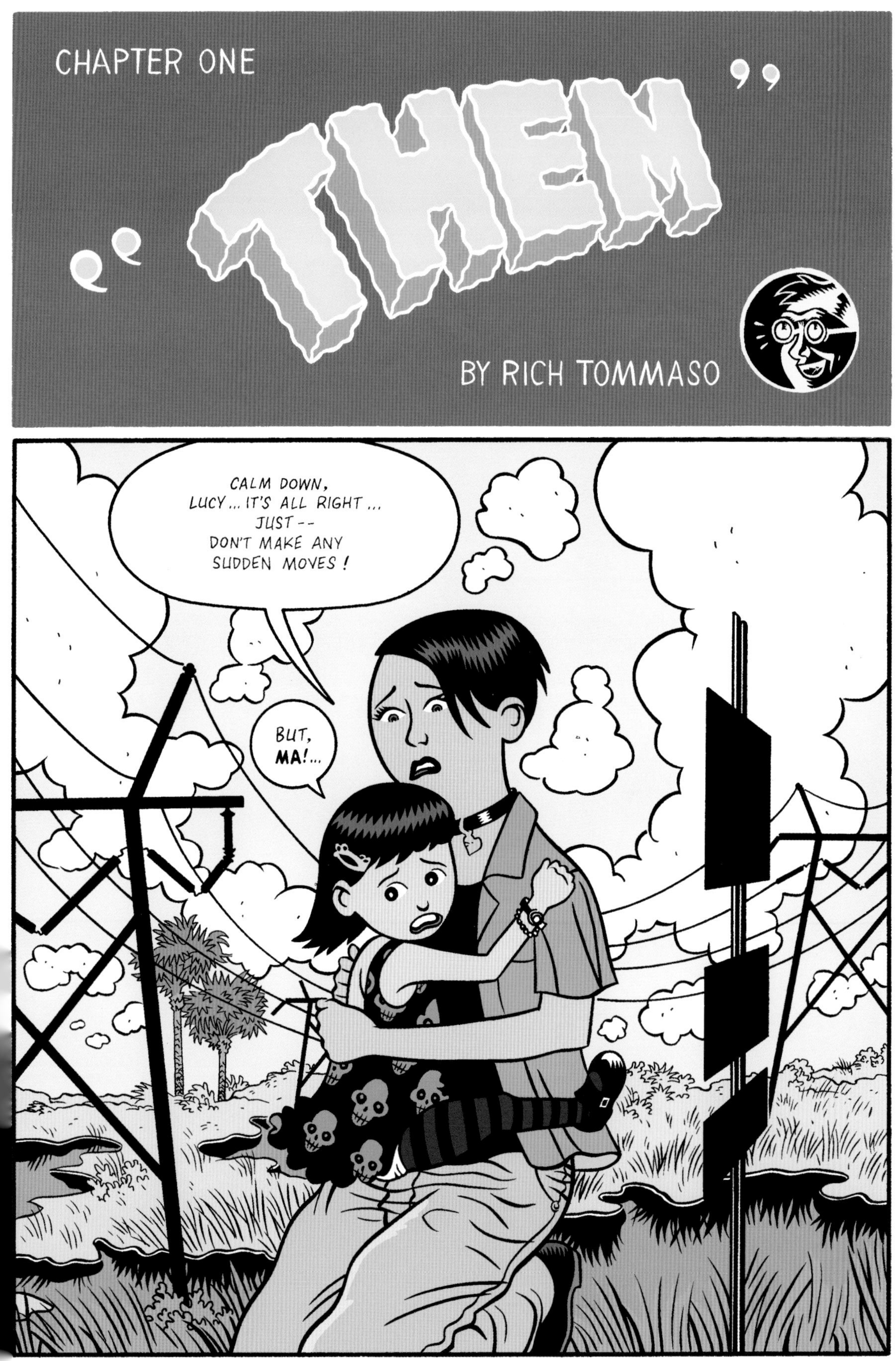

CALM DOWN, LUCY... IT'S ALL RIGHT... JUST -- DON'T MAKE ANY SUDDEN MOVES!
BUT, **MA!**...

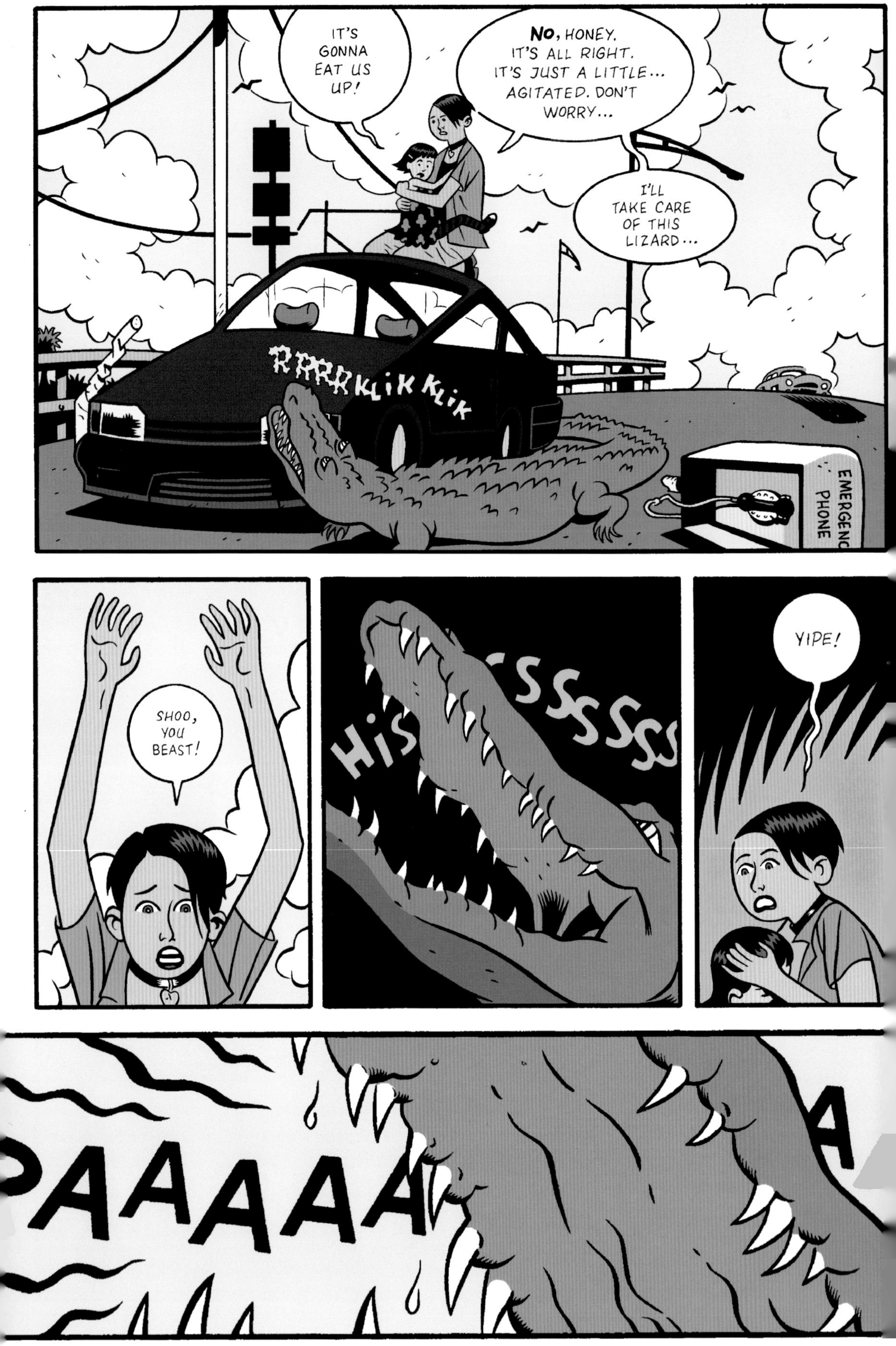
IT'S GONNA EAT US UP!
NO, HONEY. IT'S ALL RIGHT. IT'S JUST A LITTLE... AGITATED. DON'T WORRY...
I'LL TAKE CARE OF THIS LIZARD...
RRRRKLIK KLIK
EMERGENC PHONE
SHOO, YOU BEAST!
HISSSSSSS
YIPE!
AAAAAA
A

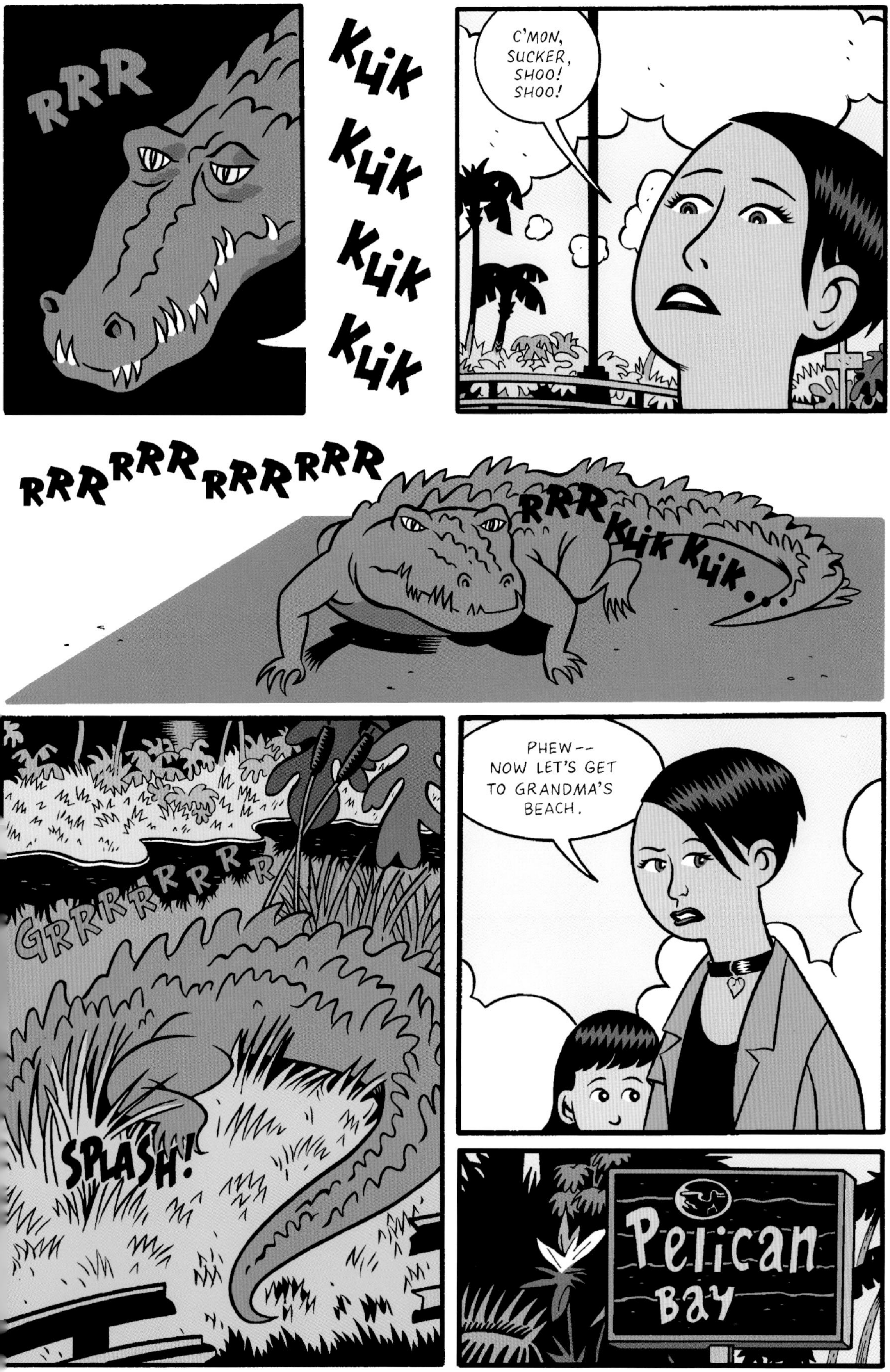
RRR
KUK
KUK
KUK
KUK
C'MON, SUCKER, SHOO! SHOO!
RRRRRRRRRRRRR
RRR
KUK KUK...
GRRRRRRRR
SPLASH!
PHEW-- NOW LET'S GET TO GRANDMA'S BEACH.
Pelican Bay

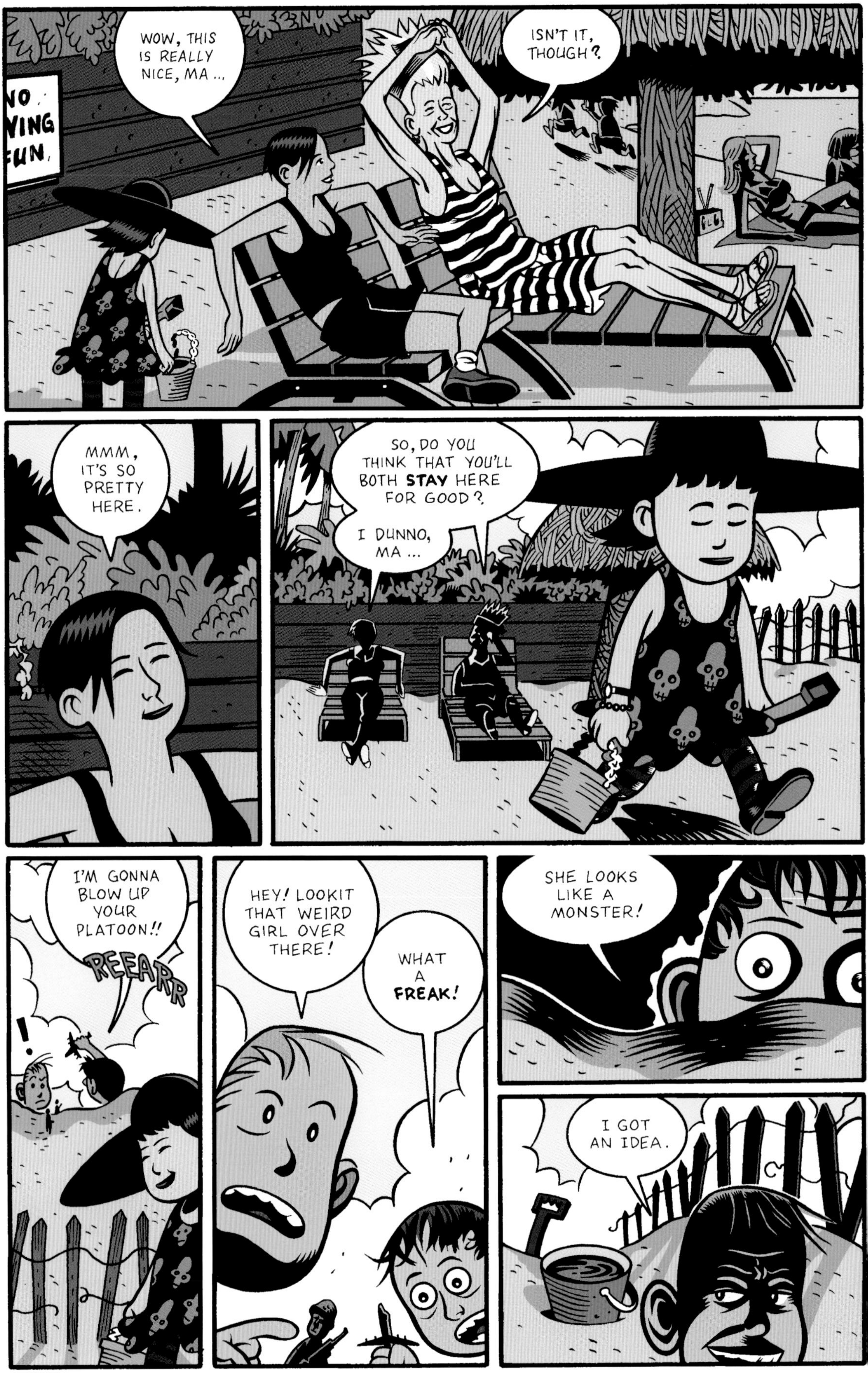
NO
WING
FUN
WOW, THIS IS REALLY NICE, MA ...
ISN'T IT, THOUGH?
MMM, IT'S SO PRETTY HERE.
SO, DO YOU THINK THAT YOU'LL BOTH **STAY** HERE FOR GOOD?
I DUNNO, MA ...
I'M GONNA BLOW UP YOUR PLATOON!!
REEARRR
!
HEY! LOOKIT THAT WEIRD GIRL OVER THERE!
WHAT A **FREAK!**
SHE LOOKS LIKE A MONSTER!
I GOT AN IDEA.

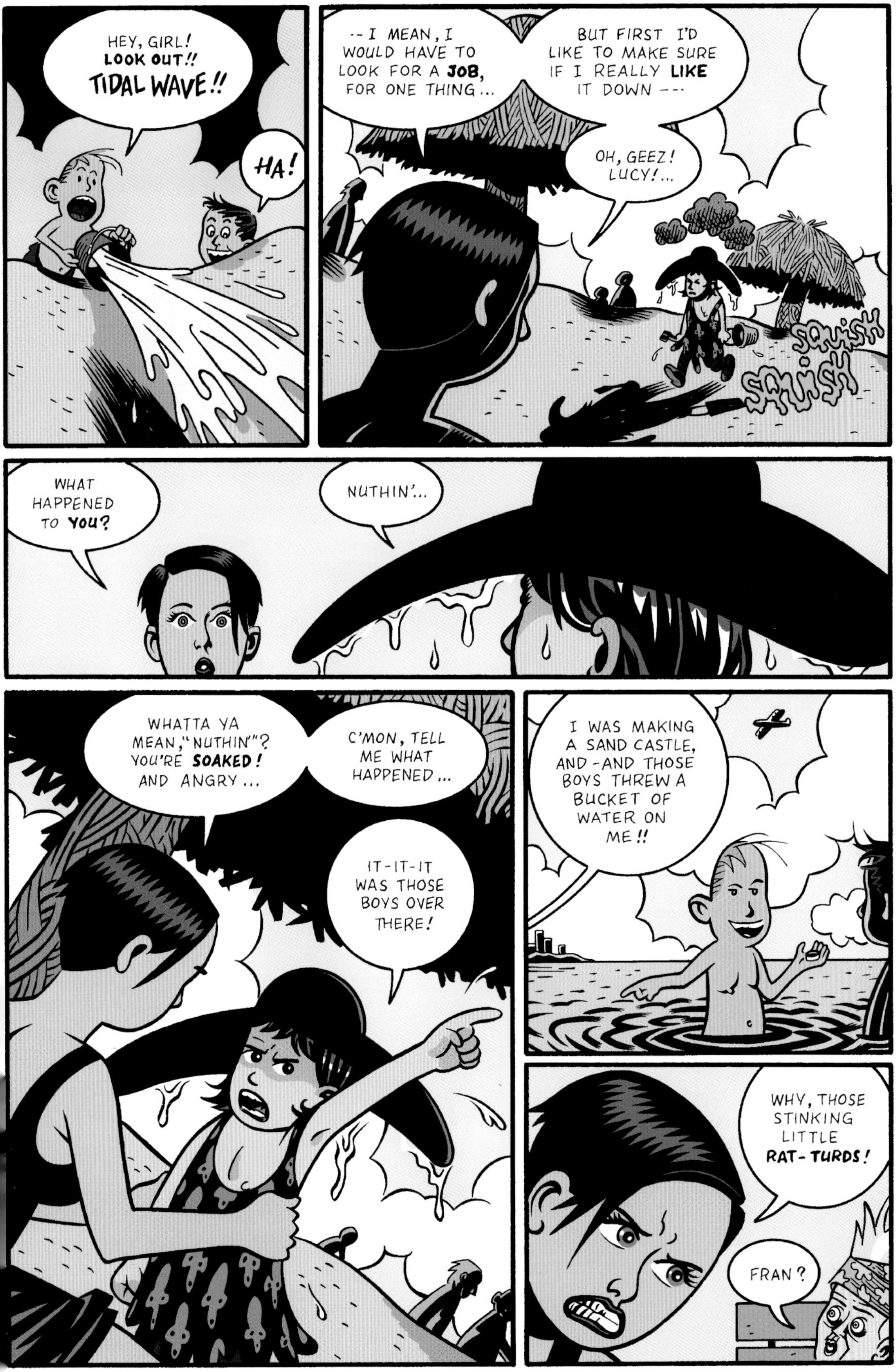
HEY, GIRL! LOOK OUT!! TIDAL WAVE!!
HA!
--I MEAN, I WOULD HAVE TO LOOK FOR A JOB, FOR ONE THING...
BUT FIRST I'D LIKE TO MAKE SURE IF I REALLY LIKE IT DOWN ---
OH, GEEZ! LUCY!...
SQUISH
SQUISH
WHAT HAPPENED TO YOU?
NUTHIN'...
WHATTA YA MEAN, "NUTHIN'"? YOU'RE SOAKED! AND ANGRY...
C'MON, TELL ME WHAT HAPPENED...
IT-IT-IT WAS THOSE BOYS OVER THERE!
I WAS MAKING A SAND CASTLE, AND-AND THOSE BOYS THREW A BUCKET OF WATER ON ME!!
WHY, THOSE STINKING LITTLE RAT-TURDS!
FRAN?

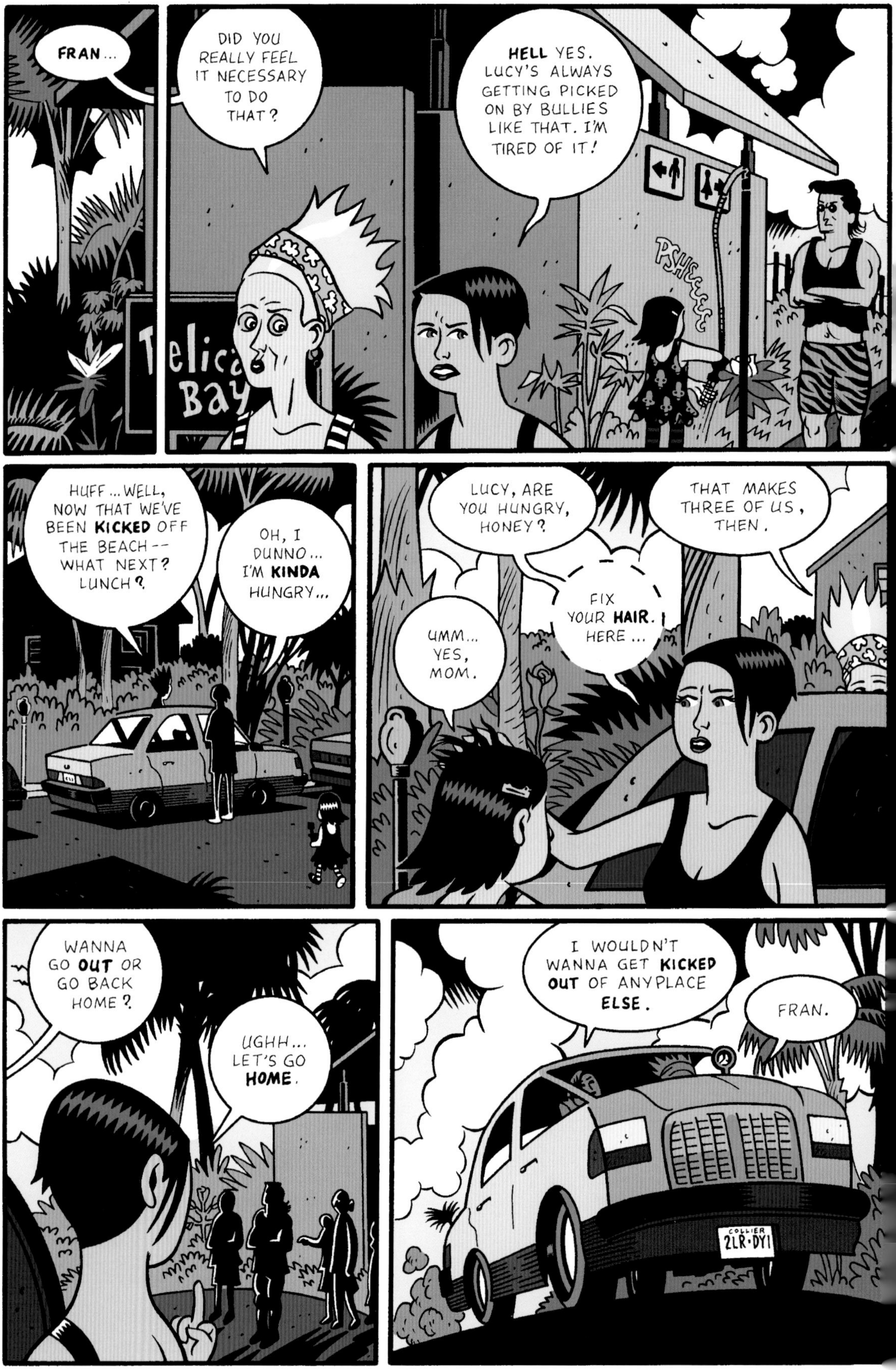
FRAN...
DID YOU REALLY FEEL IT NECESSARY TO DO THAT?
Pelica Bay
HELL YES. LUCY'S ALWAYS GETTING PICKED ON BY BULLIES LIKE THAT. I'M TIRED OF IT!
PSHEEEEE
HUFF... WELL, NOW THAT WE'VE BEEN KICKED OFF THE BEACH-- WHAT NEXT? LUNCH?
OH, I DUNNO... I'M KINDA HUNGRY...
LUCY, ARE YOU HUNGRY, HONEY?
THAT MAKES THREE OF US, THEN.
FIX YOUR HAIR. HERE...
UMM... YES, MOM.
WANNA GO OUT OR GO BACK HOME?
UGHH... LET'S GO HOME.
I WOULDN'T WANNA GET KICKED OUT OF ANYPLACE ELSE.
FRAN.
COLLIER
2LR·DY1

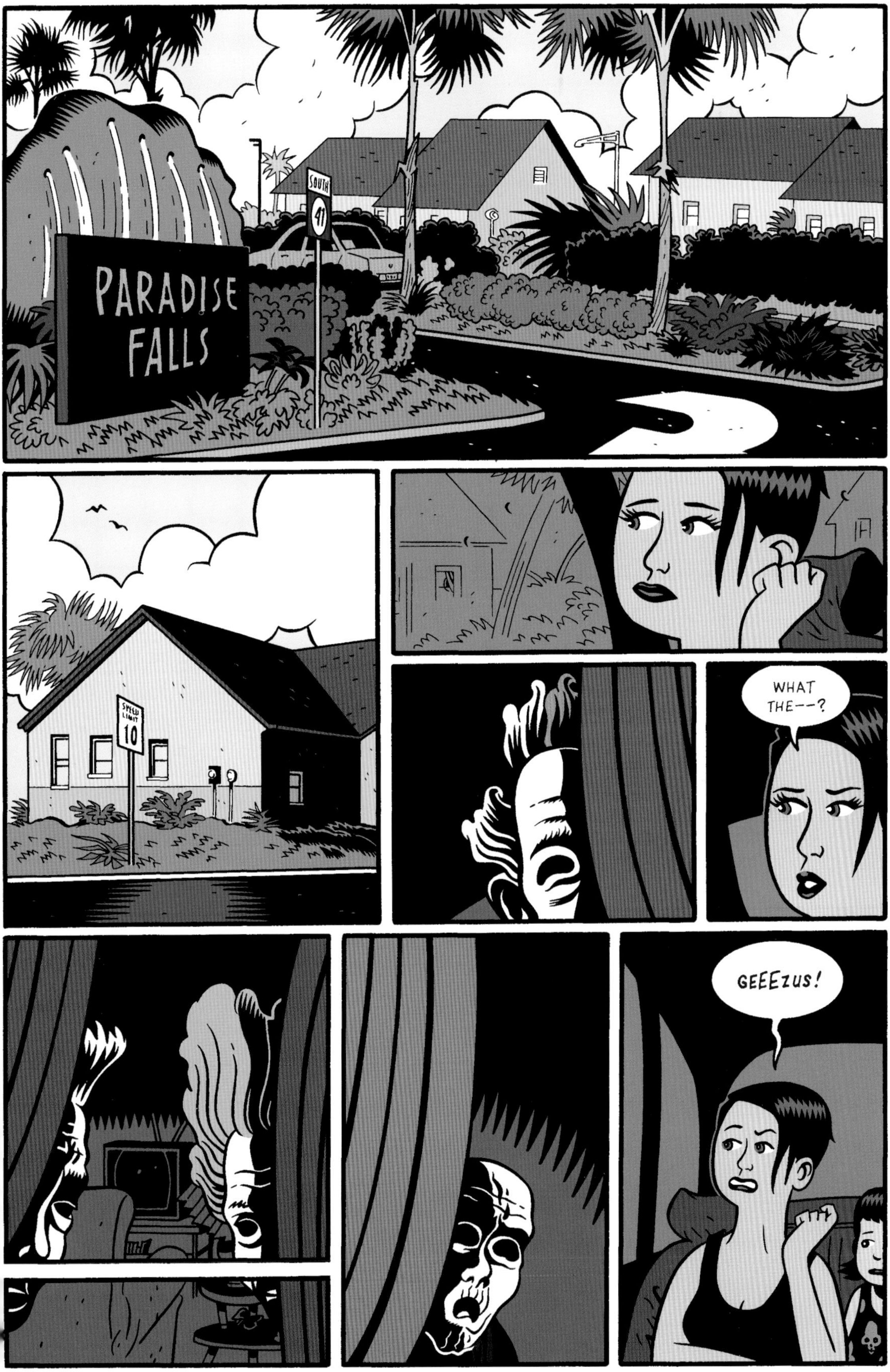
PARADISE FALLS
SOUTH
41
SPEED LIMIT
10
WHAT THE--?
GEEEzus!

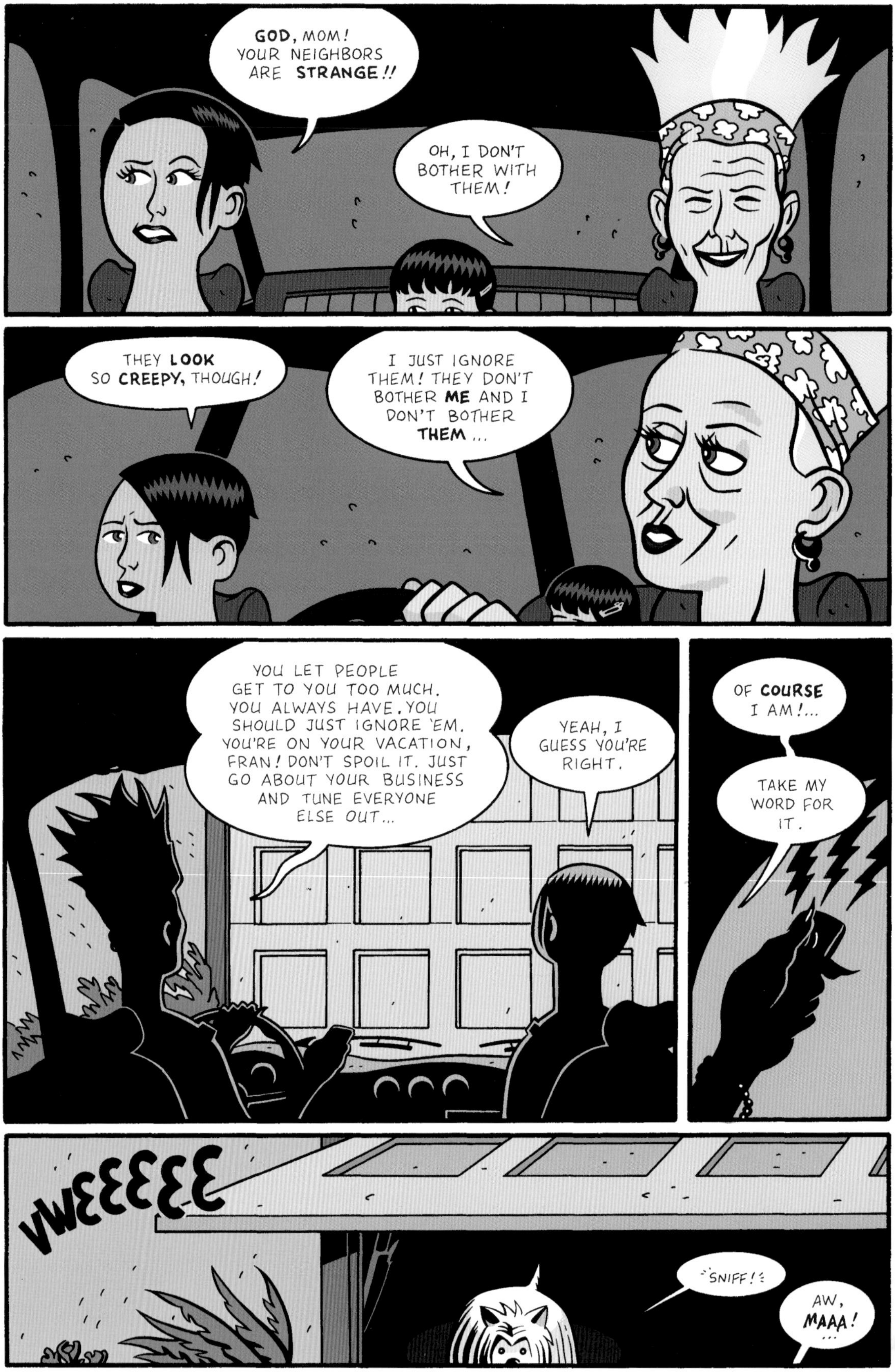
GOD, MOM! YOUR NEIGHBORS ARE STRANGE!!
OH, I DON'T BOTHER WITH THEM!
THEY LOOK SO CREEPY, THOUGH!
I JUST IGNORE THEM! THEY DON'T BOTHER ME AND I DON'T BOTHER THEM...
YOU LET PEOPLE GET TO YOU TOO MUCH. YOU ALWAYS HAVE. YOU SHOULD JUST IGNORE 'EM. YOU'RE ON YOUR VACATION, FRAN! DON'T SPOIL IT. JUST GO ABOUT YOUR BUSINESS AND TUNE EVERYONE ELSE OUT...
YEAH, I GUESS YOU'RE RIGHT.
OF COURSE I AM!...
TAKE MY WORD FOR IT.
VWEEEEE
SNIFF!
AW, MAAA! ...

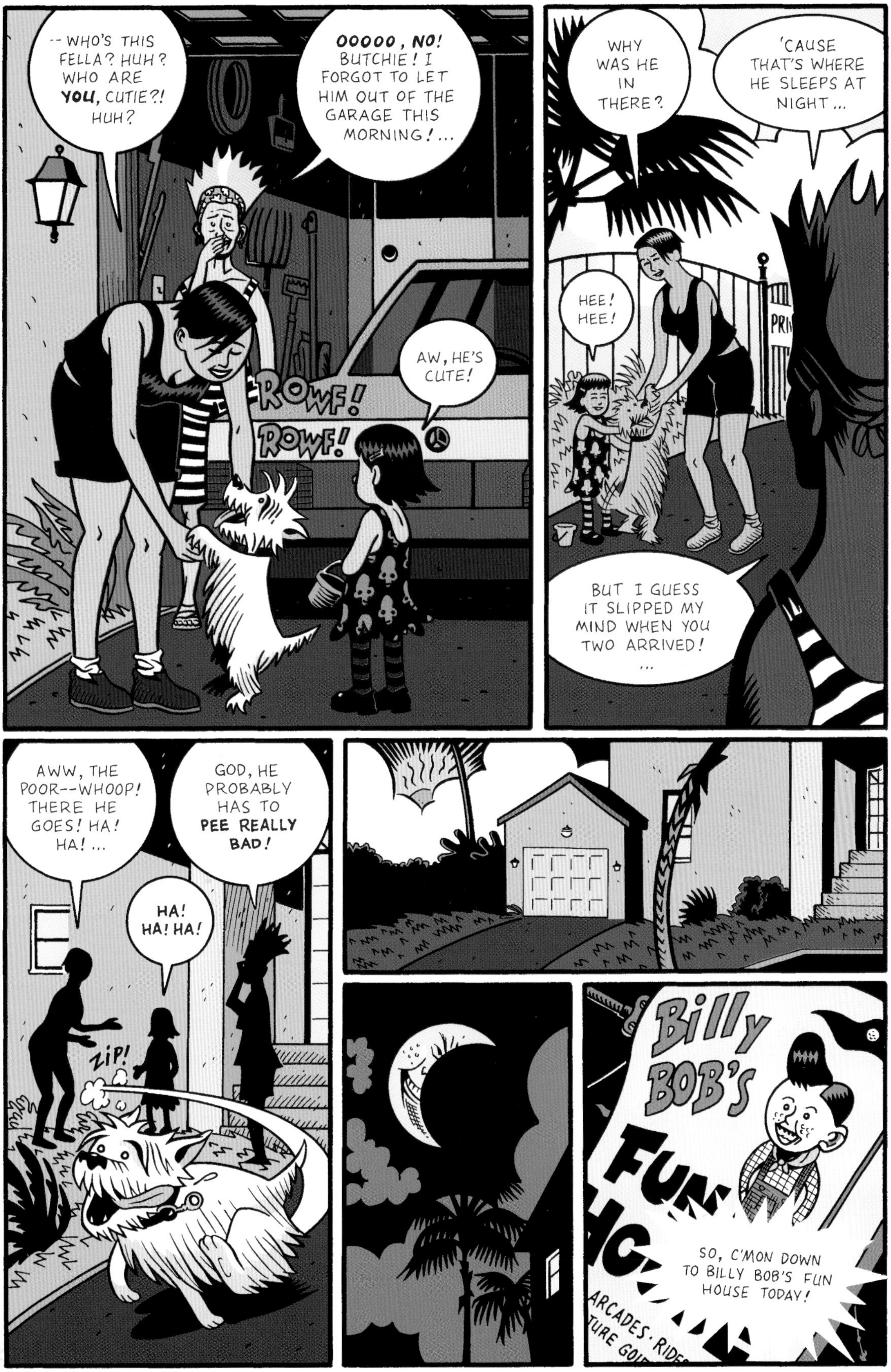
-- WHO'S THIS FELLA? HUH? WHO ARE **YOU**, CUTIE?! HUH?
OOOOO, NO! BUTCHIE! I FORGOT TO LET HIM OUT OF THE GARAGE THIS MORNING!...
ROWF!
ROWF!
AW, HE'S CUTE!
WHY WAS HE IN THERE?
'CAUSE THAT'S WHERE HE SLEEPS AT NIGHT...
HEE! HEE!
BUT I GUESS IT SLIPPED MY MIND WHEN YOU TWO ARRIVED! ...
AWW, THE POOR--WHOOP! THERE HE GOES! HA! HA! ...
GOD, HE PROBABLY HAS TO **PEE REALLY BAD!**
HA! HA! HA!
ZIP!
Billy BOB'S
SO, C'MON DOWN TO BILLY BOB'S FUN HOUSE TODAY!

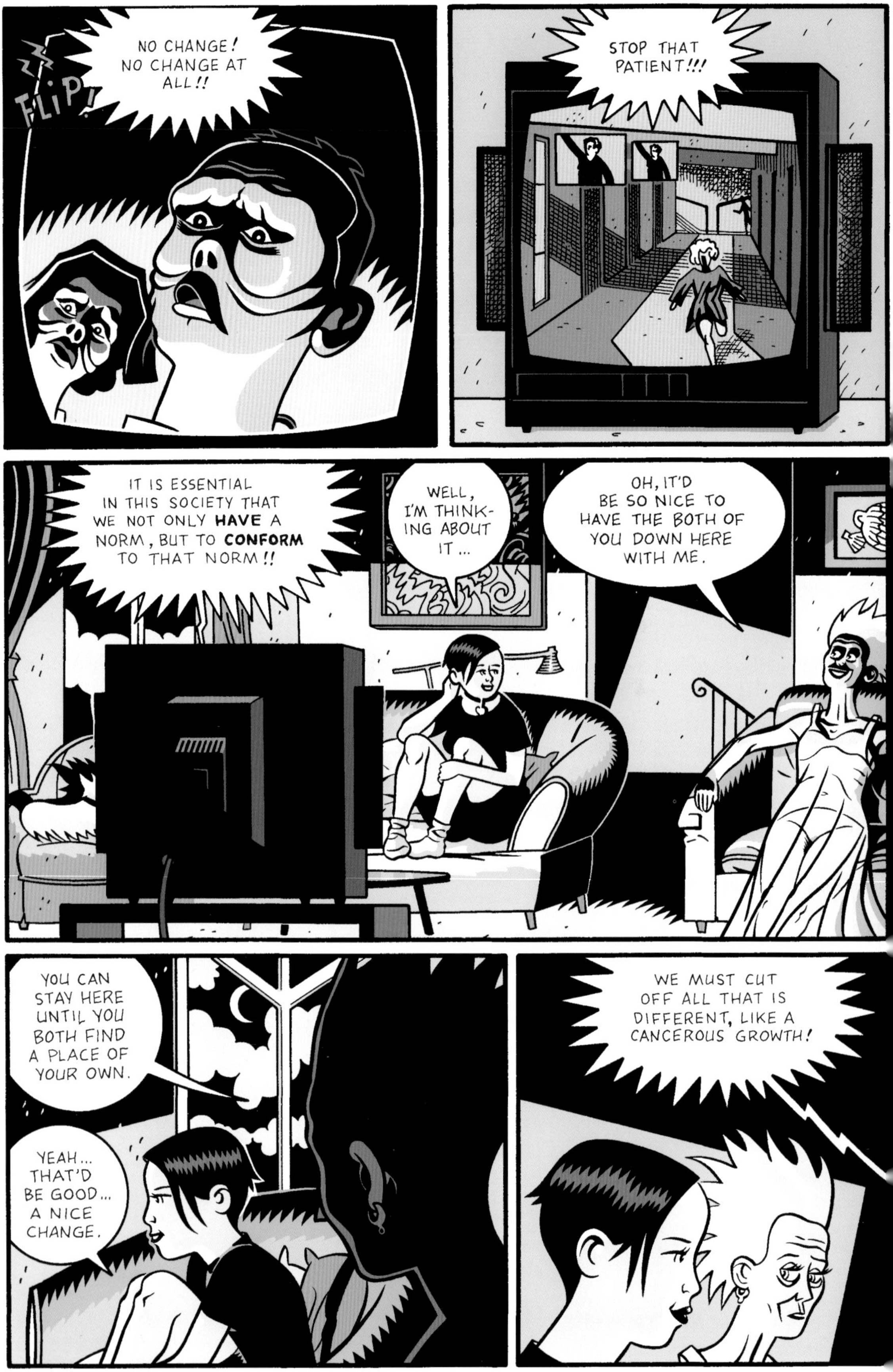
FLIP!
NO CHANGE! NO CHANGE AT ALL!!
STOP THAT PATIENT!!!
IT IS ESSENTIAL IN THIS SOCIETY THAT WE NOT ONLY **HAVE** A NORM, BUT TO **CONFORM** TO THAT NORM!!
WELL, I'M THINKING ABOUT IT...
OH, IT'D BE SO NICE TO HAVE THE BOTH OF YOU DOWN HERE WITH ME.
YOU CAN STAY HERE UNTIL YOU BOTH FIND A PLACE OF YOUR OWN.
YEAH... THAT'D BE GOOD... A NICE CHANGE.
WE MUST CUT OFF ALL THAT IS DIFFERENT, LIKE A CANCEROUS GROWTH!

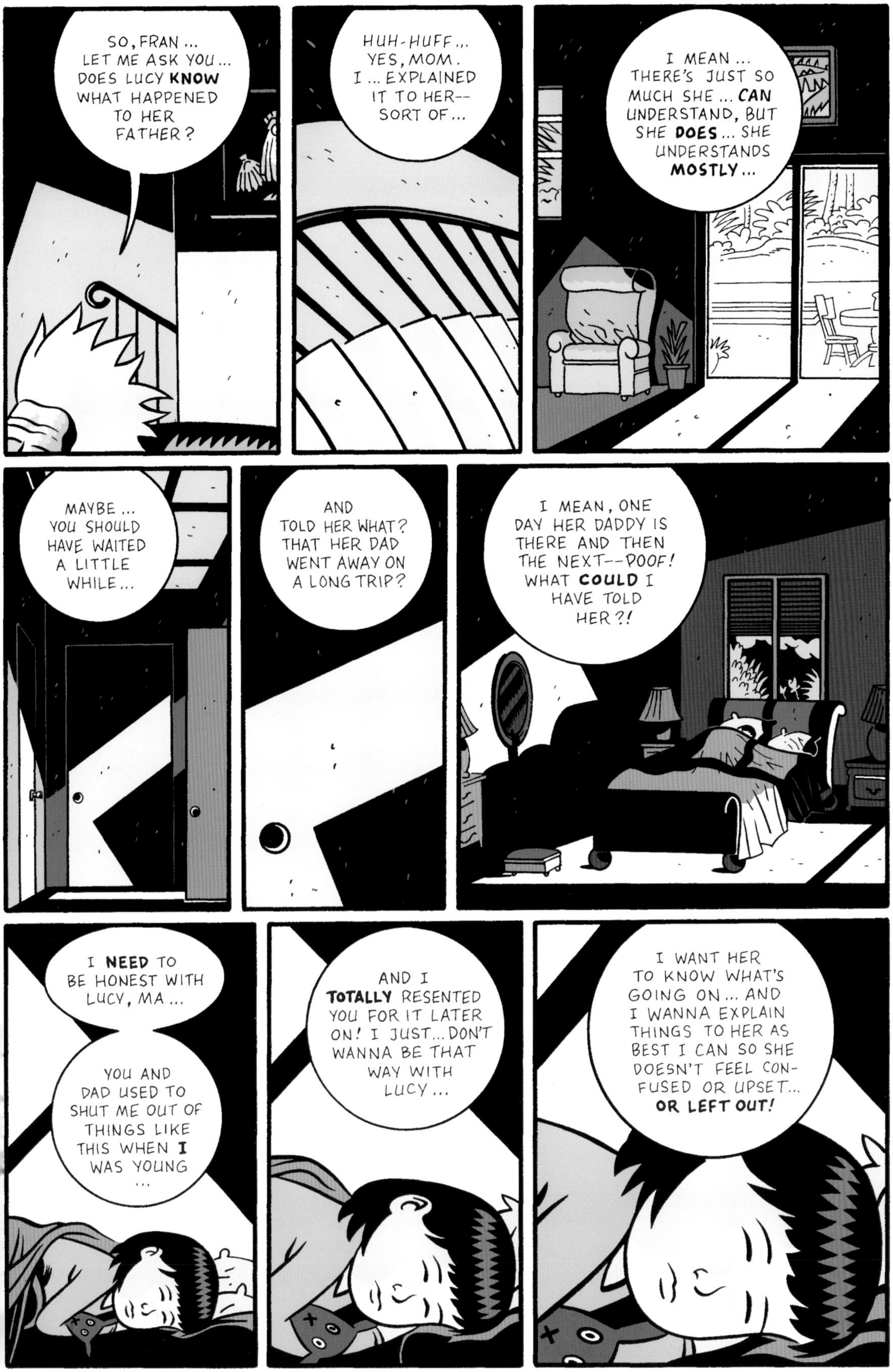
SO, FRAN ... LET ME ASK YOU ... DOES LUCY **KNOW** WHAT HAPPENED TO HER FATHER?
HUH-HUFF ... YES, MOM. I ... EXPLAINED IT TO HER-- SORT OF ...
I MEAN ... THERE'S JUST SO MUCH SHE ... **CAN** UNDERSTAND, BUT SHE **DOES** ... SHE UNDERSTANDS **MOSTLY** ...
MAYBE ... YOU SHOULD HAVE WAITED A LITTLE WHILE ...
AND TOLD HER WHAT? THAT HER DAD WENT AWAY ON A LONG TRIP?
I MEAN, ONE DAY HER DADDY IS THERE AND THEN THE NEXT--POOF! WHAT **COULD** I HAVE TOLD HER?!
I **NEED** TO BE HONEST WITH LUCY, MA ...
YOU AND DAD USED TO SHUT ME OUT OF THINGS LIKE THIS WHEN **I** WAS YOUNG ...
AND I **TOTALLY** RESENTED YOU FOR IT LATER ON! I JUST ... DON'T WANNA BE THAT WAY WITH LUCY ...
I WANT HER TO KNOW WHAT'S GOING ON ... AND I WANNA EXPLAIN THINGS TO HER AS BEST I CAN SO SHE DOESN'T FEEL CON-FUSED OR UPSET ... **OR LEFT OUT!**

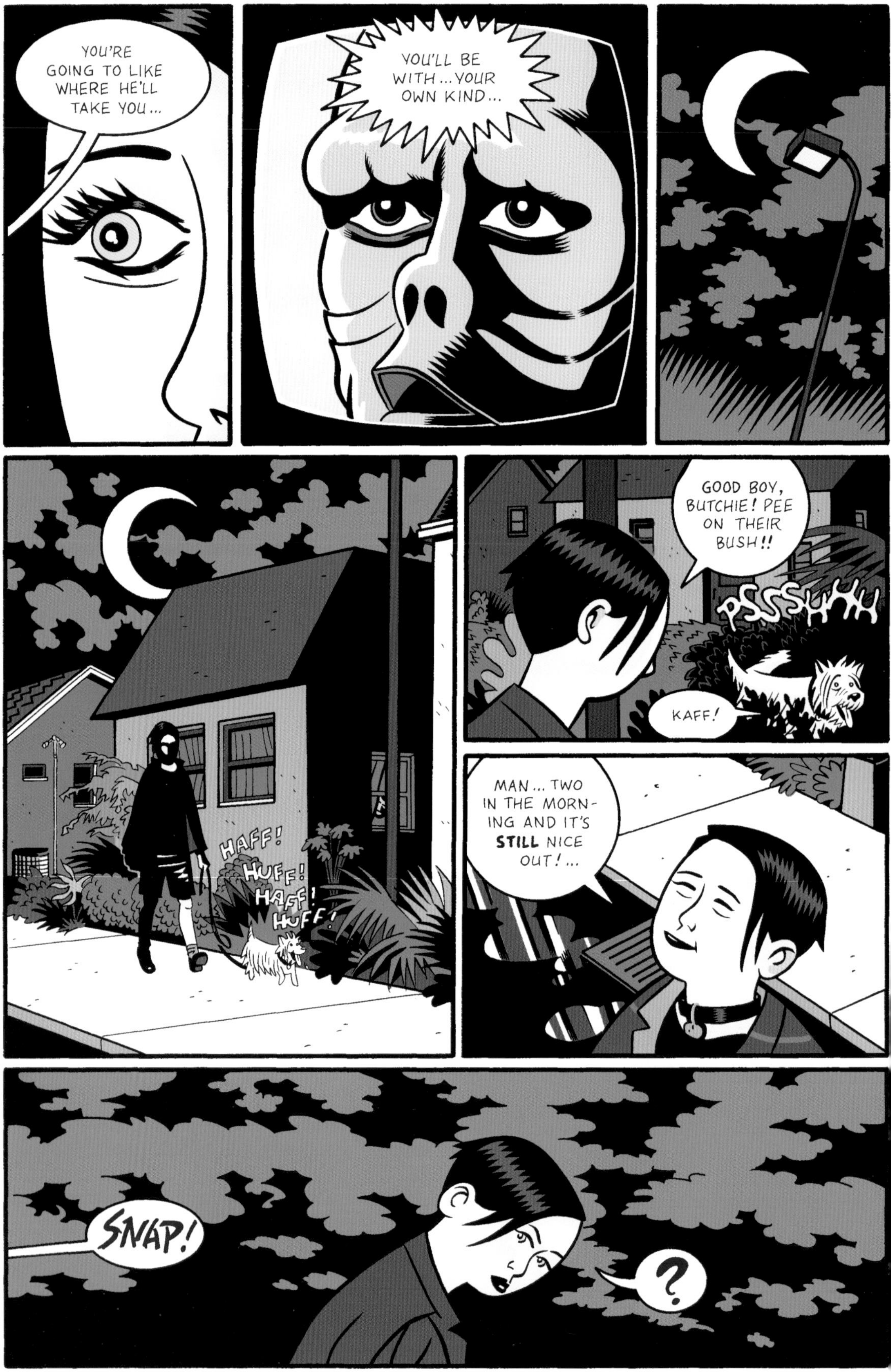
YOU'RE GOING TO LIKE WHERE HE'LL TAKE YOU...
YOU'LL BE WITH...YOUR OWN KIND...
HAFF! HUFF! HAFF! HUFF!
GOOD BOY, BUTCHIE! PEE ON THEIR BUSH!!
PSSSHHH
KAFF!
MAN... TWO IN THE MORNING AND IT'S **STILL** NICE OUT!...
SNAP!
?

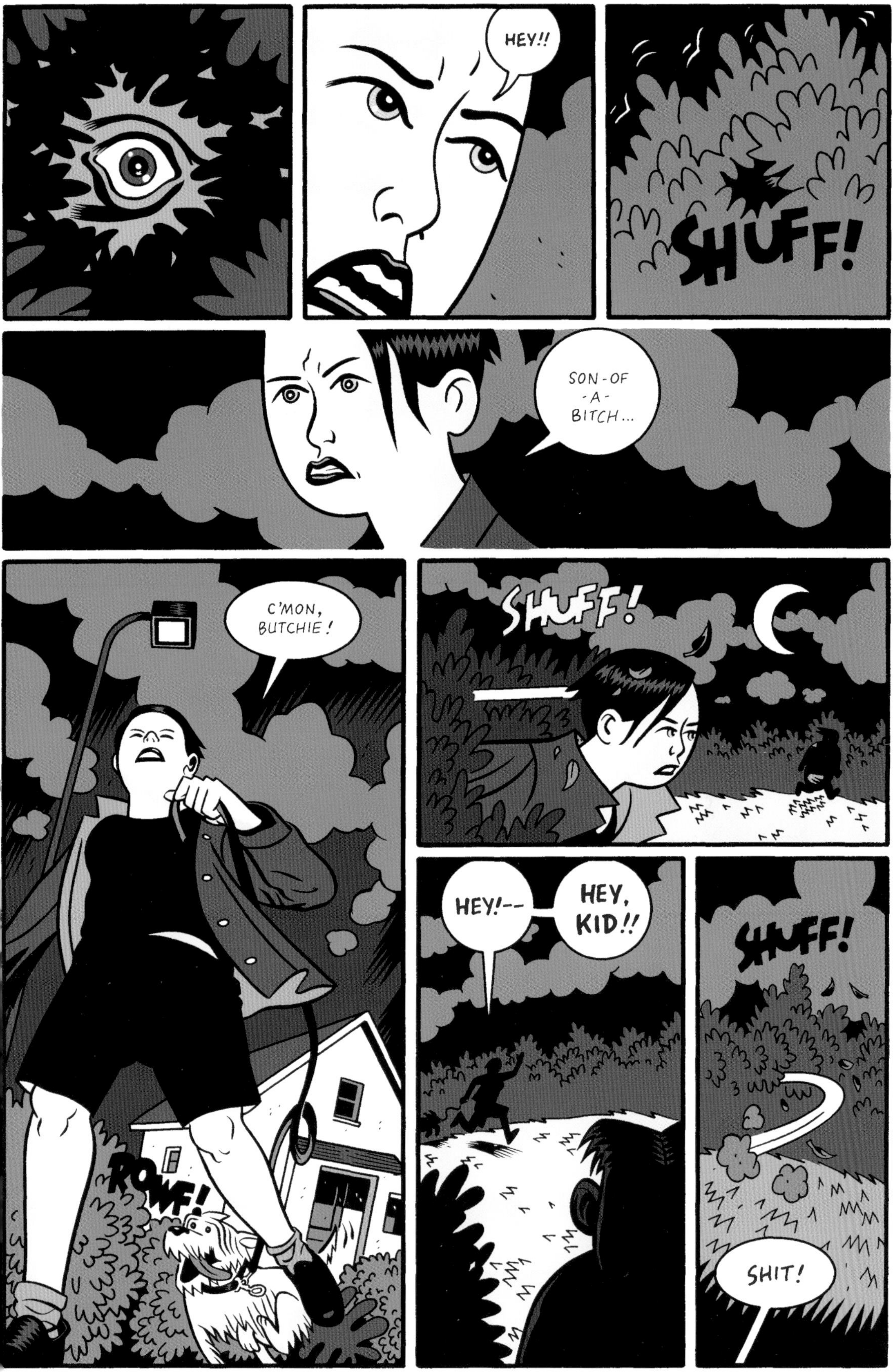
HEY!!
SHUFF!
SON-OF -A- BITCH...
C'MON, BUTCHIE!
ROWF!
SHUFF!
HEY!--
HEY, KID!!
SHUFF!
SHIT!

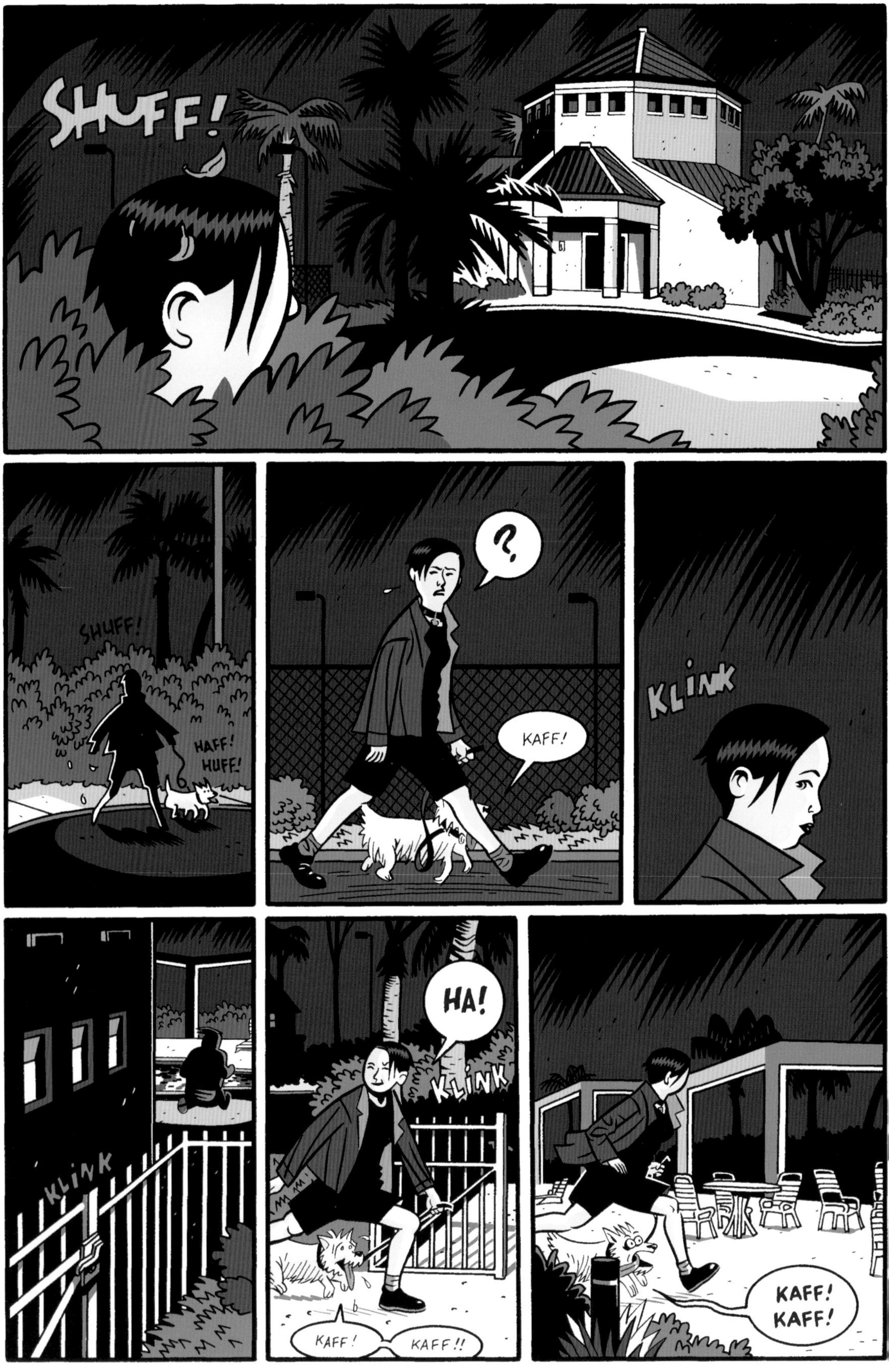
SHUFF!
SHUFF!
HAFF!
HUFF!
?
KAFF!
KLINK
KLINK
HA!
KLINK
KAFF!
KAFF!!
KAFF!
KAFF!

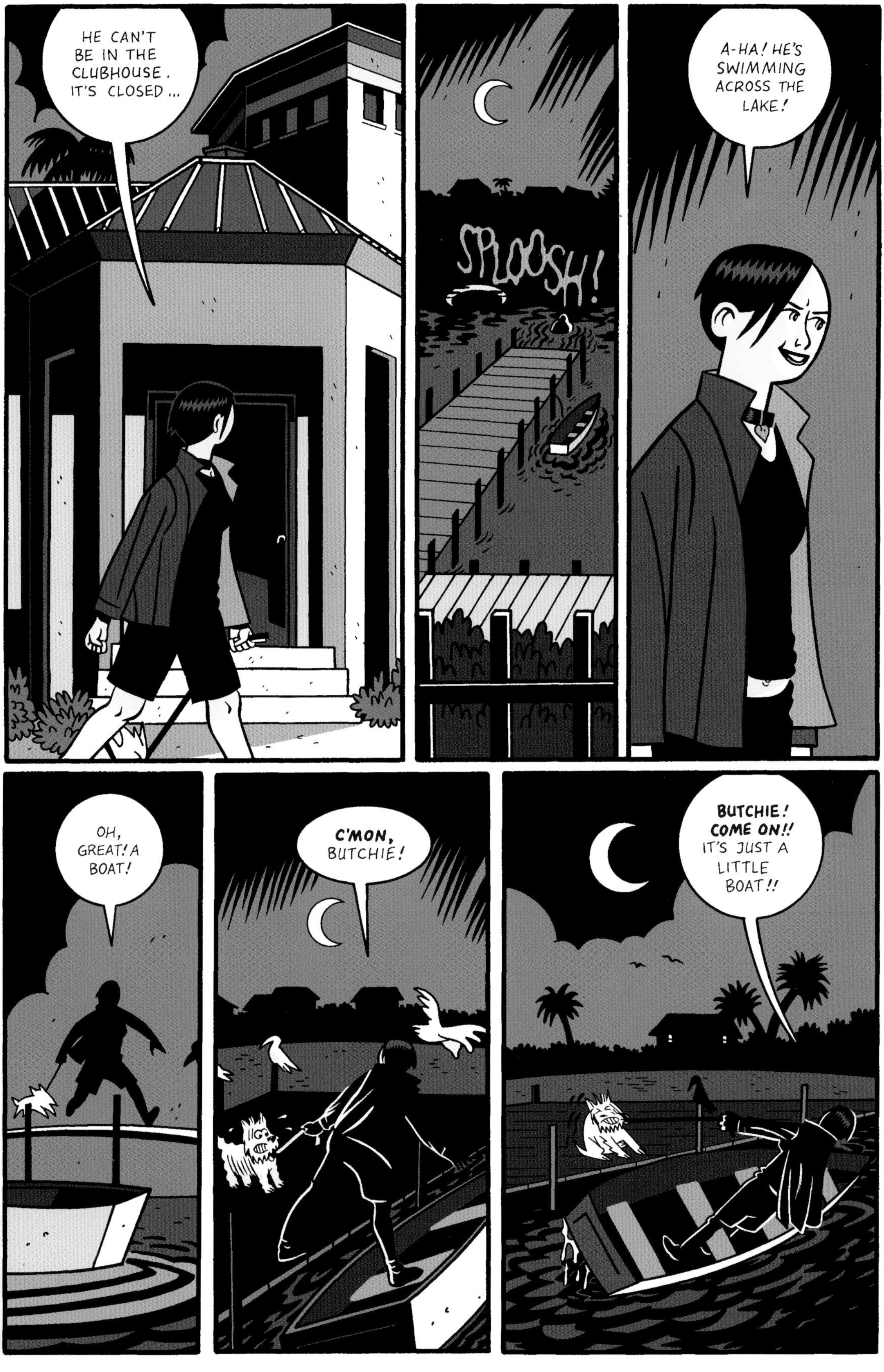
HE CAN'T BE IN THE CLUBHOUSE. IT'S CLOSED...
SPLOOSH!
A-HA! HE'S SWIMMING ACROSS THE LAKE!
OH, GREAT! A BOAT!
C'MON, BUTCHIE!
BUTCHIE! COME ON!! IT'S JUST A LITTLE BOAT!!

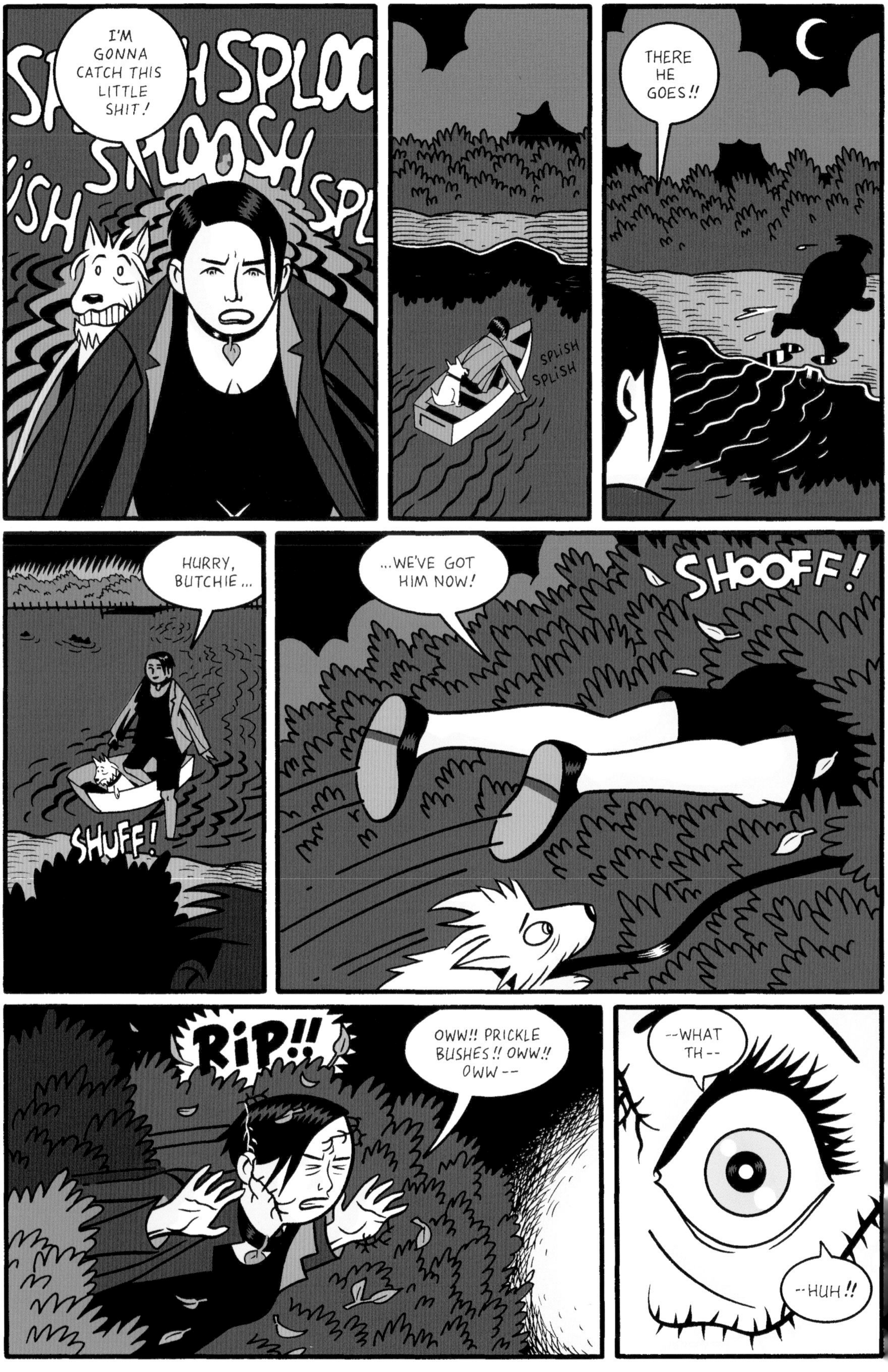
I'M GONNA CATCH THIS LITTLE SHIT!
SPLOO
SPLOOSH
SPL
SPLISH SPLISH
THERE HE GOES!!
HURRY, BUTCHIE...
SHUFF!
...WE'VE GOT HIM NOW!
SHOOFF!
RIP!!
OWW!! PRICKLE BUSHES!! OWW!! OWW--
--WHAT TH--
--HUH!!

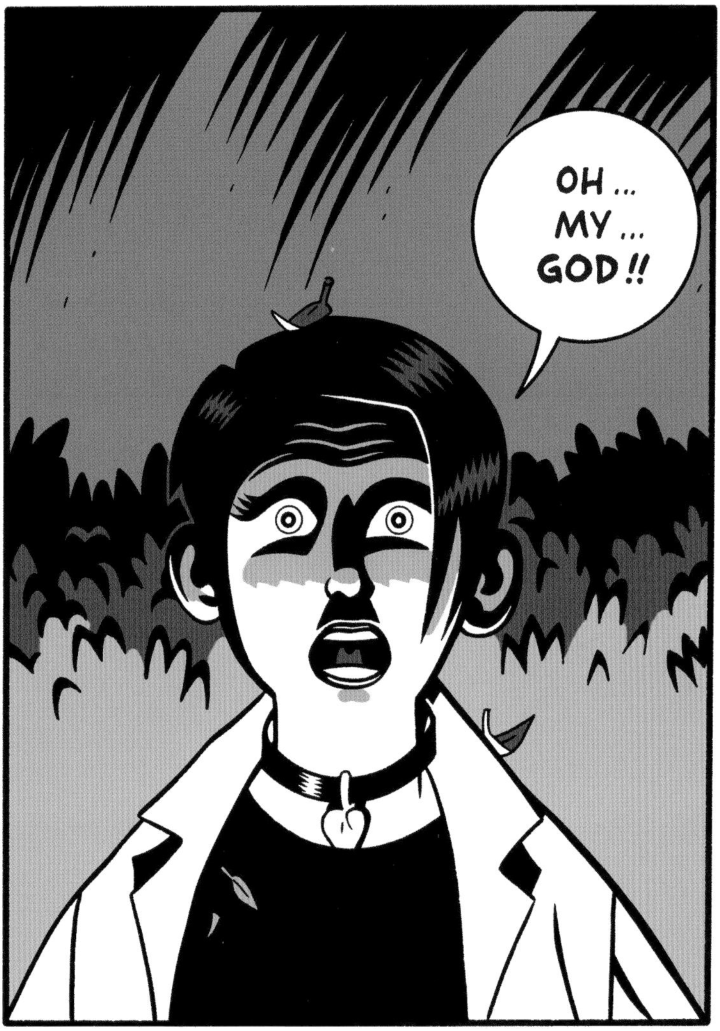
OH ... MY ... GOD !!

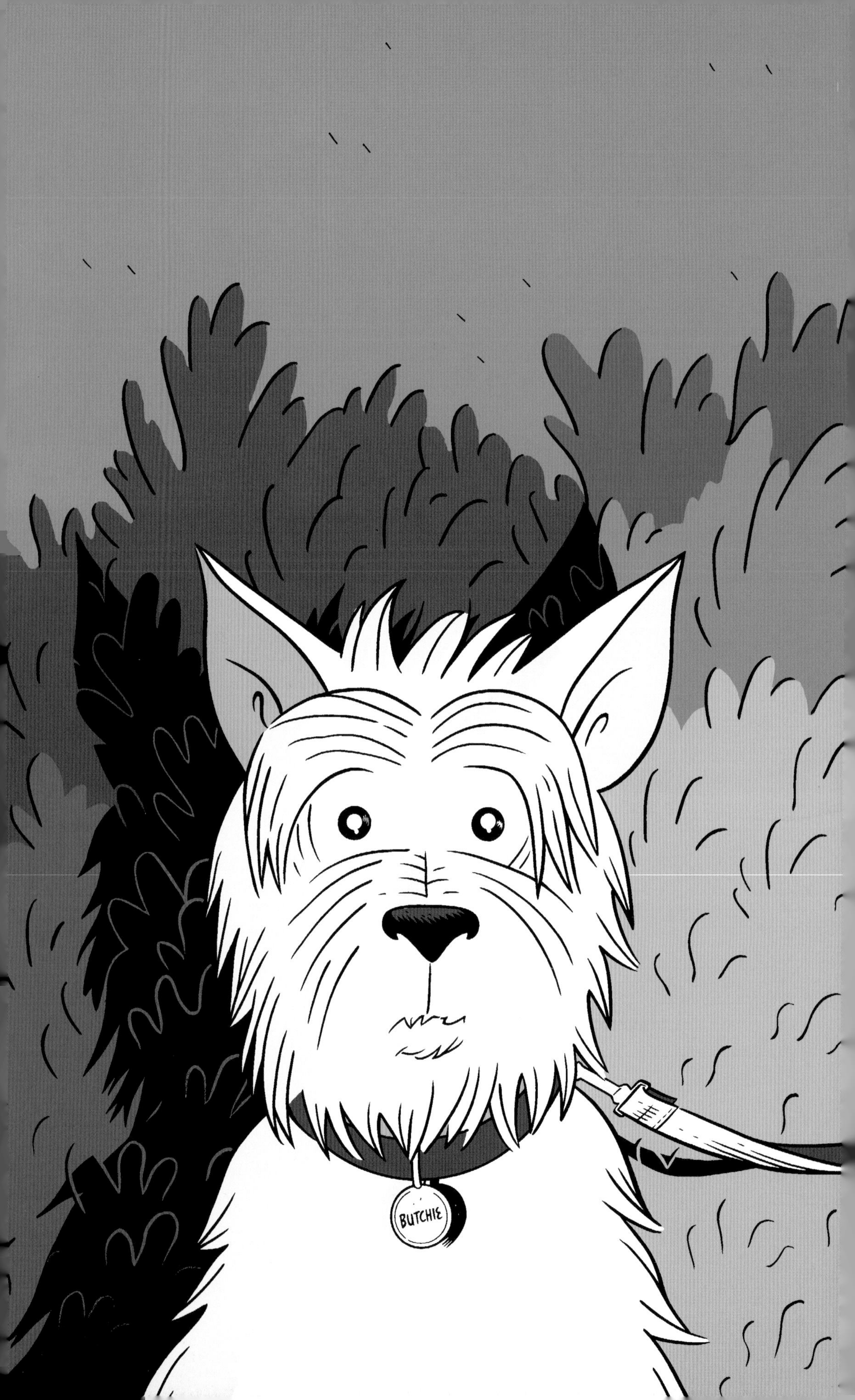
BUTCHIE

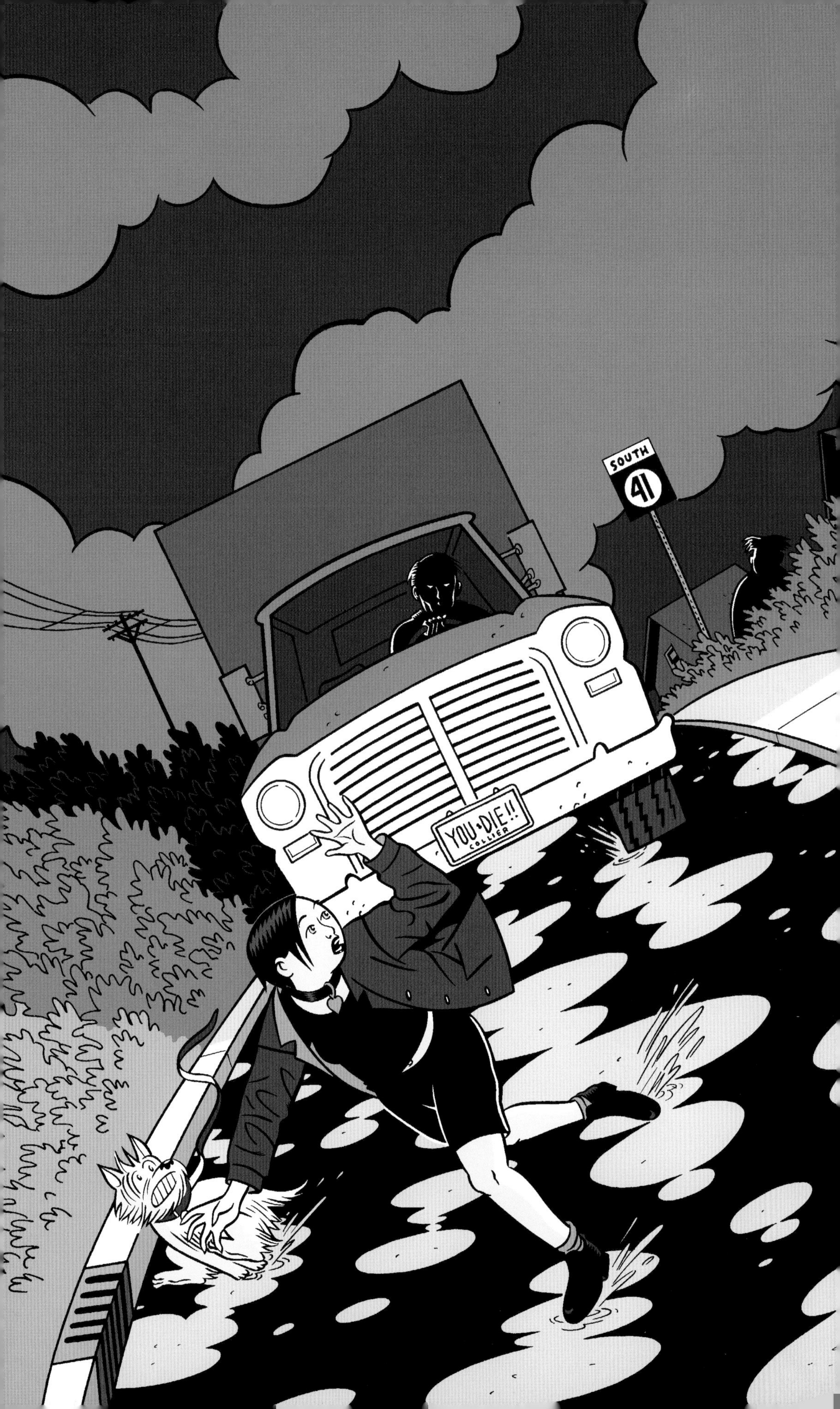
SOUTH
41
YOU•DIE!!
COLLIER

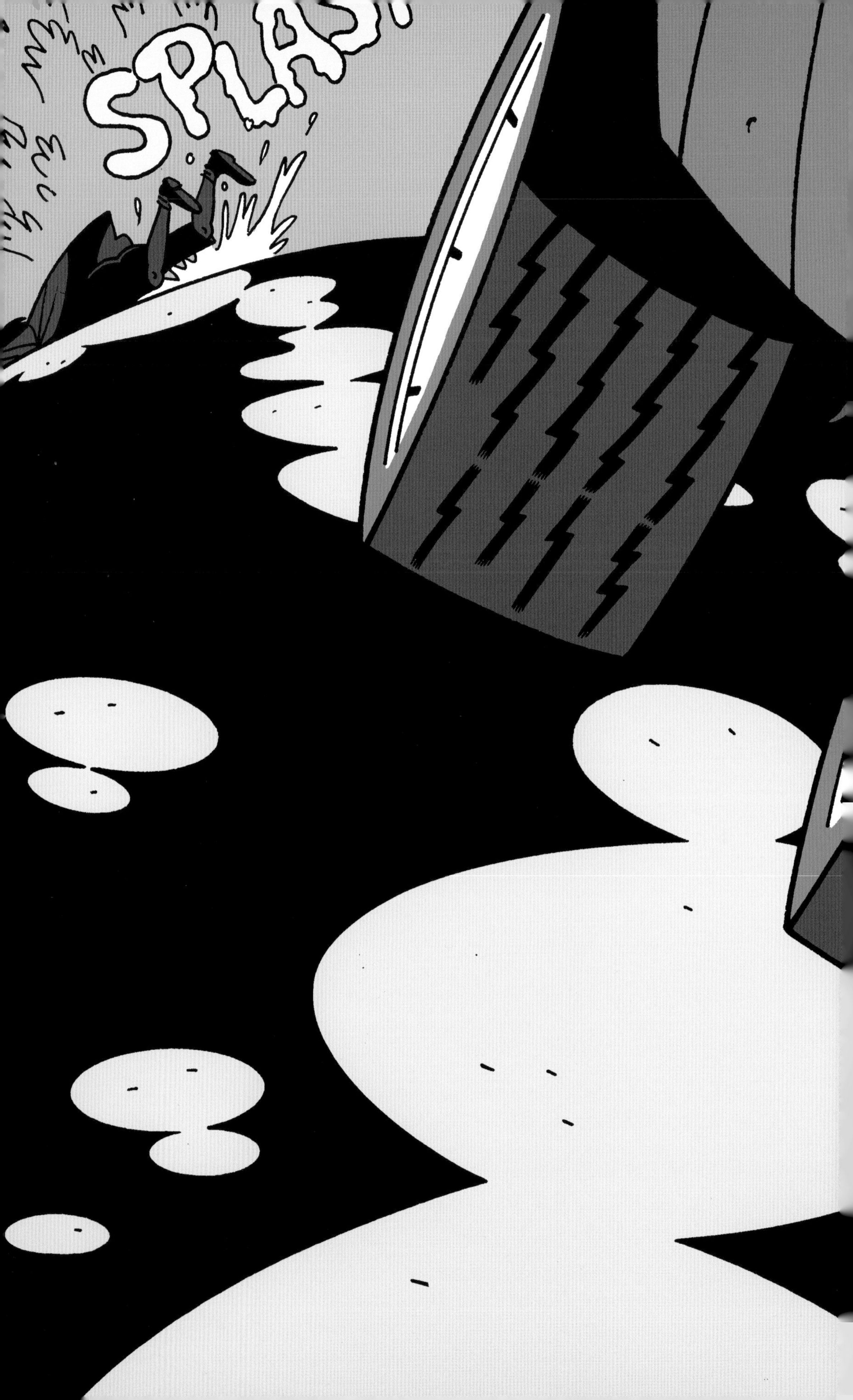
SPLAS

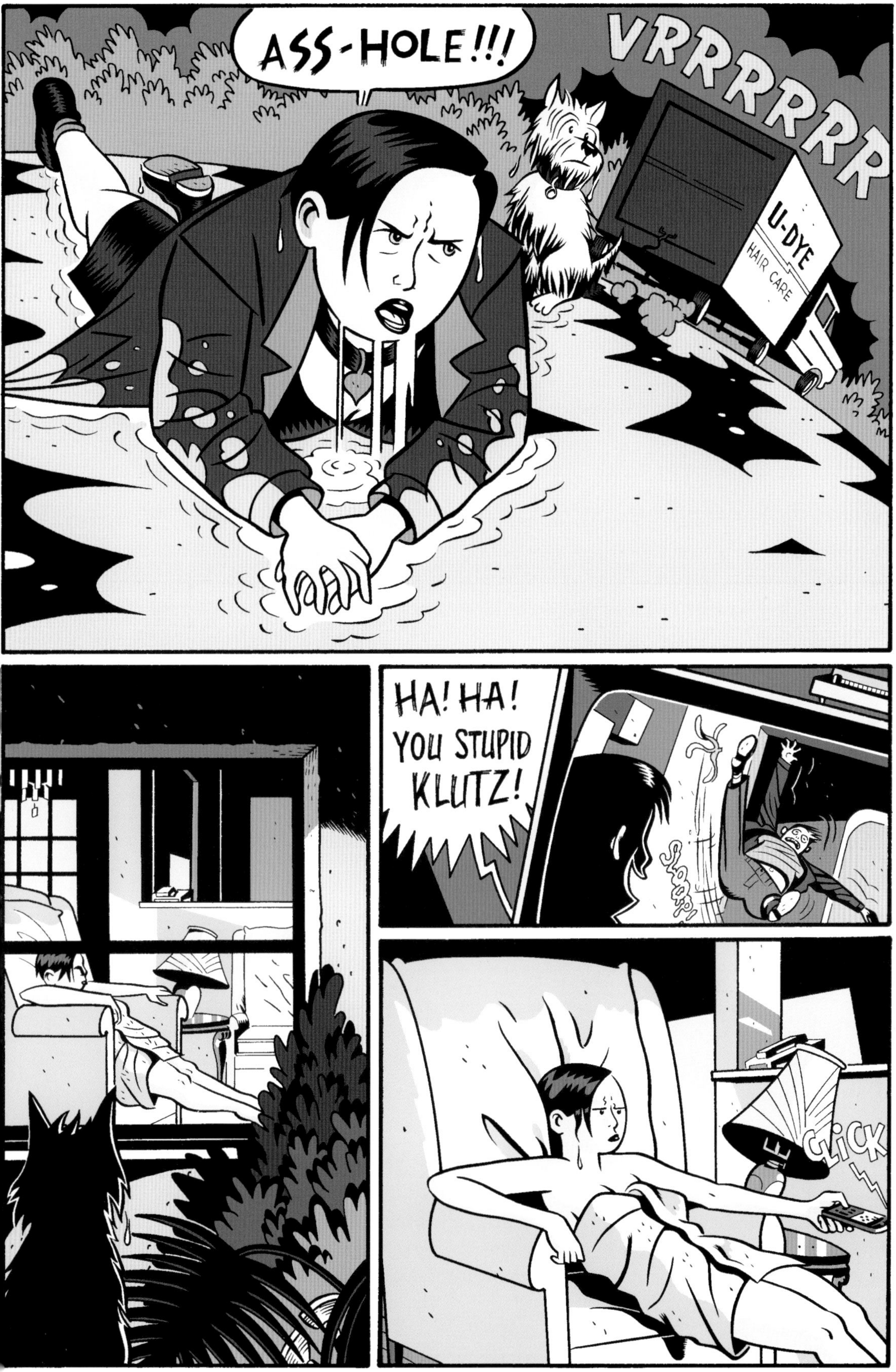
ASS-HOLE!!!
VRRRRRRR
U-DYE
HAIR CARE
HA! HA! YOU STUPID KLUTZ!
SLOP!
CLICK

Chapter 2

Dog Day Afternoon And Night

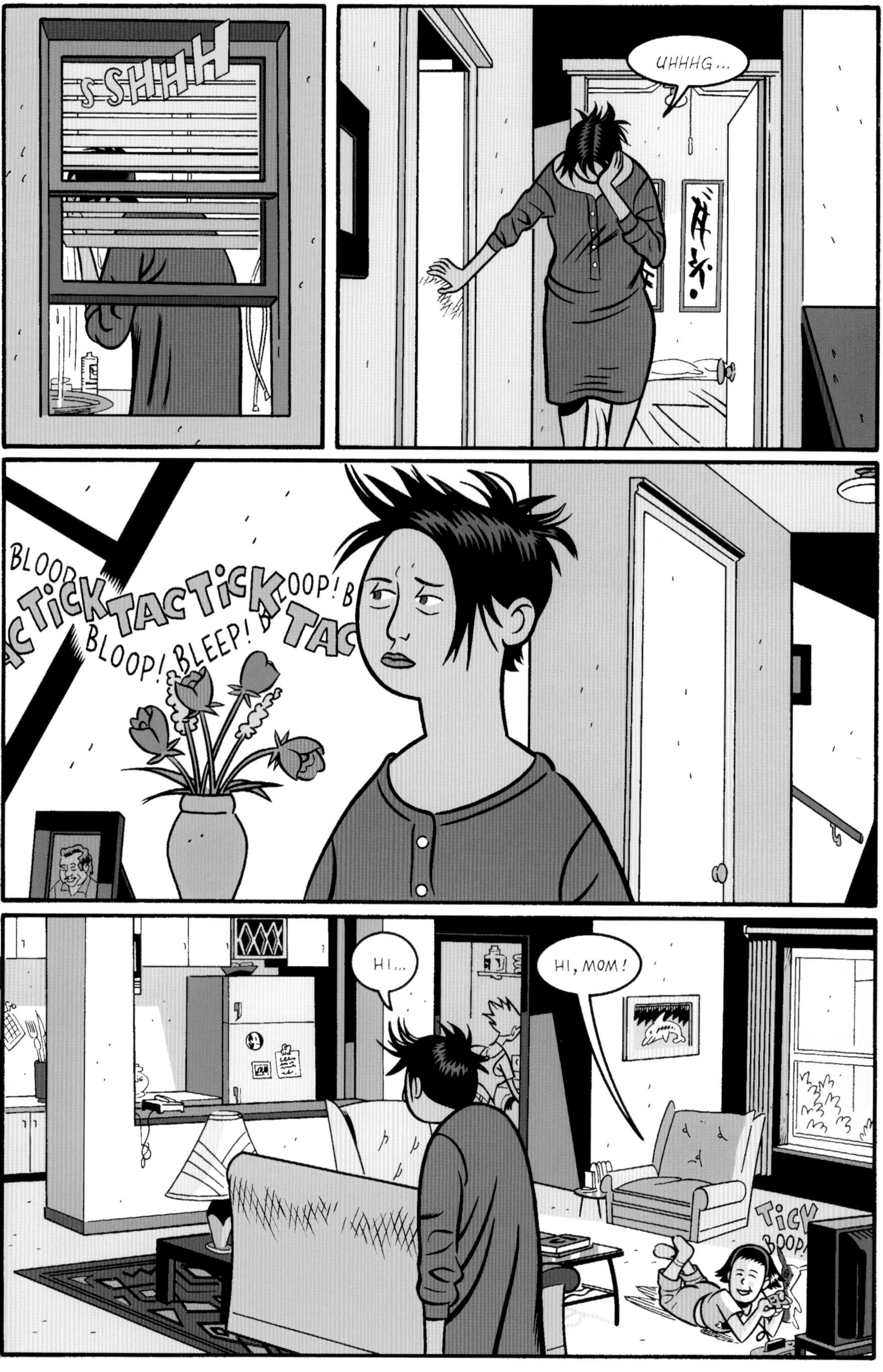

SSHHH
UHHHG...
BLOOP
TACTICKTACTICK
LOOP! B
BLOOP! BLEEP! B
TAC
HI...
HI, MOM!
TICK
BOOP!

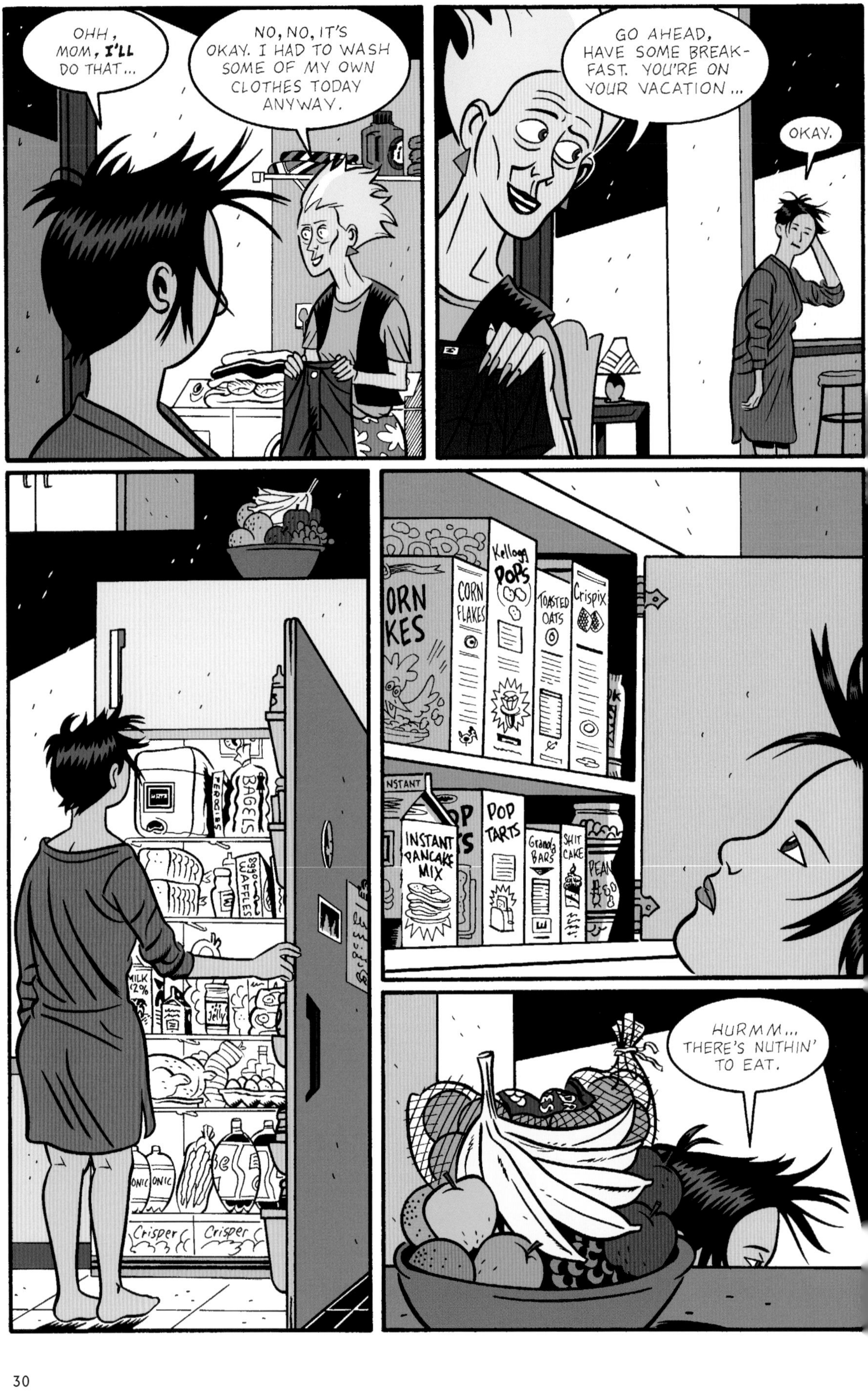
OHH, MOM, I'LL DO THAT...
NO, NO, IT'S OKAY. I HAD TO WASH SOME OF MY OWN CLOTHES TODAY ANYWAY.
GO AHEAD, HAVE SOME BREAK-FAST. YOU'RE ON YOUR VACATION...
OKAY.
BAGELS
WAFFLES
MILK 2%
Jelly
Crisper
Crisper
CORN FLAKES
Kellogg POPS
TOASTED OATS
Crispix
INSTANT PANCAKE MIX
POP TARTS
Granola BARS
SHIT CAKE
HURMM... THERE'S NUTHIN' TO EAT.

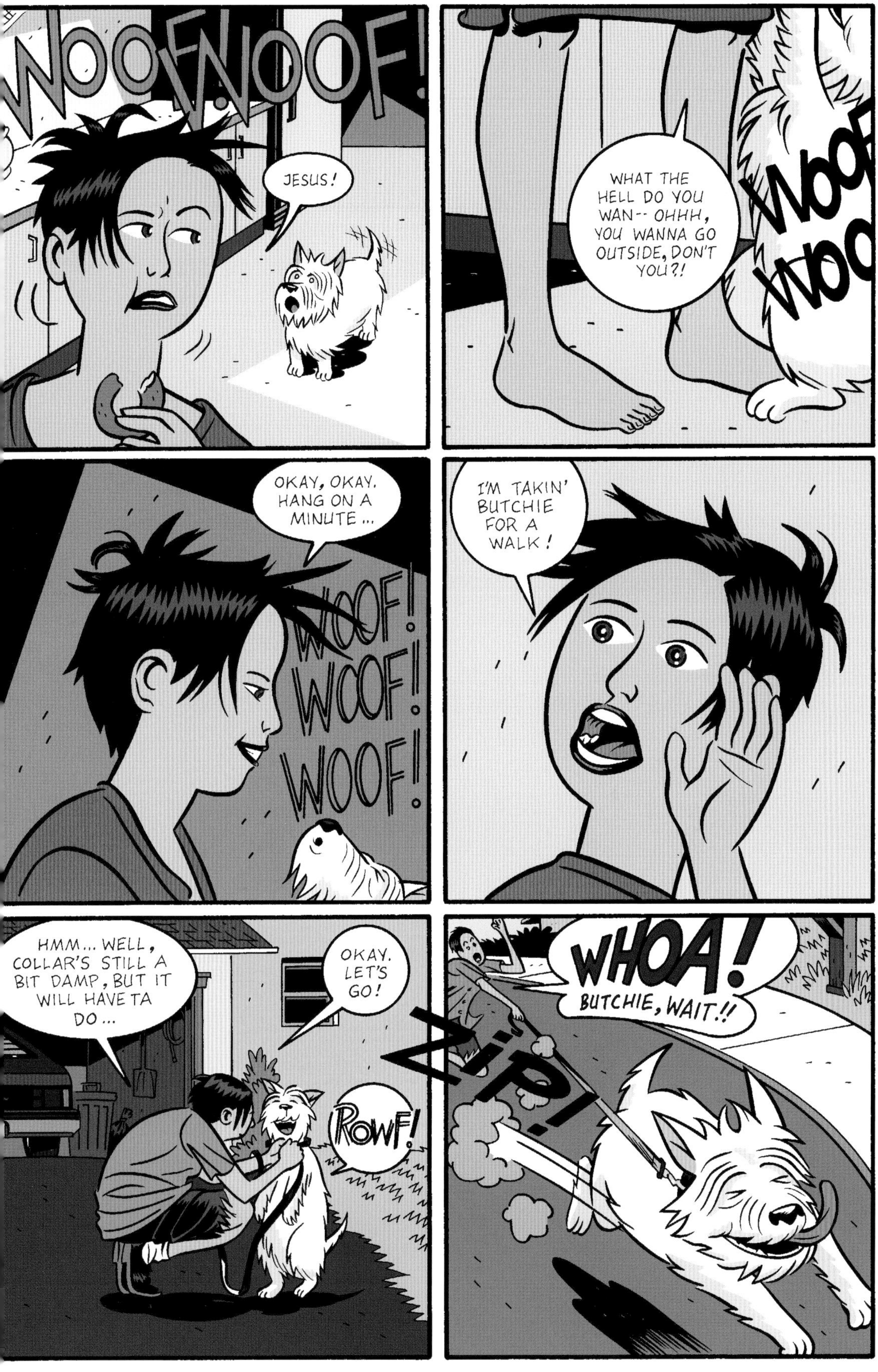
WOOF! WOOF!
JESUS!
WHAT THE HELL DO YOU WAN-- OHHH, YOU WANNA GO OUTSIDE, DON'T YOU?!
WOOF WOOF
OKAY, OKAY. HANG ON A MINUTE...
WOOF! WOOF! WOOF!
I'M TAKIN' BUTCHIE FOR A WALK!
HMM... WELL, COLLAR'S STILL A BIT DAMP, BUT IT WILL HAVE TA DO...
OKAY. LET'S GO!
ROWF!
ZIP!
WHOA!
BUTCHIE, WAIT!!

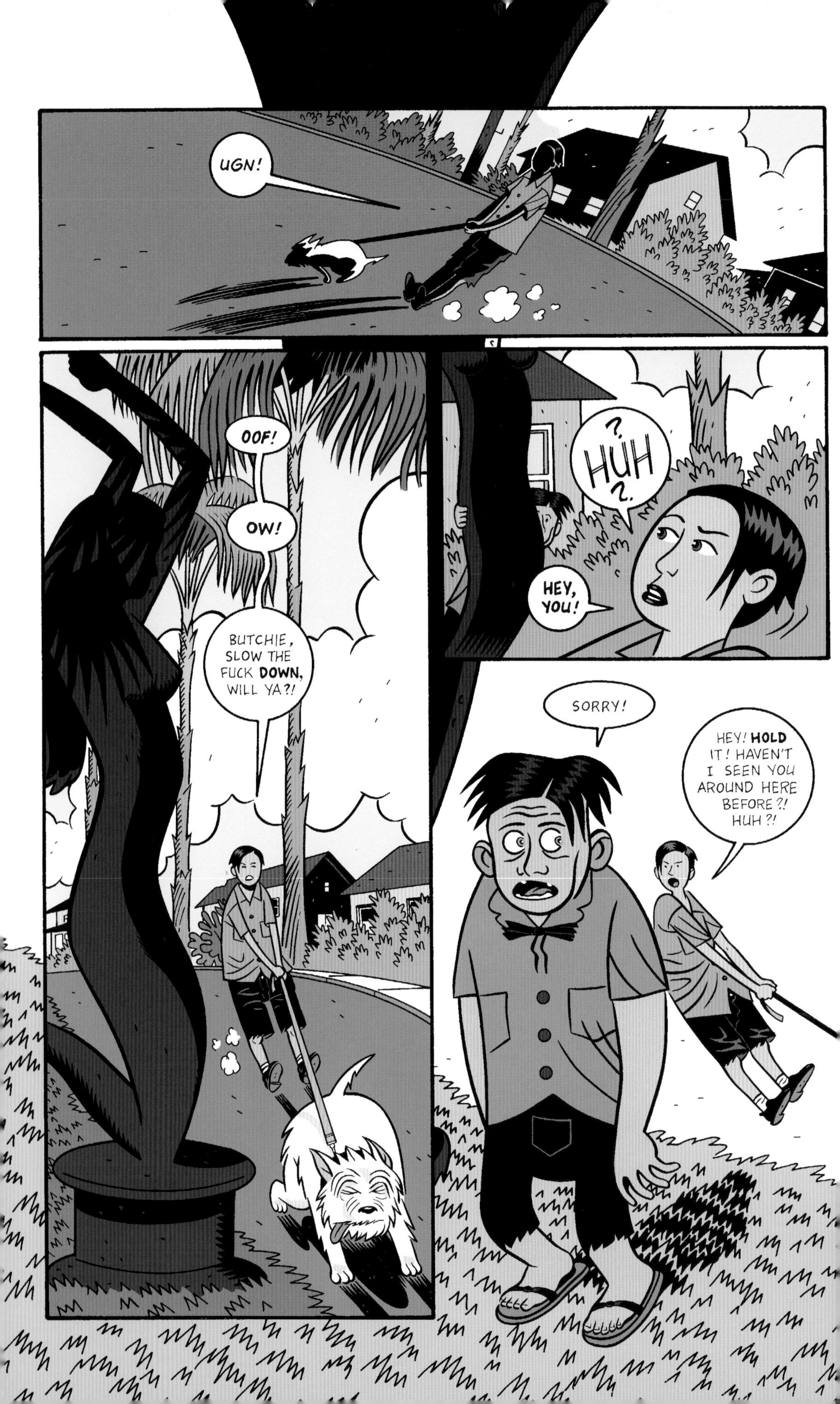
UGN!
OOF!
OW!
BUTCHIE, SLOW THE FUCK **DOWN**, WILL YA?!
?. HUH ?.
HEY, YOU!
SORRY!
HEY! **HOLD** IT! HAVEN'T I SEEN YOU AROUND HERE BEFORE?! HUH?!

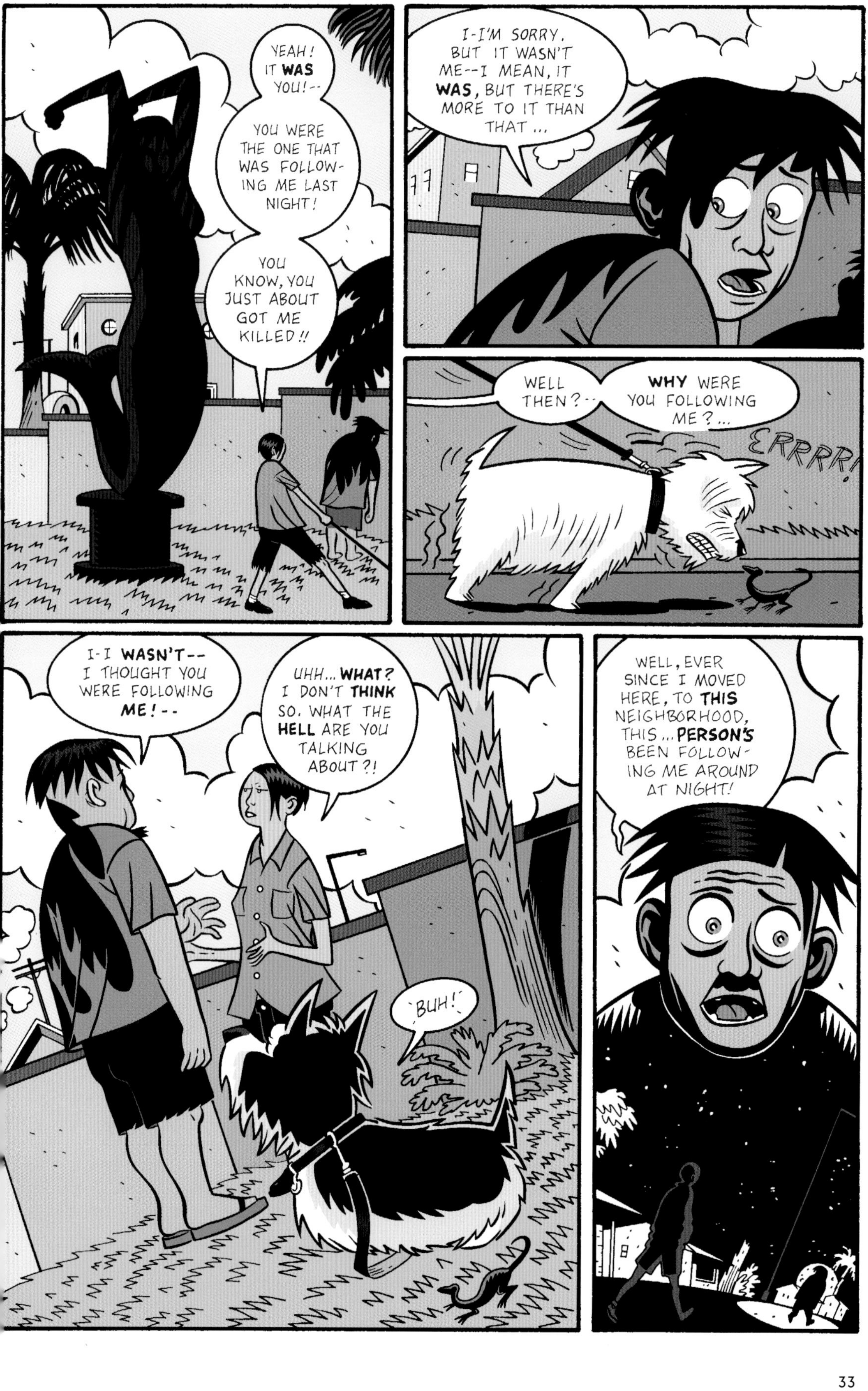

YEAH! IT **WAS** YOU!--
YOU WERE THE ONE THAT WAS FOLLOW-ING ME LAST NIGHT!
YOU KNOW, YOU JUST ABOUT GOT ME KILLED!!
I-I'M SORRY. BUT IT WASN'T ME--I MEAN, IT **WAS**, BUT THERE'S MORE TO IT THAN THAT...
WELL THEN?--
WHY WERE YOU FOLLOWING ME?...
ERRRRR!
I-I **WASN'T**-- I THOUGHT YOU WERE FOLLOWING **ME**!--
UHH... **WHAT?** I DON'T **THINK** SO. WHAT THE **HELL** ARE YOU TALKING ABOUT?!
BUH!
WELL, EVER SINCE I MOVED HERE, TO **THIS** NEIGHBORHOOD, THIS... **PERSON'S** BEEN FOLLOW-ING ME AROUND AT NIGHT!

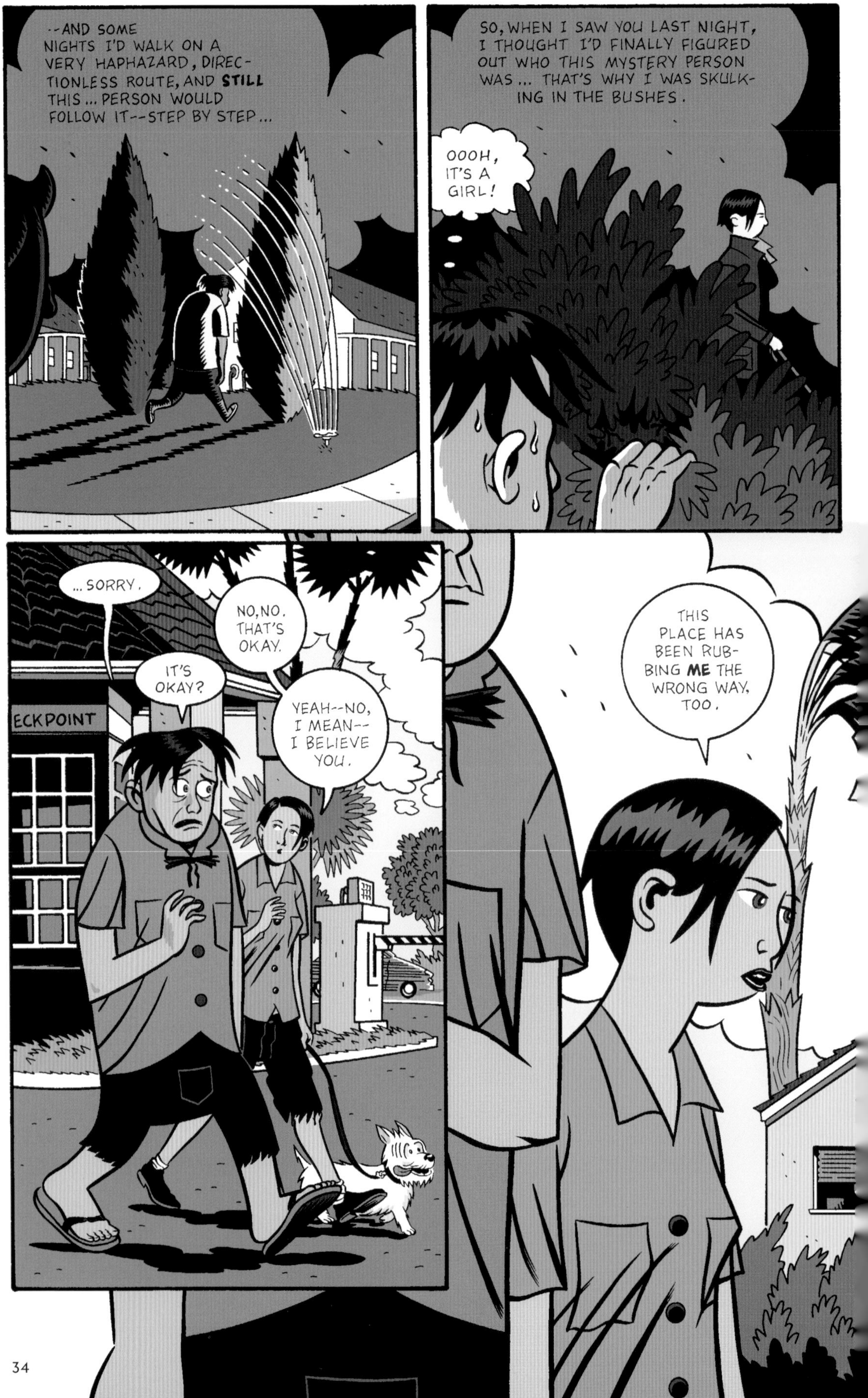
--AND SOME NIGHTS I'D WALK ON A VERY HAPHAZARD, DIRECTIONLESS ROUTE, AND STILL THIS... PERSON WOULD FOLLOW IT--STEP BY STEP...
SO, WHEN I SAW YOU LAST NIGHT, I THOUGHT I'D FINALLY FIGURED OUT WHO THIS MYSTERY PERSON WAS... THAT'S WHY I WAS SKULKING IN THE BUSHES.
OOOH, IT'S A GIRL!
...SORRY.
IT'S OKAY?
NO, NO. THAT'S OKAY.
YEAH--NO, I MEAN-- I BELIEVE YOU.
ECKPOINT
THIS PLACE HAS BEEN RUBBING ME THE WRONG WAY, TOO.

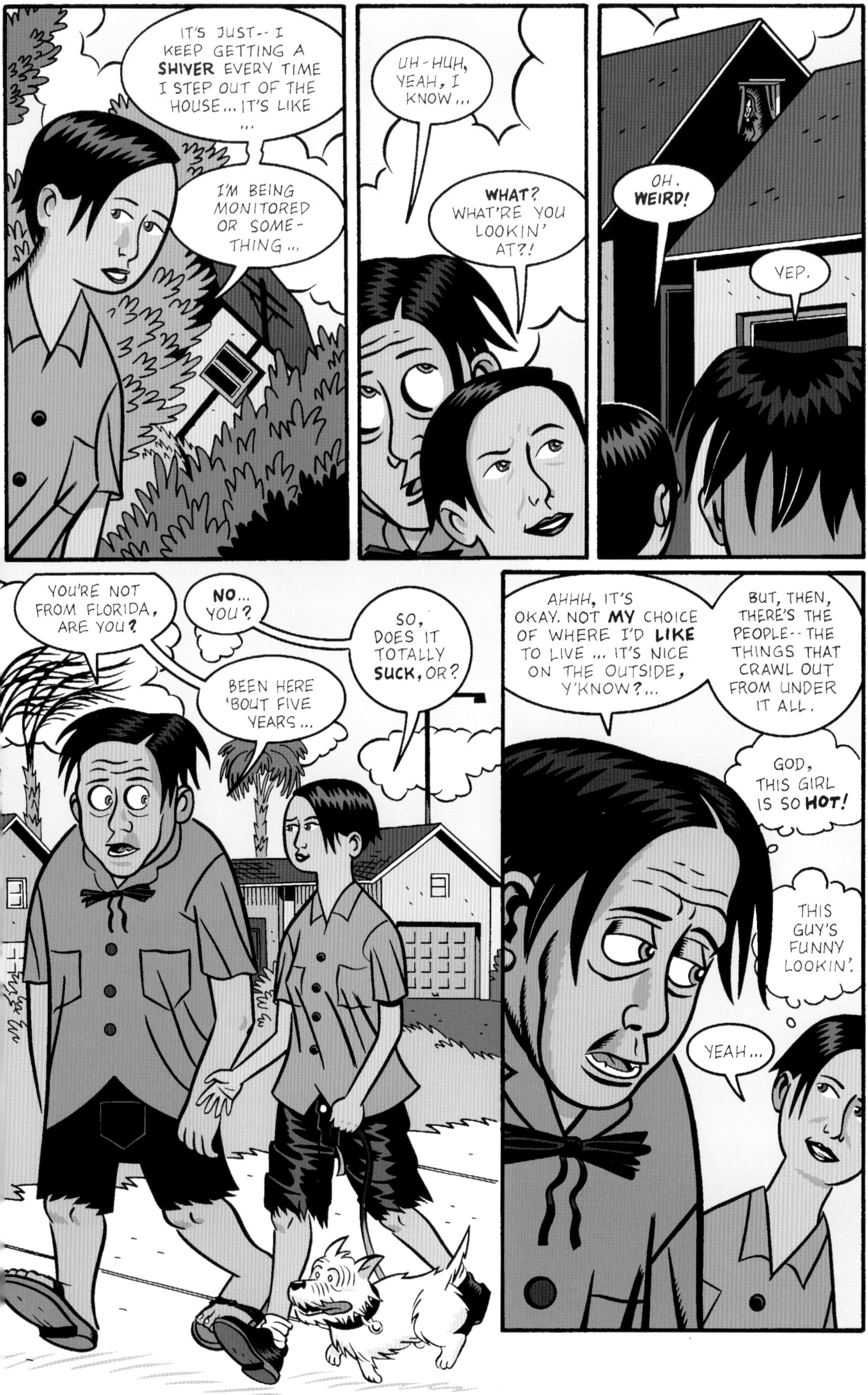
IT'S JUST-- I KEEP GETTING A SHIVER EVERY TIME I STEP OUT OF THE HOUSE... IT'S LIKE ...
I'M BEING MONITORED OR SOME-THING...
UH-HUH, YEAH, I KNOW...
WHAT? WHAT'RE YOU LOOKIN' AT?!
OH. WEIRD!
YEP.
YOU'RE NOT FROM FLORIDA, ARE YOU?
NO... YOU?
BEEN HERE 'BOUT FIVE YEARS...
SO, DOES IT TOTALLY SUCK, OR?
AHHH, IT'S OKAY. NOT MY CHOICE OF WHERE I'D LIKE TO LIVE ... IT'S NICE ON THE OUTSIDE, Y'KNOW?...
BUT, THEN, THERE'S THE PEOPLE-- THE THINGS THAT CRAWL OUT FROM UNDER IT ALL.
GOD, THIS GIRL IS SO HOT!
THIS GUY'S FUNNY LOOKIN'.
YEAH...

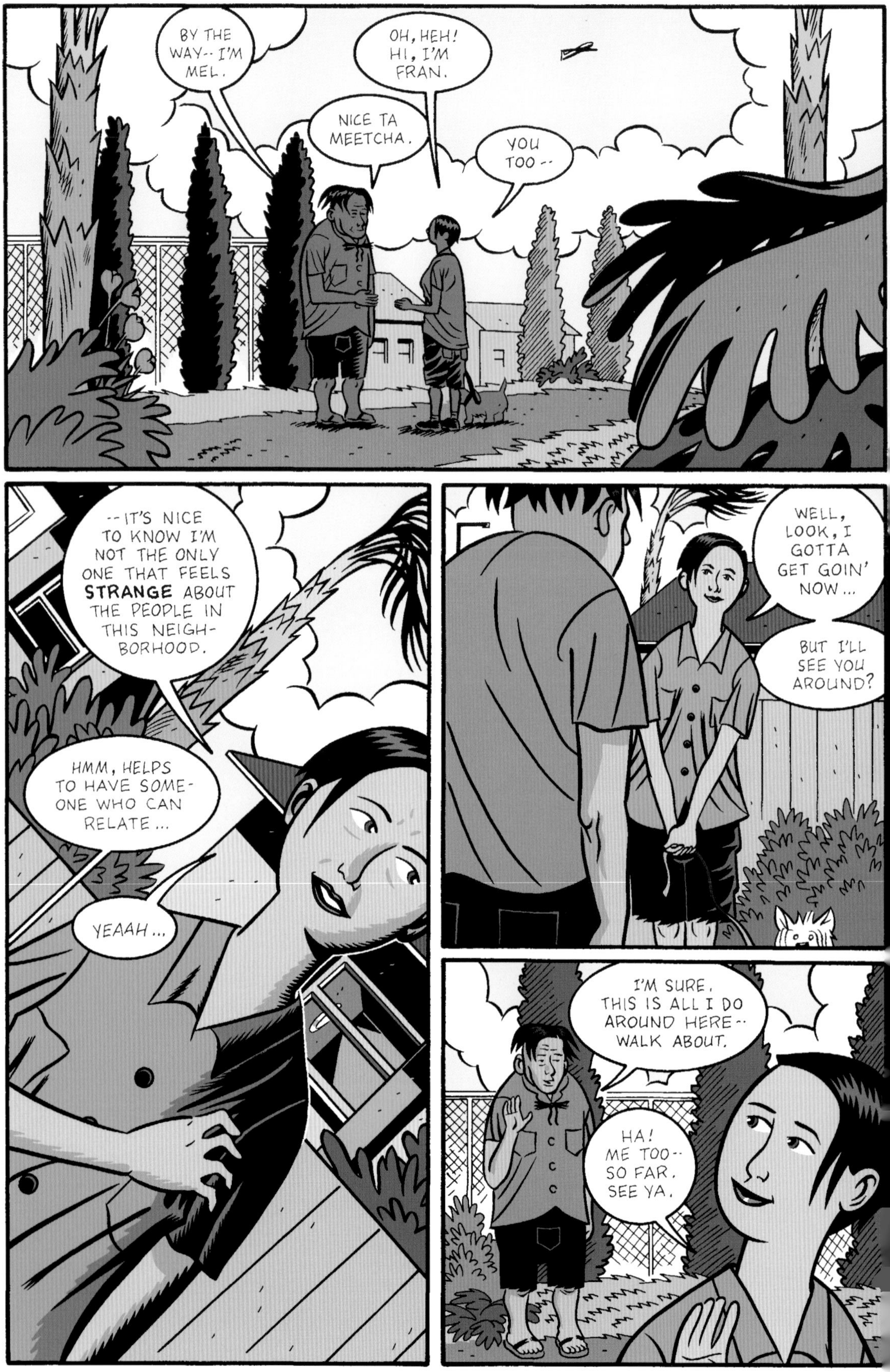
BY THE WAY-- I'M MEL.
NICE TA MEETCHA.
OH, HEH! HI, I'M FRAN.
YOU TOO --
--IT'S NICE TO KNOW I'M NOT THE ONLY ONE THAT FEELS **STRANGE** ABOUT THE PEOPLE IN THIS NEIGHBORHOOD.
HMM, HELPS TO HAVE SOMEONE WHO CAN RELATE...
YEAAH...
WELL, LOOK, I GOTTA GET GOIN' NOW...
BUT I'LL SEE YOU AROUND?
I'M SURE. THIS IS ALL I DO AROUND HERE-- WALK ABOUT.
HA! ME TOO-- SO FAR. SEE YA.

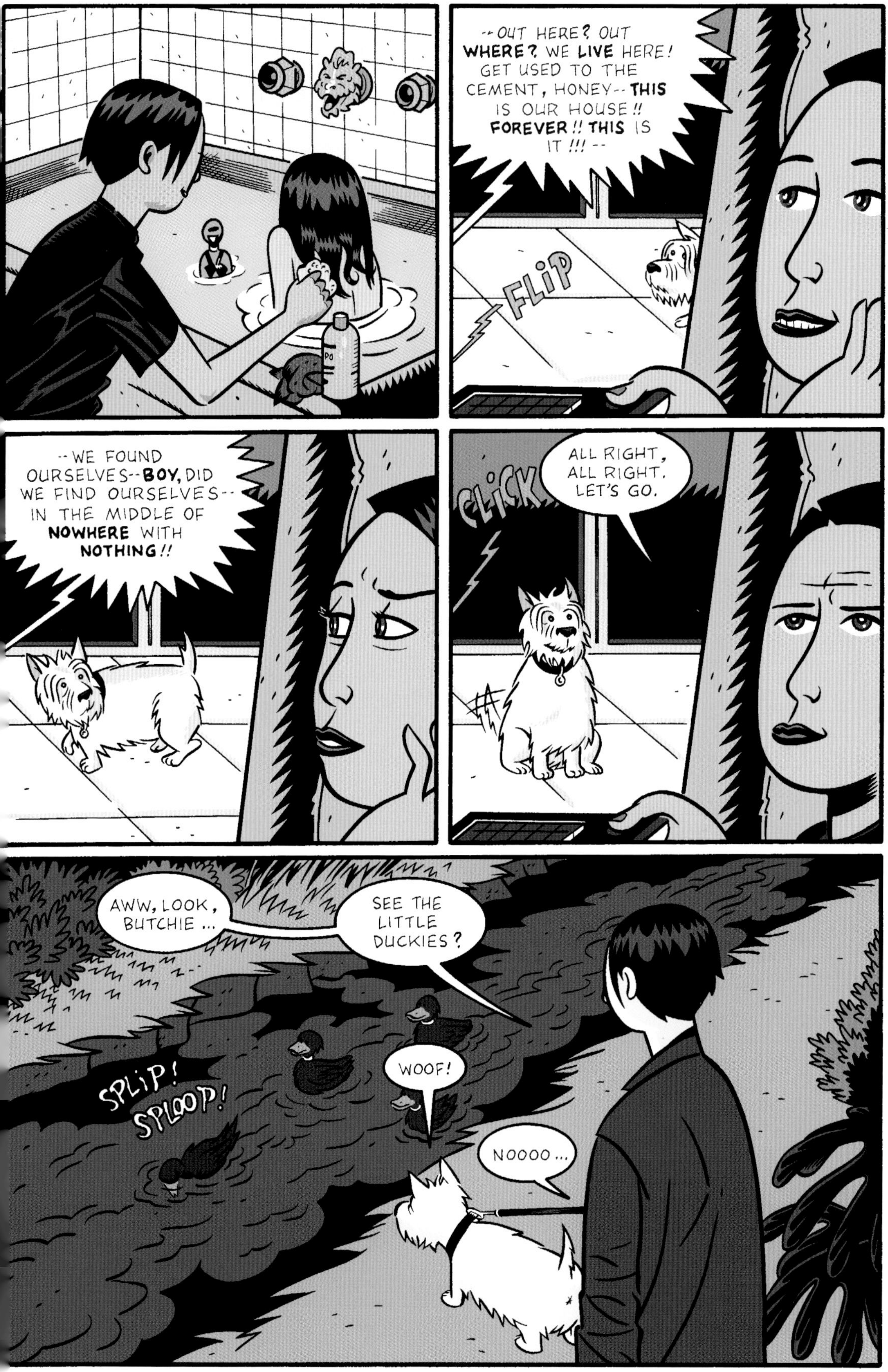
--OUT HERE? OUT WHERE? WE LIVE HERE! GET USED TO THE CEMENT, HONEY--THIS IS OUR HOUSE!! FOREVER!! THIS IS IT!!! --
FLIP
--WE FOUND OURSELVES--BOY, DID WE FIND OURSELVES--IN THE MIDDLE OF NOWHERE WITH NOTHING!!
CLICK
ALL RIGHT, ALL RIGHT. LET'S GO.
AWW, LOOK, BUTCHIE ...
SEE THE LITTLE DUCKIES?
SPLIP!
SPLOOP!
WOOF!
NOOOO ...

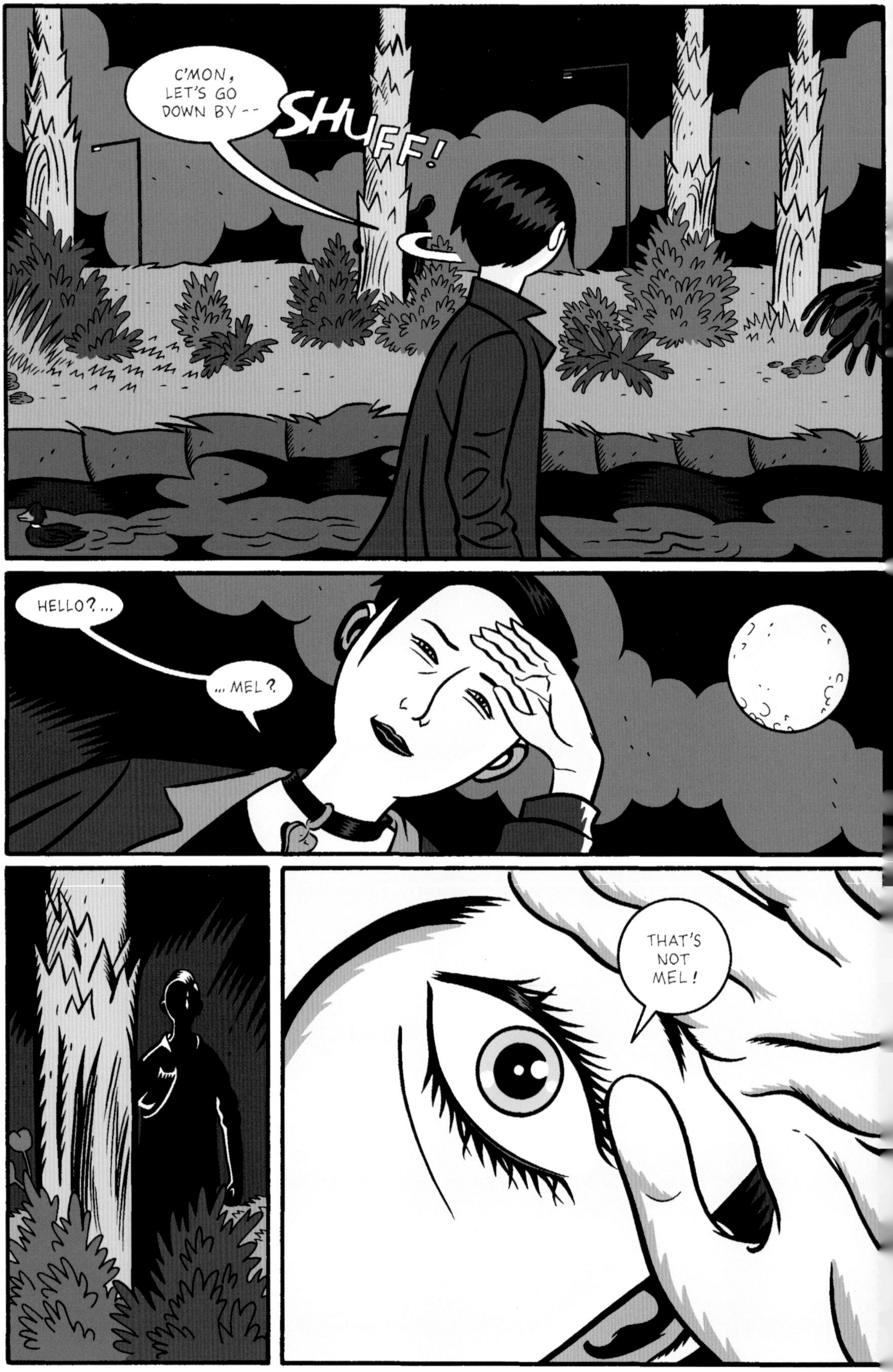
C'MON, LET'S GO DOWN BY --
SHUFF!
HELLO?...
...MEL?
THAT'S NOT MEL!

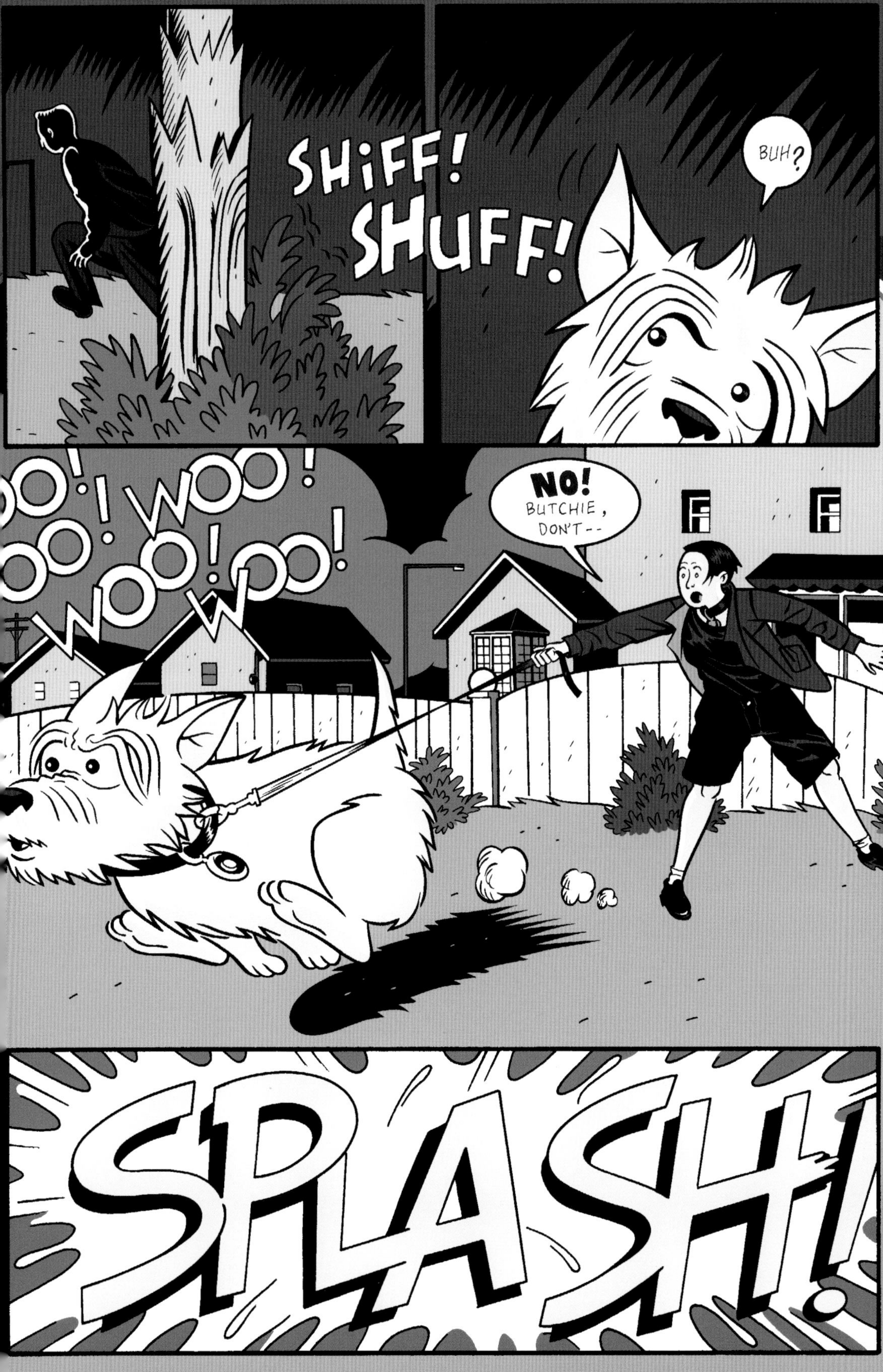
SHIFF!
SHUFF!
BUH?
WOO! WOO! WOO! WOO! WOO! WOO!
NO! BUTCHIE, DON'T--
SPLASH!

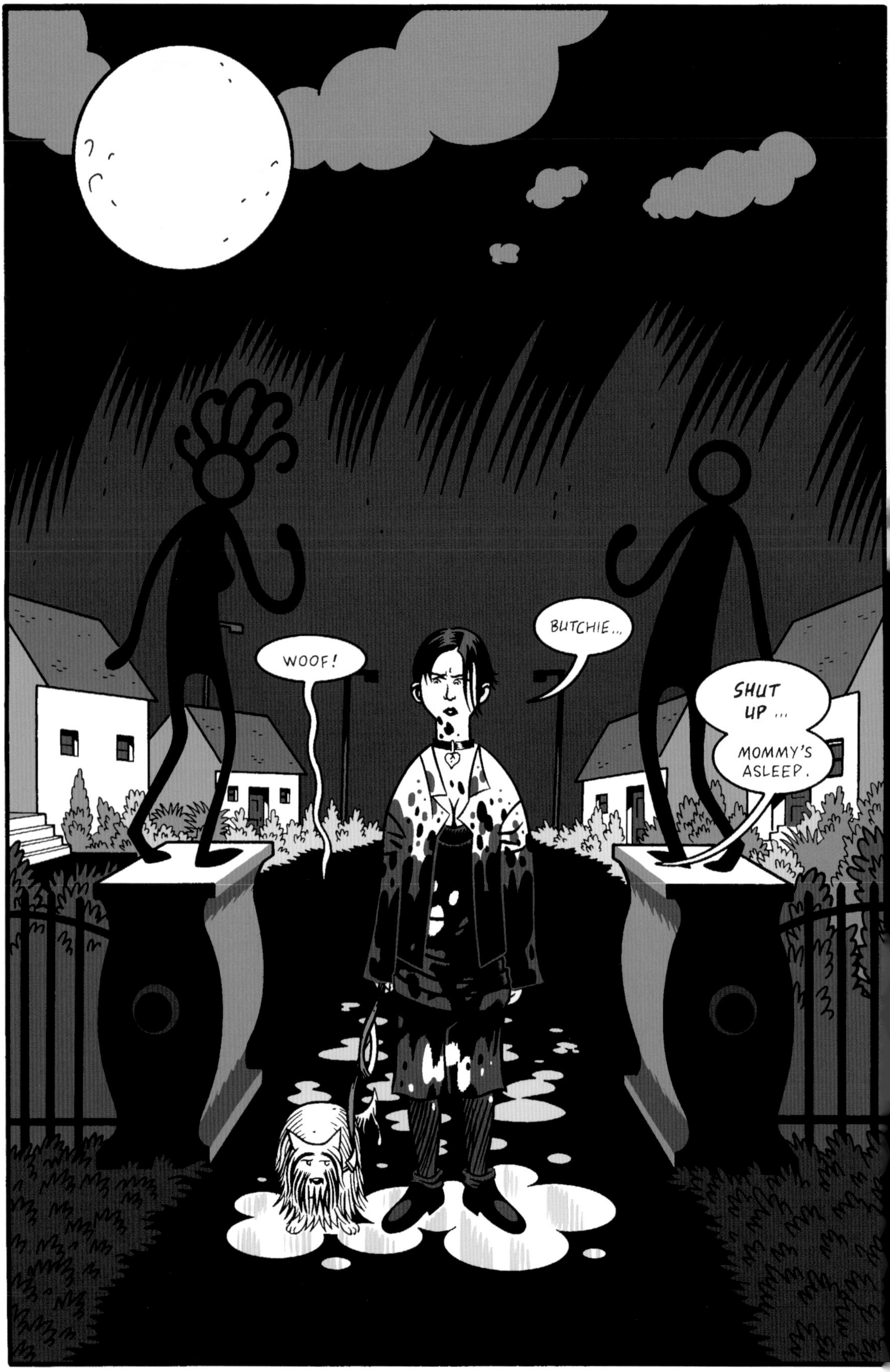
WOOF!
BUTCHIE...
SHUT UP...
MOMMY'S ASLEEP.

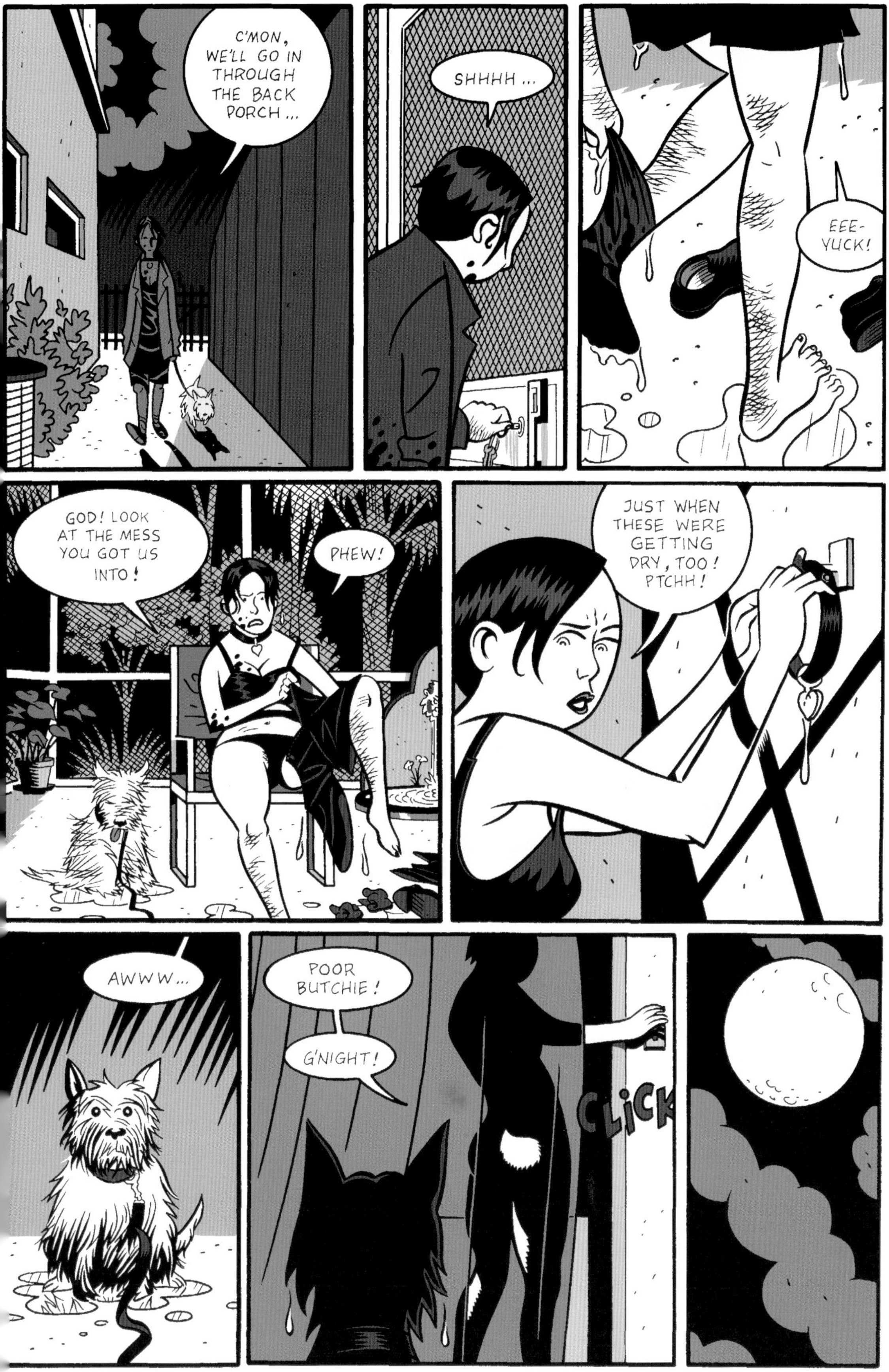
C'MON, WE'LL GO IN THROUGH THE BACK PORCH...
SHHHH...
EEE-YUCK!
GOD! LOOK AT THE MESS YOU GOT US INTO!
PHEW!
JUST WHEN THESE WERE GETTING DRY, TOO! PTCHH!
AWWW...
POOR BUTCHIE!
G'NIGHT!
CLICK

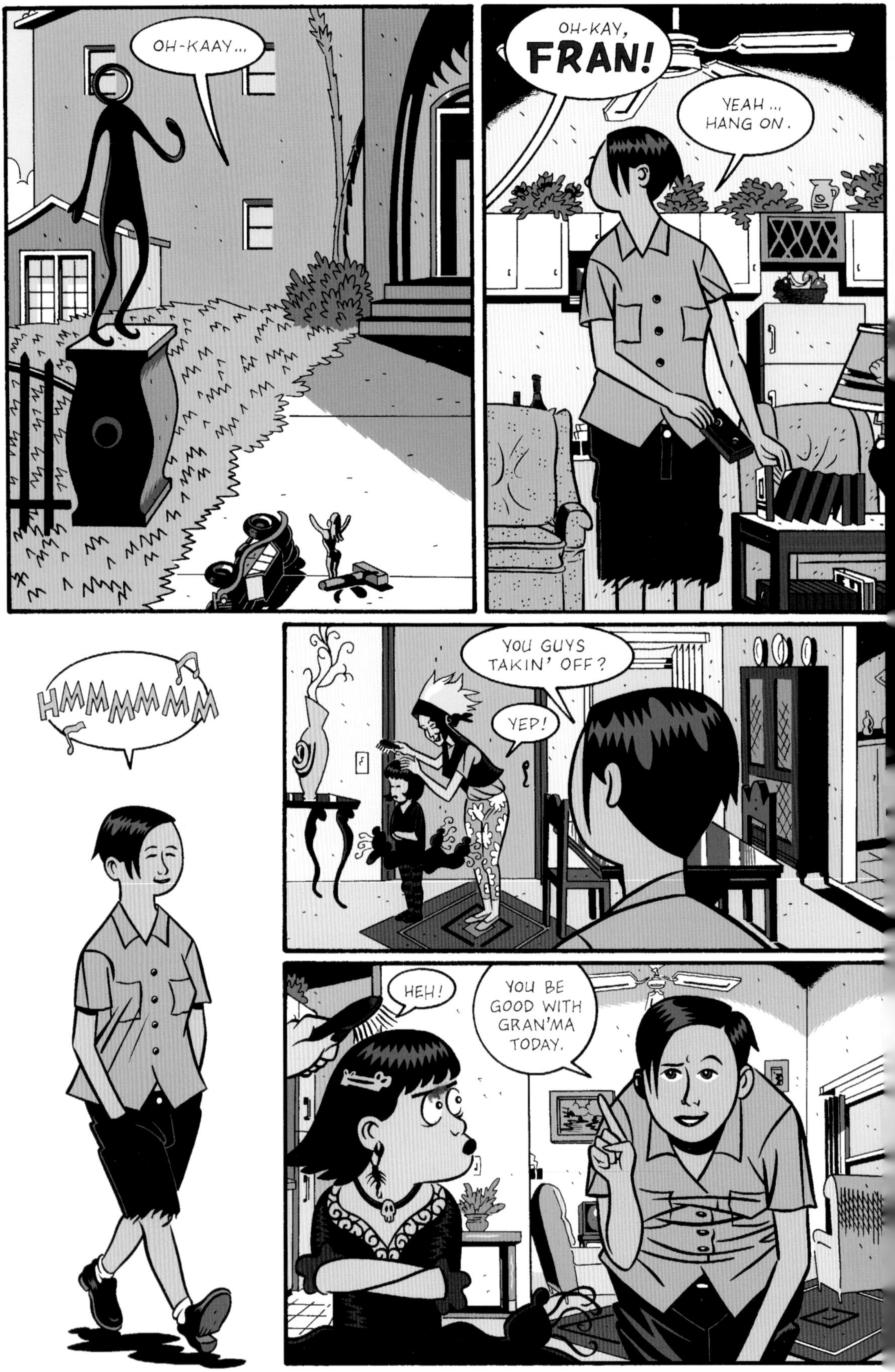
OH-KAAY...
OH-KAY, FRAN!
YEAH... HANG ON.
HMMMMMMM
YOU GUYS TAKIN' OFF?
YEP!
HEH!
YOU BE GOOD WITH GRAN'MA TODAY.

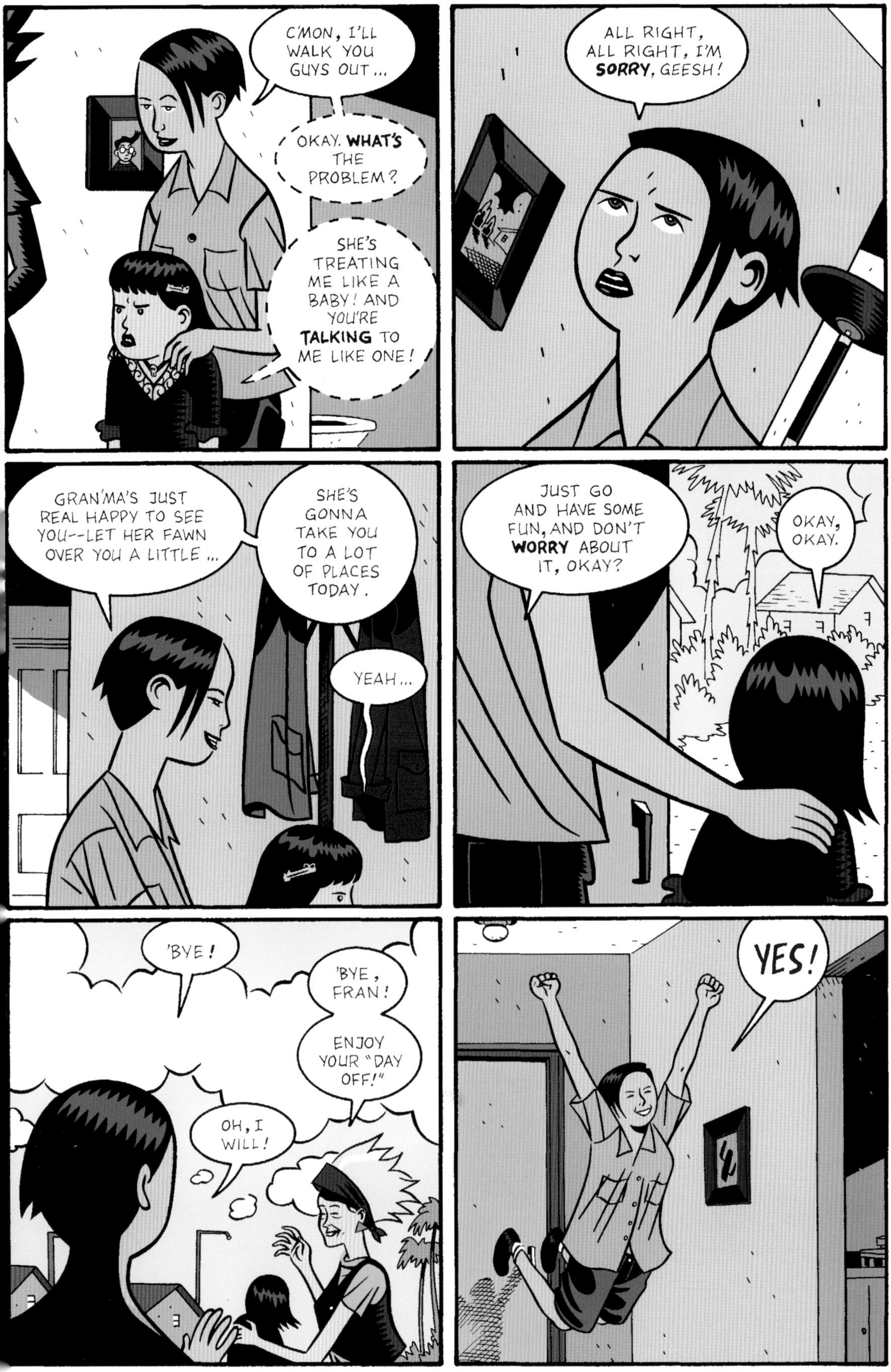
C'MON, I'LL WALK YOU GUYS OUT...
OKAY. WHAT'S THE PROBLEM?
SHE'S TREATING ME LIKE A BABY! AND YOU'RE TALKING TO ME LIKE ONE!
ALL RIGHT, ALL RIGHT, I'M SORRY, GEESH!
GRAN'MA'S JUST REAL HAPPY TO SEE YOU--LET HER FAWN OVER YOU A LITTLE...
SHE'S GONNA TAKE YOU TO A LOT OF PLACES TODAY.
YEAH...
JUST GO AND HAVE SOME FUN, AND DON'T WORRY ABOUT IT, OKAY?
OKAY, OKAY.
'BYE!
'BYE, FRAN!
ENJOY YOUR "DAY OFF!"
OH, I WILL!
YES!

chapter three

Signs

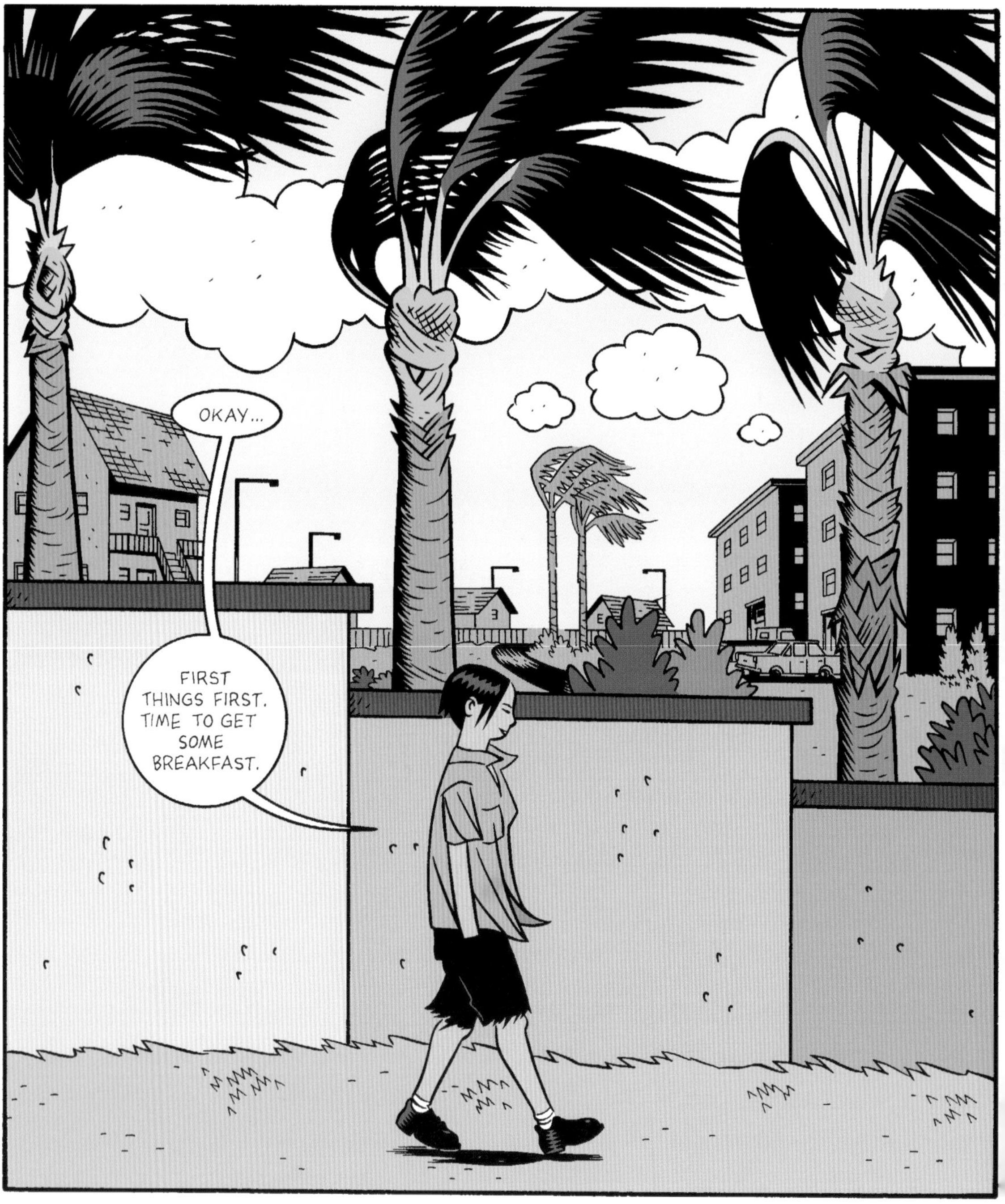
OKAY...
FIRST THINGS FIRST. TIME TO GET SOME BREAKFAST.

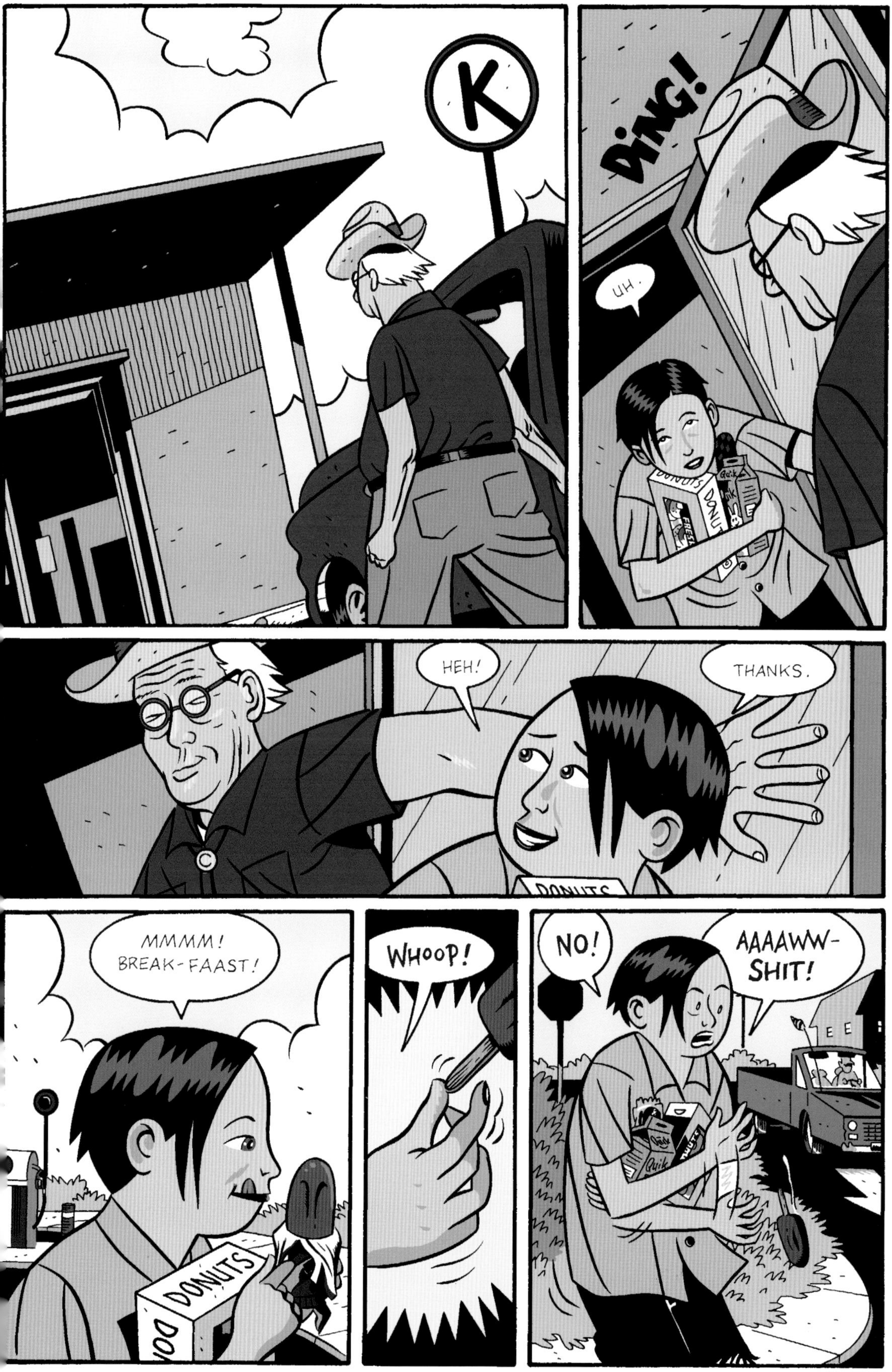
DING!
UH.
HEH!
THANKS.
DONUTS
MMMM! BREAK-FAAST!
DONUTS
WHOOP!
NO!
AAAAWW-SHIT!

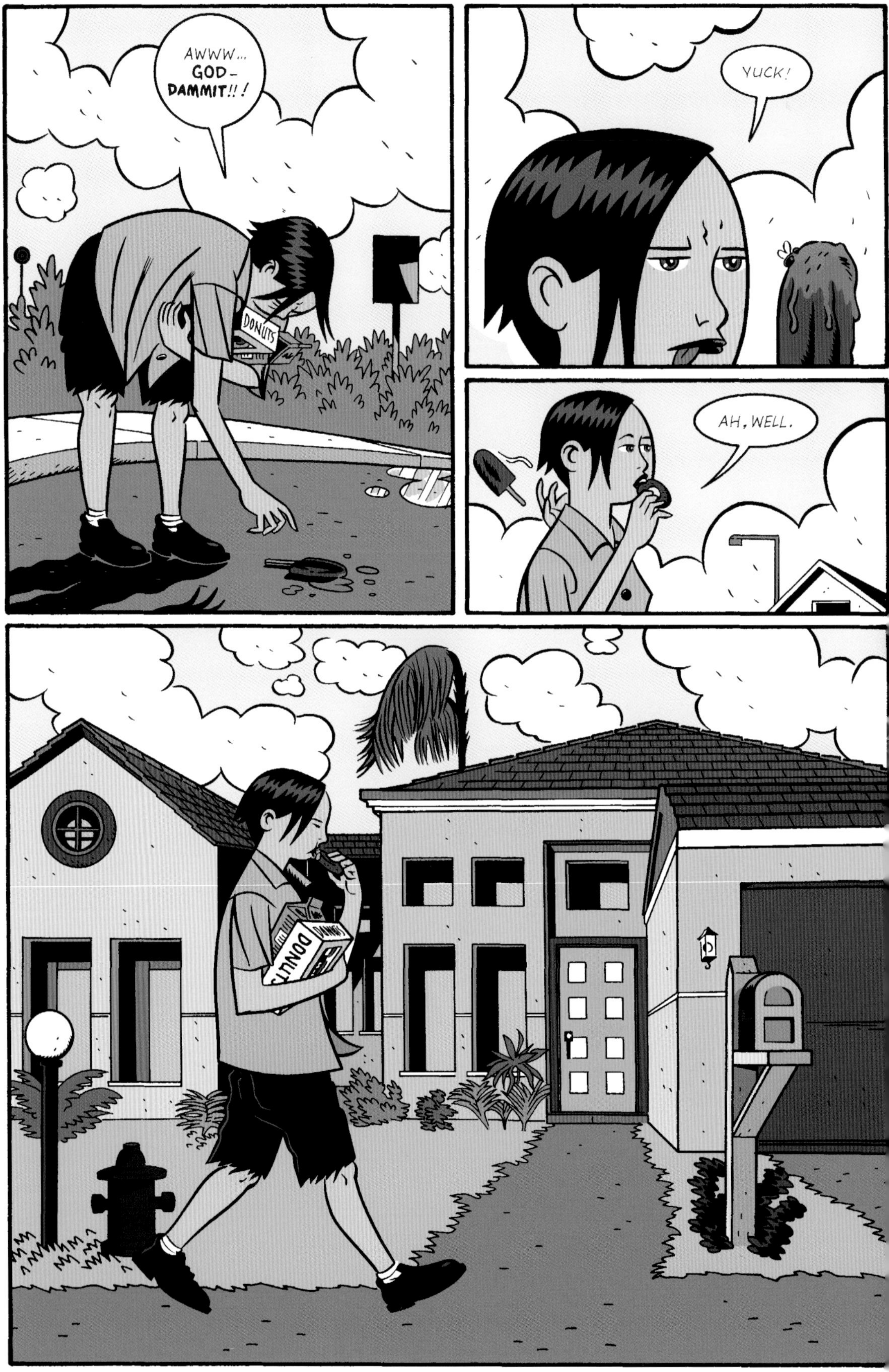
AWWW... GOD-DAMMIT!!!
DONUTS
YUCK!
AH, WELL.
DONUTS

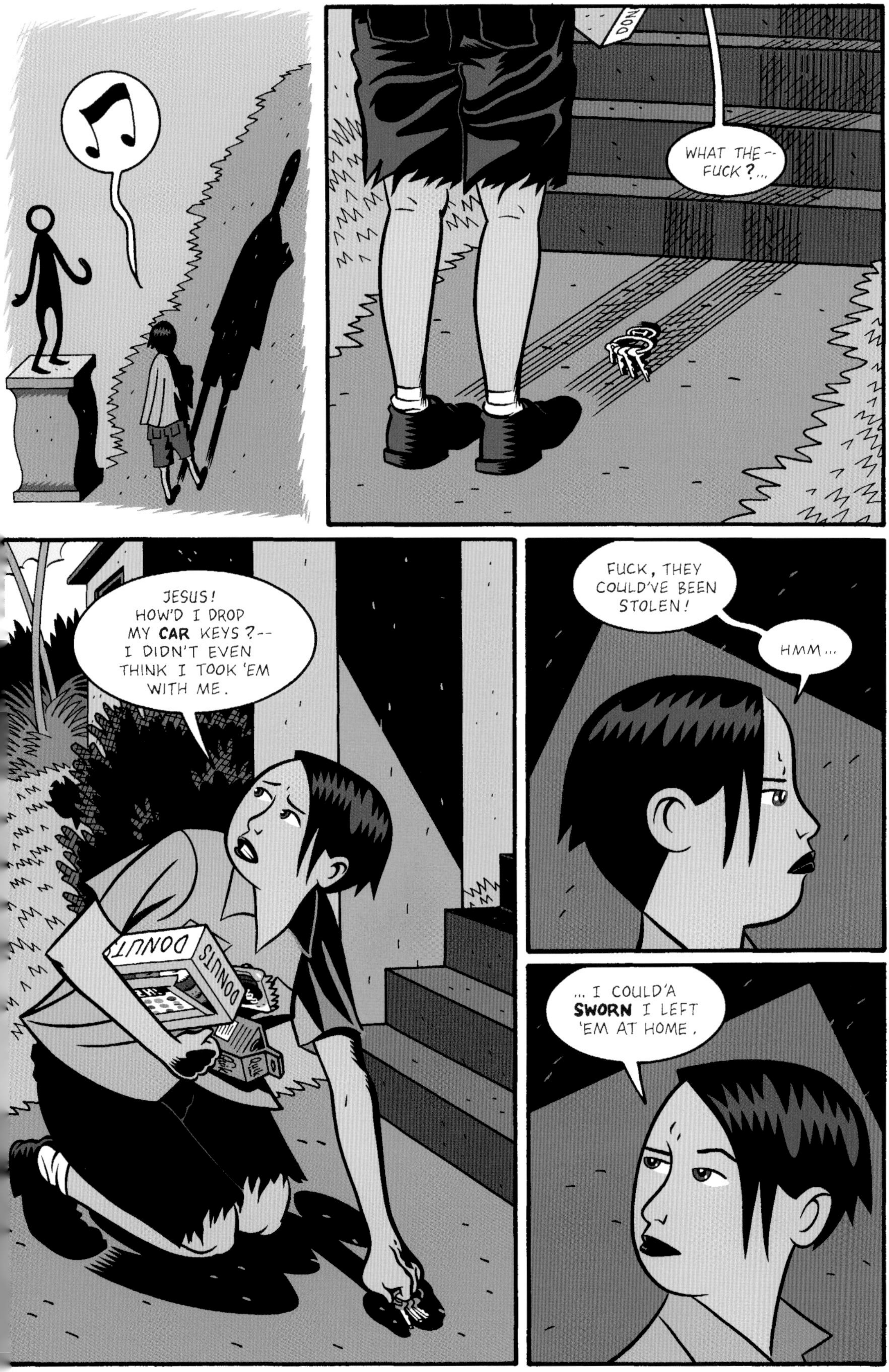
WHAT THE-- FUCK?...
JESUS! HOW'D I DROP MY CAR KEYS?-- I DIDN'T EVEN THINK I TOOK 'EM WITH ME.
DONUTS
FUCK, THEY COULD'VE BEEN STOLEN!
HMM...
... I COULD'A SWORN I LEFT 'EM AT HOME.

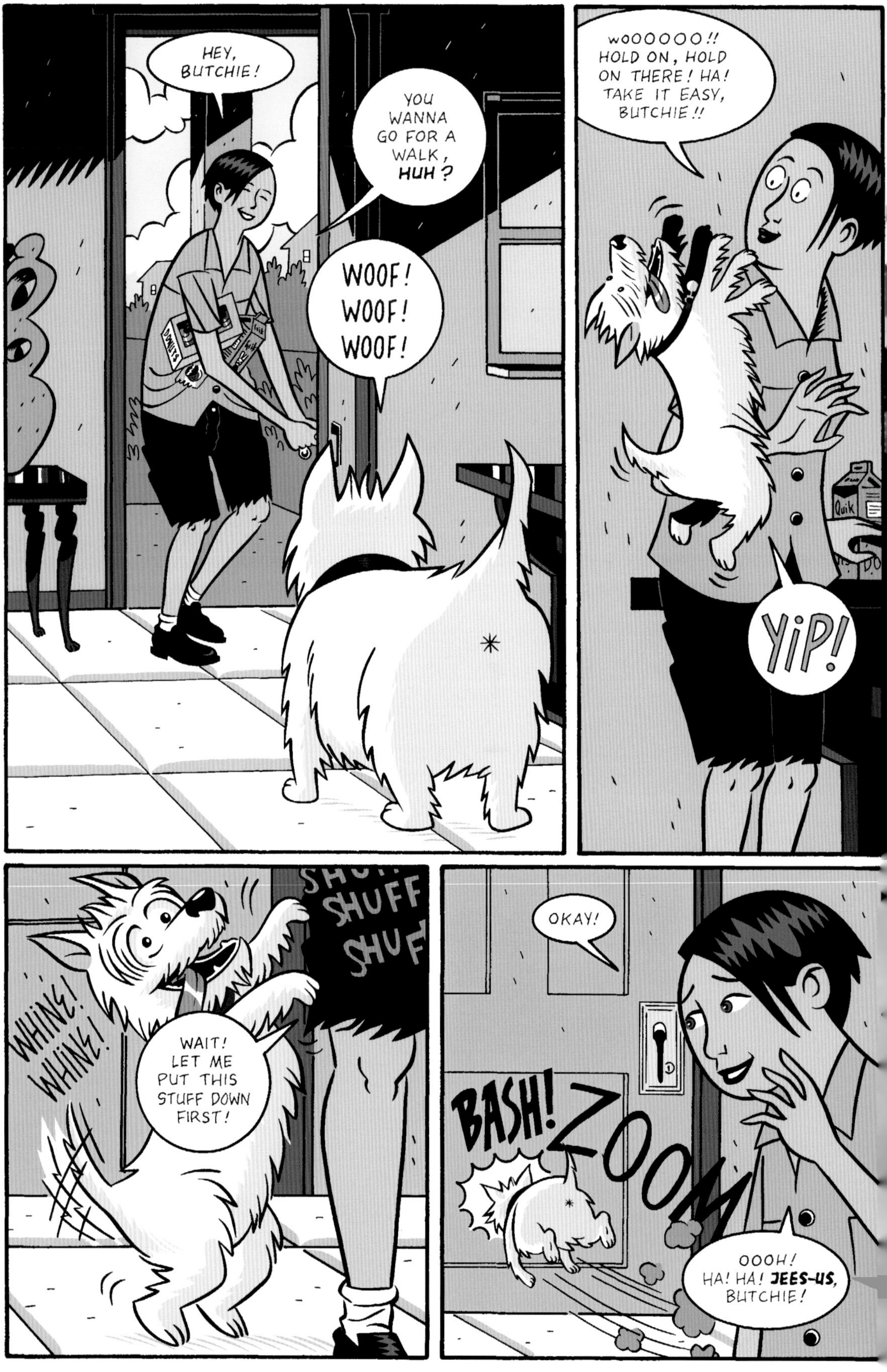
HEY, BUTCHIE!
YOU WANNA GO FOR A WALK, **HUH**?
WOOF! WOOF! WOOF!
WOOOOOO!! HOLD ON, HOLD ON THERE! HA! TAKE IT EASY, BUTCHIE!!
YiP!
SHUFF SHUFF SHUF
WHINE! WHINE!
WAIT! LET ME PUT THIS STUFF DOWN FIRST!
OKAY!
BASH!
ZOOM
OOOH! HA! HA! **JEES-US**, BUTCHIE!

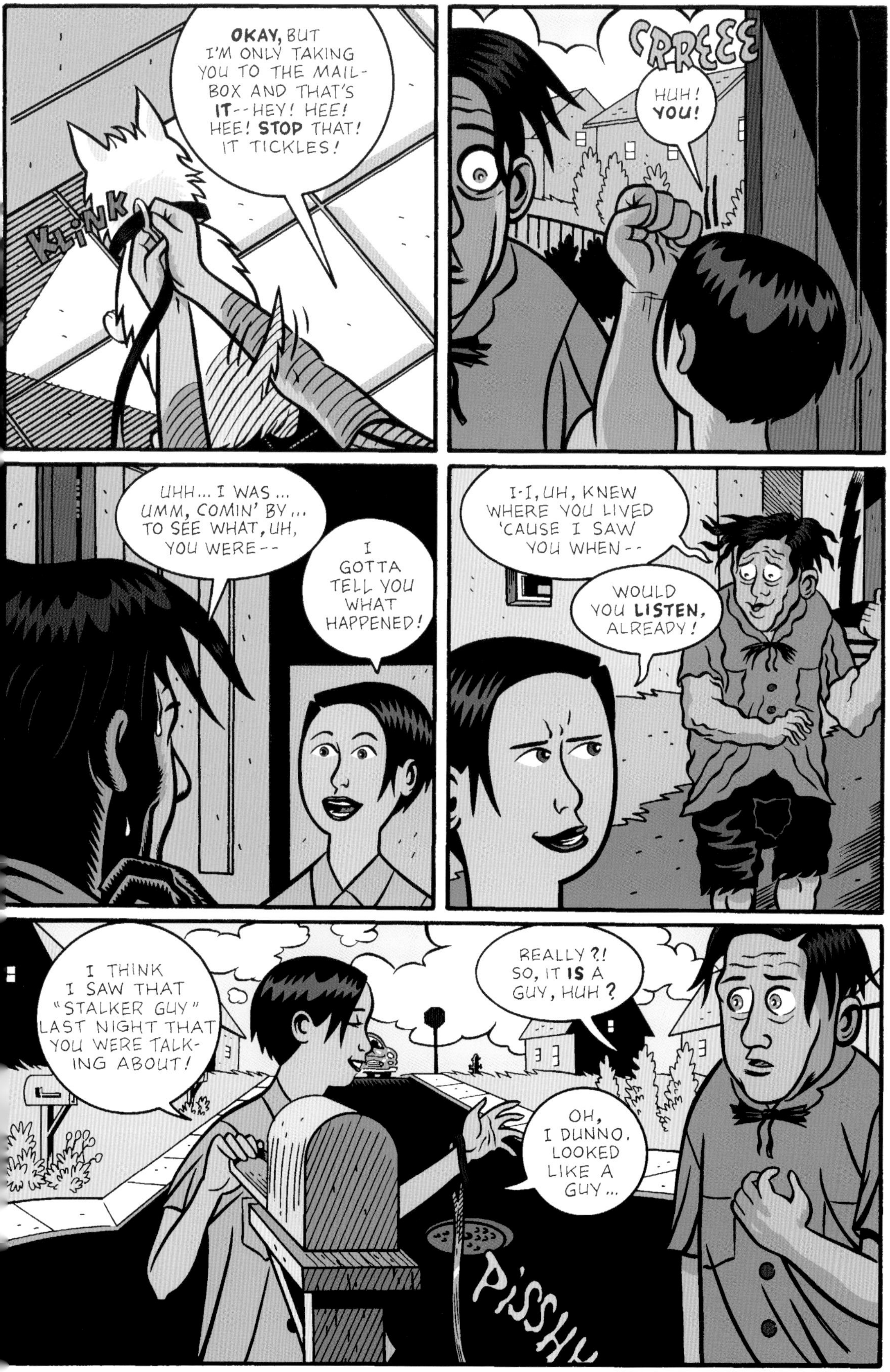

OKAY, BUT I'M ONLY TAKING YOU TO THE MAIL-BOX AND THAT'S IT--HEY! HEE! HEE! STOP THAT! IT TICKLES!
KLINK
CRREEE
HUH! YOU!
UHH... I WAS... UMM, COMIN' BY... TO SEE WHAT, UH, YOU WERE--
I GOTTA TELL YOU WHAT HAPPENED!
I-I, UH, KNEW WHERE YOU LIVED 'CAUSE I SAW YOU WHEN--
WOULD YOU LISTEN, ALREADY!
I THINK I SAW THAT "STALKER GUY" LAST NIGHT THAT YOU WERE TALK-ING ABOUT!
REALLY?! SO, IT IS A GUY, HUH?
OH, I DUNNO. LOOKED LIKE A GUY...
PISSH

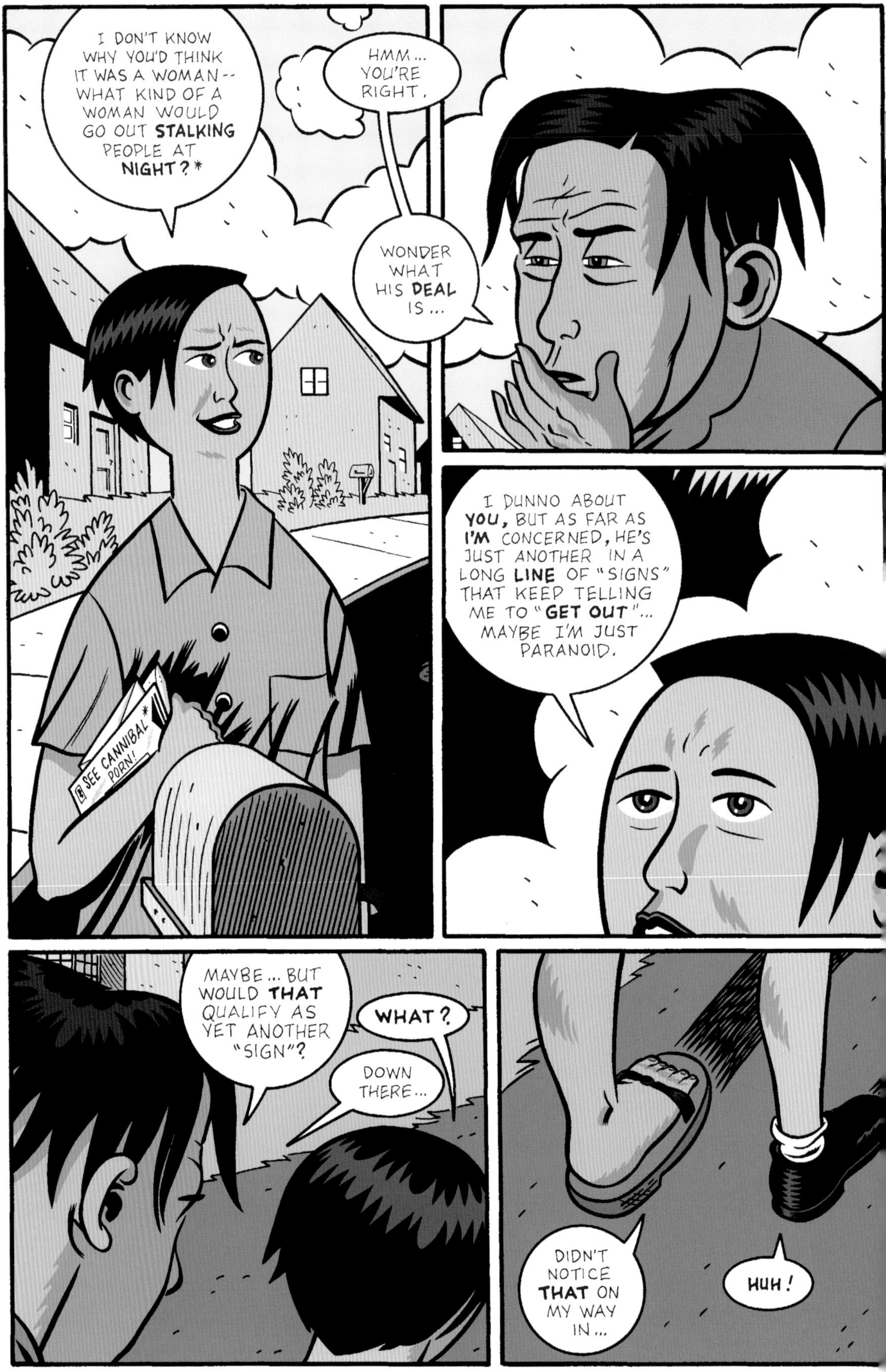
I DON'T KNOW WHY YOU'D THINK IT WAS A WOMAN-- WHAT KIND OF A WOMAN WOULD GO OUT STALKING PEOPLE AT NIGHT?*
HMM... YOU'RE RIGHT.
WONDER WHAT HIS DEAL IS...
* SEE CANNIBAL PORN!
I DUNNO ABOUT YOU, BUT AS FAR AS I'M CONCERNED, HE'S JUST ANOTHER IN A LONG LINE OF "SIGNS" THAT KEEP TELLING ME TO "GET OUT"... MAYBE I'M JUST PARANOID.
MAYBE... BUT WOULD THAT QUALIFY AS YET ANOTHER "SIGN"?
WHAT?
DOWN THERE...
DIDN'T NOTICE THAT ON MY WAY IN...
HUH!

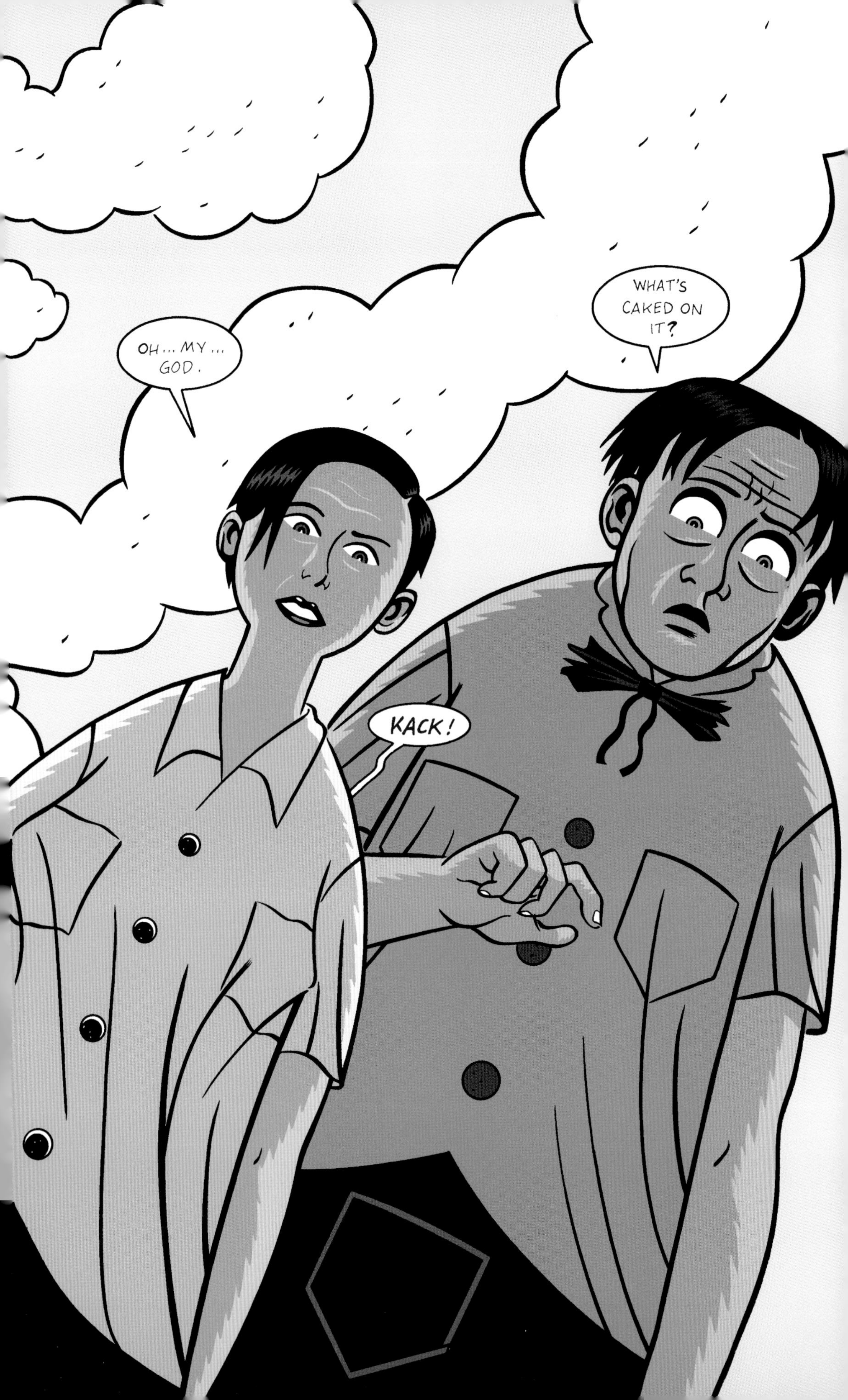
OH... MY... GOD.
WHAT'S CAKED ON IT?
KACK!

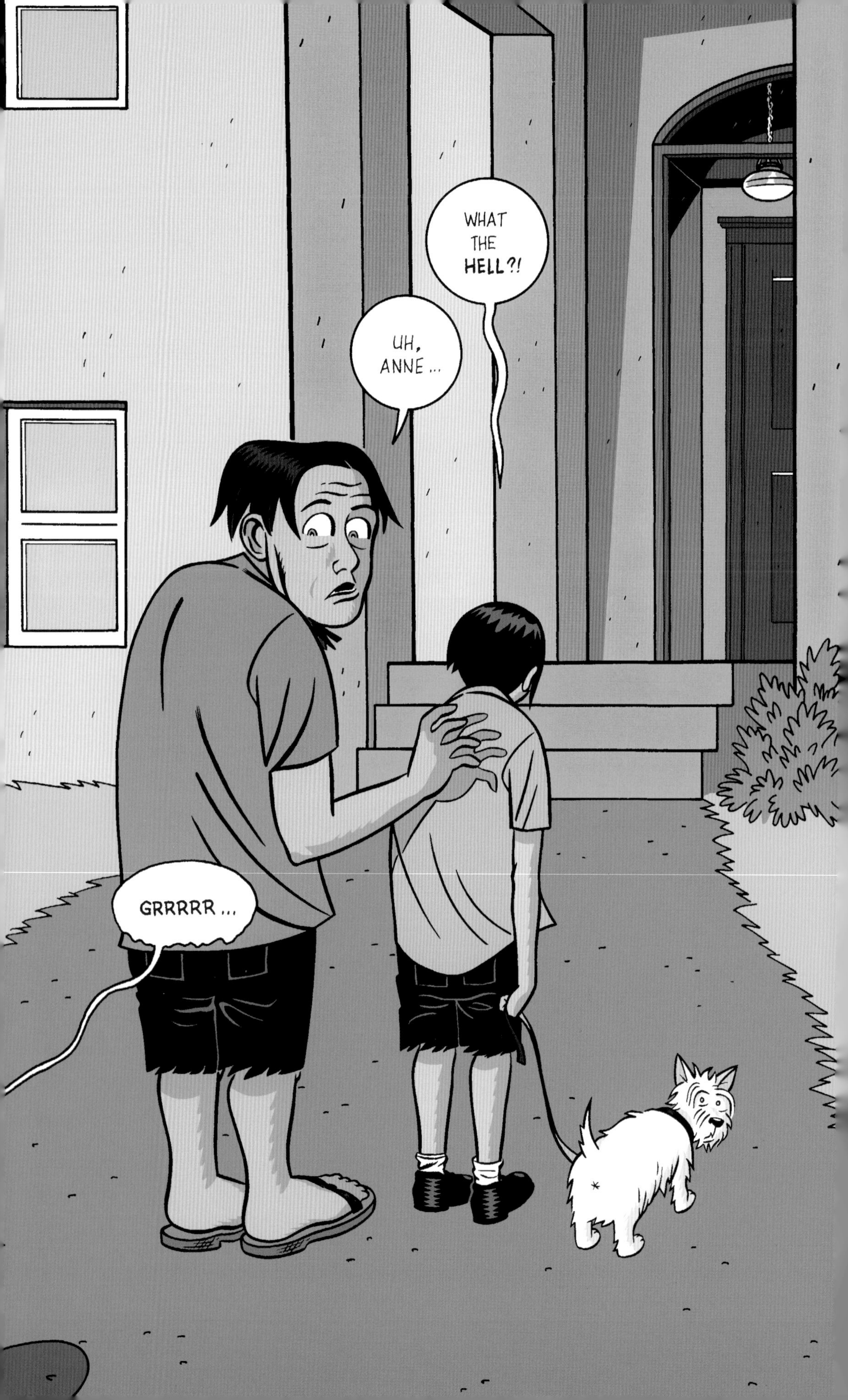
WHAT THE HELL?!
UH, ANNE ...
GRRRRR ...

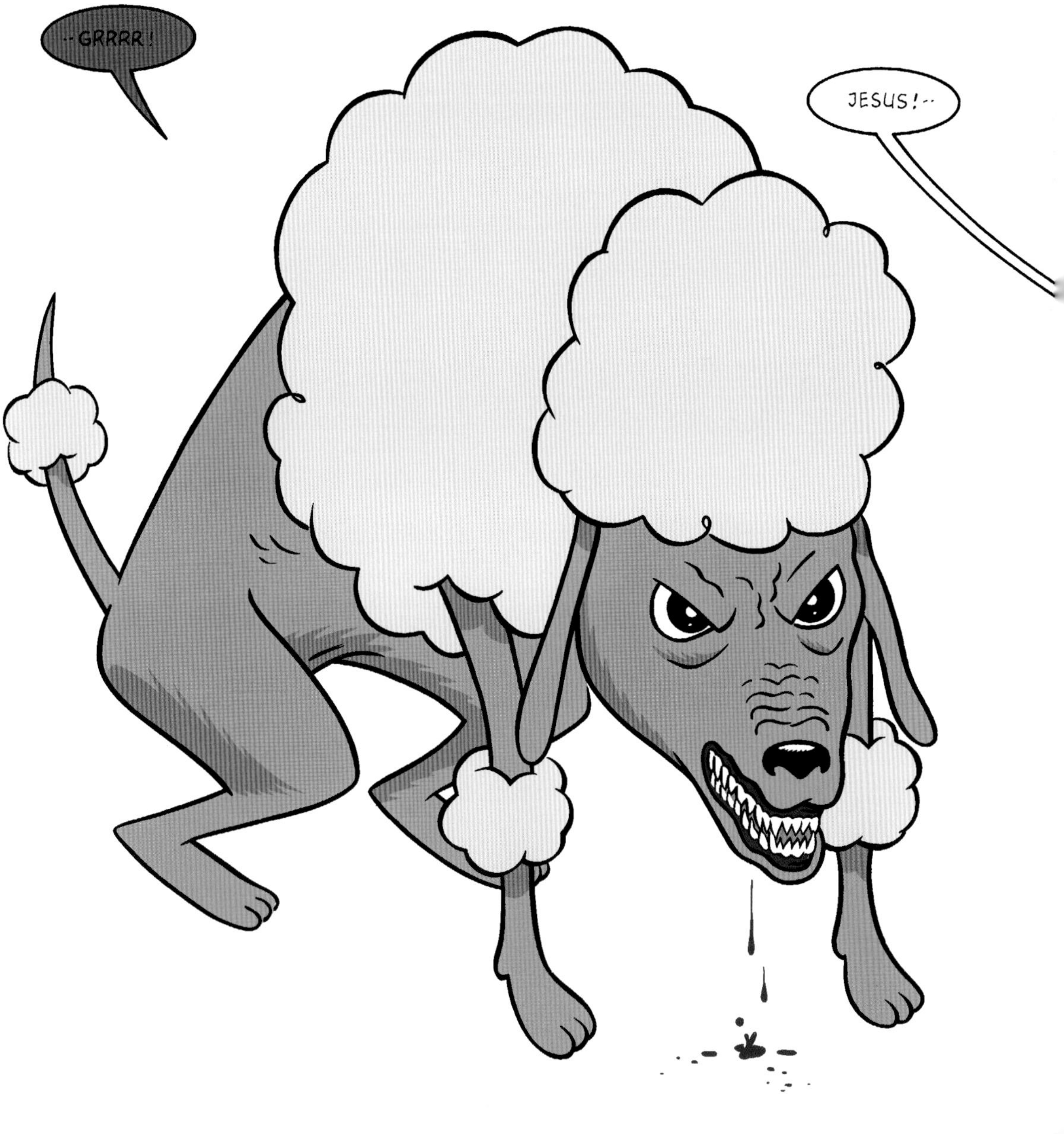

--GRRRR!
JESUS!--

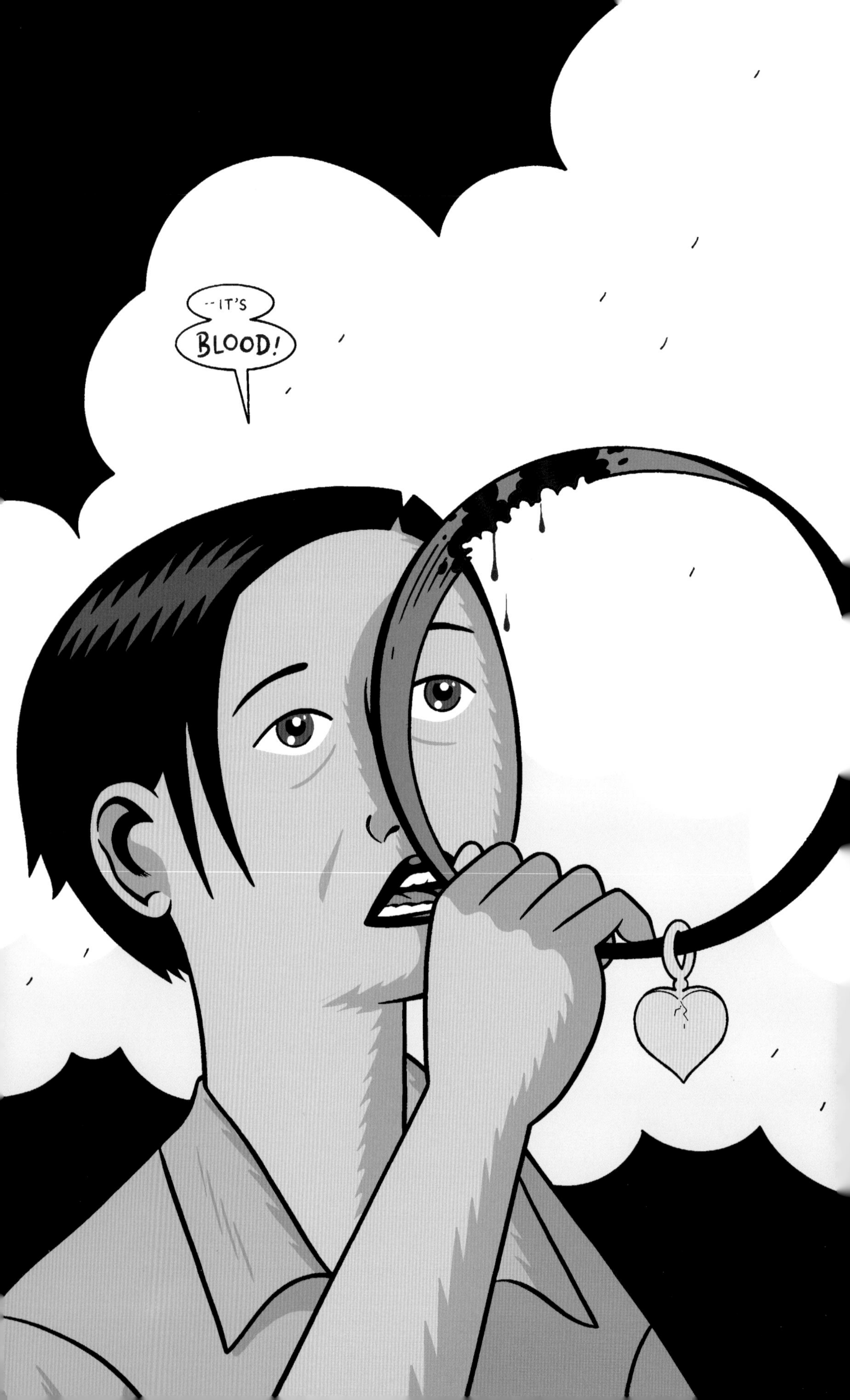
--IT'S
BLOOD!

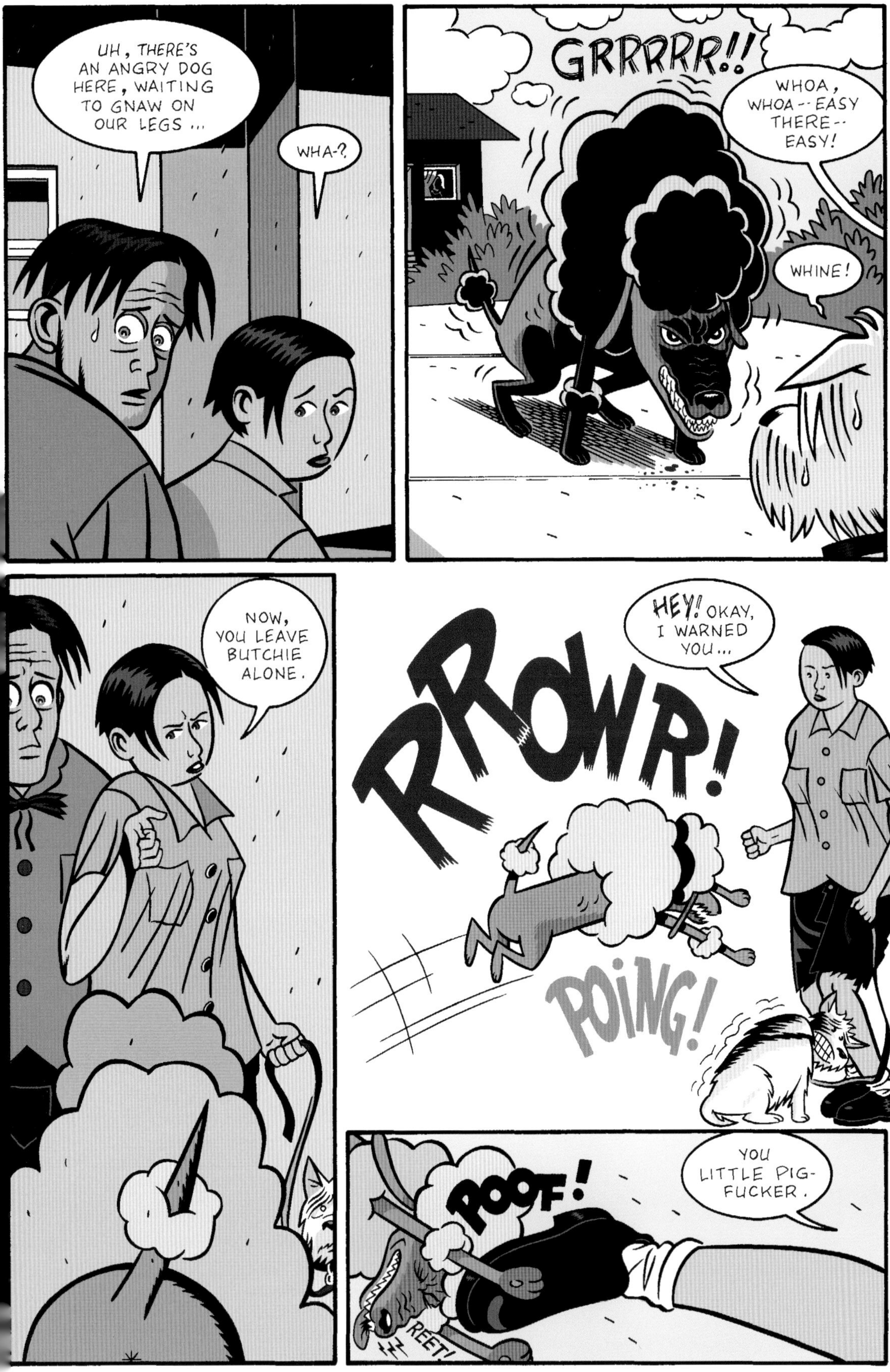
UH, THERE'S AN ANGRY DOG HERE, WAITING TO GNAW ON OUR LEGS...
WHA-?
GRRRRR!!
WHOA, WHOA--EASY THERE--EASY!
WHINE!
NOW, YOU LEAVE BUTCHIE ALONE.
HEY! OKAY, I WARNED YOU...
RROWR!
POING!
POOF!
YOU LITTLE PIG-FUCKER.
REET!

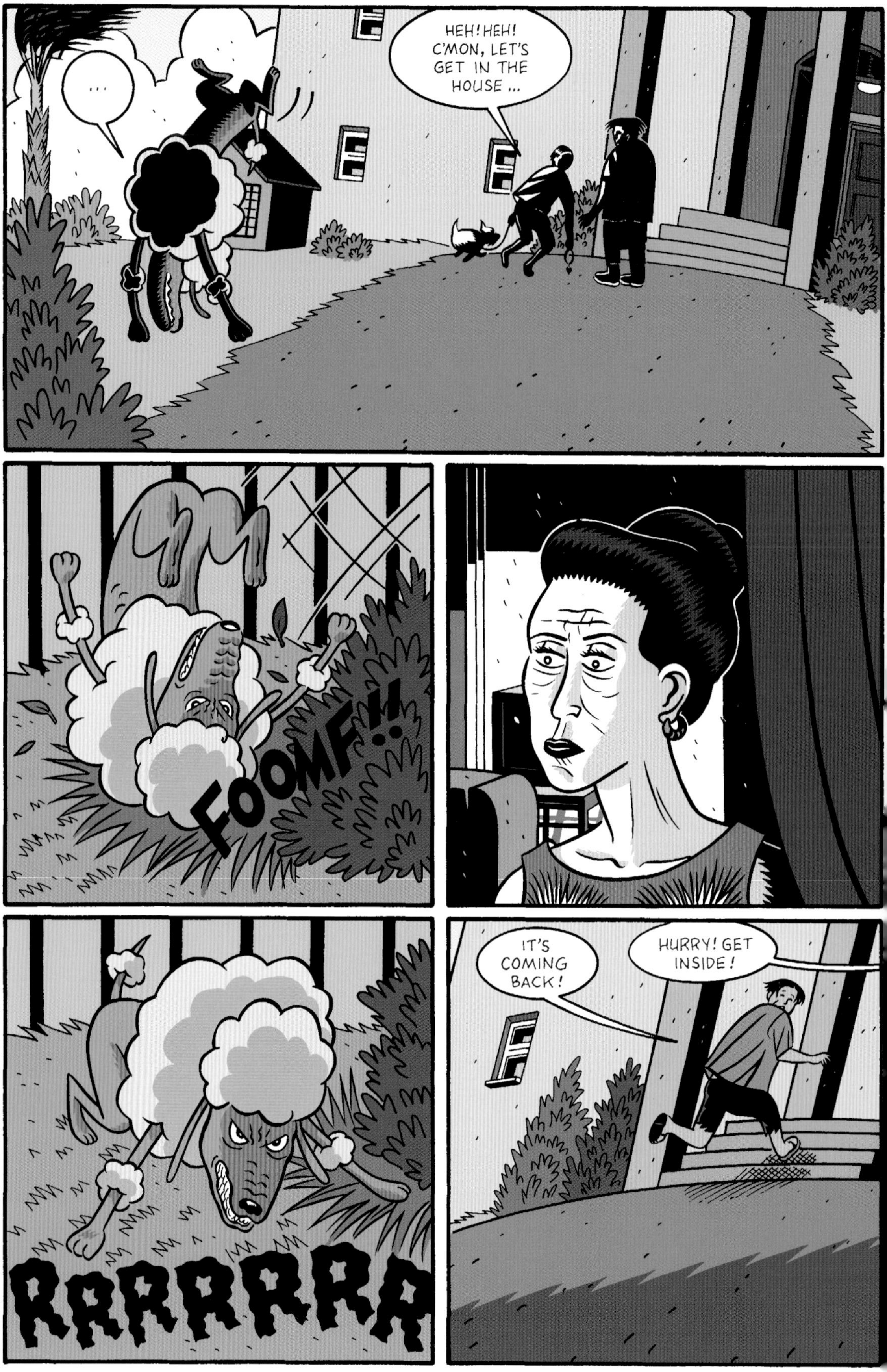
...
HEH! HEH! C'MON, LET'S GET IN THE HOUSE ...
FOOMF!!
RRRRRRA
IT'S COMING BACK!
HURRY! GET INSIDE!

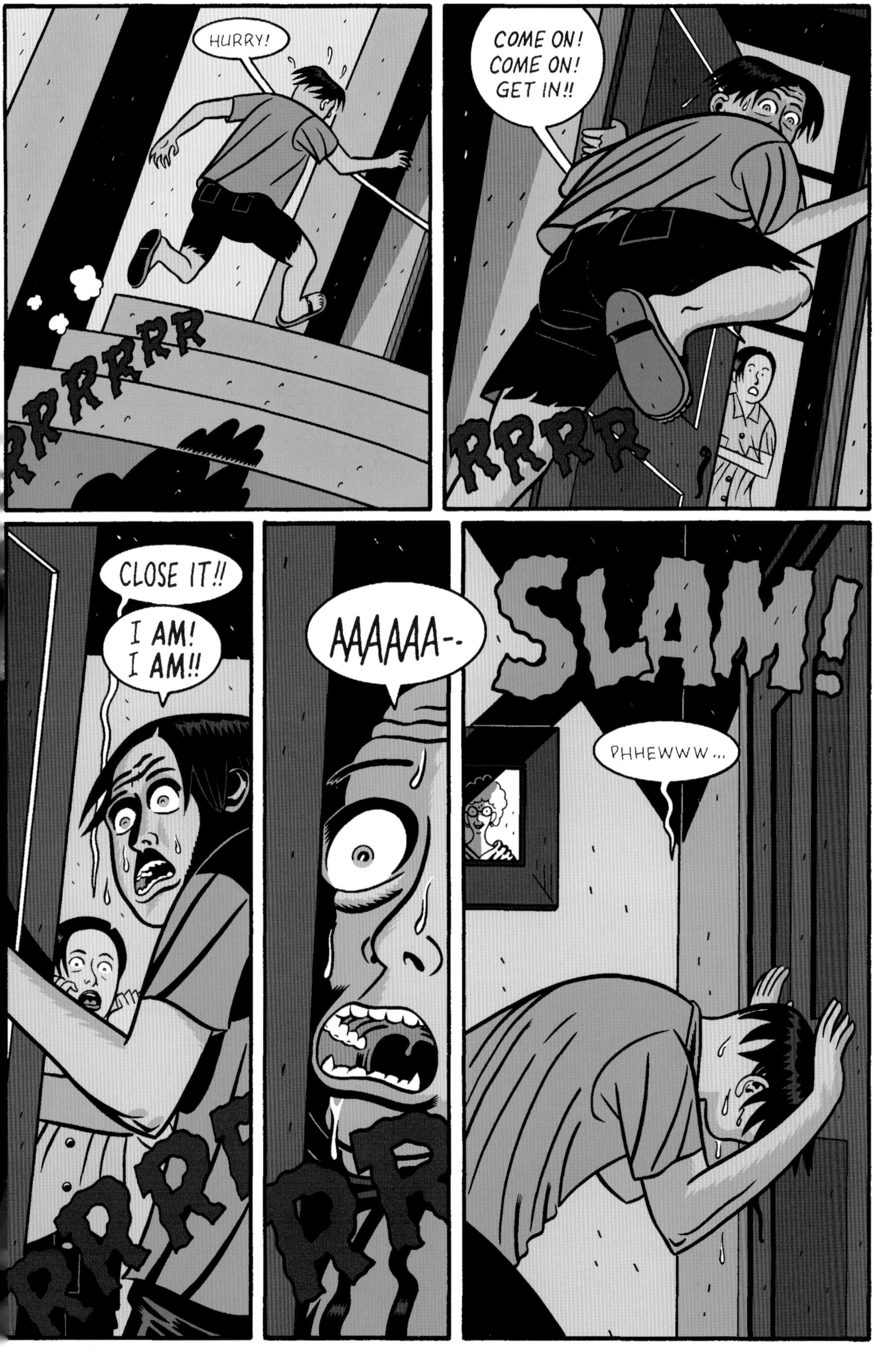
HURRY!
RRRRRRR
COME ON! COME ON! GET IN!!
RRRR
CLOSE IT!!
I AM! I AM!!
AAAAAA-.
SLAM!
PHHEWWW...

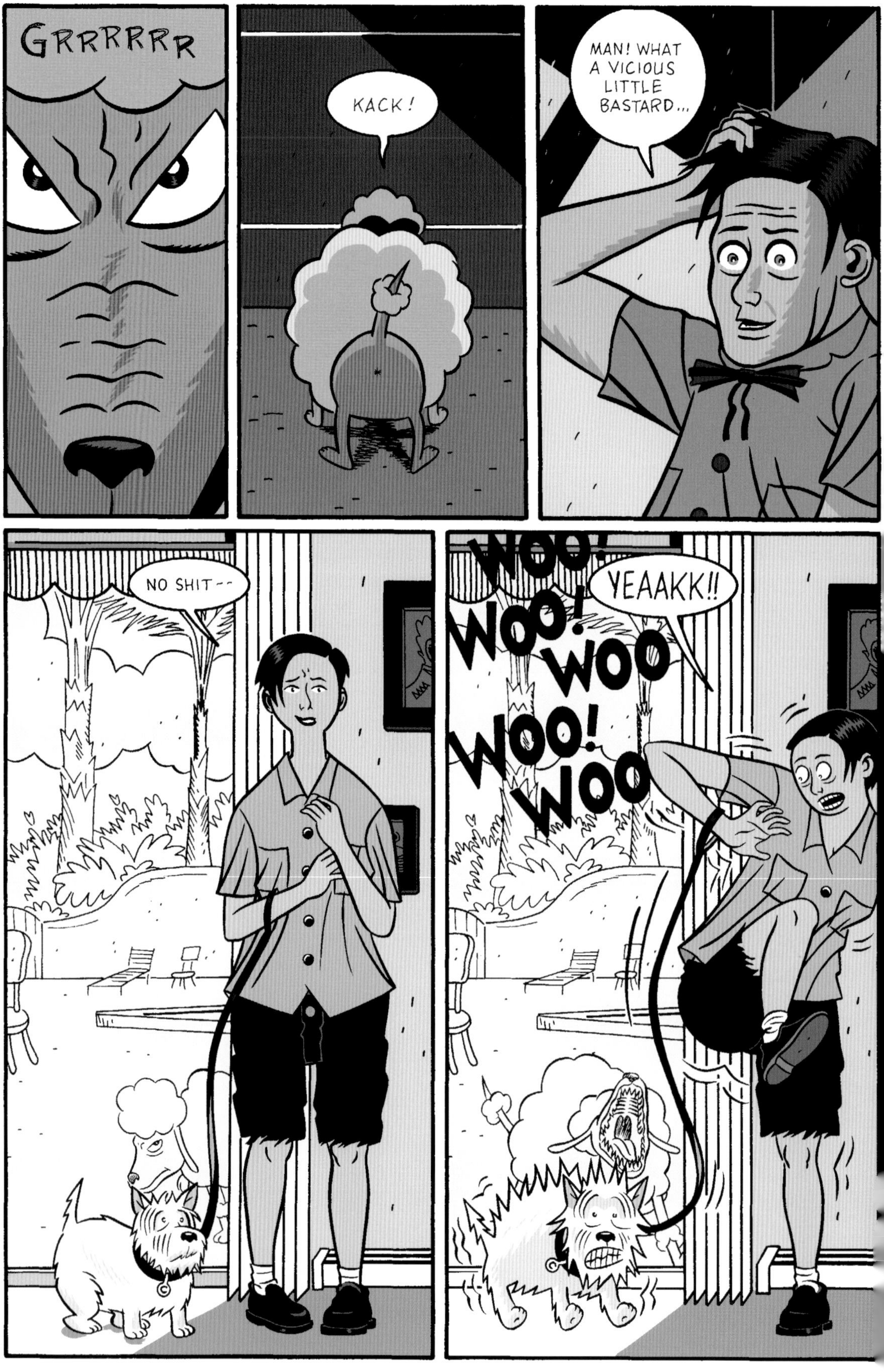
GRRRRRR
KACK!
MAN! WHAT A VICIOUS LITTLE BASTARD...
NO SHIT--
WOO!
YEAAKK!!
WOO!
WOO
WOO!
WOO

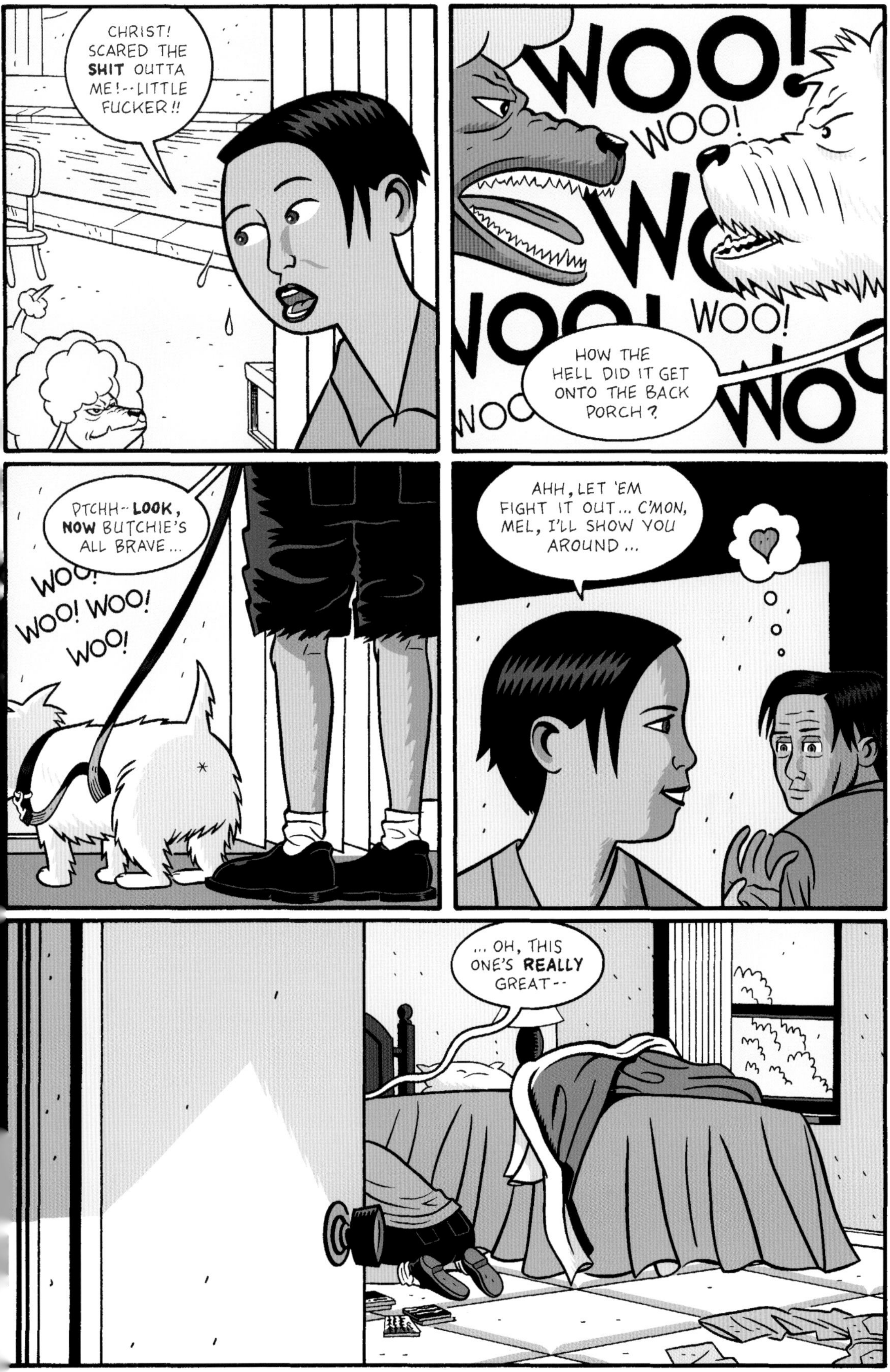
CHRIST! SCARED THE **SHIT** OUTTA ME!--LITTLE FUCKER!!
WOO!
WOO!
WOO!
HOW THE HELL DID IT GET ONTO THE BACK PORCH?
PTCHH--**LOOK, NOW** BUTCHIE'S ALL BRAVE...
WOO! WOO!
WOO!
AHH, LET 'EM FIGHT IT OUT... C'MON, MEL, I'LL SHOW YOU AROUND...
...OH, THIS ONE'S **REALLY** GREAT--

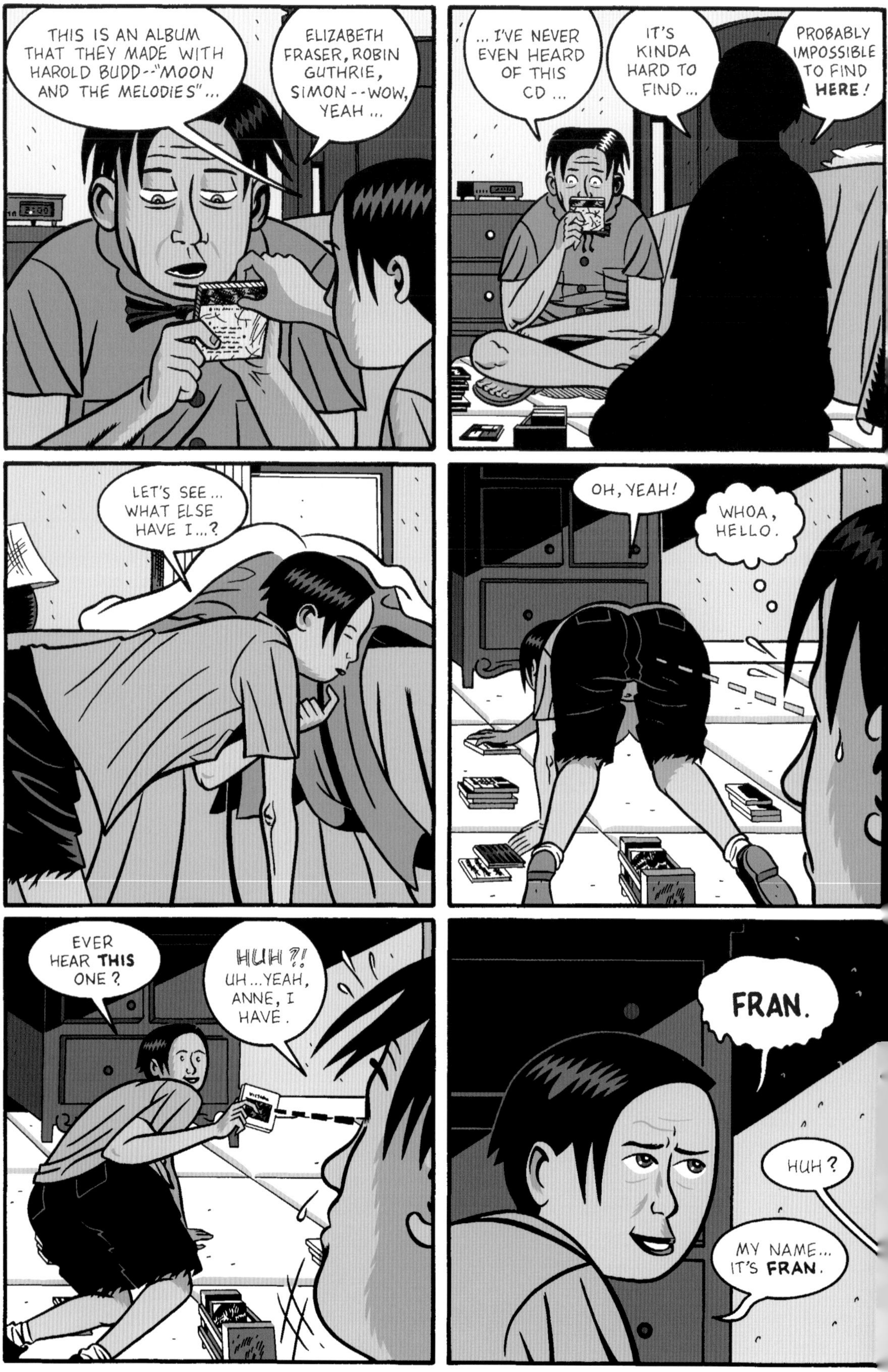

THIS IS AN ALBUM THAT THEY MADE WITH HAROLD BUDD--"MOON AND THE MELODIES"...
ELIZABETH FRASER, ROBIN GUTHRIE, SIMON--WOW, YEAH...
...I'VE NEVER EVEN HEARD OF THIS CD...
IT'S KINDA HARD TO FIND...
PROBABLY IMPOSSIBLE TO FIND **HERE**!
LET'S SEE... WHAT ELSE HAVE I...?
OH, YEAH!
WHOA, HELLO.
EVER HEAR **THIS** ONE?
HUH?! UH...YEAH, ANNE, I HAVE.
FRAN.
HUH?
MY NAME... IT'S **FRAN**.

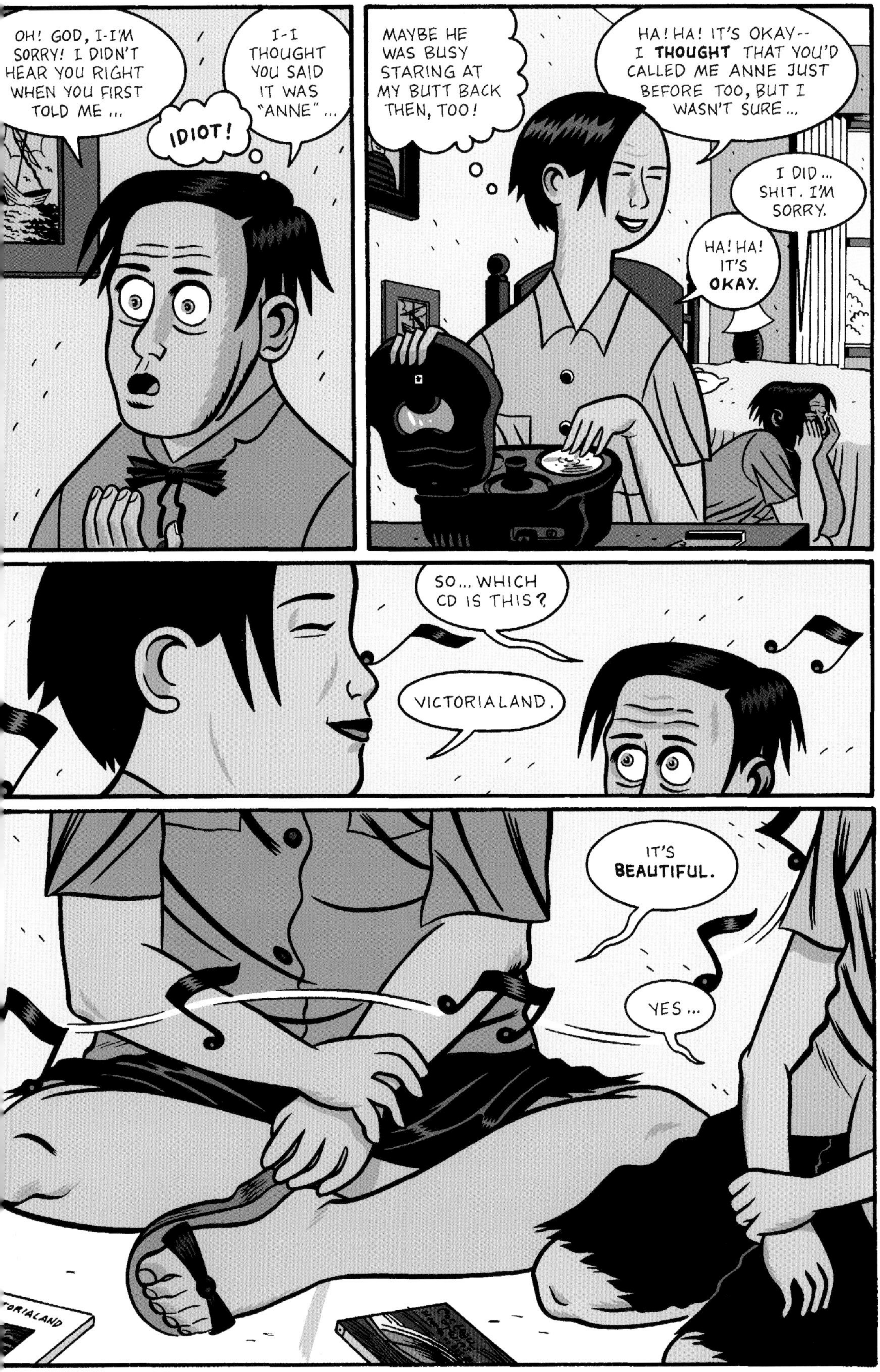
OH! GOD, I-I'M SORRY! I DIDN'T HEAR YOU RIGHT WHEN YOU FIRST TOLD ME ...
IDIOT!
I-I THOUGHT YOU SAID IT WAS "ANNE" ...
MAYBE HE WAS BUSY STARING AT MY BUTT BACK THEN, TOO!
HA! HA! IT'S OKAY-- I THOUGHT THAT YOU'D CALLED ME ANNE JUST BEFORE TOO, BUT I WASN'T SURE ...
I DID ... SHIT. I'M SORRY.
HA! HA! IT'S OKAY.
SO ... WHICH CD IS THIS?
VICTORIALAND.
IT'S BEAUTIFUL.
YES ...

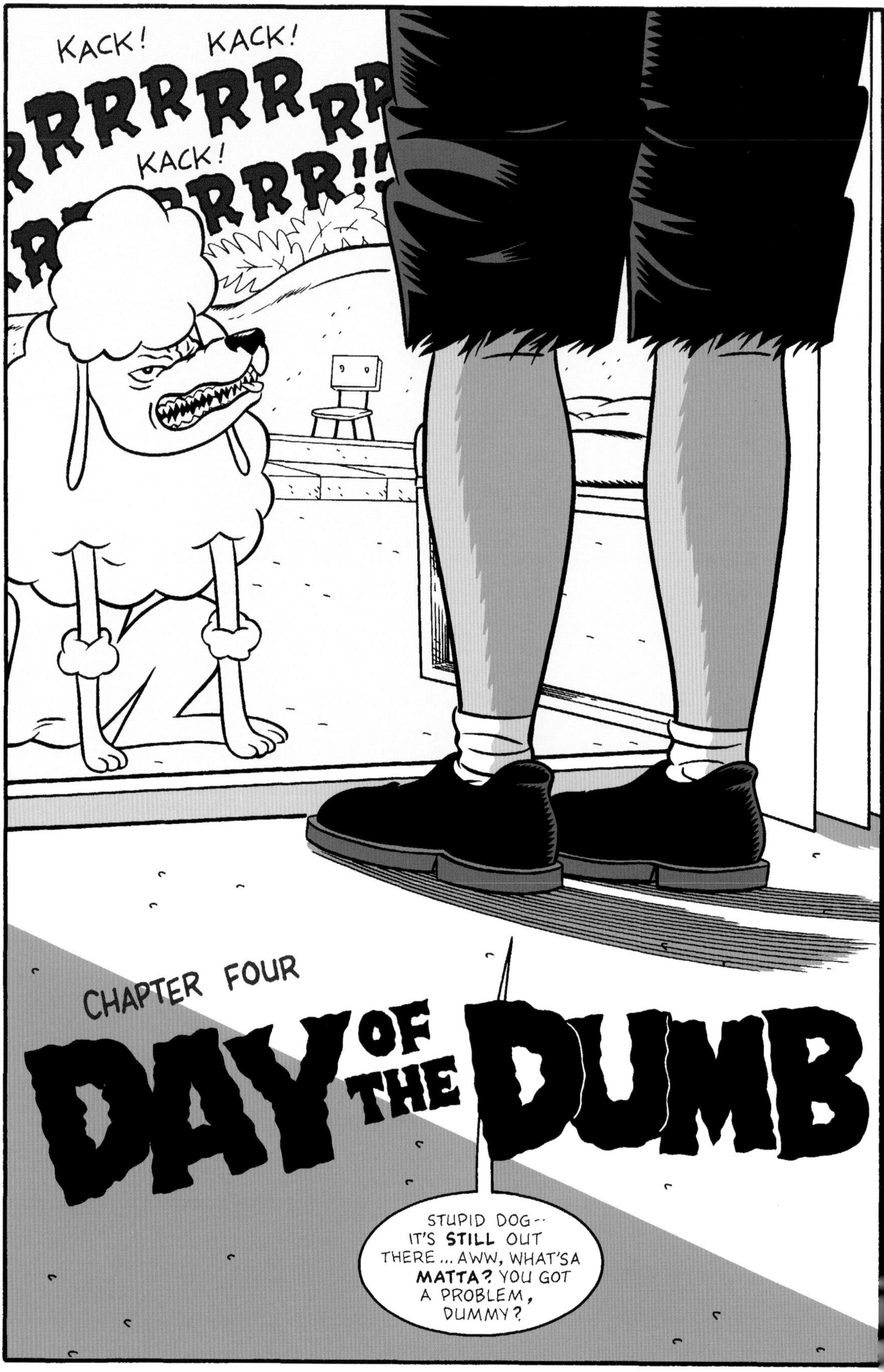
KACK! KACK!
RRRRRRRRRR
KACK!
RRRRRRR!!
CHAPTER FOUR
DAY OF THE DUMB
STUPID DOG-- IT'S **STILL** OUT THERE... AWW, WHAT'SA **MATTA?** YOU GOT A PROBLEM, DUMMY?

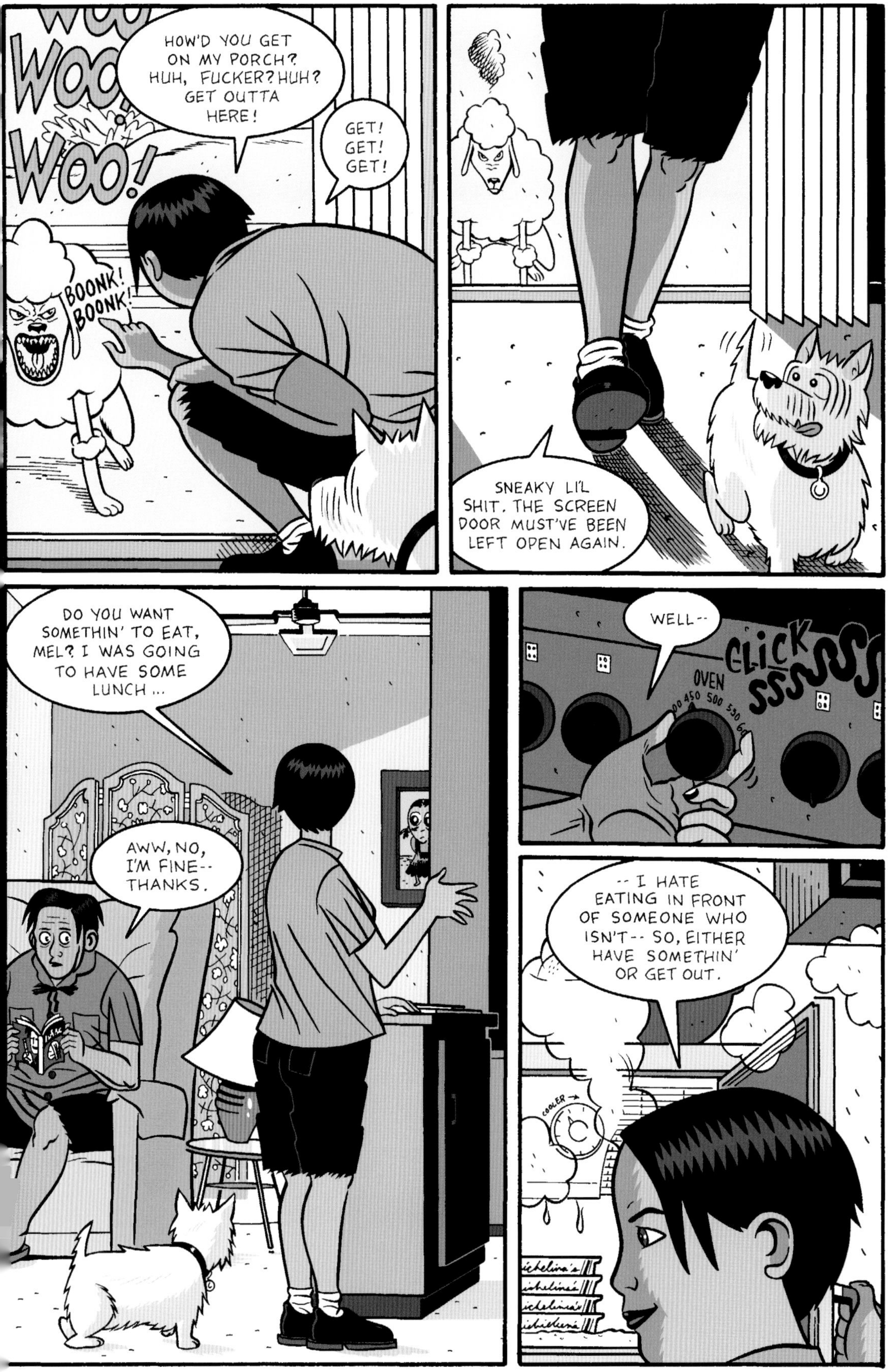
WOO WOO! WOO!
HOW'D YOU GET ON MY PORCH? HUH, FUCKER? HUH? GET OUTTA HERE!
GET! GET! GET!
BOONK! BOONK!
SNEAKY LI'L SHIT. THE SCREEN DOOR MUST'VE BEEN LEFT OPEN AGAIN.
DO YOU WANT SOMETHIN' TO EAT, MEL? I WAS GOING TO HAVE SOME LUNCH ...
AWW, NO, I'M FINE-- THANKS.
WELL--
CLICK SSSSSSS
OVEN
-- I HATE EATING IN FRONT OF SOMEONE WHO ISN'T-- SO, EITHER HAVE SOMETHIN' OR GET OUT.
COOLER

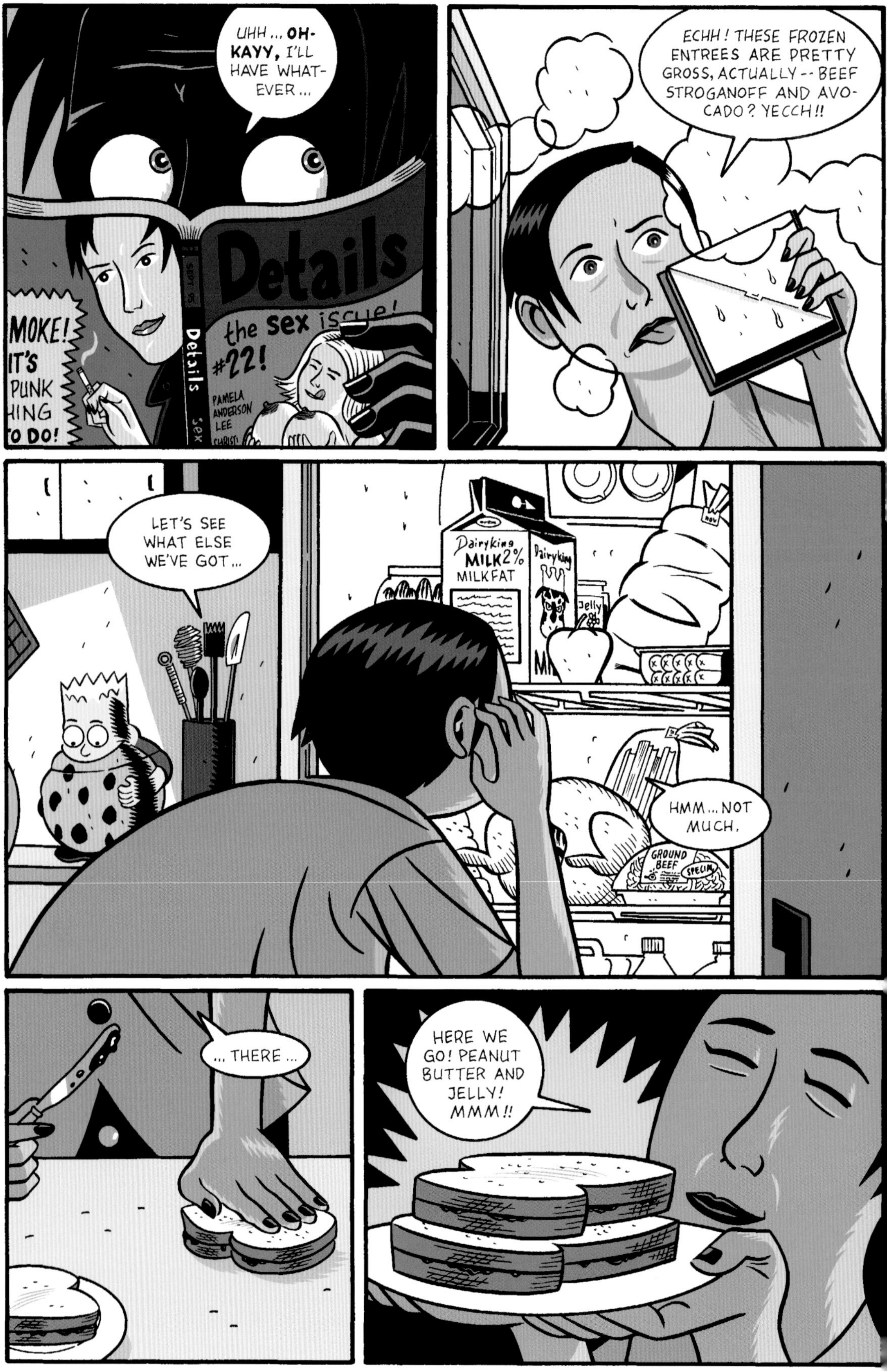
UHH... OH-KAYY, I'LL HAVE WHAT-EVER...
Details
the sex issue!
#22!
PAMELA ANDERSON LEE
ECHH! THESE FROZEN ENTREES ARE PRETTY GROSS, ACTUALLY -- BEEF STROGANOFF AND AVO-CADO? YECCH!!
LET'S SEE WHAT ELSE WE'VE GOT...
Dairyking MILK 2% MILKFAT
Jelly
HMM... NOT MUCH.
GROUND BEEF
... THERE ...
HERE WE GO! PEANUT BUTTER AND JELLY! MMM!!

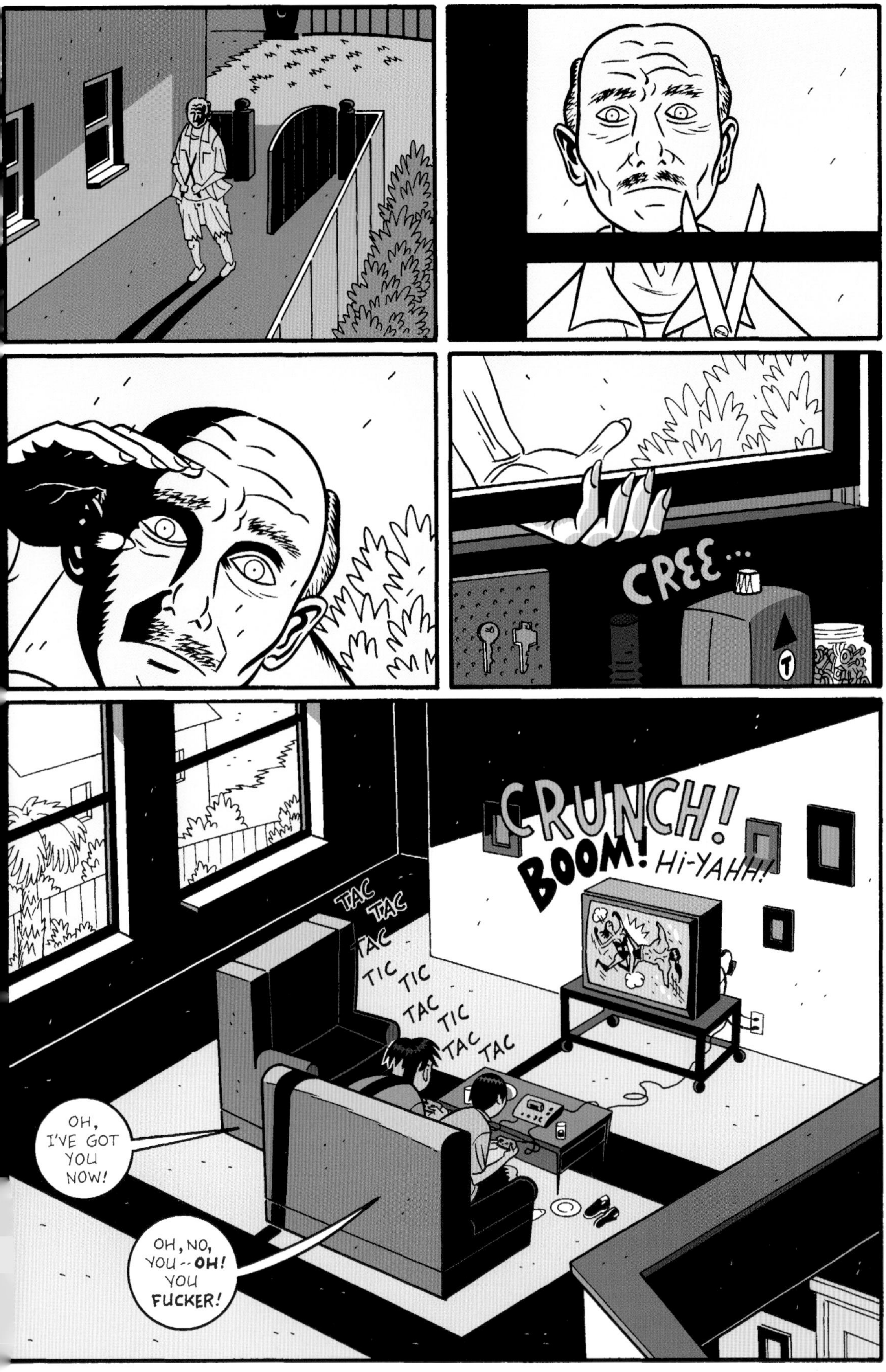
CREE...
CRUNCH!
BOOM!
Hi-YAHH!
TAC TAC TAC
TIC TIC
TAC TIC TAC TAC
OH, I'VE GOT YOU NOW!
OH, NO, YOU--OH! YOU FUCKER!

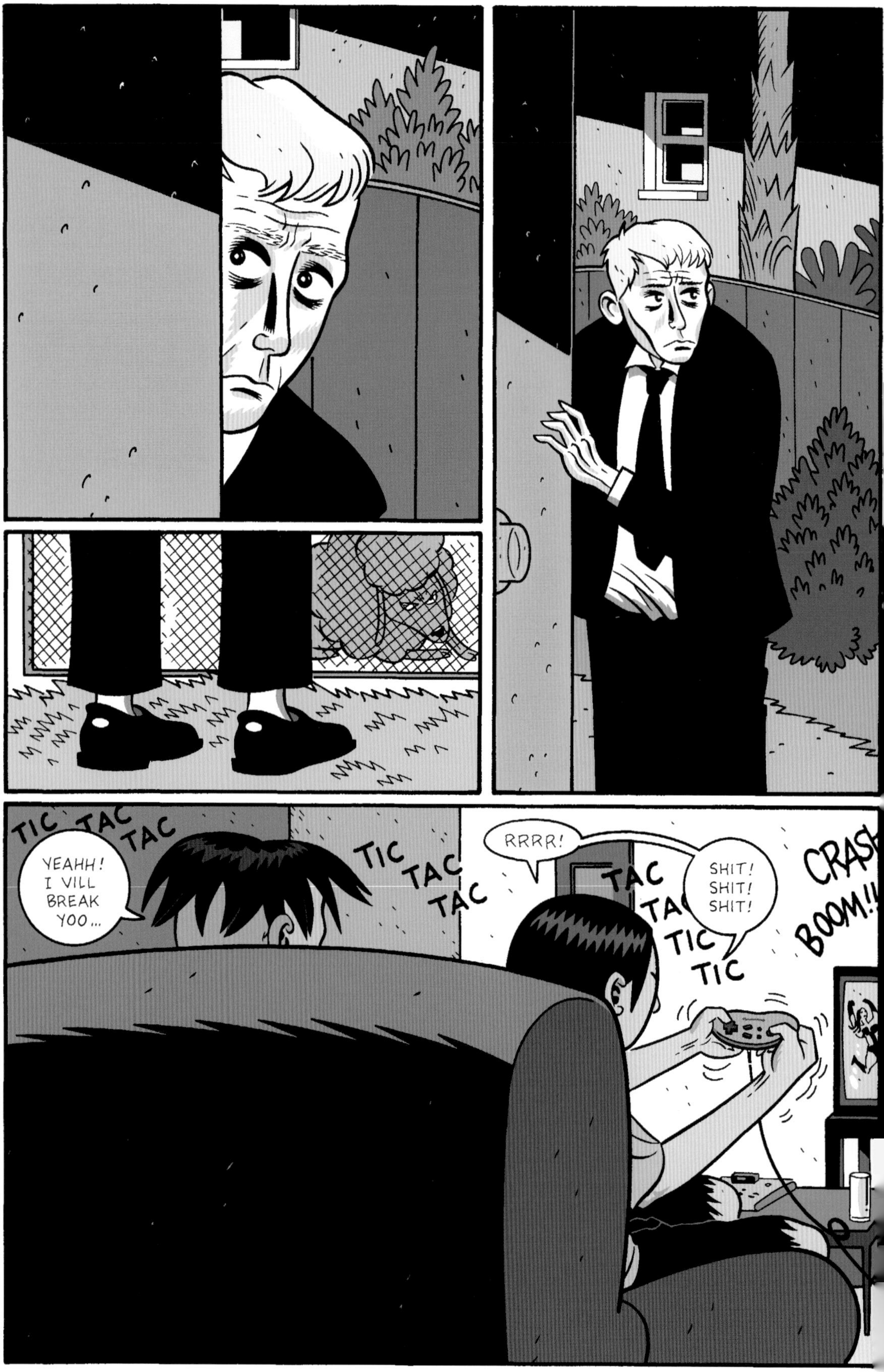
TIC TAC TAC
YEAHH! I VILL BREAK YOO...
TIC TAC TAC
RRRR!
TAC TAC TIC TIC
SHIT! SHIT! SHIT!
CRASH BOOM!!

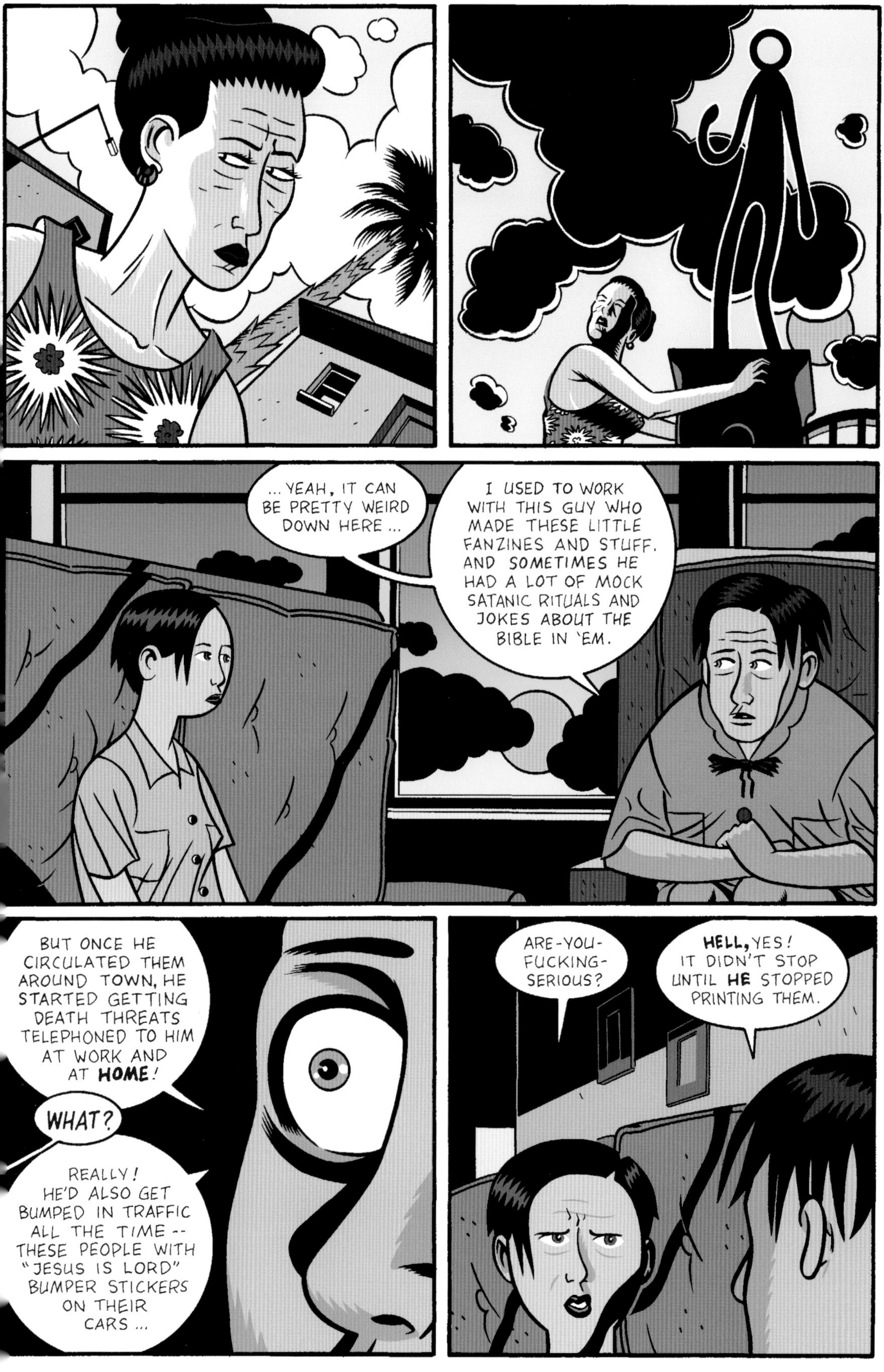
...YEAH, IT CAN BE PRETTY WEIRD DOWN HERE...
I USED TO WORK WITH THIS GUY WHO MADE THESE LITTLE FANZINES AND STUFF. AND SOMETIMES HE HAD A LOT OF MOCK SATANIC RITUALS AND JOKES ABOUT THE BIBLE IN 'EM.
BUT ONCE HE CIRCULATED THEM AROUND TOWN, HE STARTED GETTING DEATH THREATS TELEPHONED TO HIM AT WORK AND AT **HOME**!
WHAT?
REALLY! HE'D ALSO GET BUMPED IN TRAFFIC ALL THE TIME -- THESE PEOPLE WITH "JESUS IS LORD" BUMPER STICKERS ON THEIR CARS...
ARE-YOU-FUCKING-SERIOUS?
HELL, YES! IT DIDN'T STOP UNTIL **HE** STOPPED PRINTING THEM.

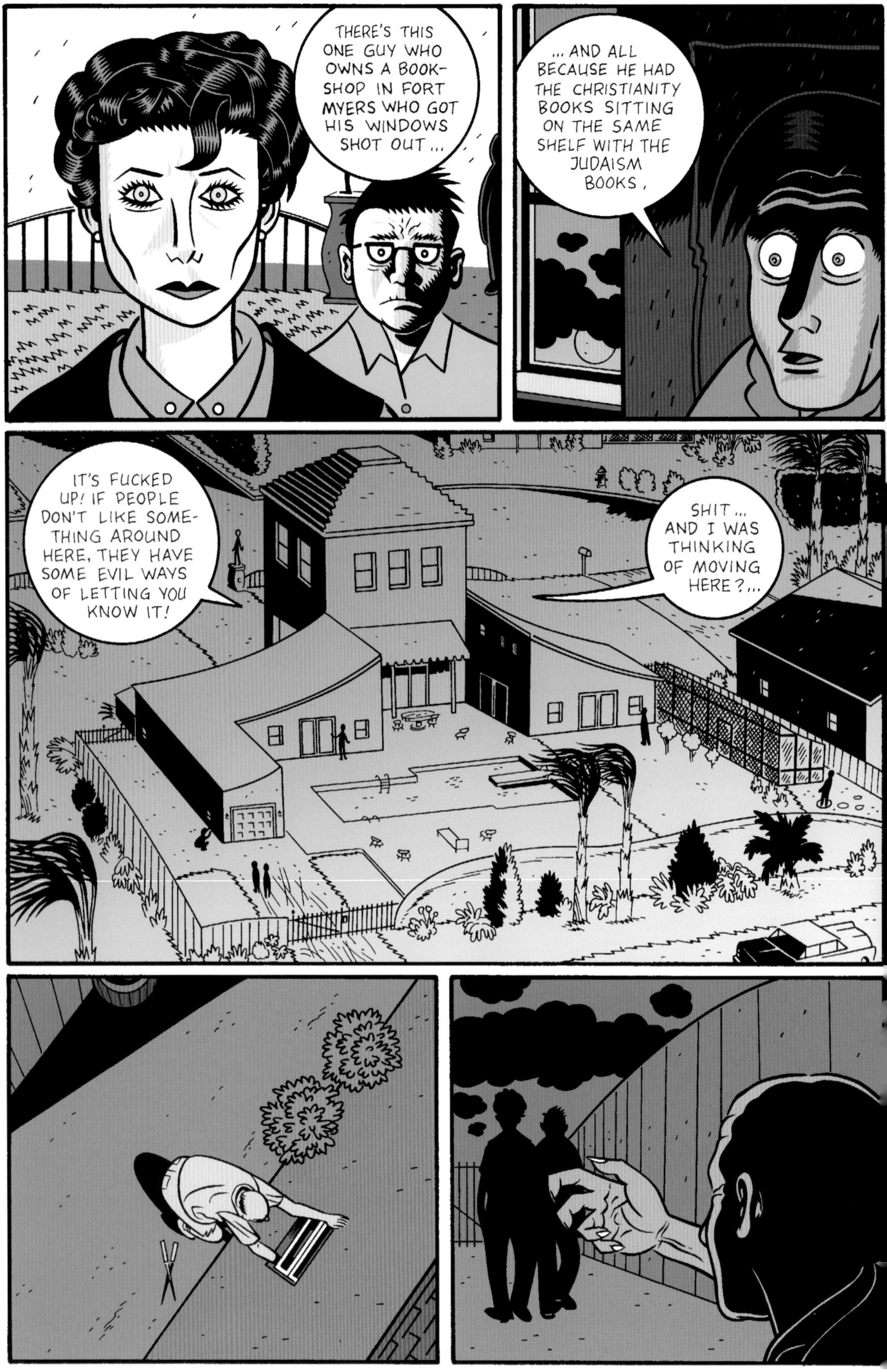
THERE'S THIS ONE GUY WHO OWNS A BOOK-SHOP IN FORT MYERS WHO GOT HIS WINDOWS SHOT OUT...
...AND ALL BECAUSE HE HAD THE CHRISTIANITY BOOKS SITTING ON THE SAME SHELF WITH THE JUDAISM BOOKS.
IT'S FUCKED UP! IF PEOPLE DON'T LIKE SOME-THING AROUND HERE, THEY HAVE SOME EVIL WAYS OF LETTING YOU KNOW IT!
SHIT... AND I WAS THINKING OF MOVING HERE?...

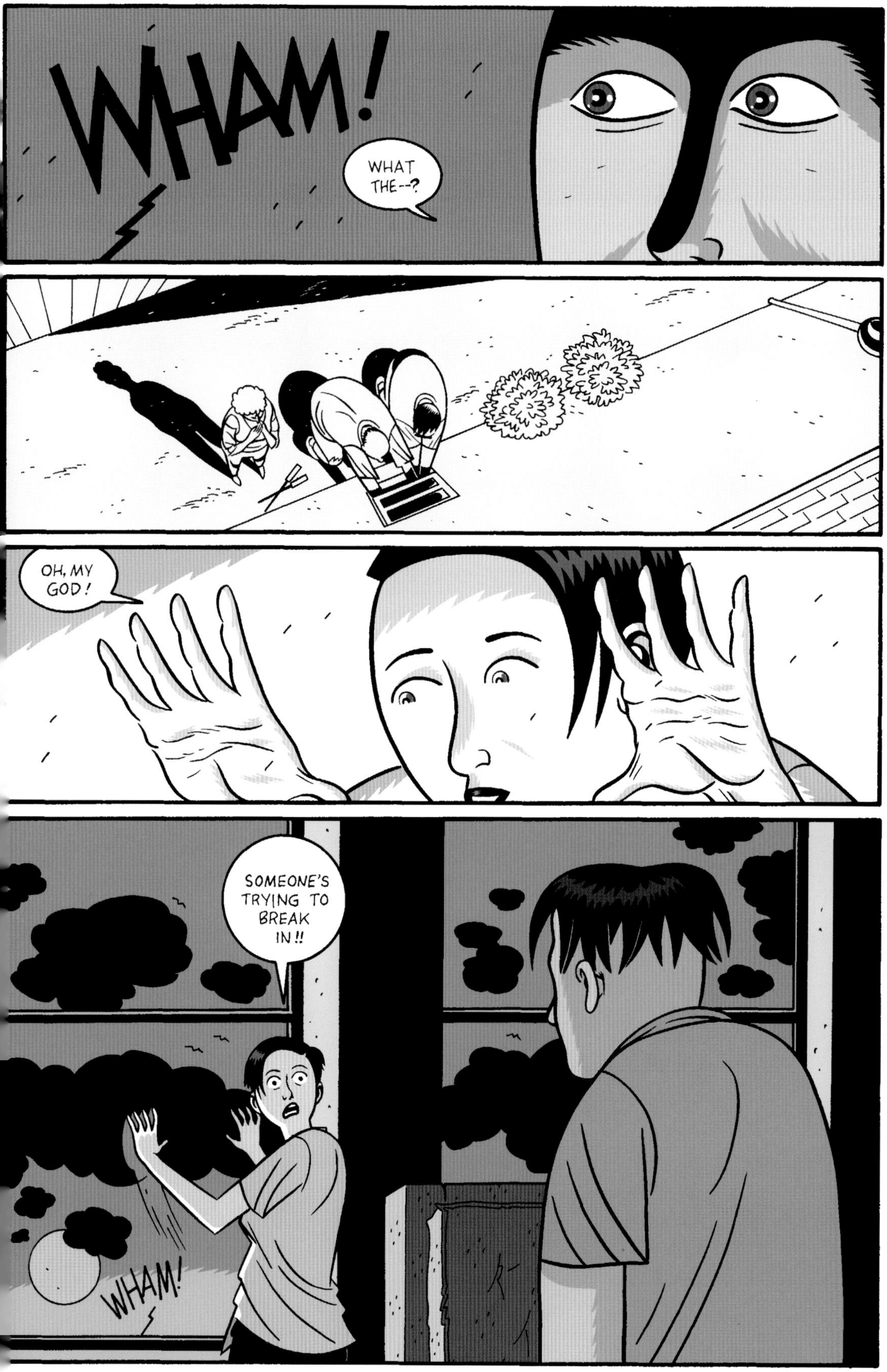
WHAM!
WHAT THE--?
OH, MY GOD!
SOMEONE'S TRYING TO BREAK IN!!
WHAM!

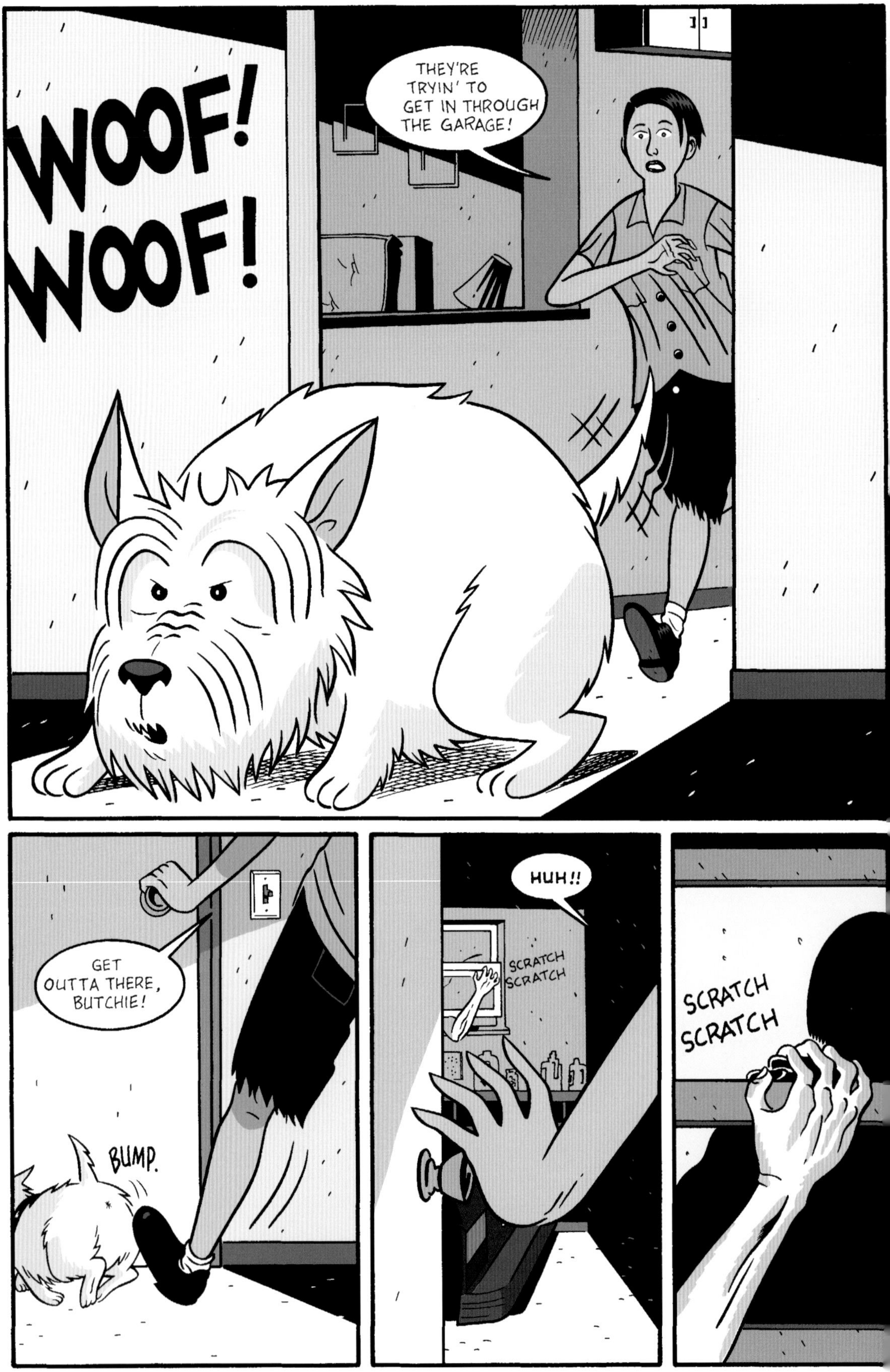
WOOF! WOOF!
THEY'RE TRYIN' TO GET IN THROUGH THE GARAGE!
GET OUTTA THERE, BUTCHIE!
BUMP.
HUH!!
SCRATCH SCRATCH
SCRATCH SCRATCH

SCREE

SCREE

NO!

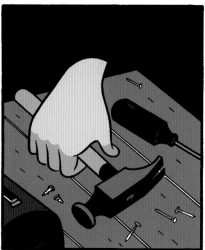

MMNN--

KREEE

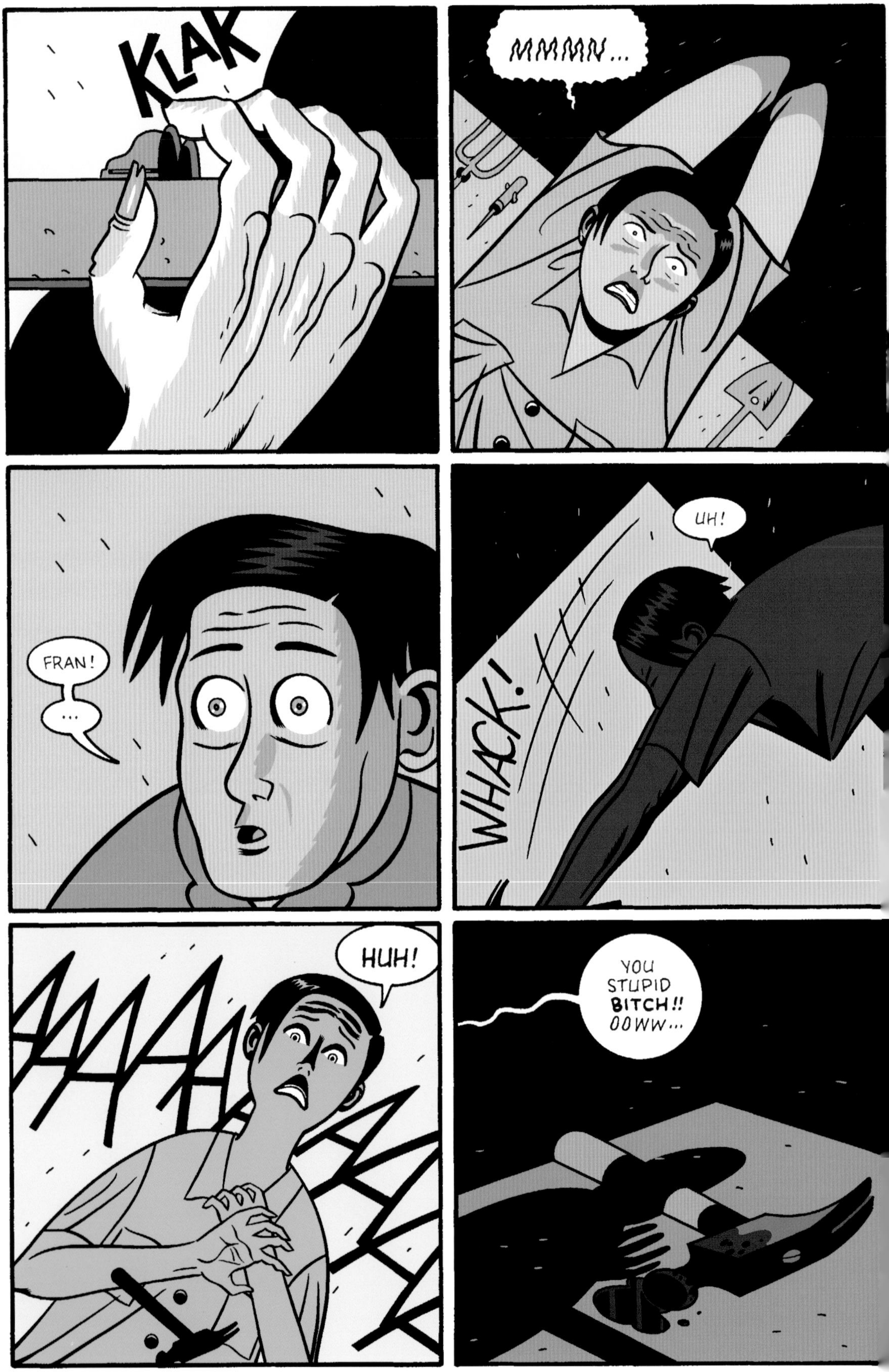
KLAK
MMMN...
FRAN!
...
UH!
WHACK!
HUH!
YOU STUPID **BITCH!!** OOWW...

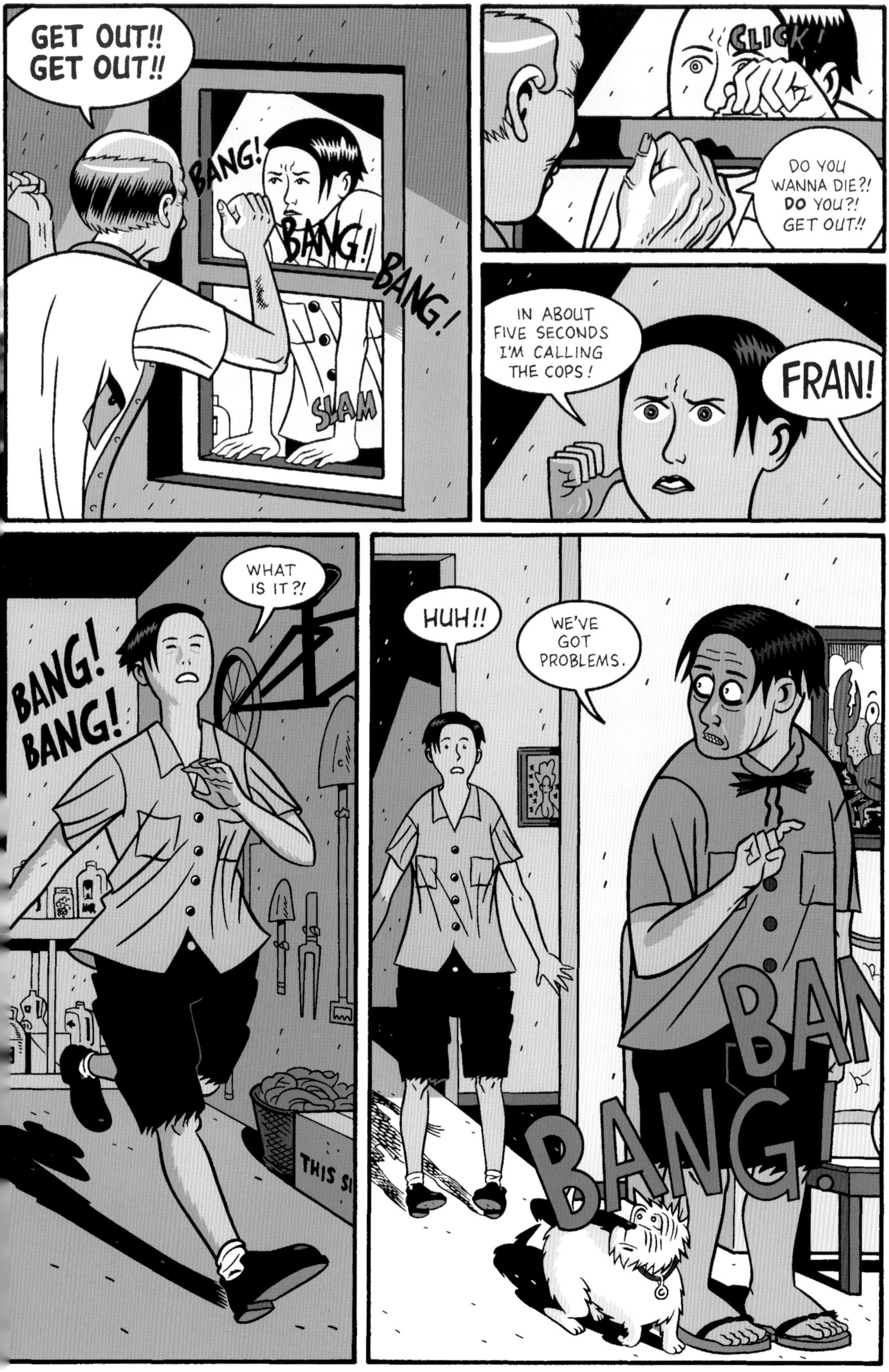
GET OUT!! GET OUT!!
BANG!
BANG!
BANG!
SLAM
CLICK!
DO YOU WANNA DIE?! DO YOU?! GET OUT!!
IN ABOUT FIVE SECONDS I'M CALLING THE COPS!
FRAN!
WHAT IS IT?!
BANG! BANG!
HUH!!
WE'VE GOT PROBLEMS.
BANG!
BAN
THIS S

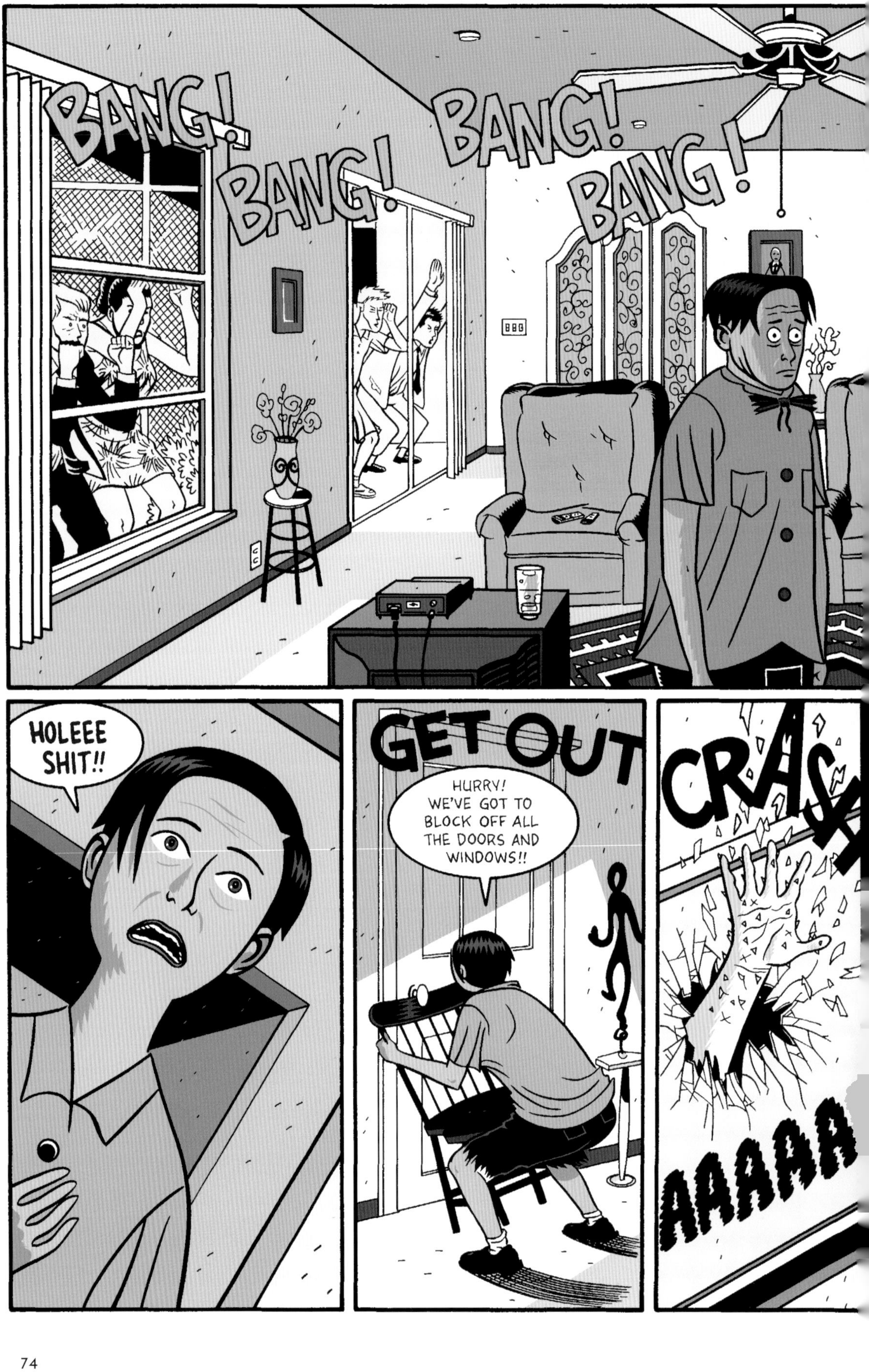
BANG! BANG! BANG! BANG!
HOLEEE SHIT!!
GET OUT
HURRY! WE'VE GOT TO BLOCK OFF ALL THE DOORS AND WINDOWS!!
CRASH
AAAAA

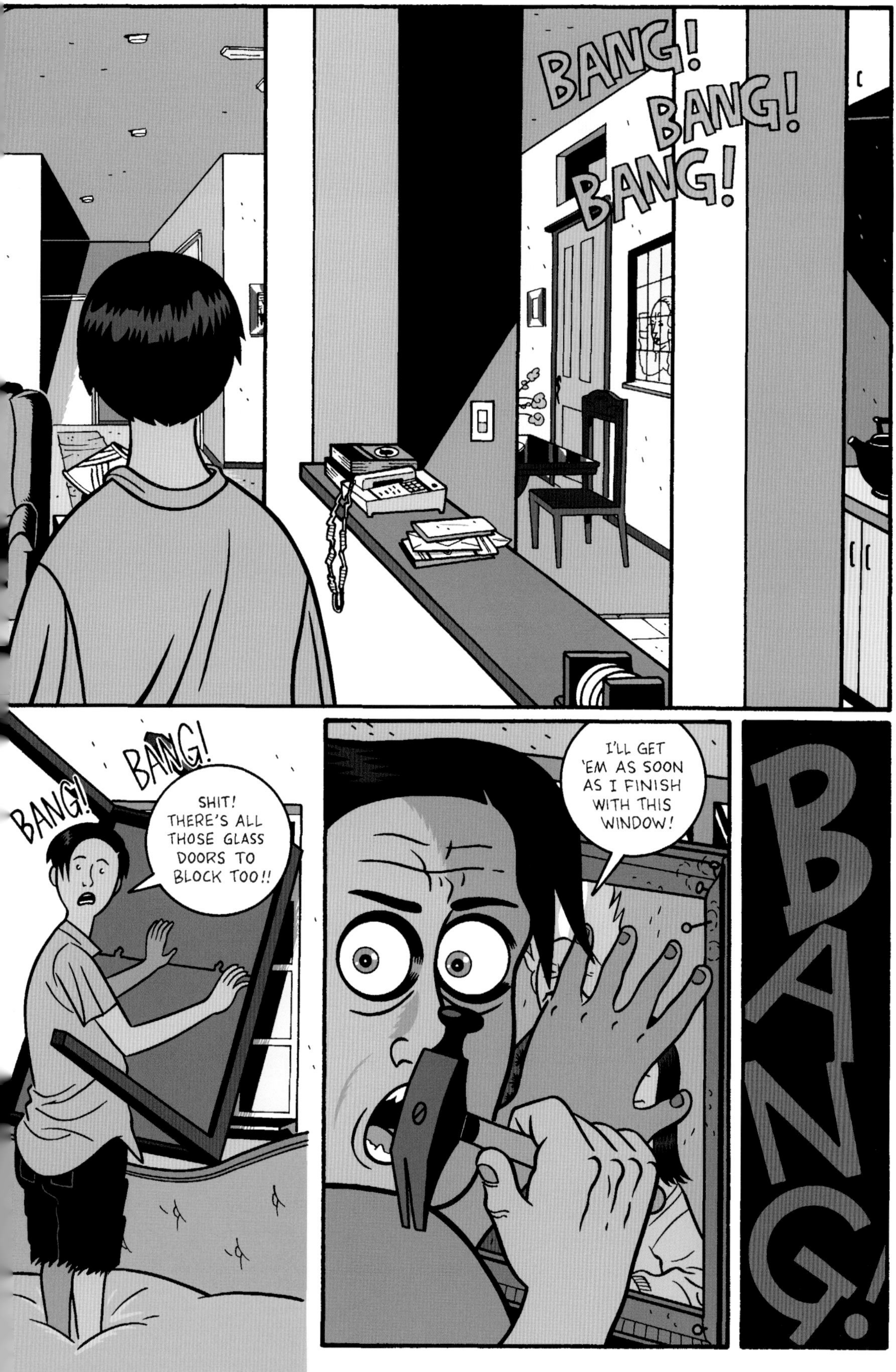
BANG!
BANG!
BANG!
BANG!
BANG!
SHIT! THERE'S ALL THOSE GLASS DOORS TO BLOCK TOO!!
I'LL GET 'EM AS SOON AS I FINISH WITH THIS WINDOW!
BANG!

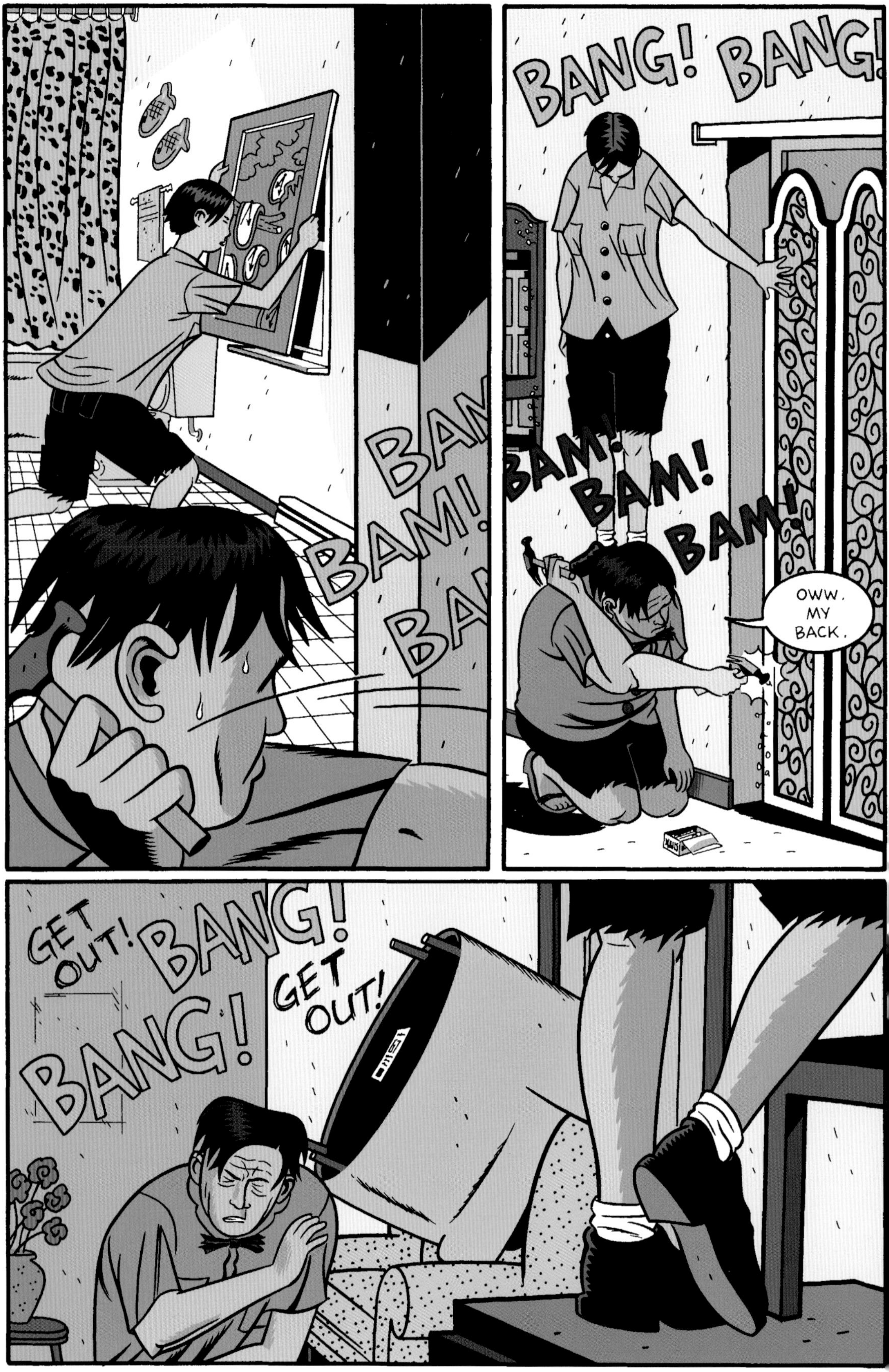
BAM!
BAM!
BAM!
BANG! BANG!
BAM!
BAM!
BAM!
OWW. MY BACK.
GET OUT!
BANG!
BANG!
GET OUT!

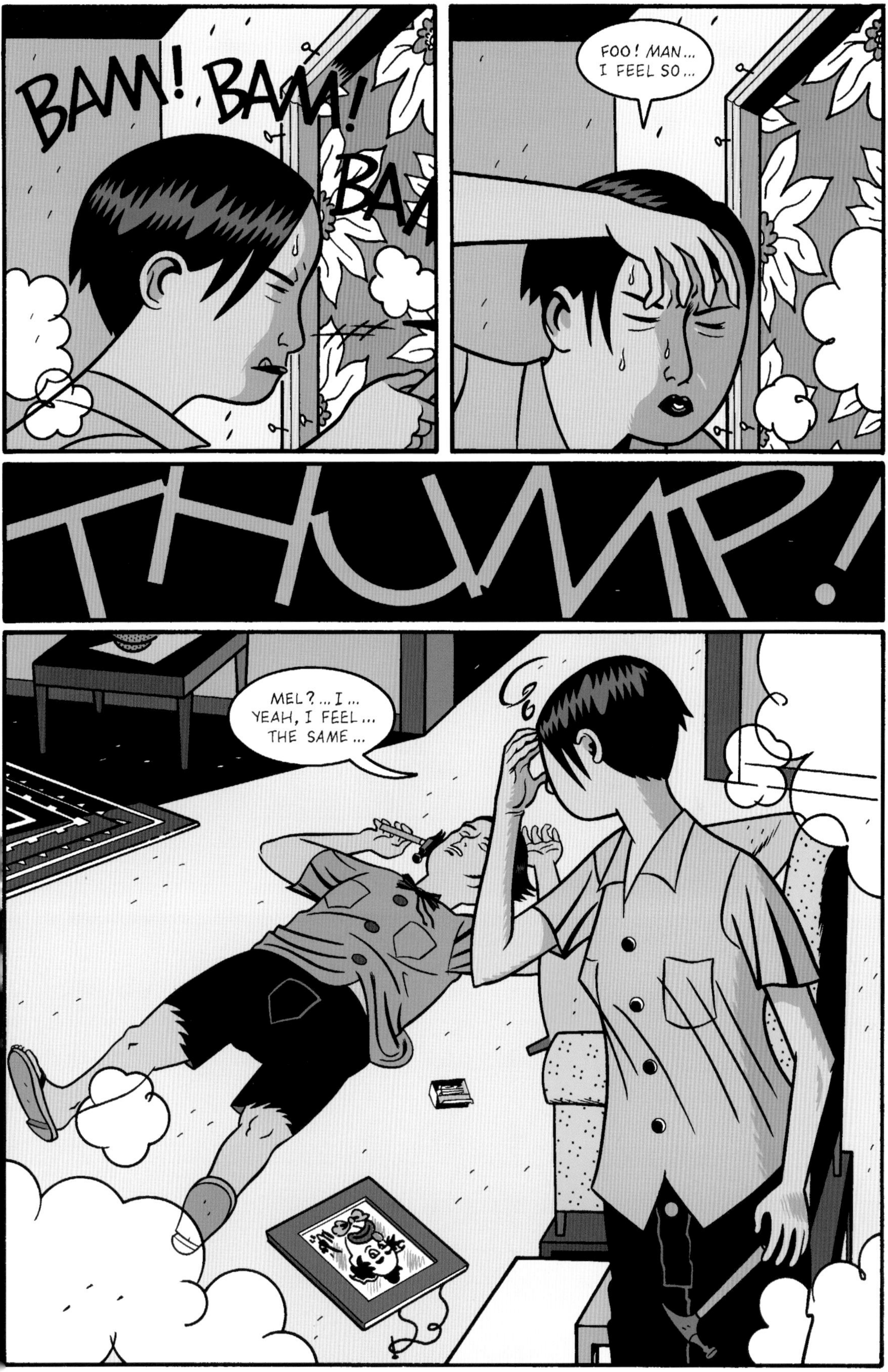

BAM! BAM!
BAM
FOO! MAN...
I FEEL SO...
THUMP!
MEL?... I...
YEAH, I FEEL...
THE SAME...

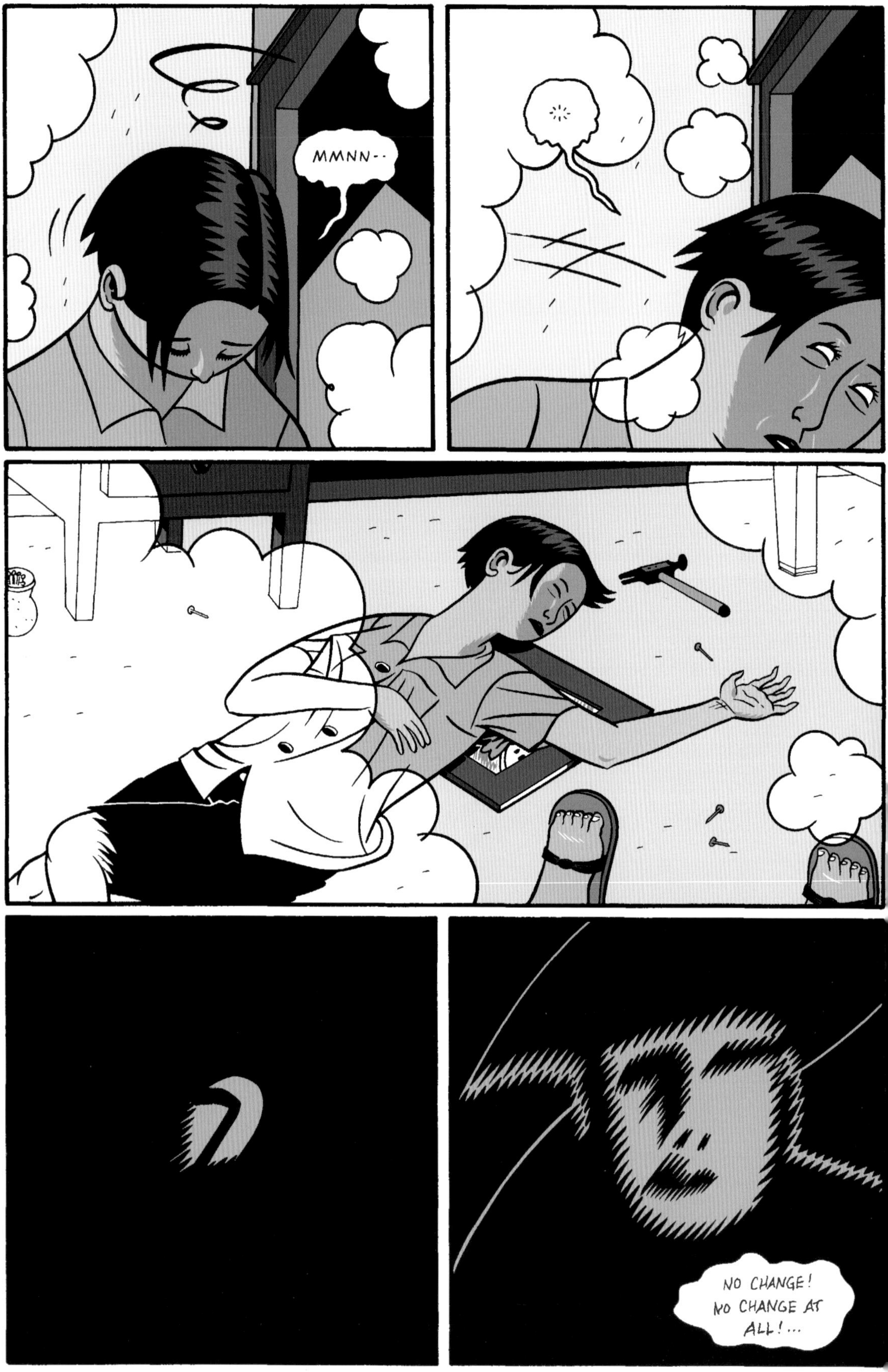
MMNN--
NO CHANGE! NO CHANGE AT ALL!...

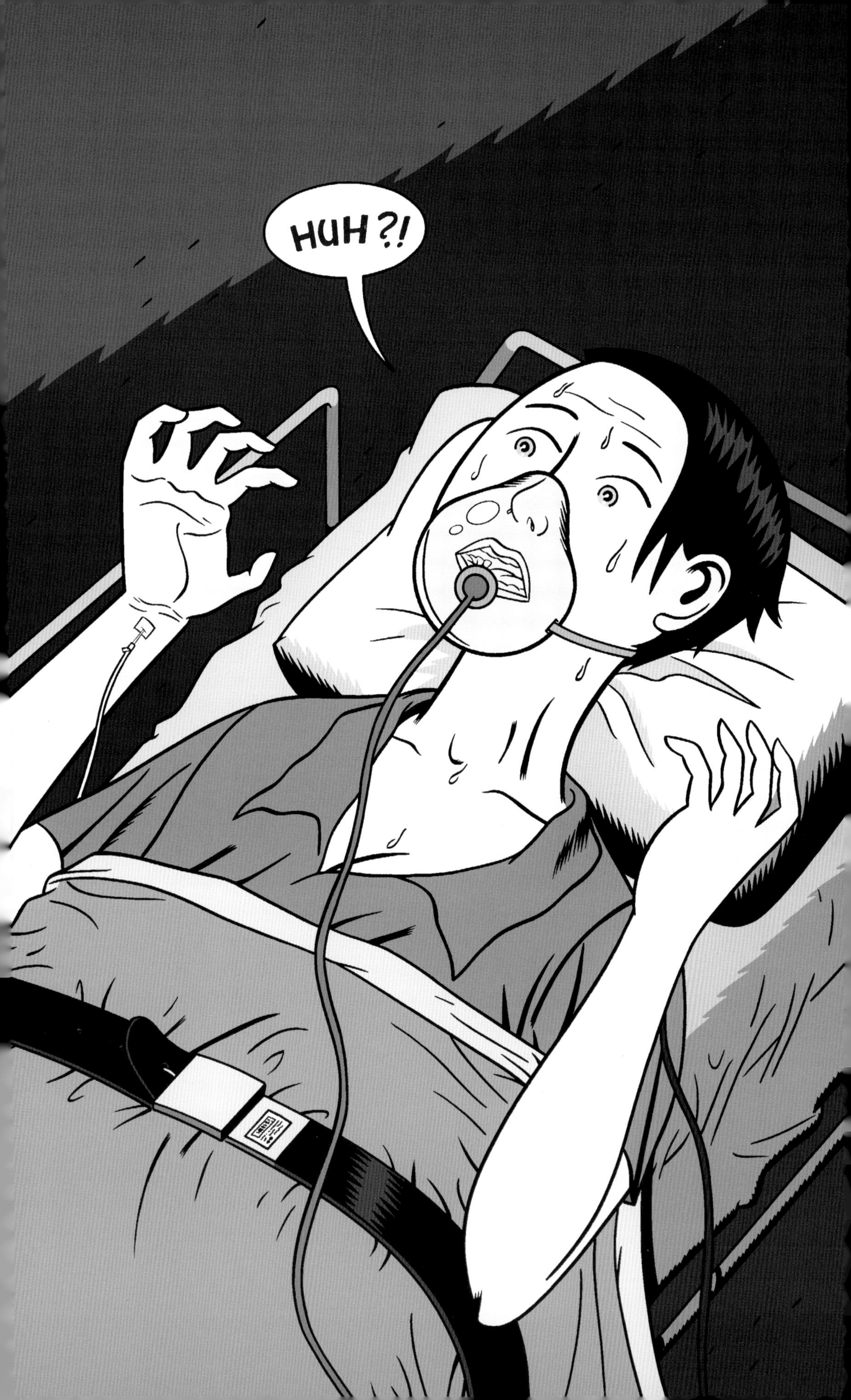
HUH ?!

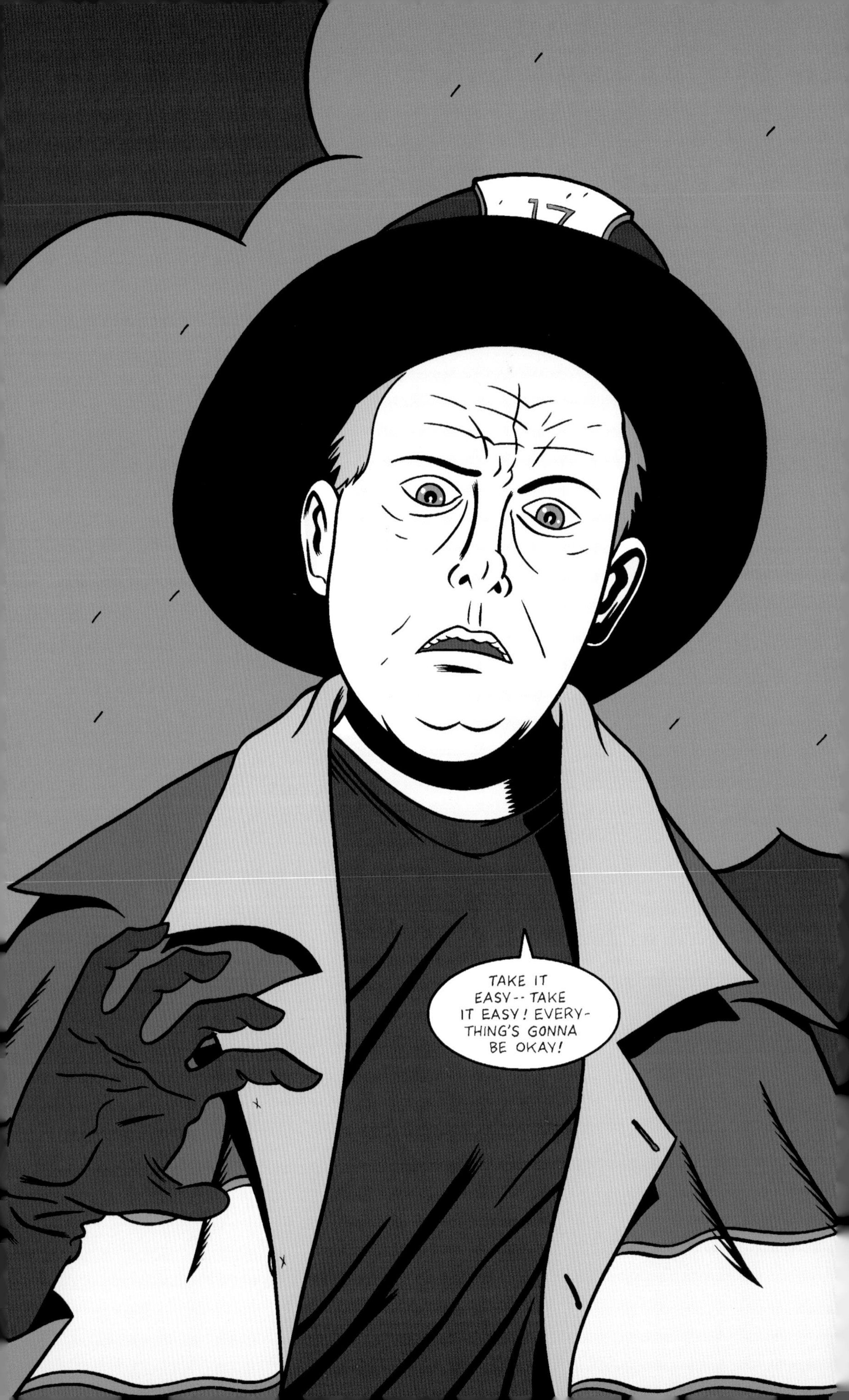
17
TAKE IT EASY-- TAKE IT EASY! EVERY-THING'S GONNA BE OKAY!

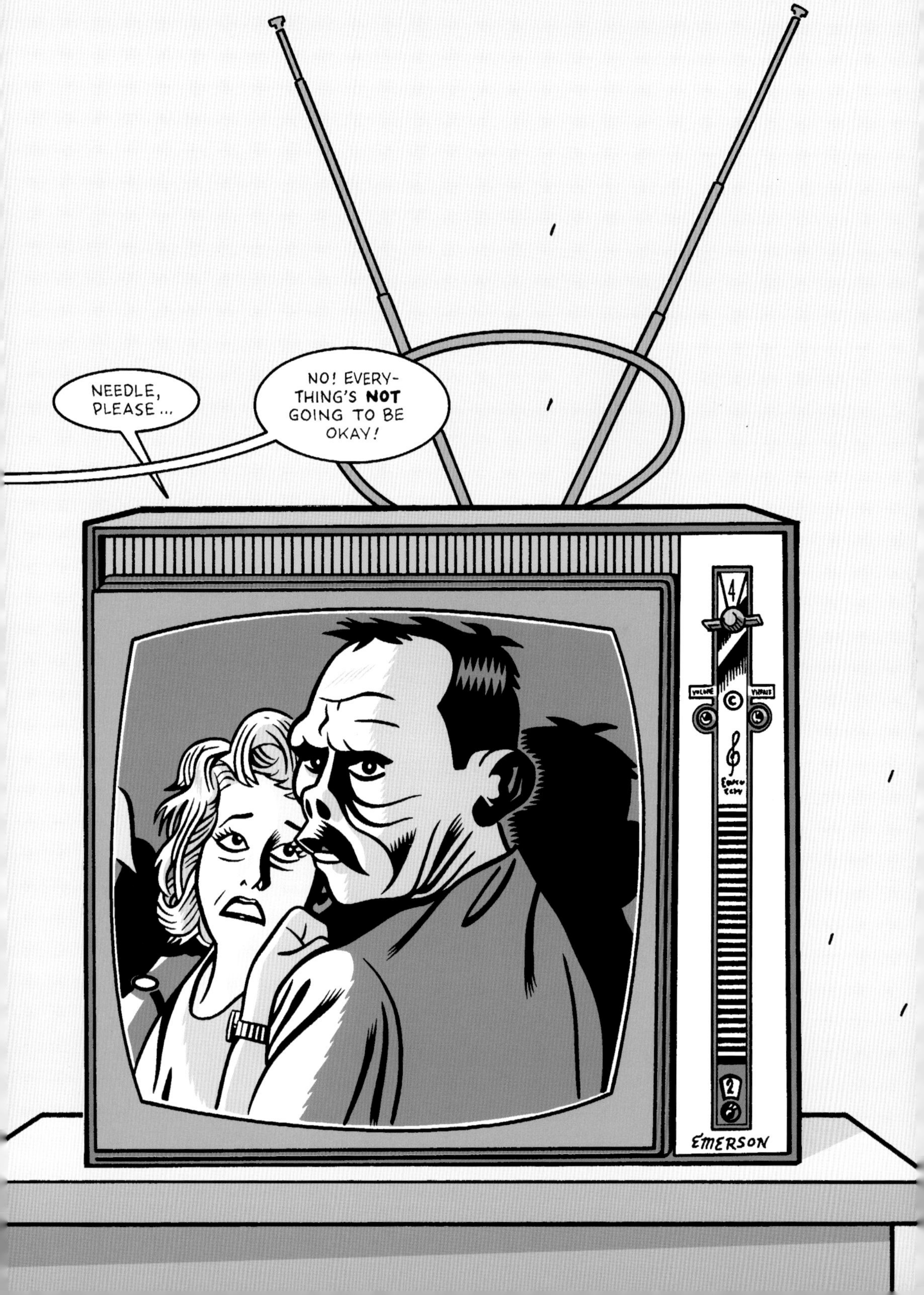
NEEDLE, PLEASE ...
NO! EVERYTHING'S **NOT** GOING TO BE OKAY!
EMERSON

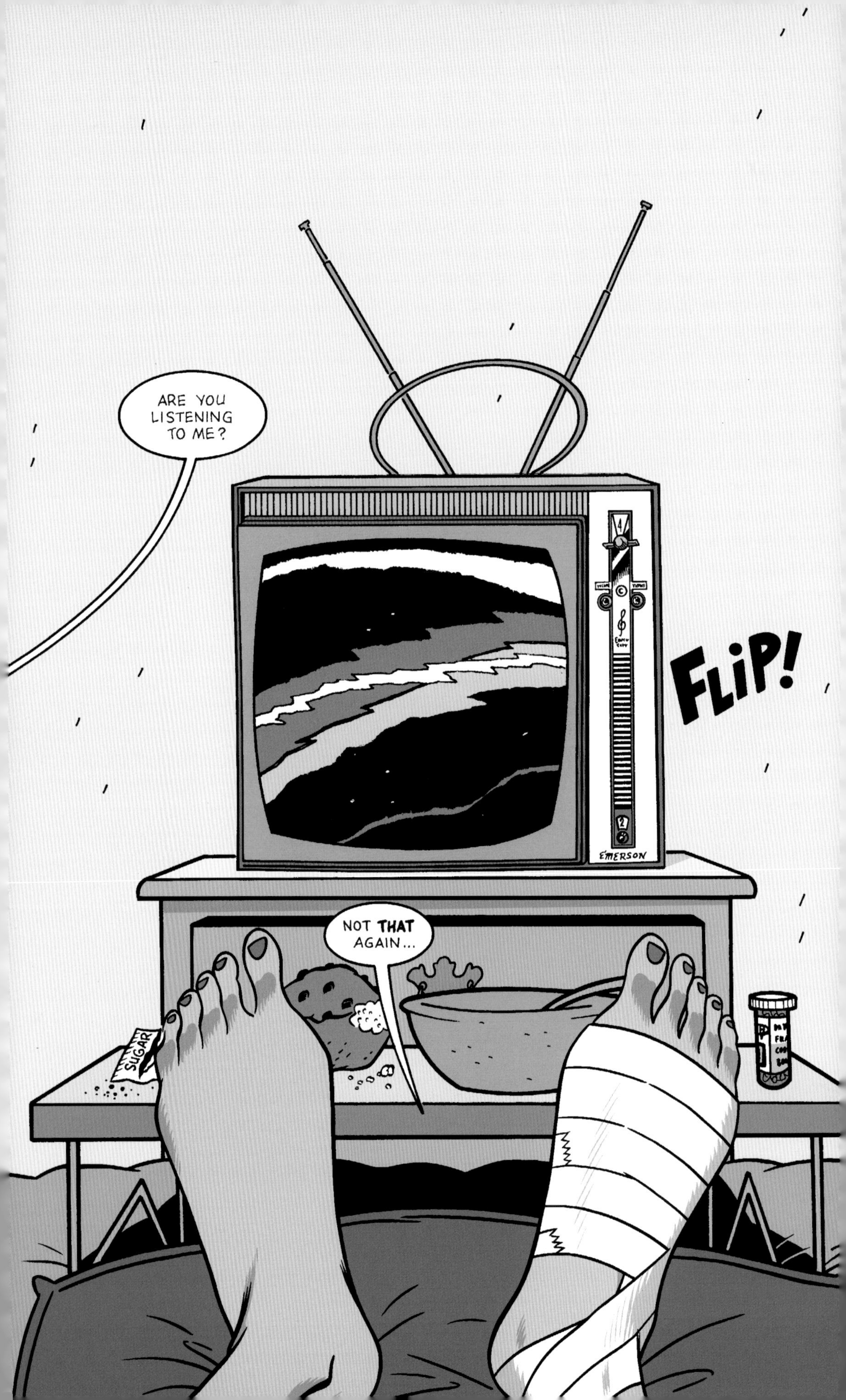

ARE YOU LISTENING TO ME?
EMERSON
FLIP!
NOT **THAT** AGAIN...
SUGAR

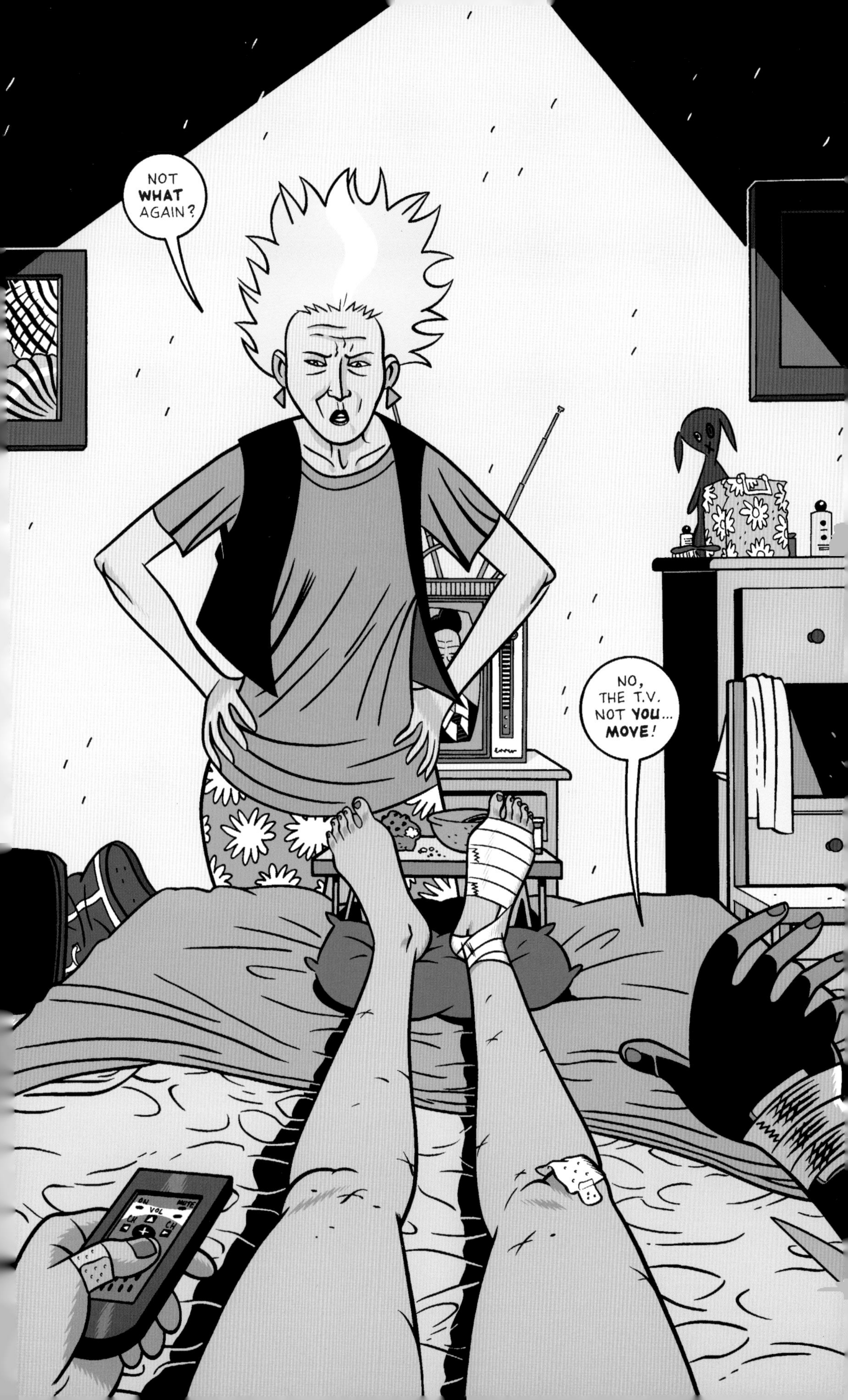
NOT **WHAT** AGAIN?
NO, THE T.V. NOT **YOU**... **MOVE**!

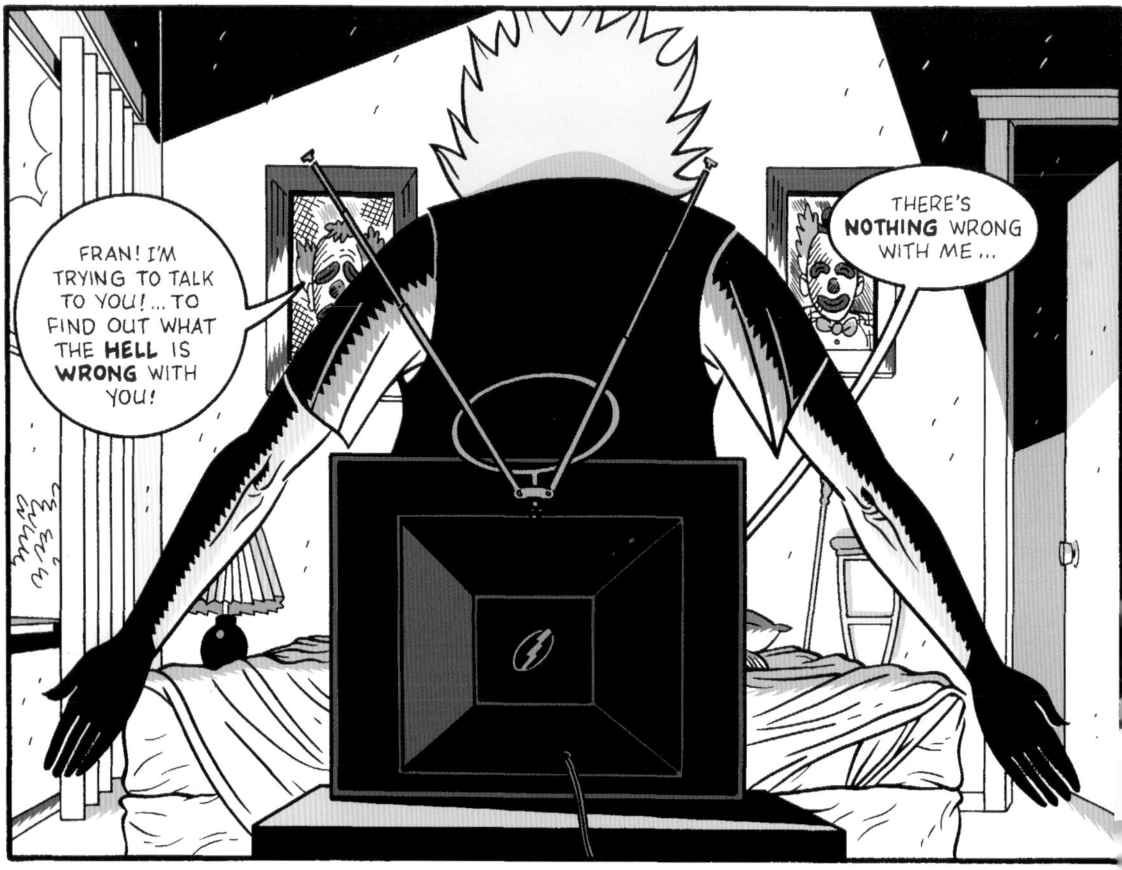
FRAN! I'M TRYING TO TALK TO YOU!...TO FIND OUT WHAT THE **HELL** IS **WRONG** WITH YOU!
THERE'S **NOTHING** WRONG WITH ME...

CHAPTER FIVE

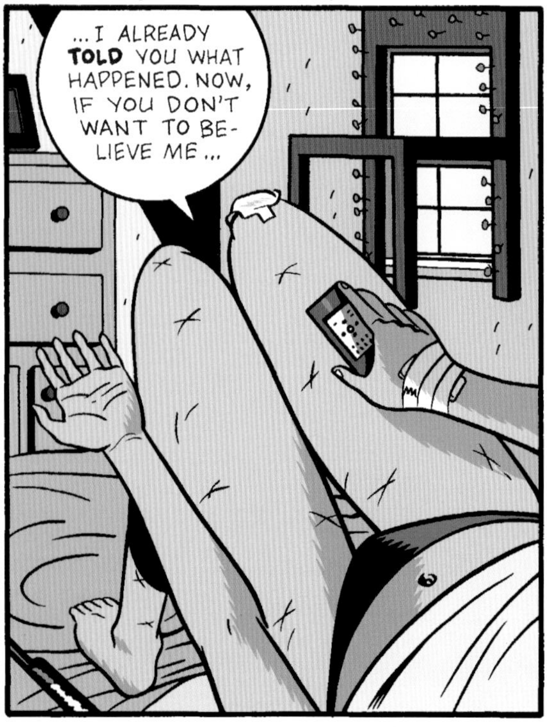
...I ALREADY **TOLD** YOU WHAT HAPPENED. NOW, IF YOU DON'T WANT TO BE-LIEVE ME...

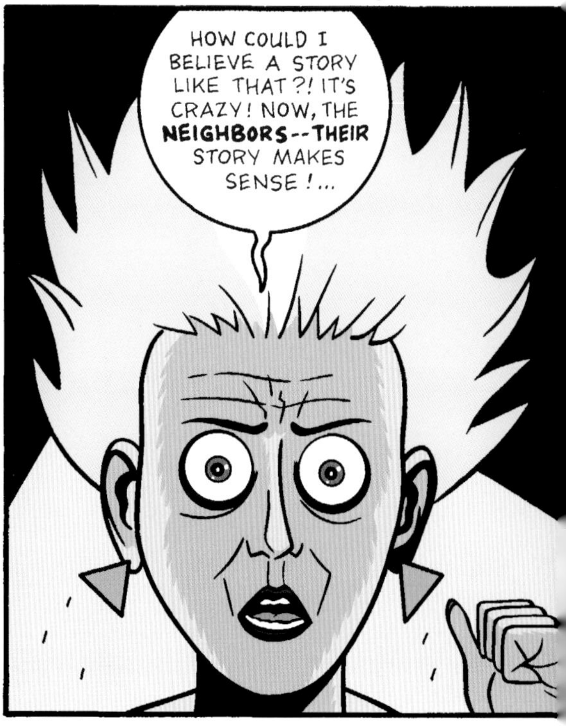
HOW COULD I BELIEVE A STORY LIKE THAT?! IT'S CRAZY! NOW, THE **NEIGHBORS--THEIR** STORY MAKES SENSE!...

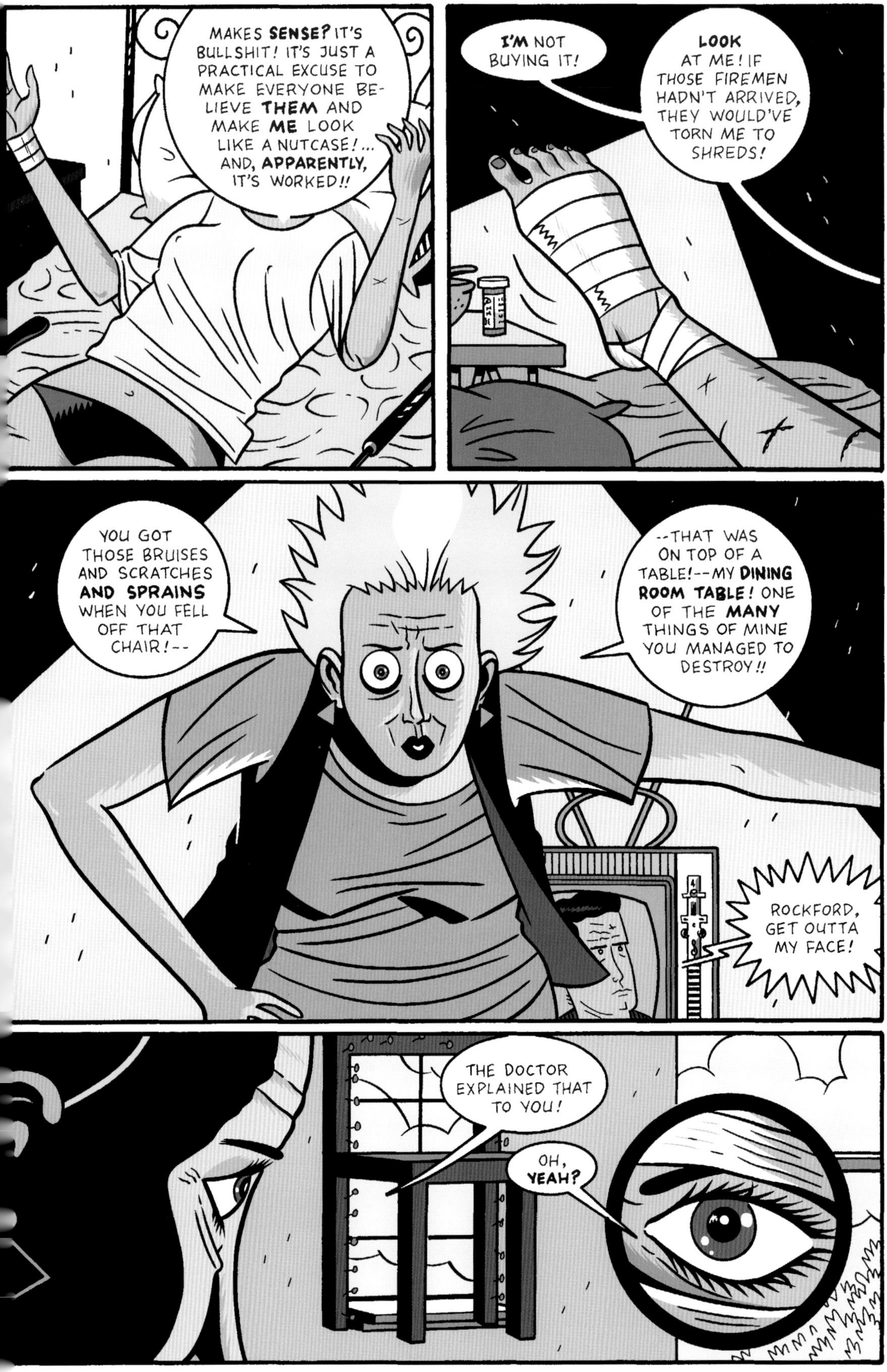
MAKES SENSE? IT'S BULLSHIT! IT'S JUST A PRACTICAL EXCUSE TO MAKE EVERYONE BELIEVE THEM AND MAKE ME LOOK LIKE A NUTCASE!... AND, APPARENTLY, IT'S WORKED!!
I'M NOT BUYING IT!
LOOK AT ME! IF THOSE FIREMEN HADN'T ARRIVED, THEY WOULD'VE TORN ME TO SHREDS!
YOU GOT THOSE BRUISES AND SCRATCHES AND SPRAINS WHEN YOU FELL OFF THAT CHAIR!--
--THAT WAS ON TOP OF A TABLE!--MY DINING ROOM TABLE! ONE OF THE MANY THINGS OF MINE YOU MANAGED TO DESTROY!!
ROCKFORD, GET OUTTA MY FACE!
THE DOCTOR EXPLAINED THAT TO YOU!
OH, YEAH?

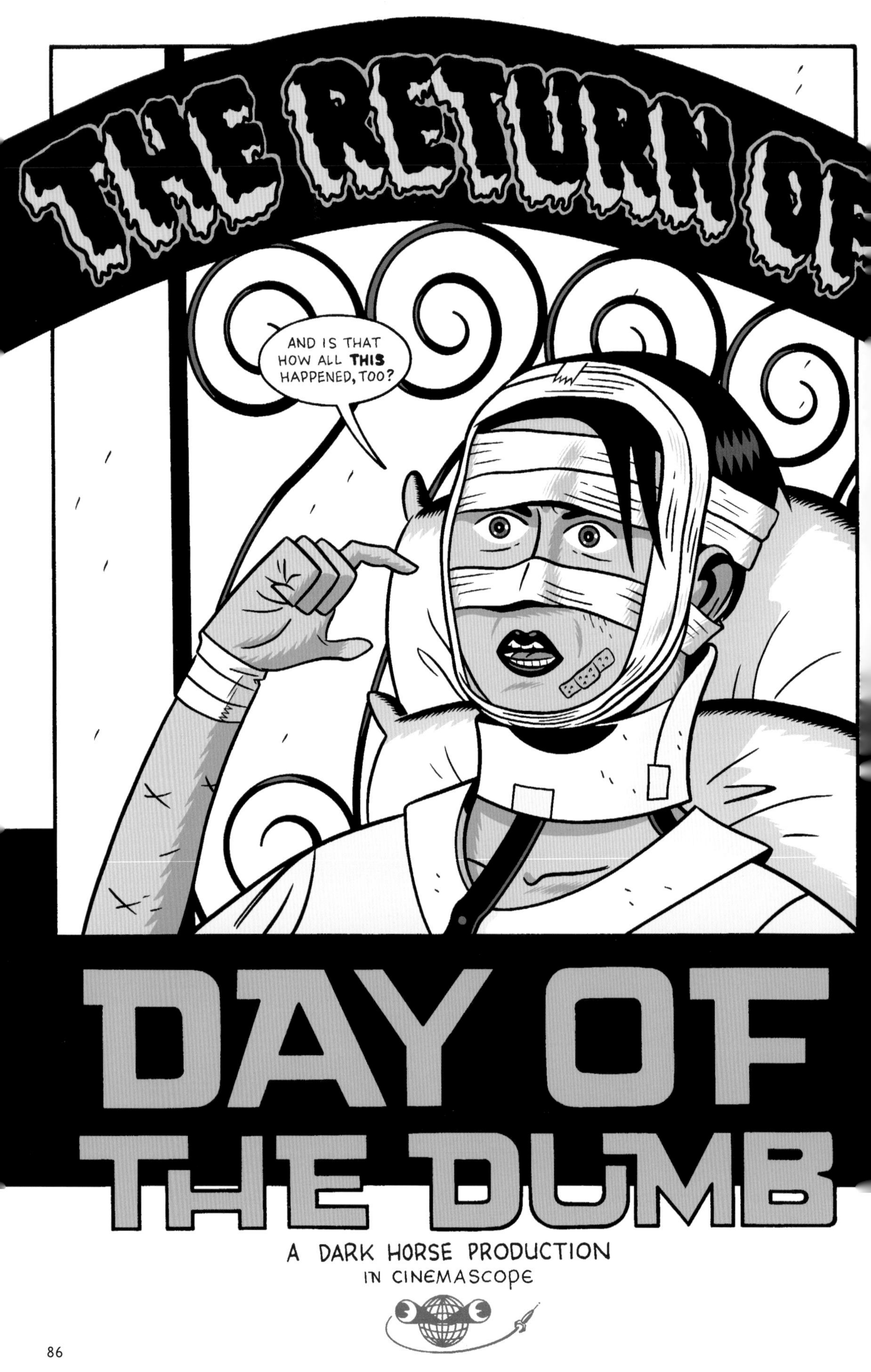
THE RETURN OF
AND IS THAT HOW ALL **THIS** HAPPENED, TOO?
DAY OF THE DUMB
A DARK HORSE PRODUCTION
IN CINEMASCOPE

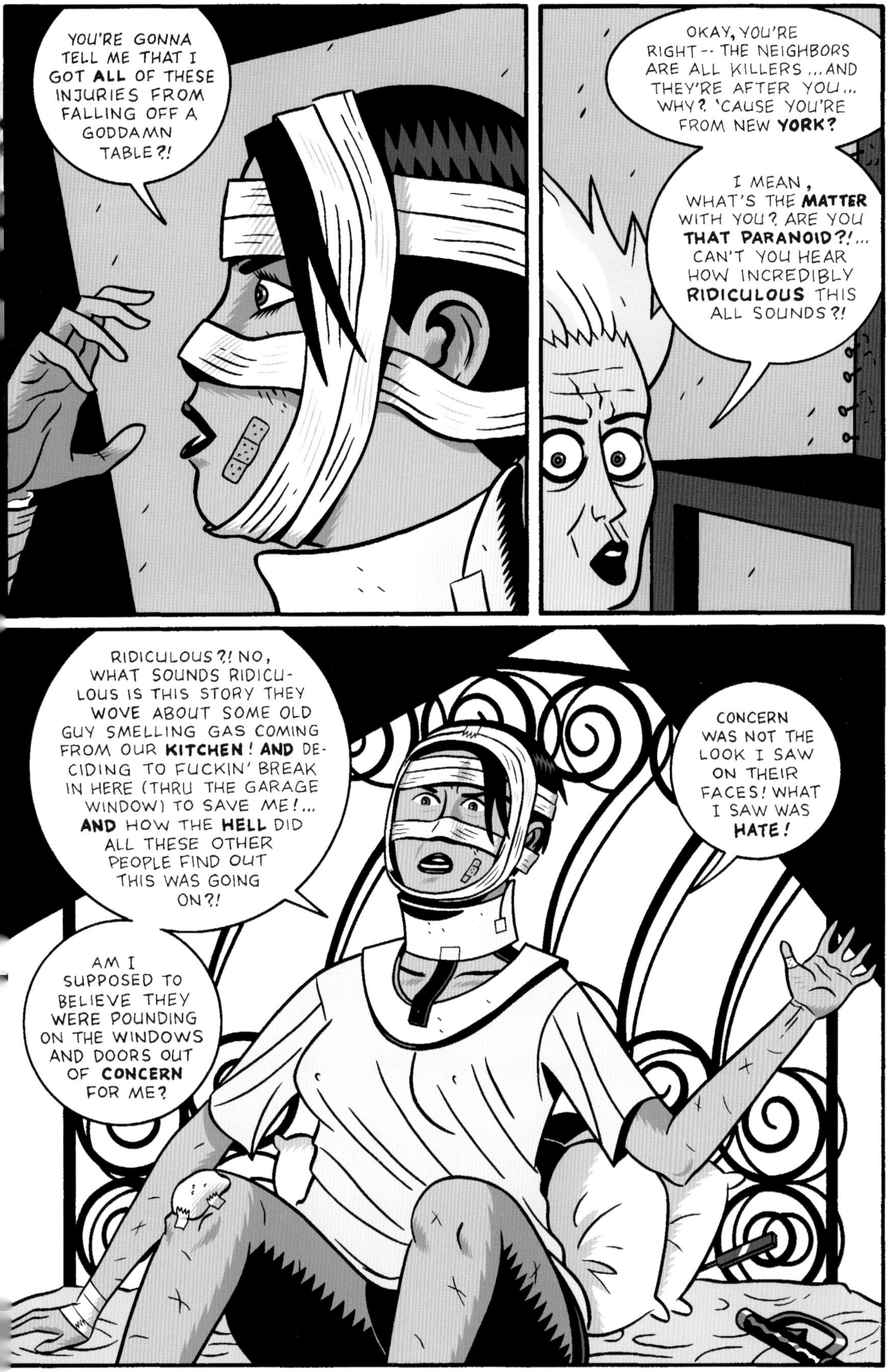
YOU'RE GONNA TELL ME THAT I GOT ALL OF THESE INJURIES FROM FALLING OFF A GODDAMN TABLE?!
OKAY, YOU'RE RIGHT -- THE NEIGHBORS ARE ALL KILLERS ... AND THEY'RE AFTER YOU... WHY? 'CAUSE YOU'RE FROM NEW YORK?
I MEAN, WHAT'S THE MATTER WITH YOU? ARE YOU THAT PARANOID?!... CAN'T YOU HEAR HOW INCREDIBLY RIDICULOUS THIS ALL SOUNDS?!
RIDICULOUS?! NO, WHAT SOUNDS RIDICULOUS IS THIS STORY THEY WOVE ABOUT SOME OLD GUY SMELLING GAS COMING FROM OUR KITCHEN! AND DECIDING TO FUCKIN' BREAK IN HERE (THRU THE GARAGE WINDOW) TO SAVE ME!... AND HOW THE HELL DID ALL THESE OTHER PEOPLE FIND OUT THIS WAS GOING ON?!
AM I SUPPOSED TO BELIEVE THEY WERE POUNDING ON THE WINDOWS AND DOORS OUT OF CONCERN FOR ME?
CONCERN WAS NOT THE LOOK I SAW ON THEIR FACES! WHAT I SAW WAS HATE!

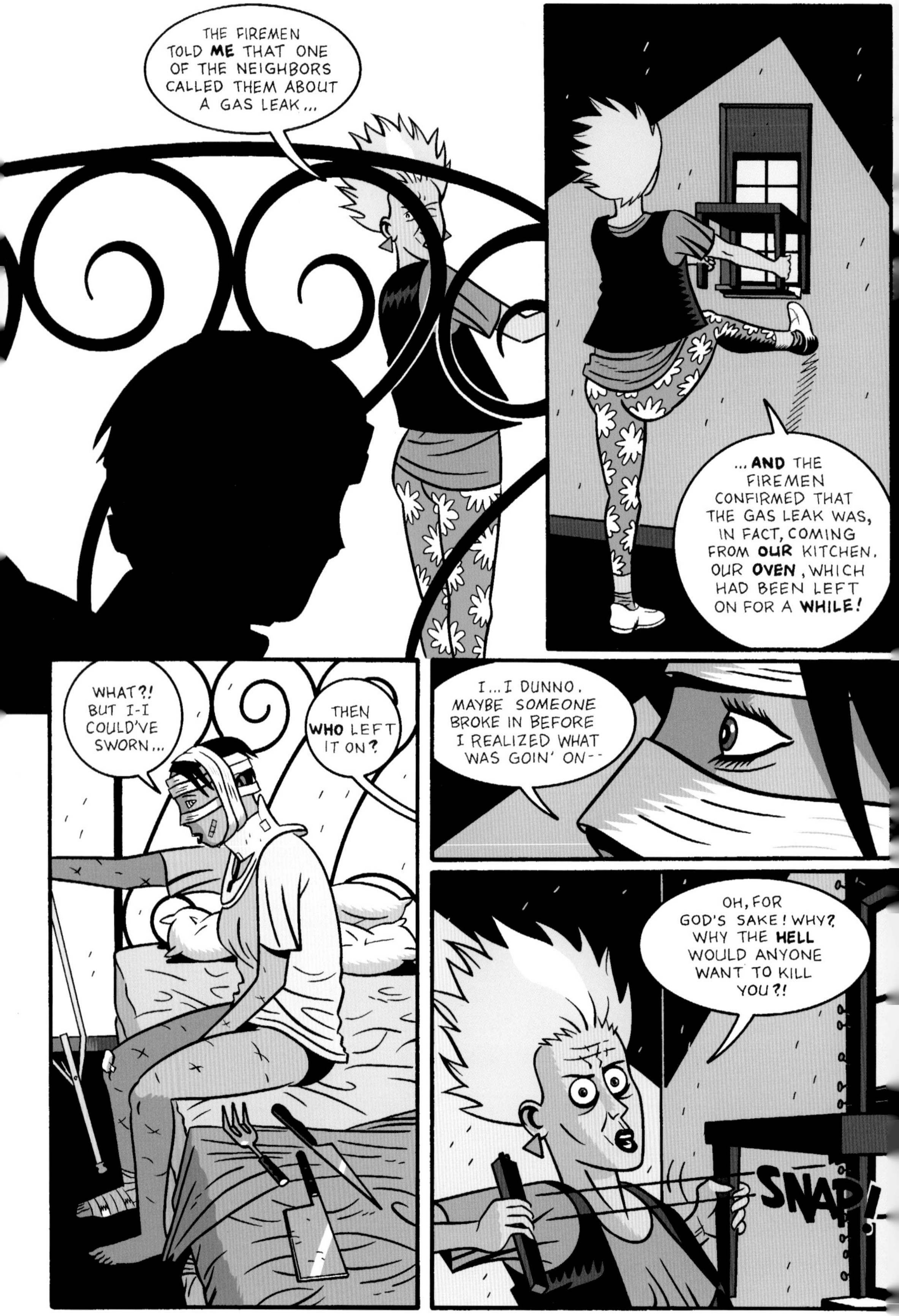
THE FIREMEN TOLD **ME** THAT ONE OF THE NEIGHBORS CALLED THEM ABOUT A GAS LEAK...
...**AND** THE FIREMEN CONFIRMED THAT THE GAS LEAK WAS, IN FACT, COMING FROM **OUR** KITCHEN. OUR **OVEN**, WHICH HAD BEEN LEFT ON FOR A **WHILE**!
WHAT?! BUT I-I COULD'VE SWORN...
THEN **WHO** LEFT IT ON?
I...I DUNNO. MAYBE SOMEONE BROKE IN BEFORE I REALIZED WHAT WAS GOIN' ON--
OH, FOR GOD'S SAKE! WHY? WHY THE **HELL** WOULD ANYONE WANT TO KILL YOU?!
SNAP!

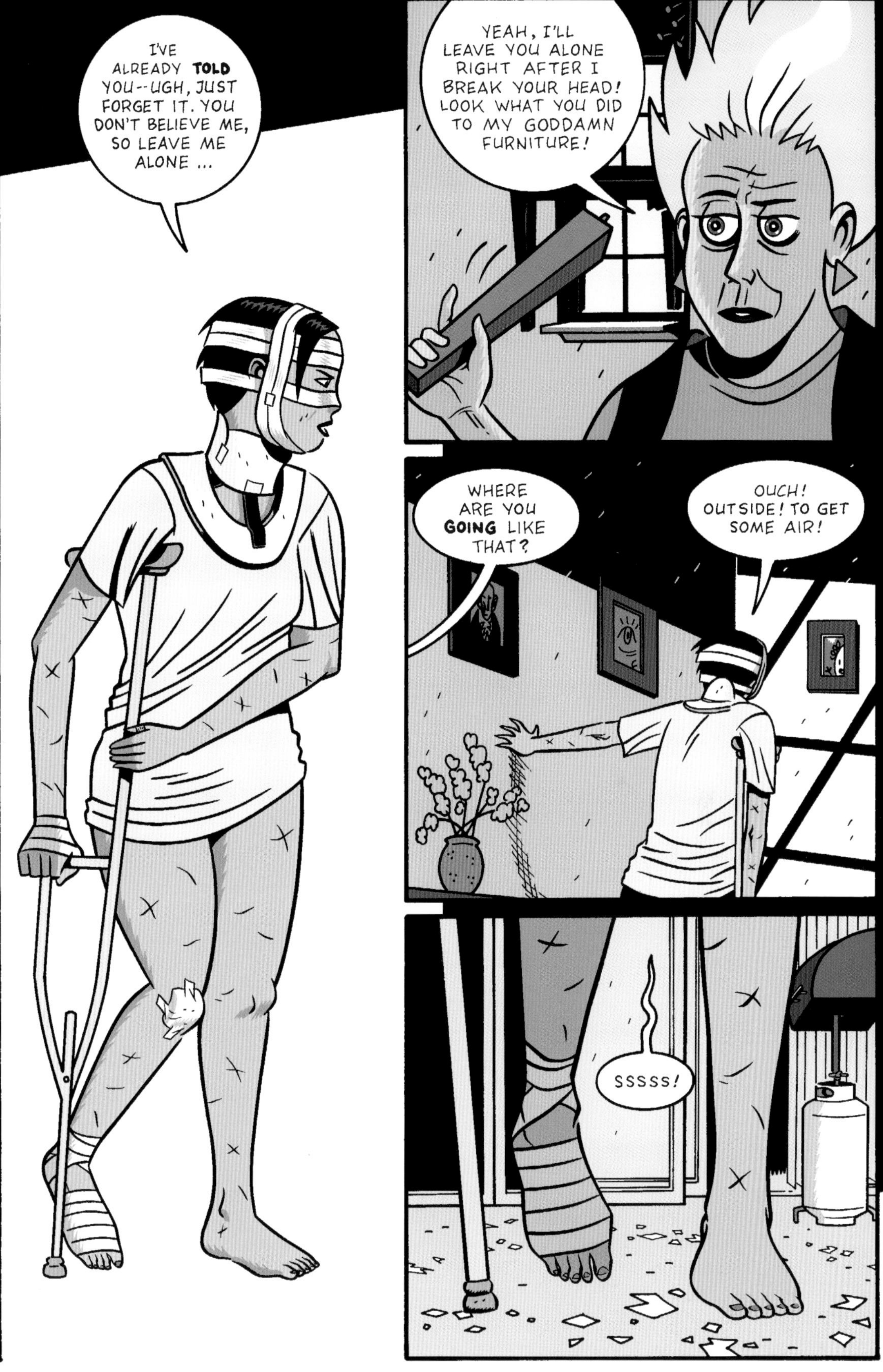
I'VE ALREADY TOLD YOU--UGH, JUST FORGET IT. YOU DON'T BELIEVE ME, SO LEAVE ME ALONE ...
YEAH, I'LL LEAVE YOU ALONE RIGHT AFTER I BREAK YOUR HEAD! LOOK WHAT YOU DID TO MY GODDAMN FURNITURE!
WHERE ARE YOU GOING LIKE THAT?
OUCH! OUTSIDE! TO GET SOME AIR!
SSSSS!

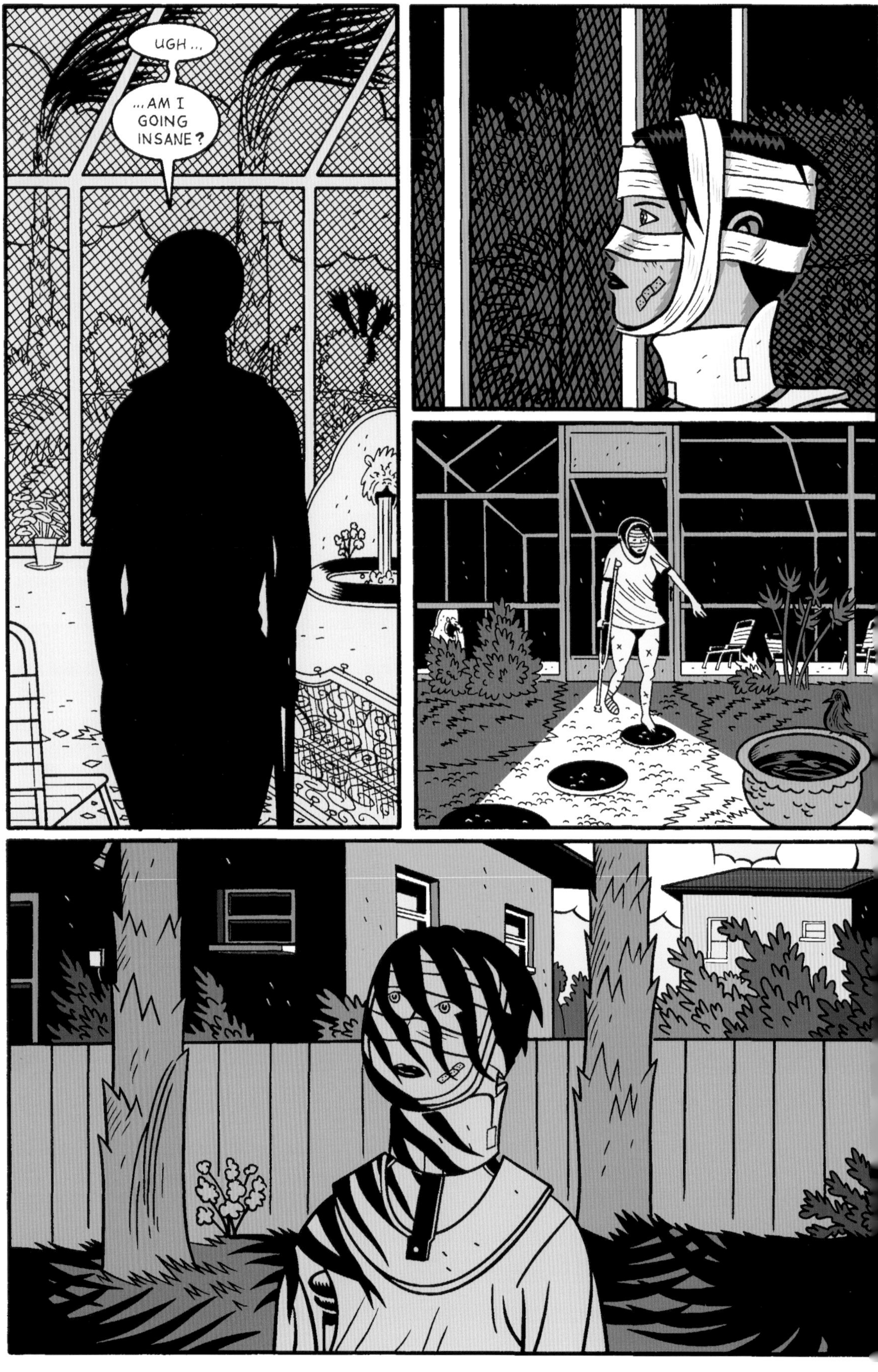
UGH...
...AM I GOING INSANE?

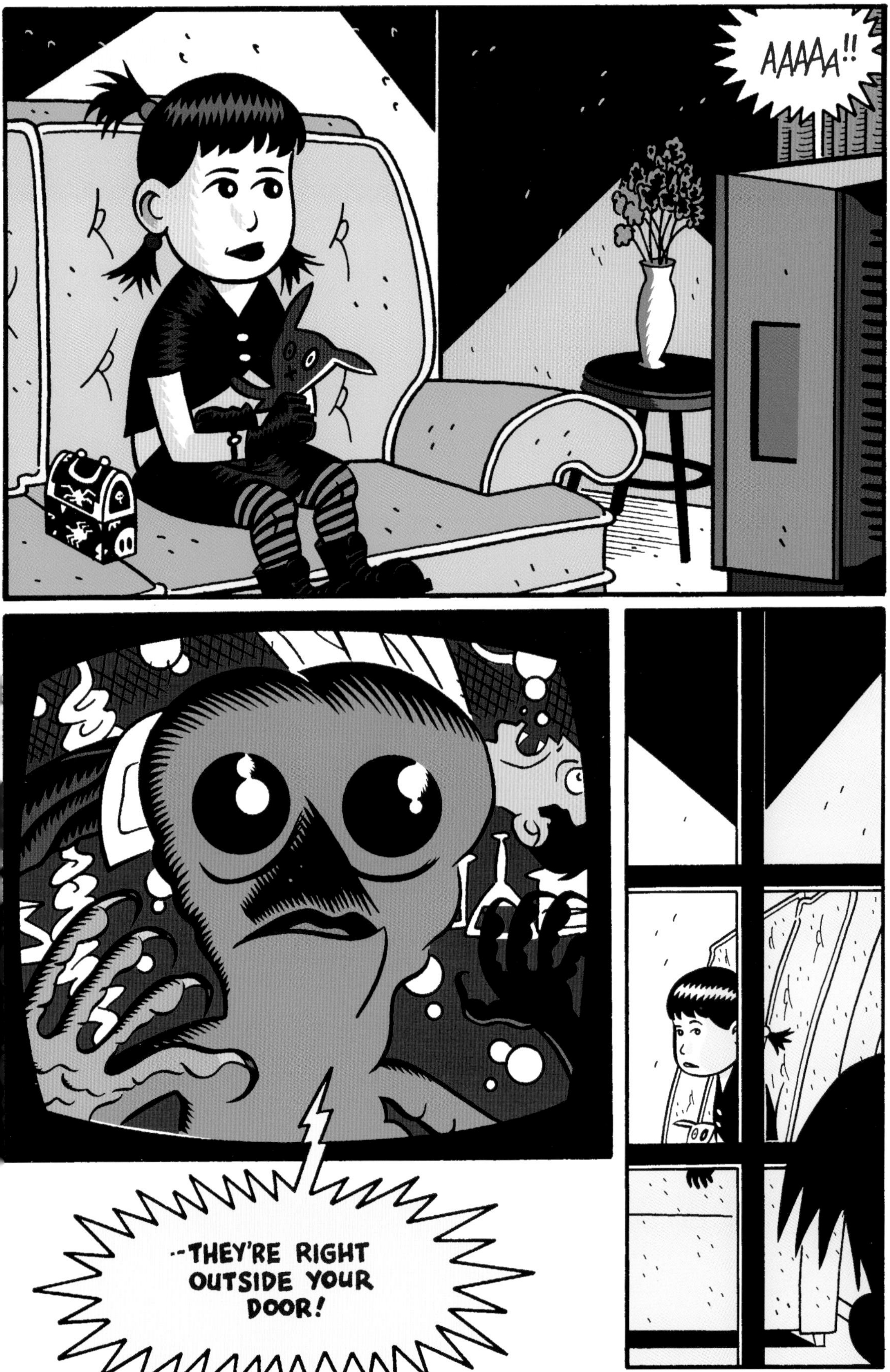
AAAAA!!
--THEY'RE RIGHT OUTSIDE YOUR DOOR!

HUH?
WHO THE...?
WHO'S **THAT**?

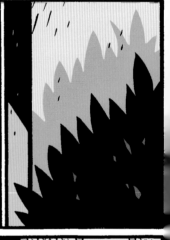

AAAHAA-GRAN-
MAA!!

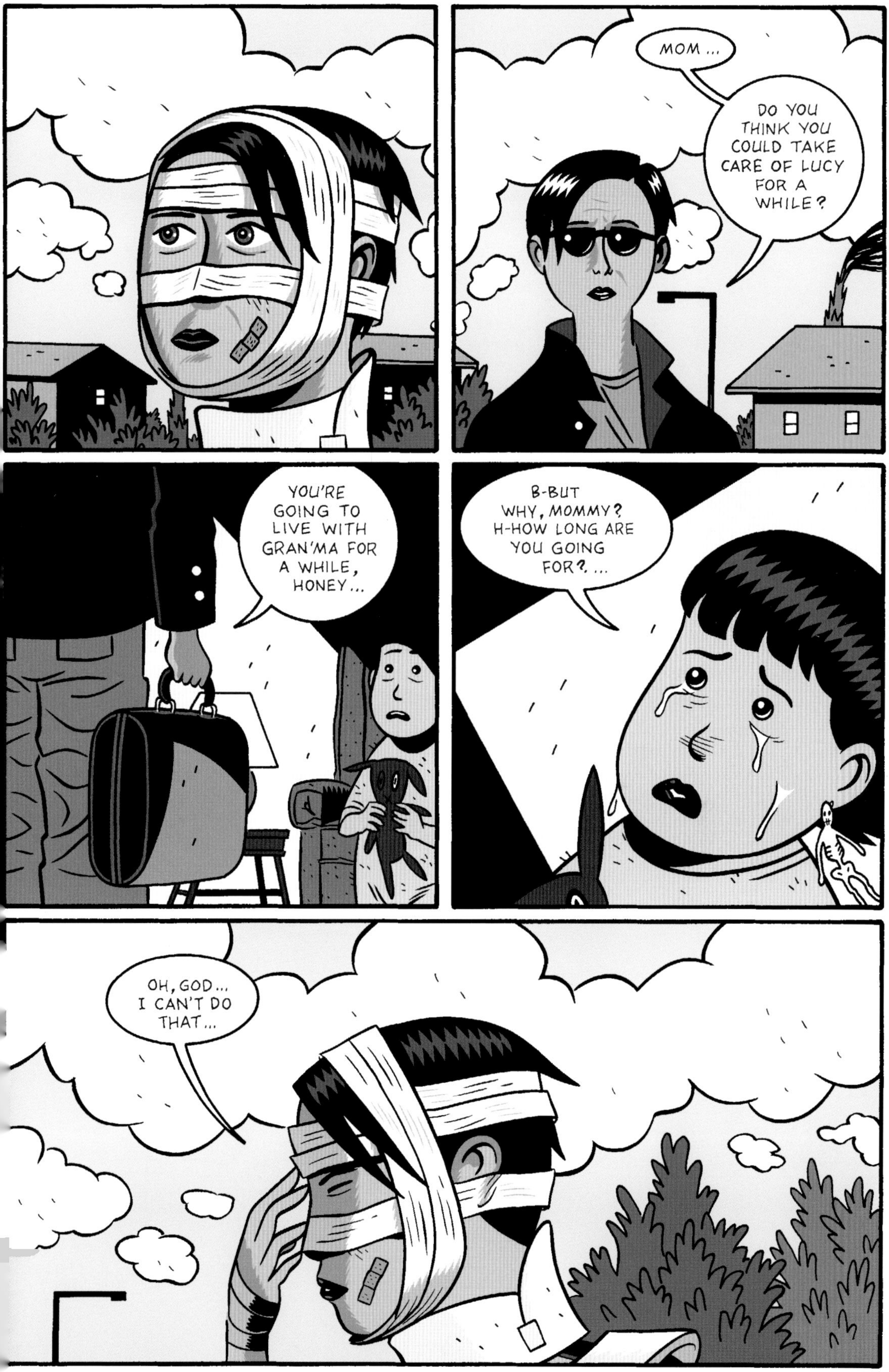
MOM...
DO YOU THINK YOU COULD TAKE CARE OF LUCY FOR A WHILE?
YOU'RE GOING TO LIVE WITH GRAN'MA FOR A WHILE, HONEY...
B-BUT WHY, MOMMY? H-HOW LONG ARE YOU GOING FOR?...
OH, GOD... I CAN'T DO THAT...

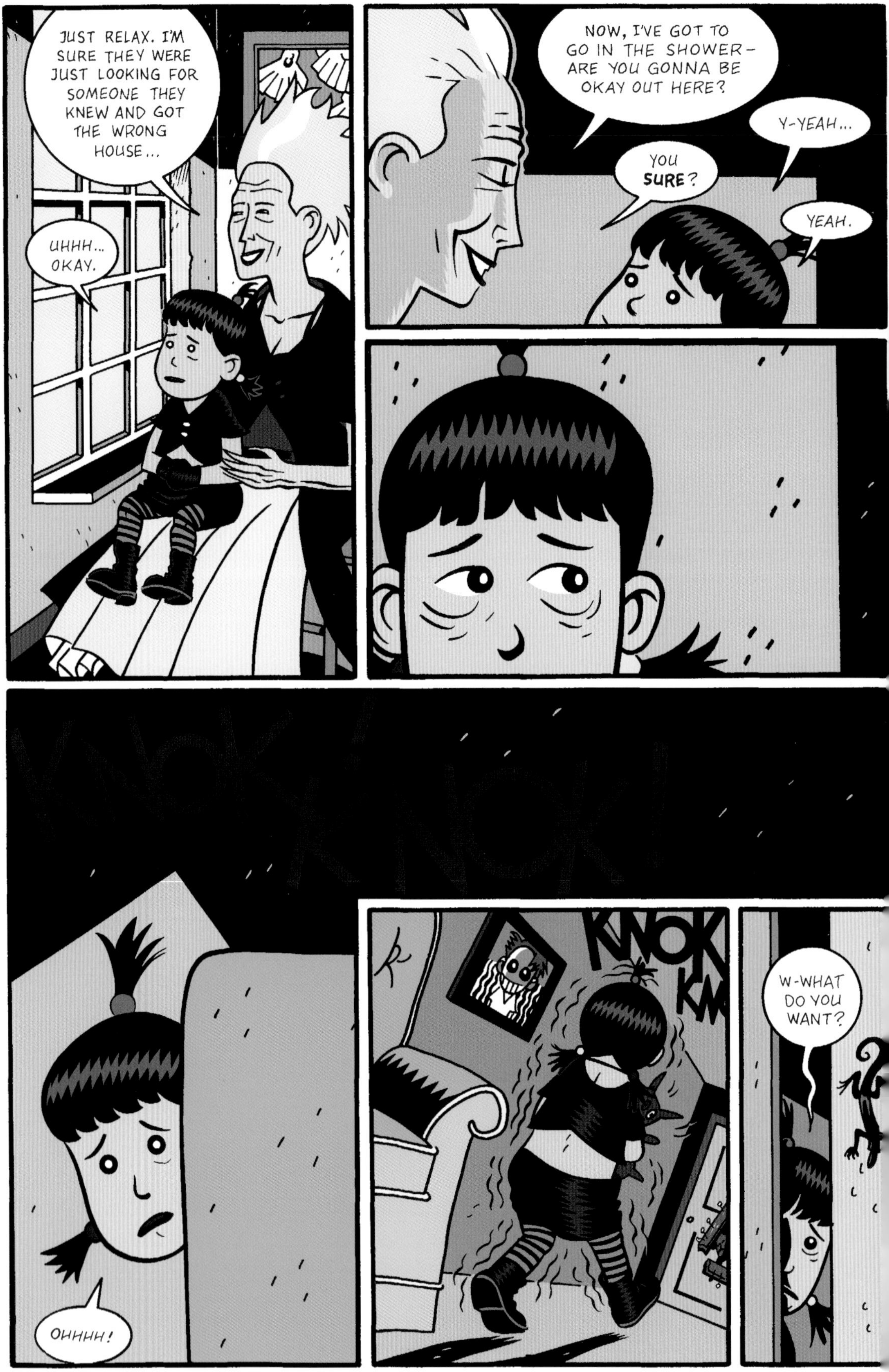
JUST RELAX. I'M SURE THEY WERE JUST LOOKING FOR SOMEONE THEY KNEW AND GOT THE WRONG HOUSE...
UHHH... OKAY.
NOW, I'VE GOT TO GO IN THE SHOWER- ARE YOU GONNA BE OKAY OUT HERE?
YOU **SURE**?
Y-YEAH...
YEAH.
KNOK! KNOK!
OHHHH!
KNOK
W-WHAT DO YOU WANT?

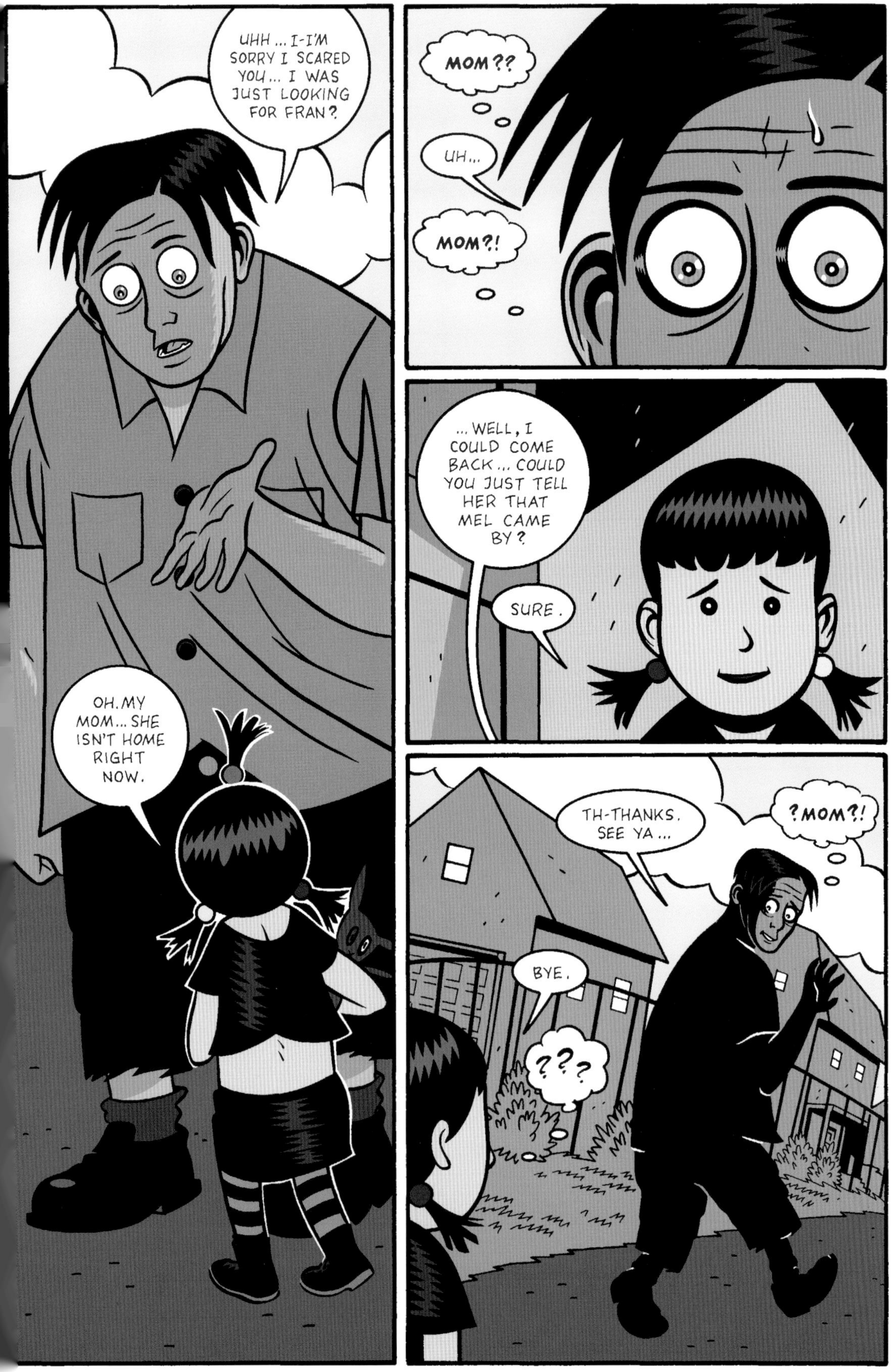
UHH ... I-I'M SORRY I SCARED YOU ... I WAS JUST LOOKING FOR FRAN?
OH. MY MOM ... SHE ISN'T HOME RIGHT NOW.
MOM??
UH ...
MOM?!
... WELL, I COULD COME BACK ... COULD YOU JUST TELL HER THAT MEL CAME BY?
SURE.
TH-THANKS. SEE YA ...
?MOM?!
BYE.
???

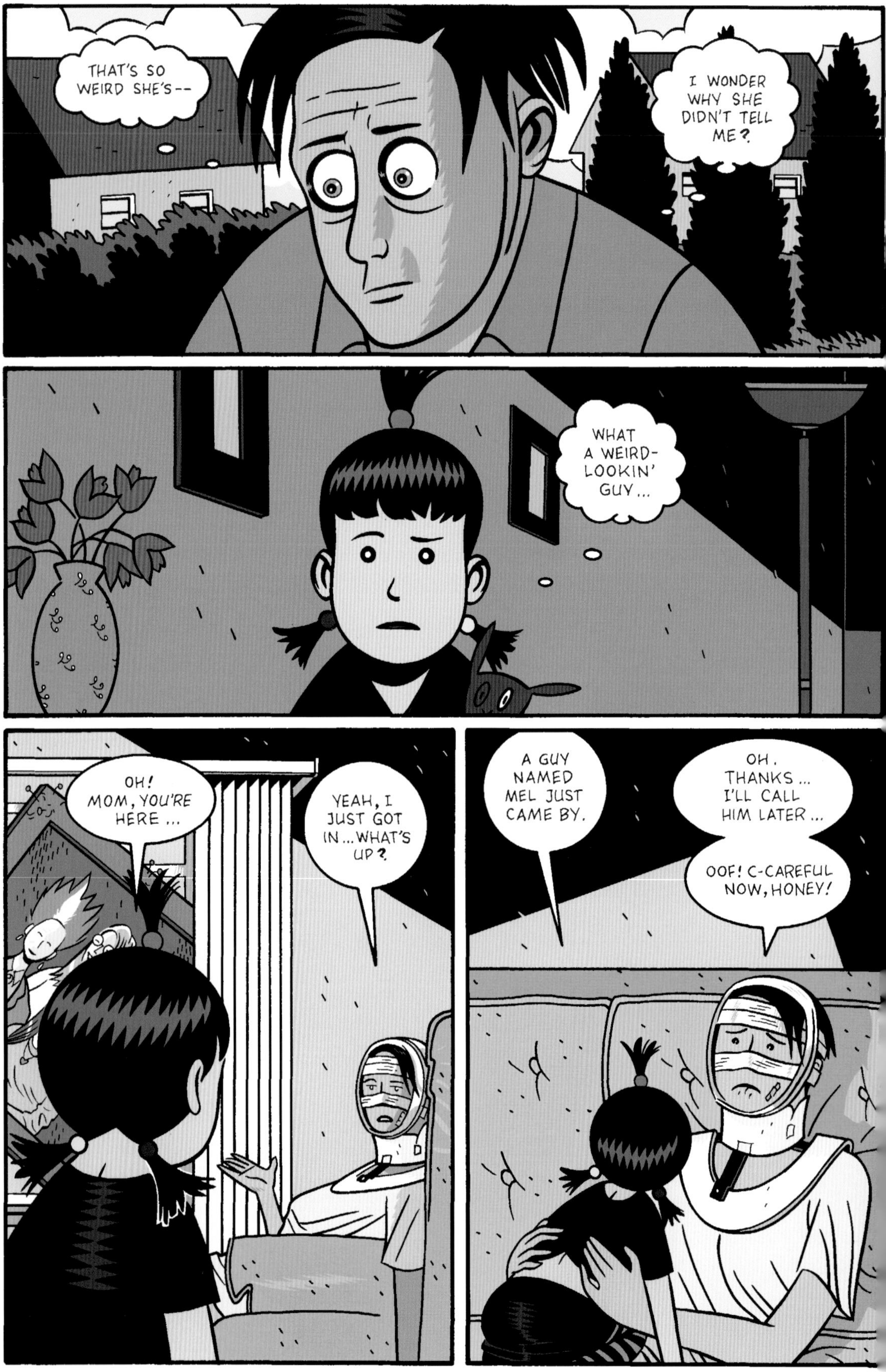
THAT'S SO WEIRD SHE'S--
I WONDER WHY SHE DIDN'T TELL ME?
WHAT A WEIRD-LOOKIN' GUY...
OH! MOM, YOU'RE HERE...
YEAH, I JUST GOT IN... WHAT'S UP?
A GUY NAMED MEL JUST CAME BY.
OH. THANKS... I'LL CALL HIM LATER...
OOF! C-CAREFUL NOW, HONEY!

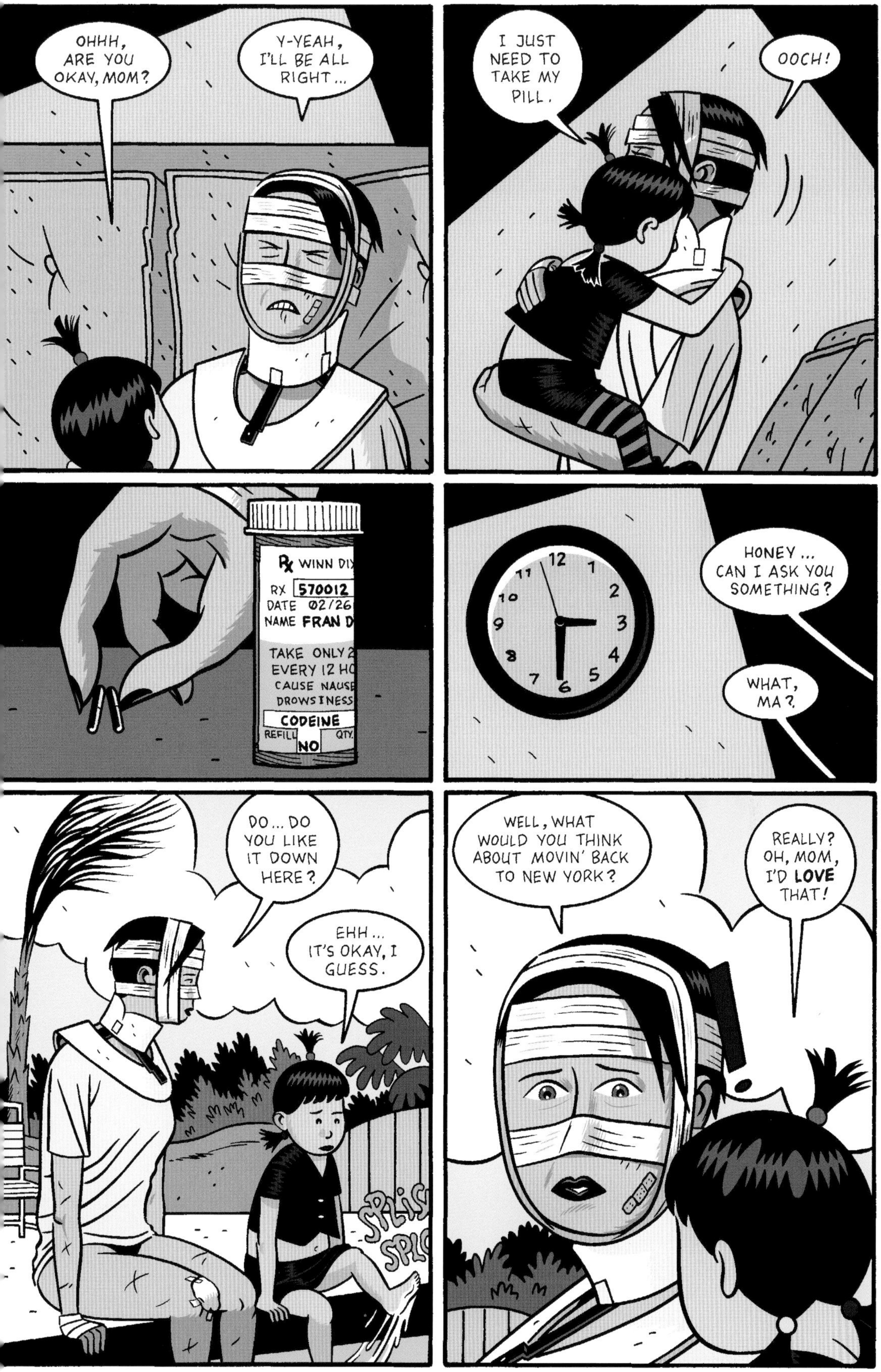
OHHH, ARE YOU OKAY, MOM?
Y-YEAH, I'LL BE ALL RIGHT...
I JUST NEED TO TAKE MY PILL.
OOCH!
Rx WINN DI
RX 570012
DATE 02/26
NAME FRAN D
TAKE ONLY 2
EVERY 12 HO
CAUSE NAUSE
DROWSINESS
CODEINE
REFILL NO
QTY.
HONEY... CAN I ASK YOU SOMETHING?
WHAT, MA?
DO... DO YOU LIKE IT DOWN HERE?
EHH... IT'S OKAY, I GUESS.
WELL, WHAT WOULD YOU THINK ABOUT MOVIN' BACK TO NEW YORK?
REALLY? OH, MOM, I'D **LOVE** THAT!

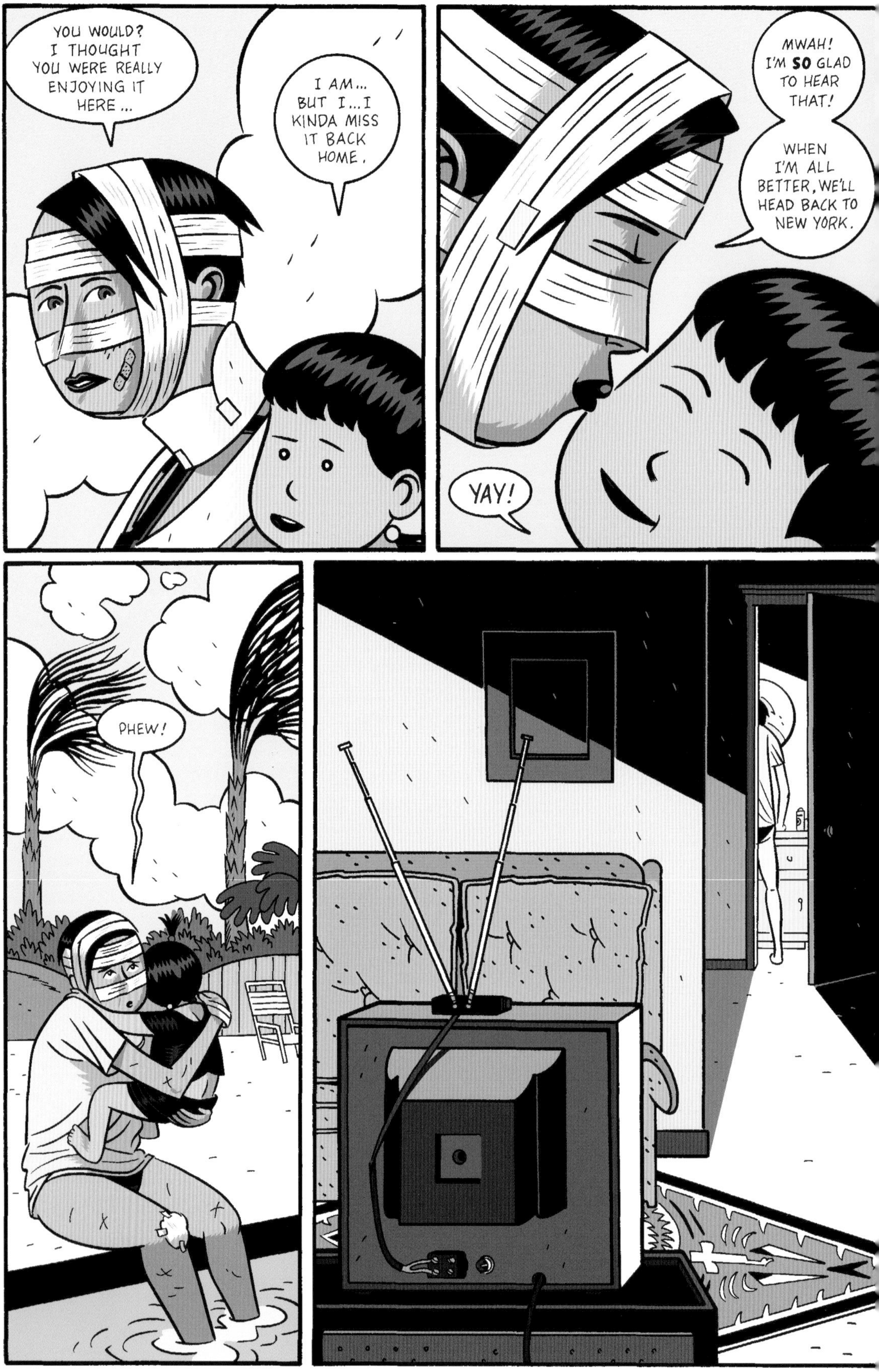
YOU WOULD? I THOUGHT YOU WERE REALLY ENJOYING IT HERE...
I AM... BUT I...I KINDA MISS IT BACK HOME.
MWAH! I'M SO GLAD TO HEAR THAT!
WHEN I'M ALL BETTER, WE'LL HEAD BACK TO NEW YORK.
YAY!
PHEW!

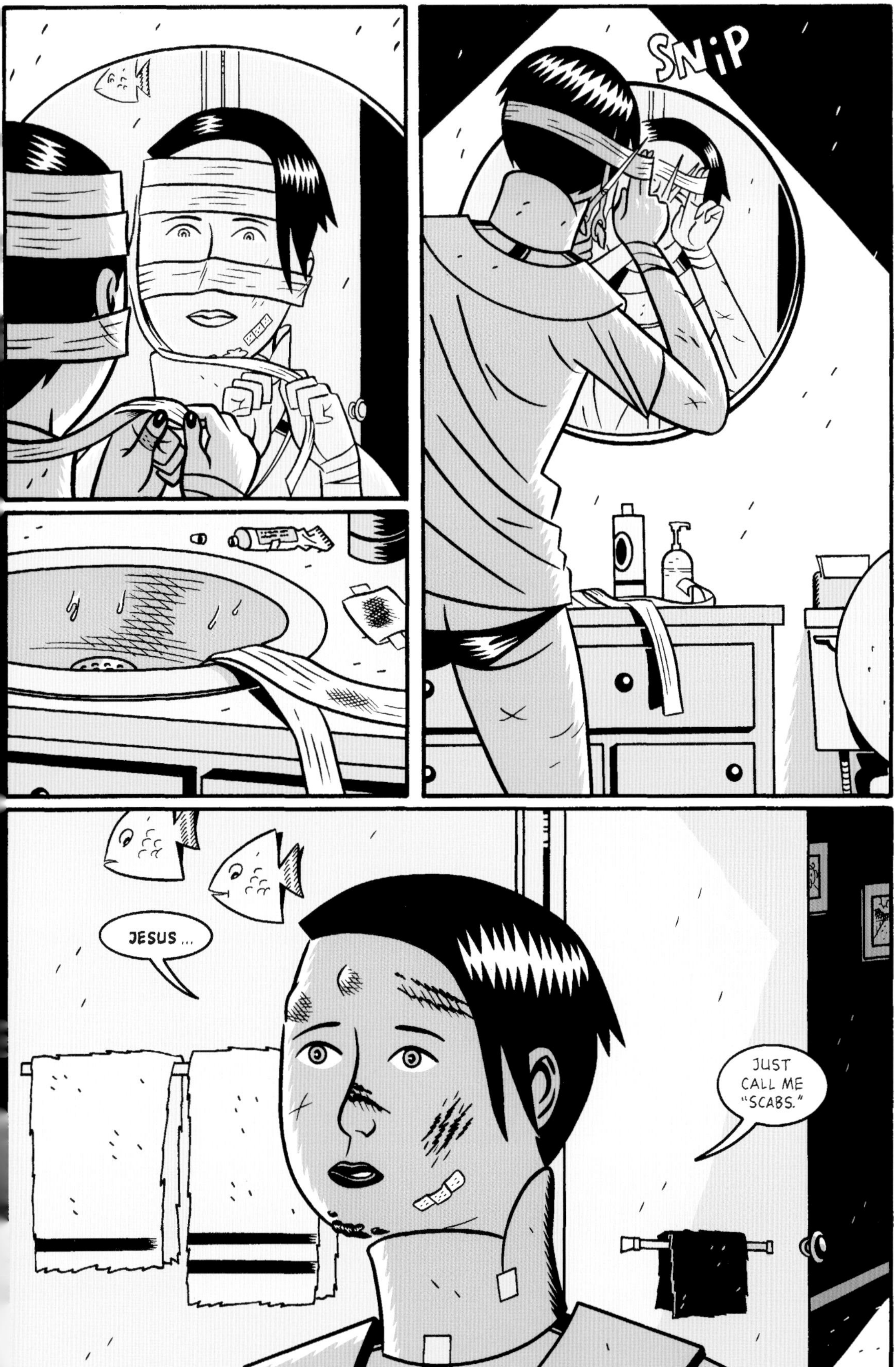
SNIP
JESUS...
JUST CALL ME "SCABS."

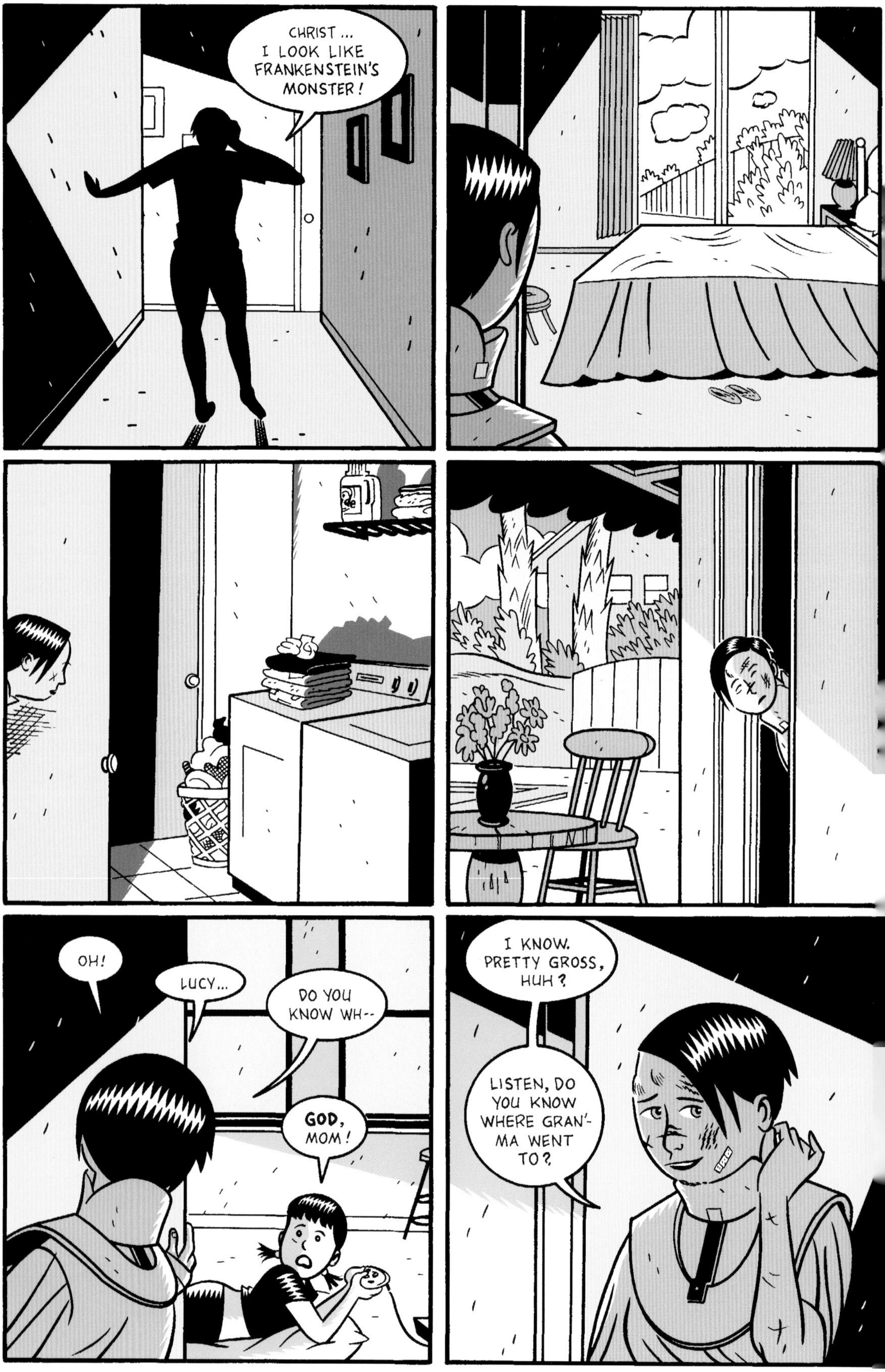
CHRIST ... I LOOK LIKE FRANKENSTEIN'S MONSTER!
OH!
LUCY...
DO YOU KNOW WH--
GOD, MOM!
I KNOW. PRETTY GROSS, HUH?
LISTEN, DO YOU KNOW WHERE GRAN'-MA WENT TO?

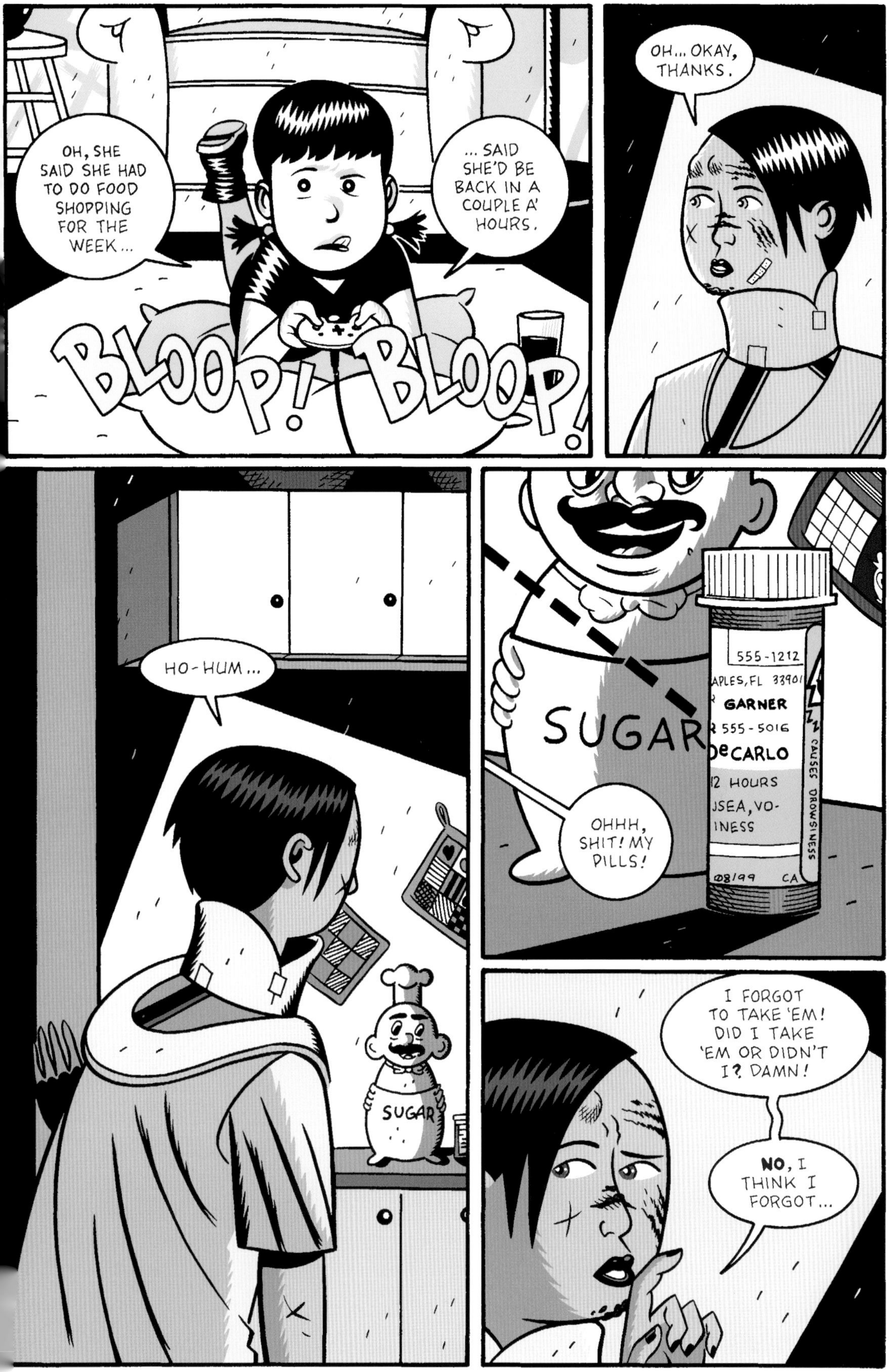
OH, SHE SAID SHE HAD TO DO FOOD SHOPPING FOR THE WEEK...
... SAID SHE'D BE BACK IN A COUPLE A' HOURS.
BLOOP! BLOOP!
OH... OKAY, THANKS.
HO-HUM...
SUGAR
555-1212
APLES, FL 33901
GARNER
R 555-5016
DeCARLO
12 HOURS
USEA, VO-
INESS
CAUSES DROWSINESS
08/99 CA
OHHH, SHIT! MY PILLS!
I FORGOT TO TAKE 'EM! DID I TAKE 'EM OR DIDN'T I? DAMN!
NO, I THINK I FORGOT...

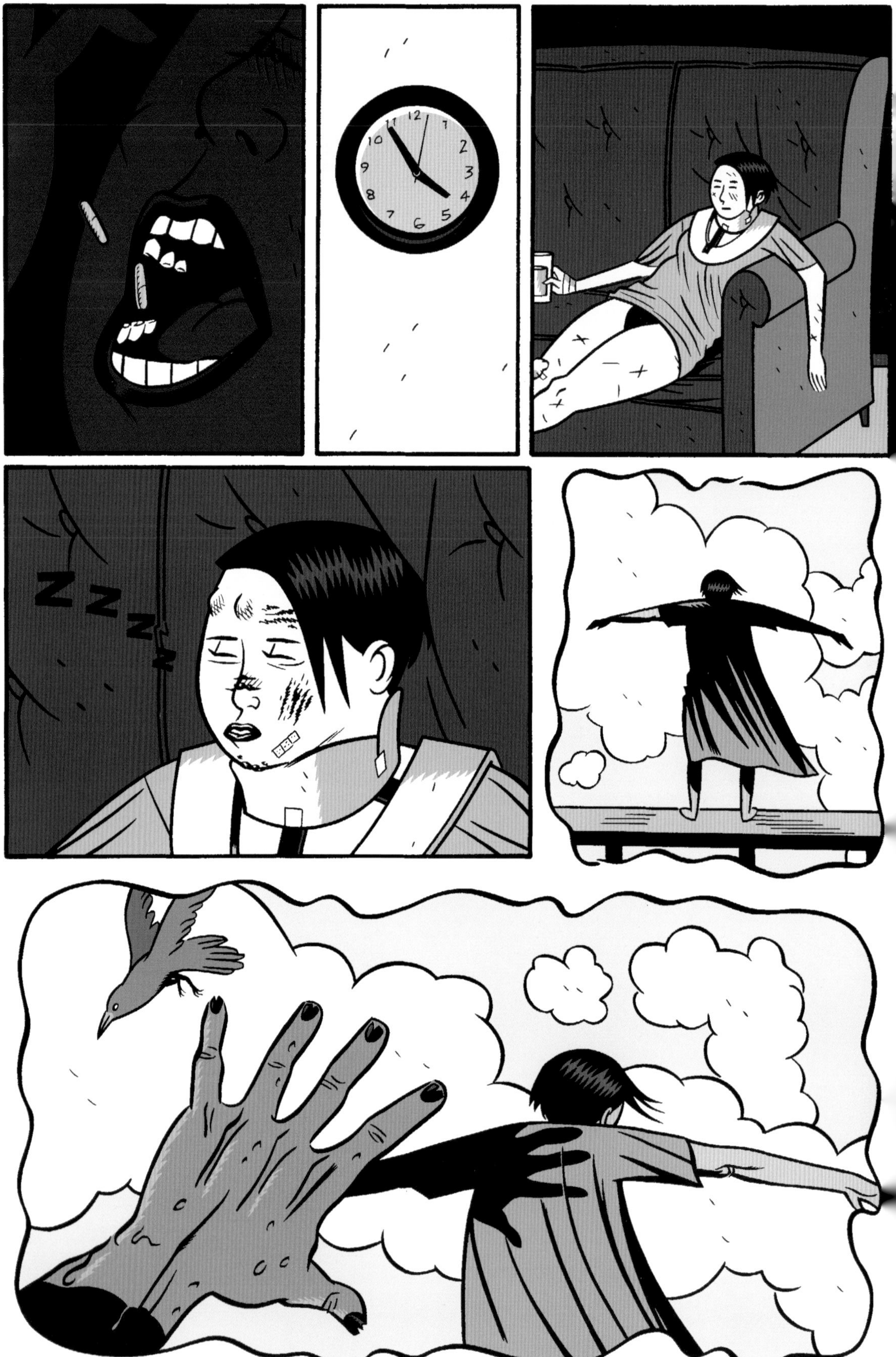
Z Z Z Z

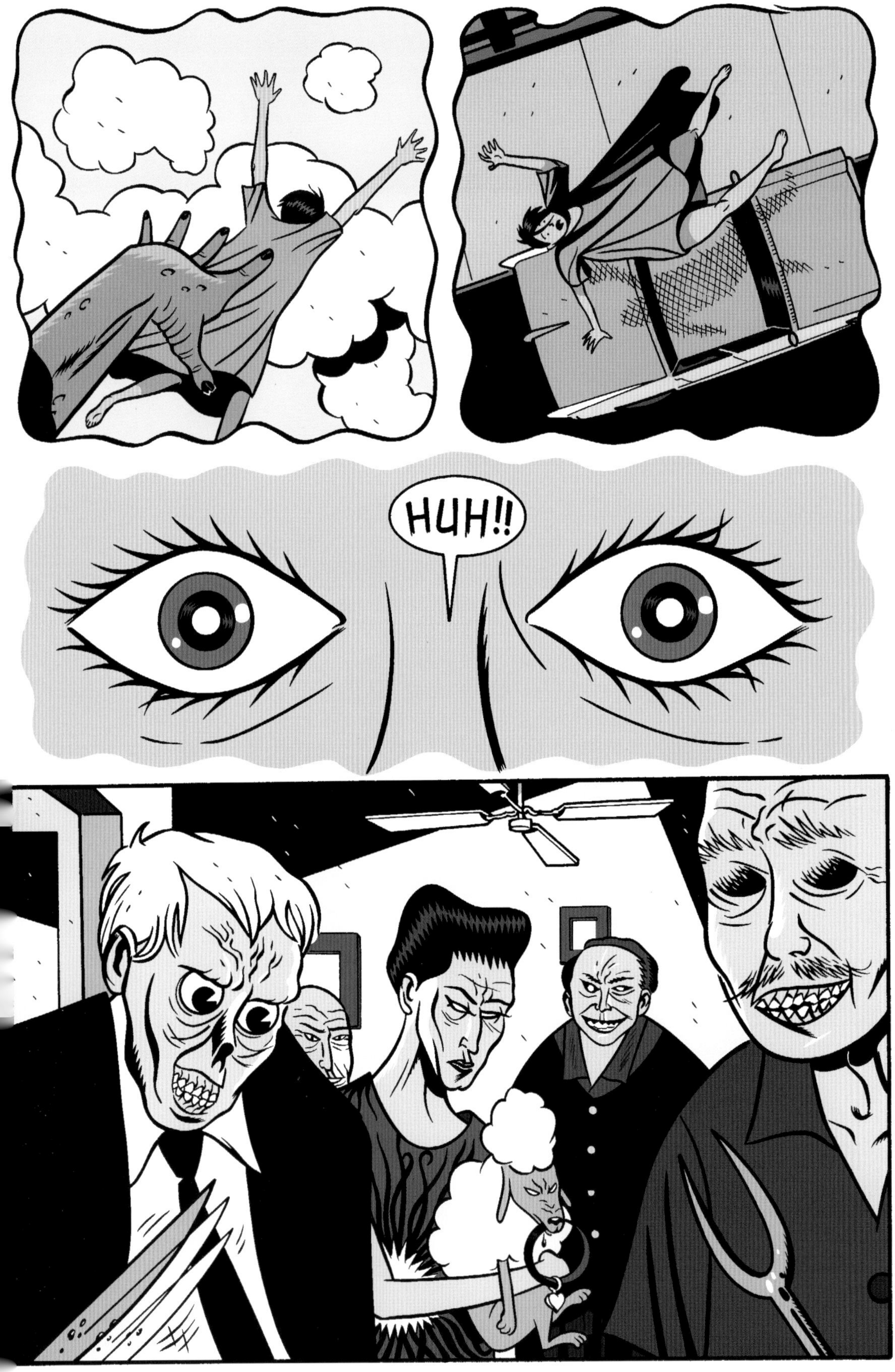
HUH!!

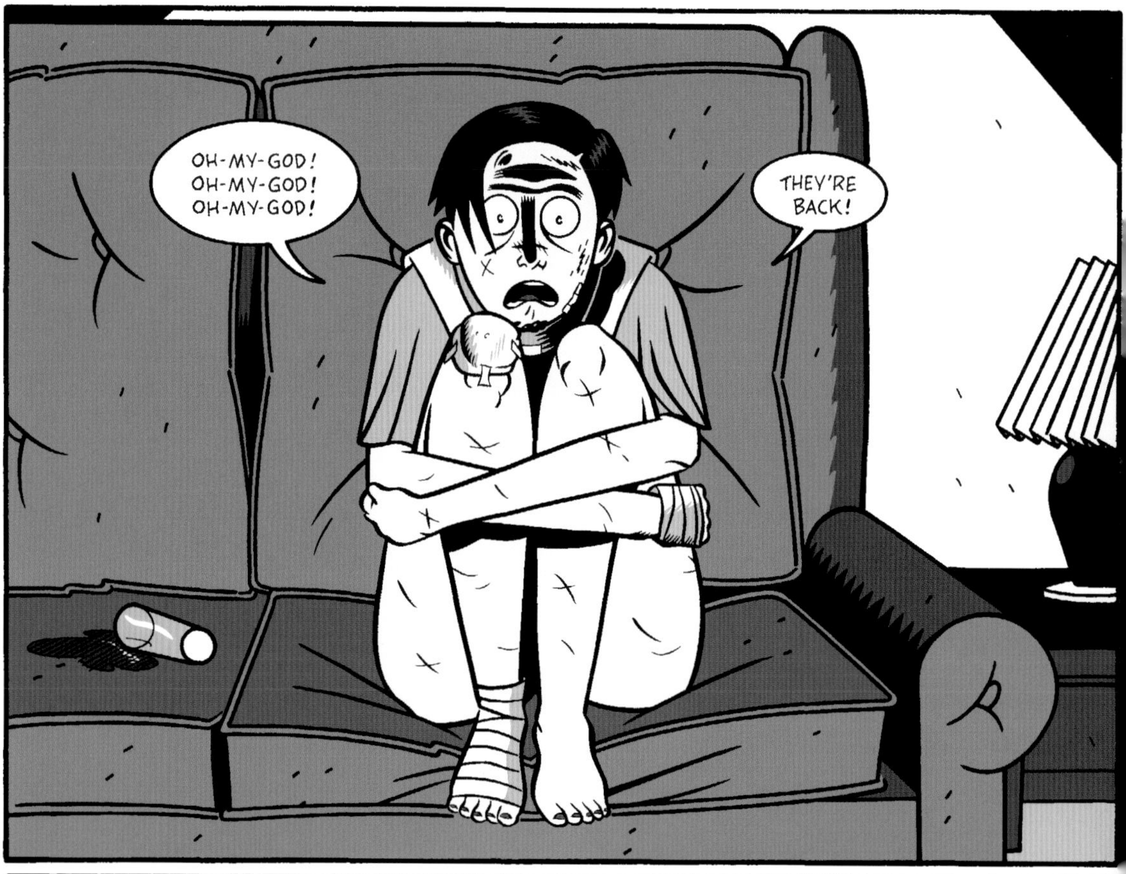
OH-MY-GOD!
OH-MY-GOD!
OH-MY-GOD!
THEY'RE BACK!

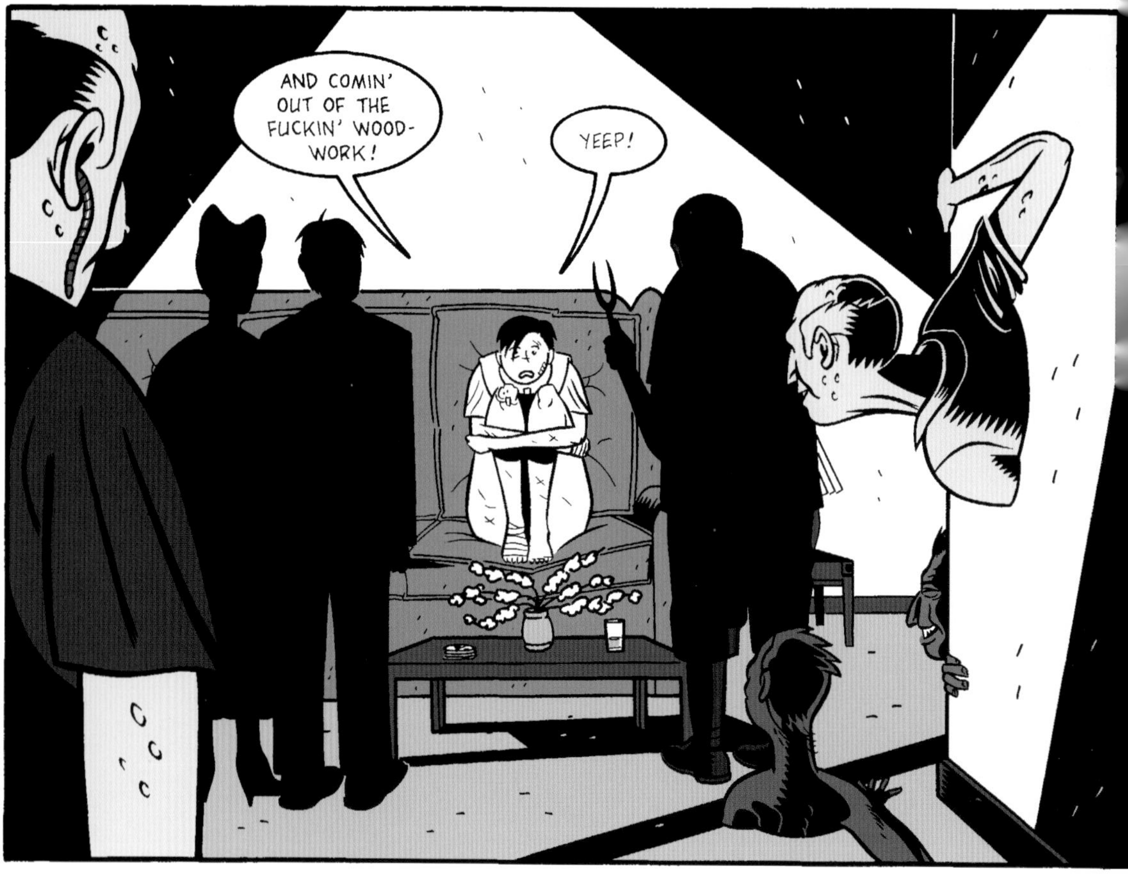
AND COMIN' OUT OF THE FUCKIN' WOOD-WORK!
YEEP!

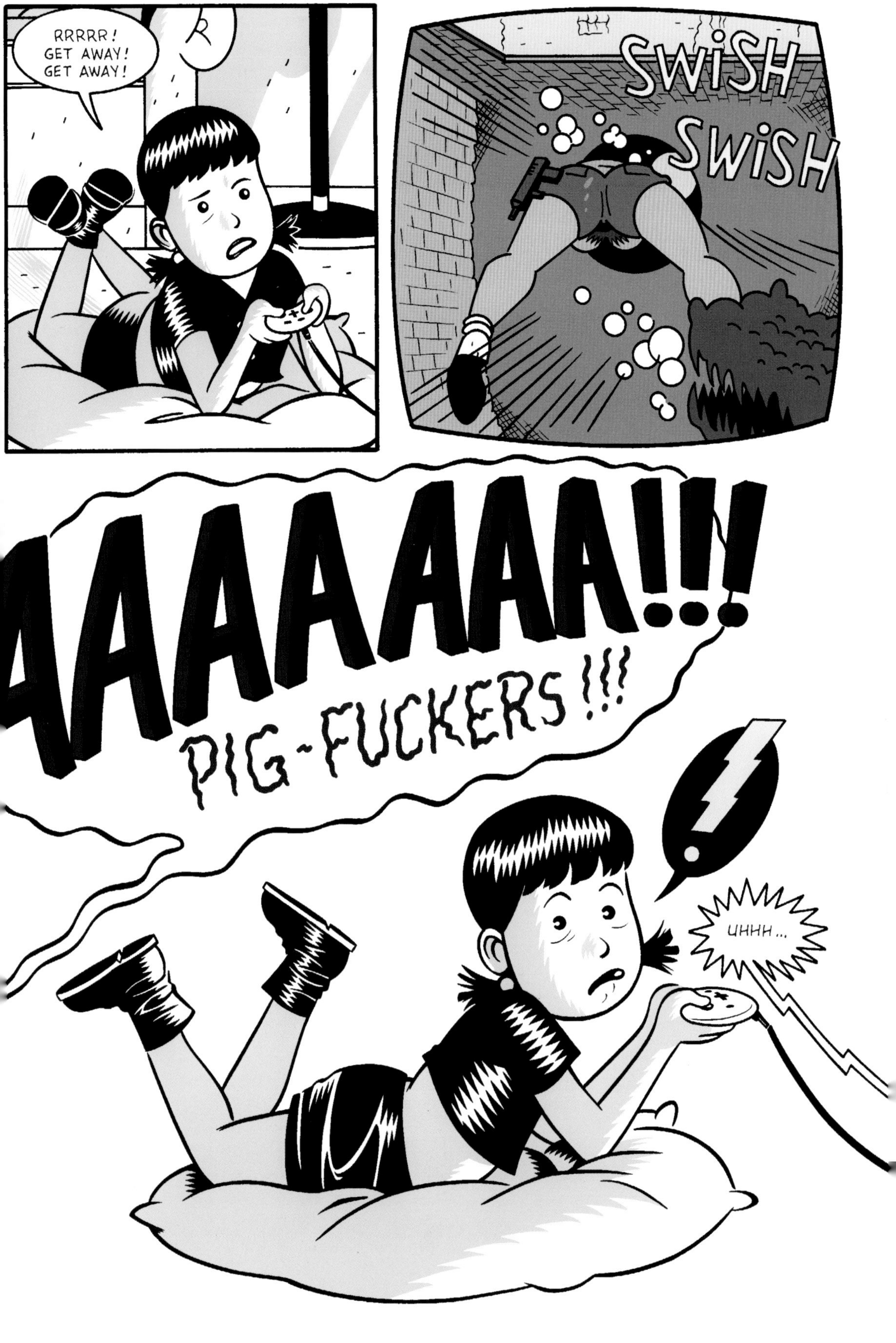
RRRRR! GET AWAY! GET AWAY!
SWISH
SWISH
AAAAAAA!!!
PIG-FUCKERS!!!
UHHH...

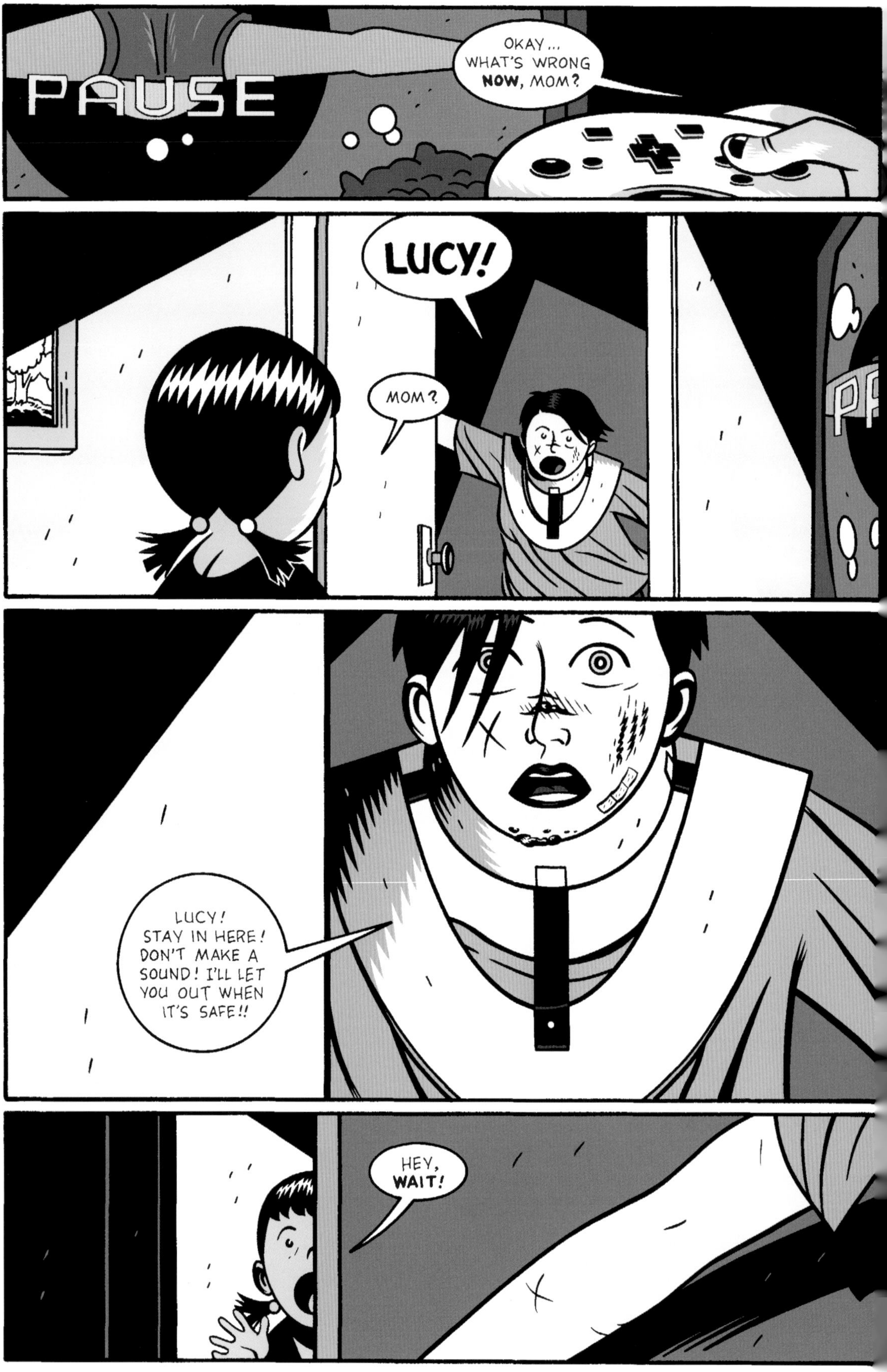
PAUSE
OKAY... WHAT'S WRONG NOW, MOM?
LUCY!
MOM?
LUCY! STAY IN HERE! DON'T MAKE A SOUND! I'LL LET YOU OUT WHEN IT'S SAFE!!
HEY, WAIT!

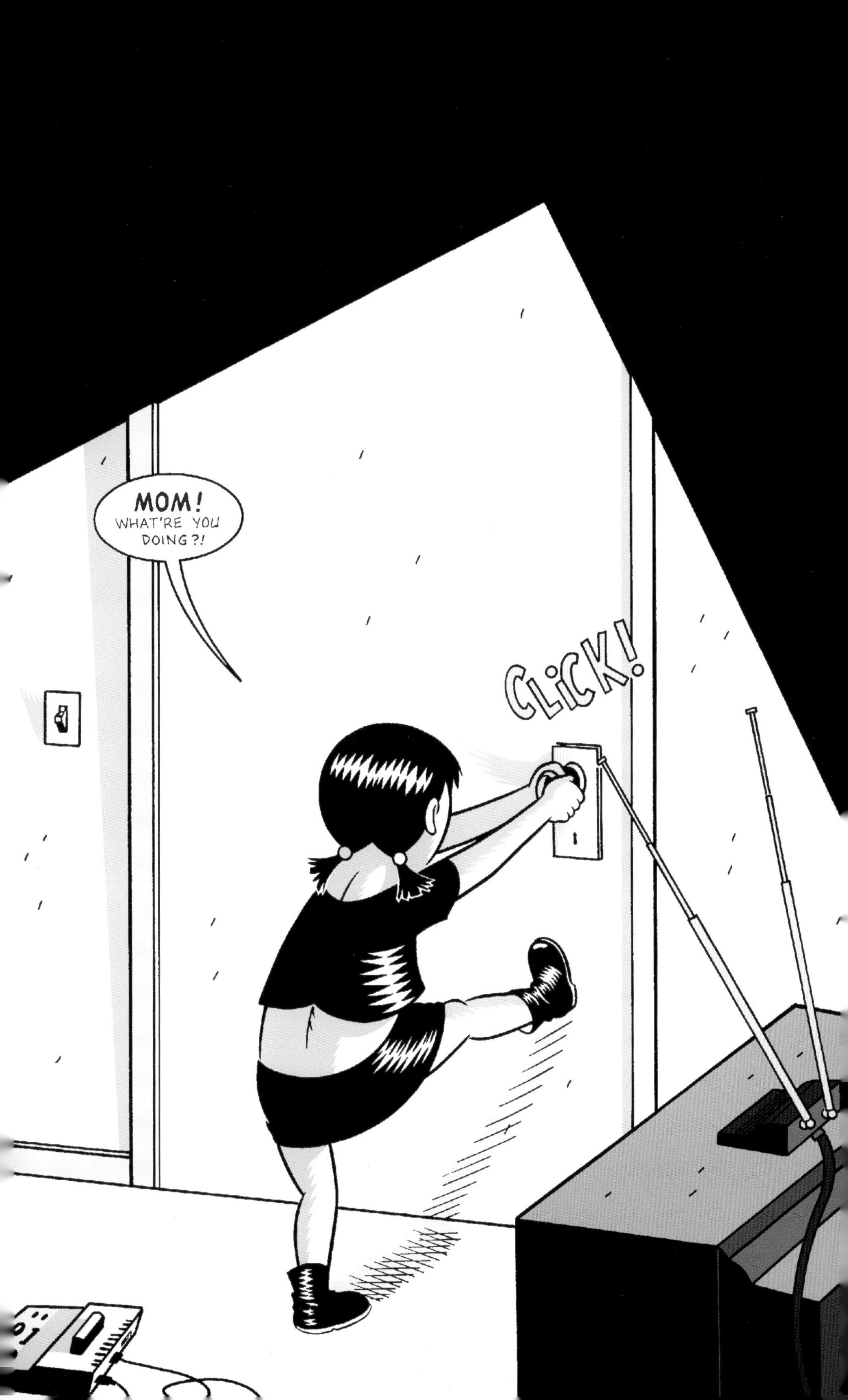
MOM! WHAT'RE YOU DOING?!
CLICK!

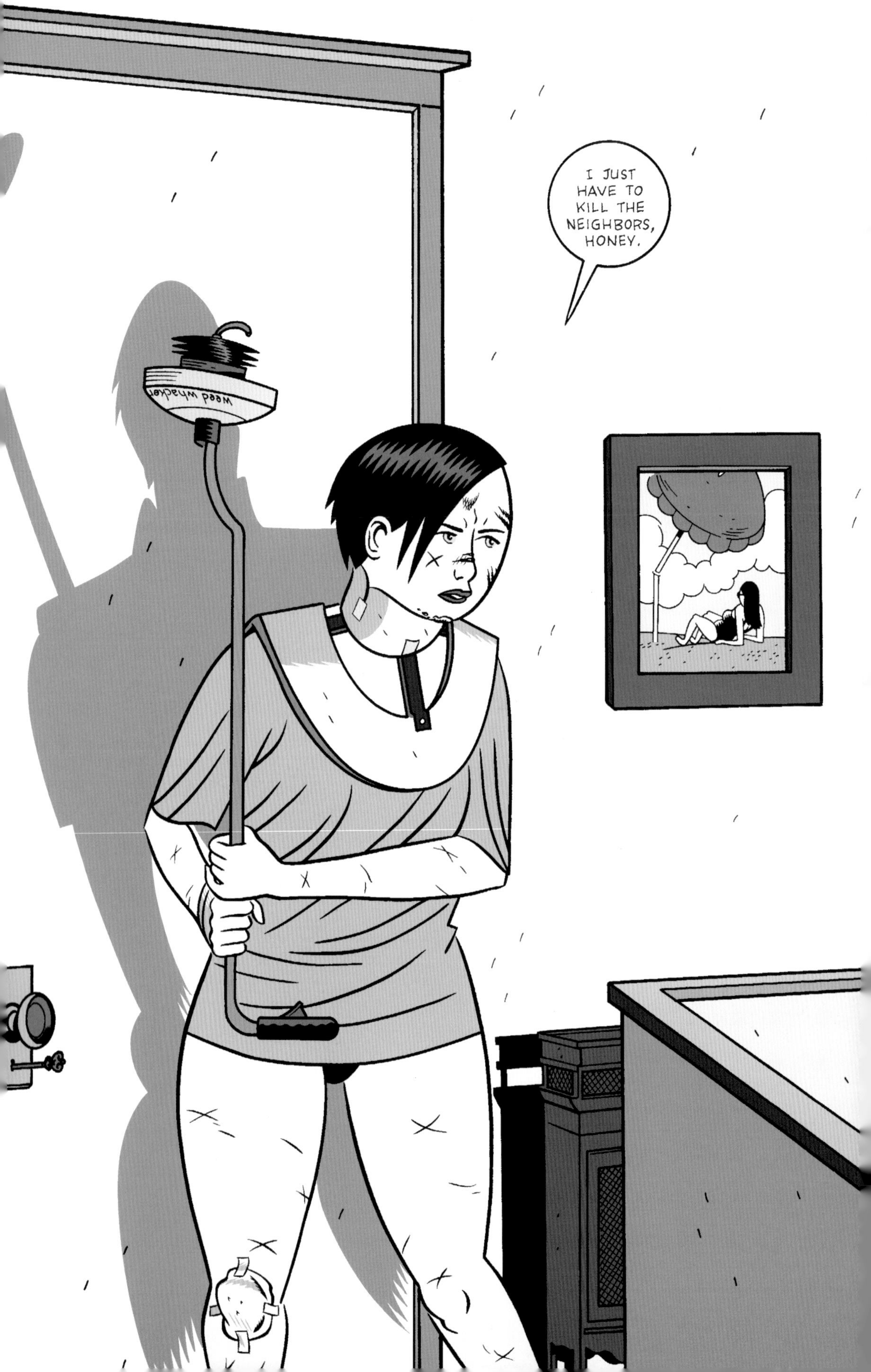
I JUST HAVE TO KILL THE NEIGHBORS, HONEY.
weed whacker

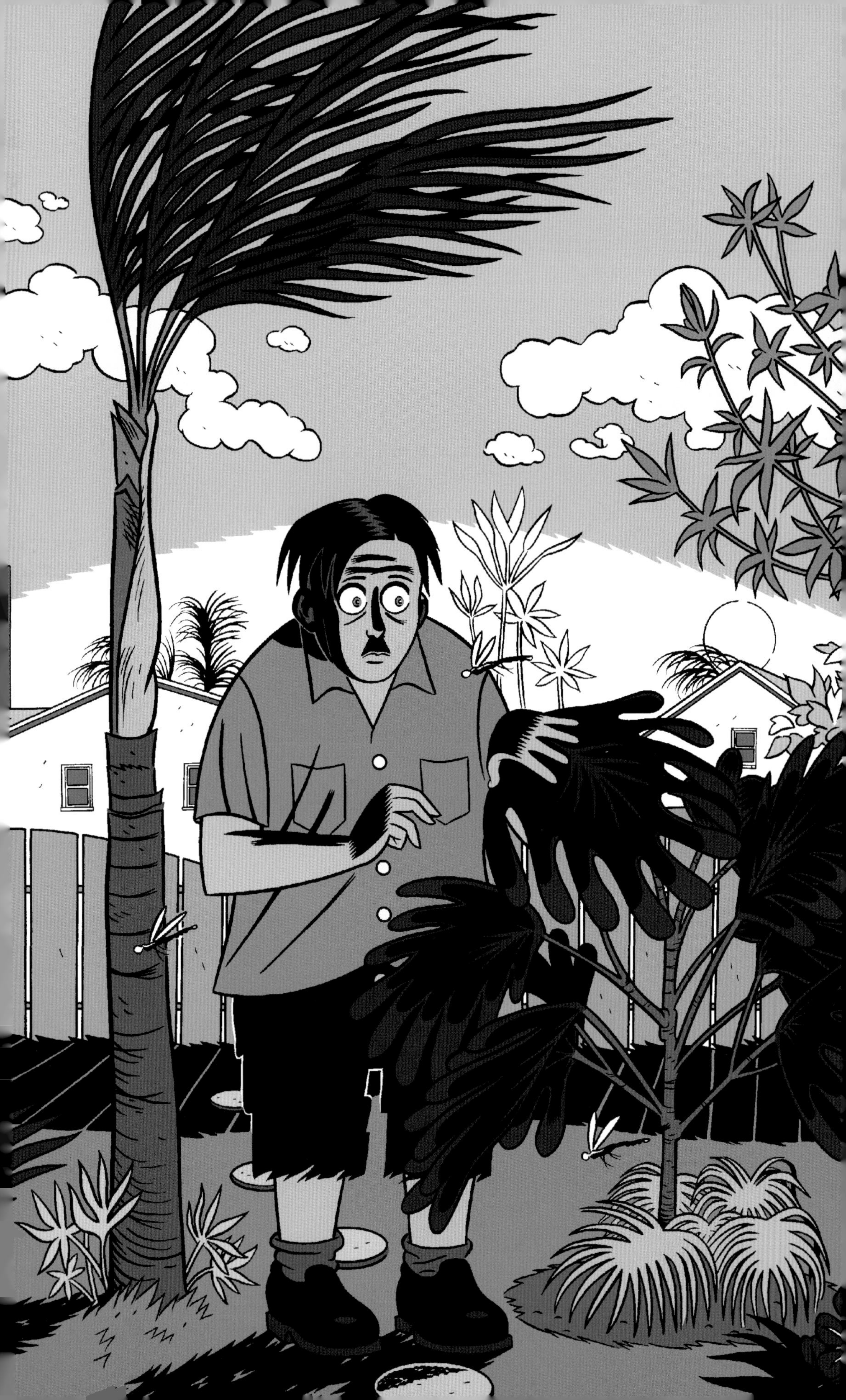

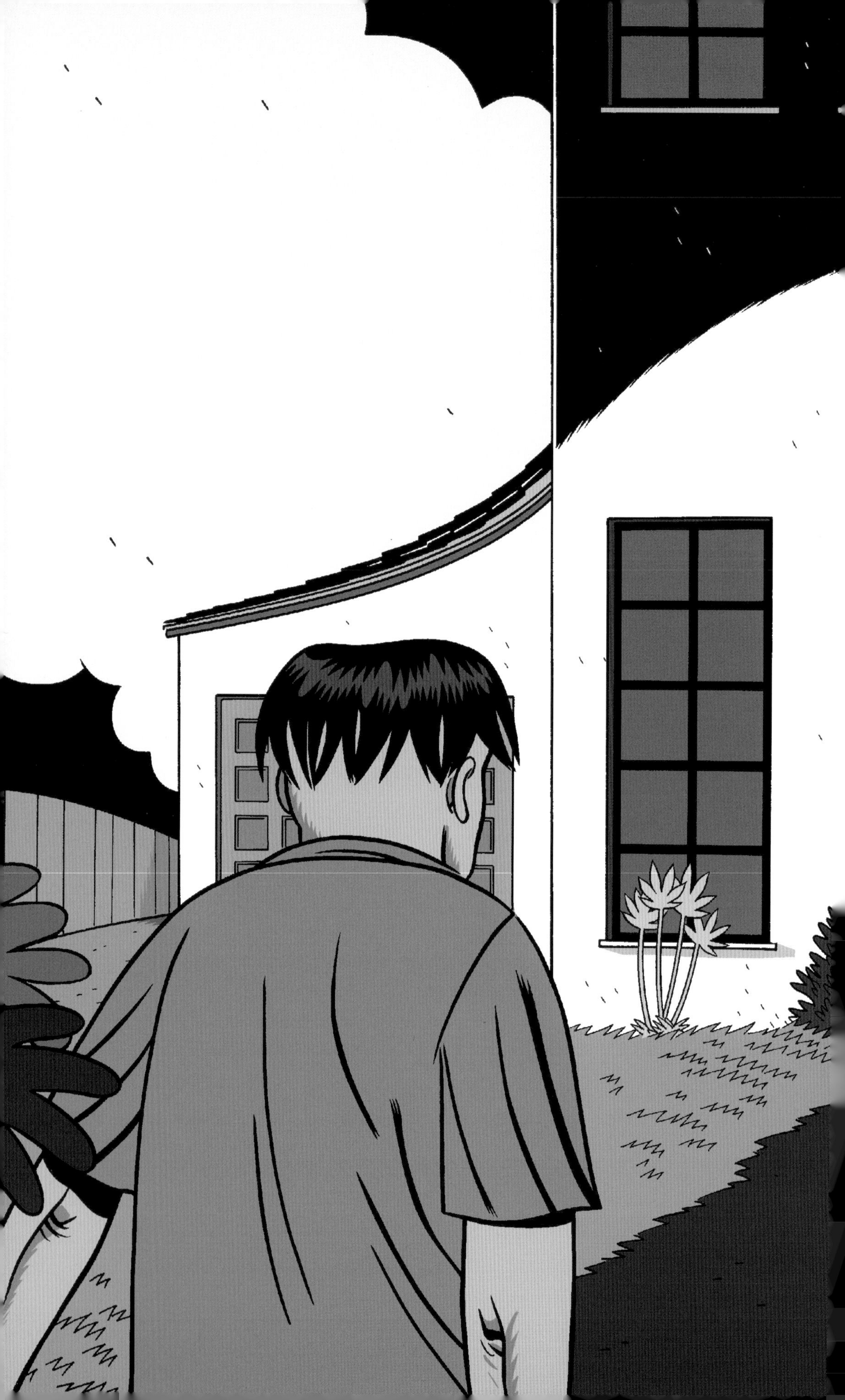

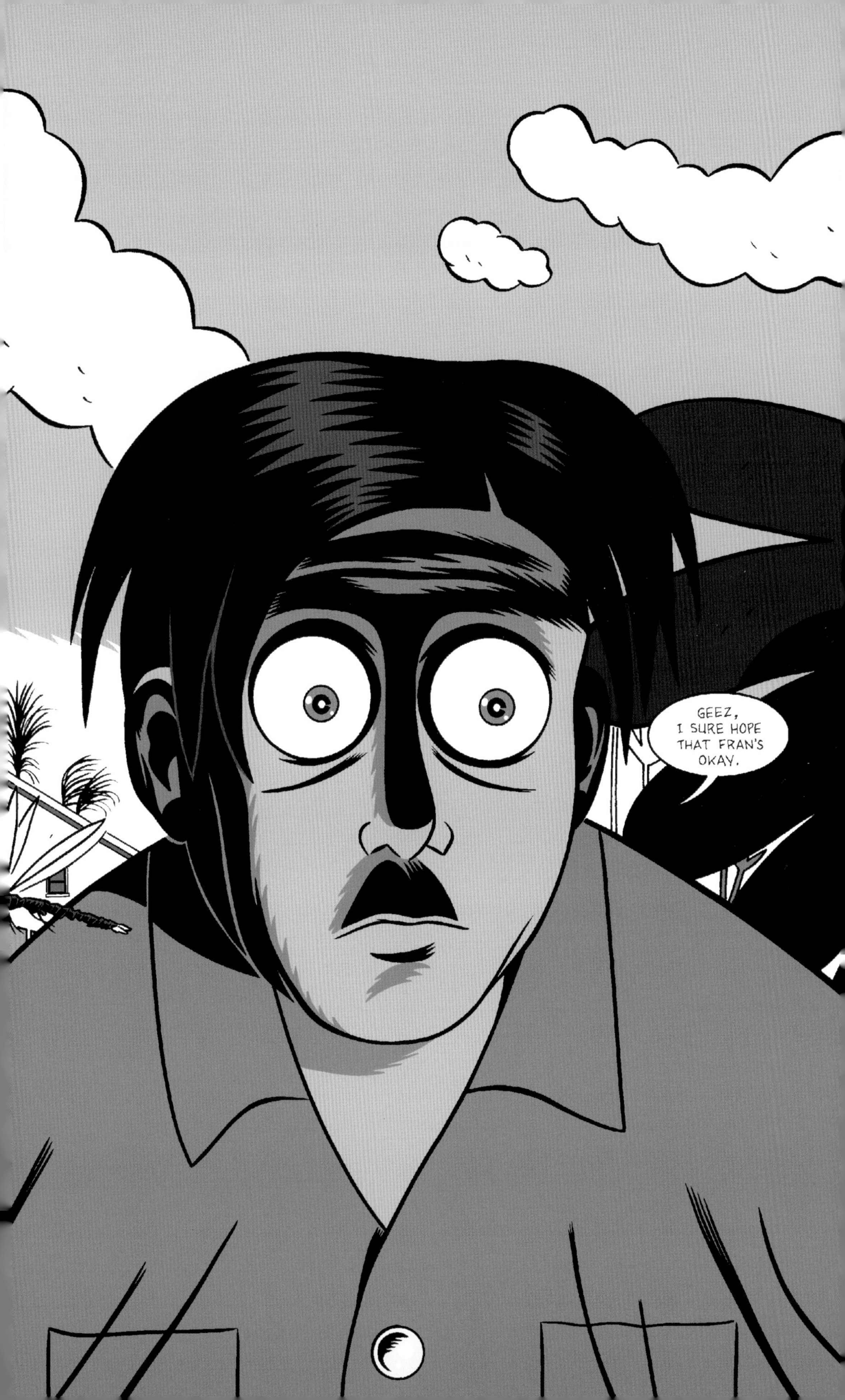
GEEZ, I SURE HOPE THAT FRAN'S OKAY.

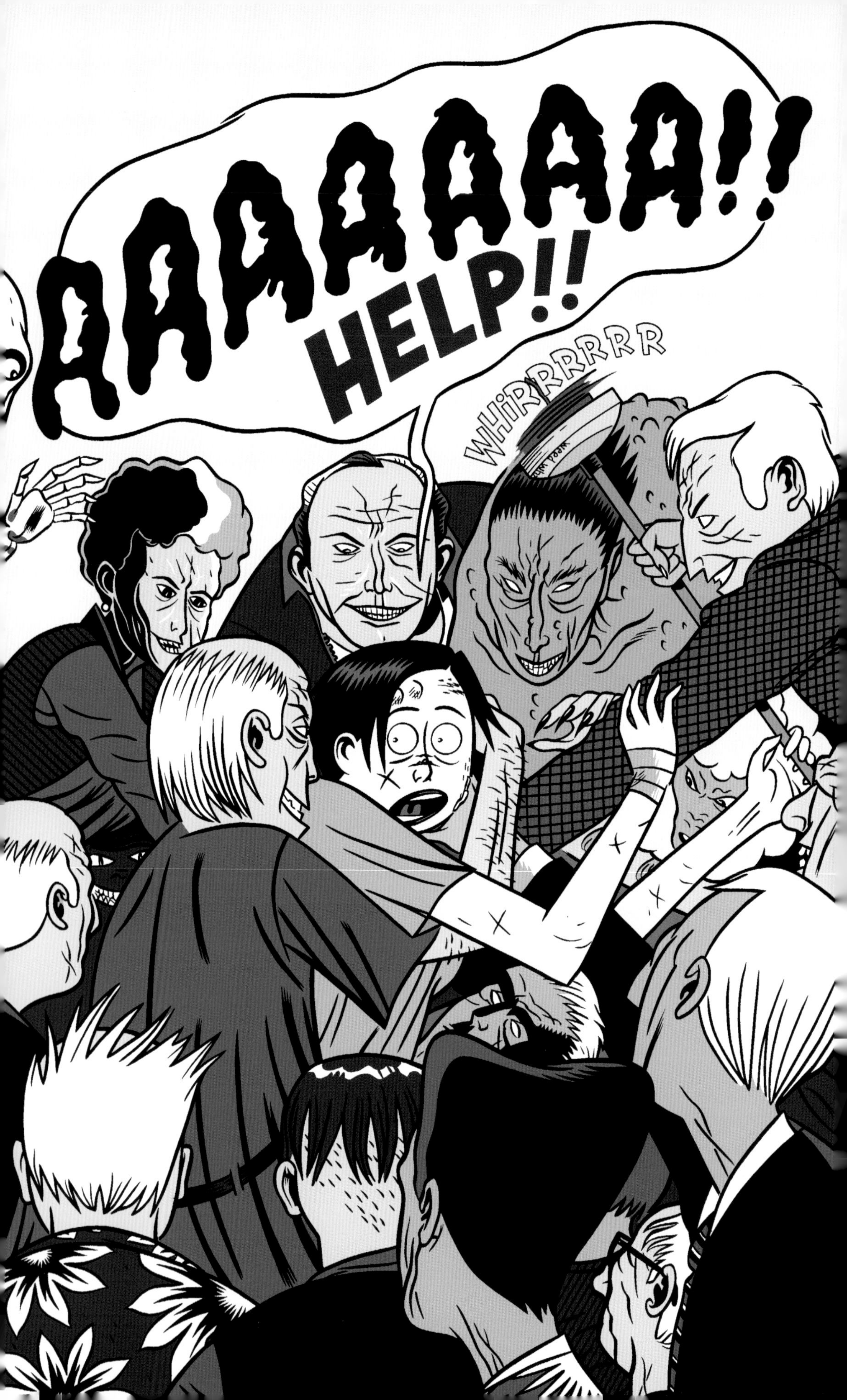
AAAAAAA!!
HELP!!
WHiRRRRRR

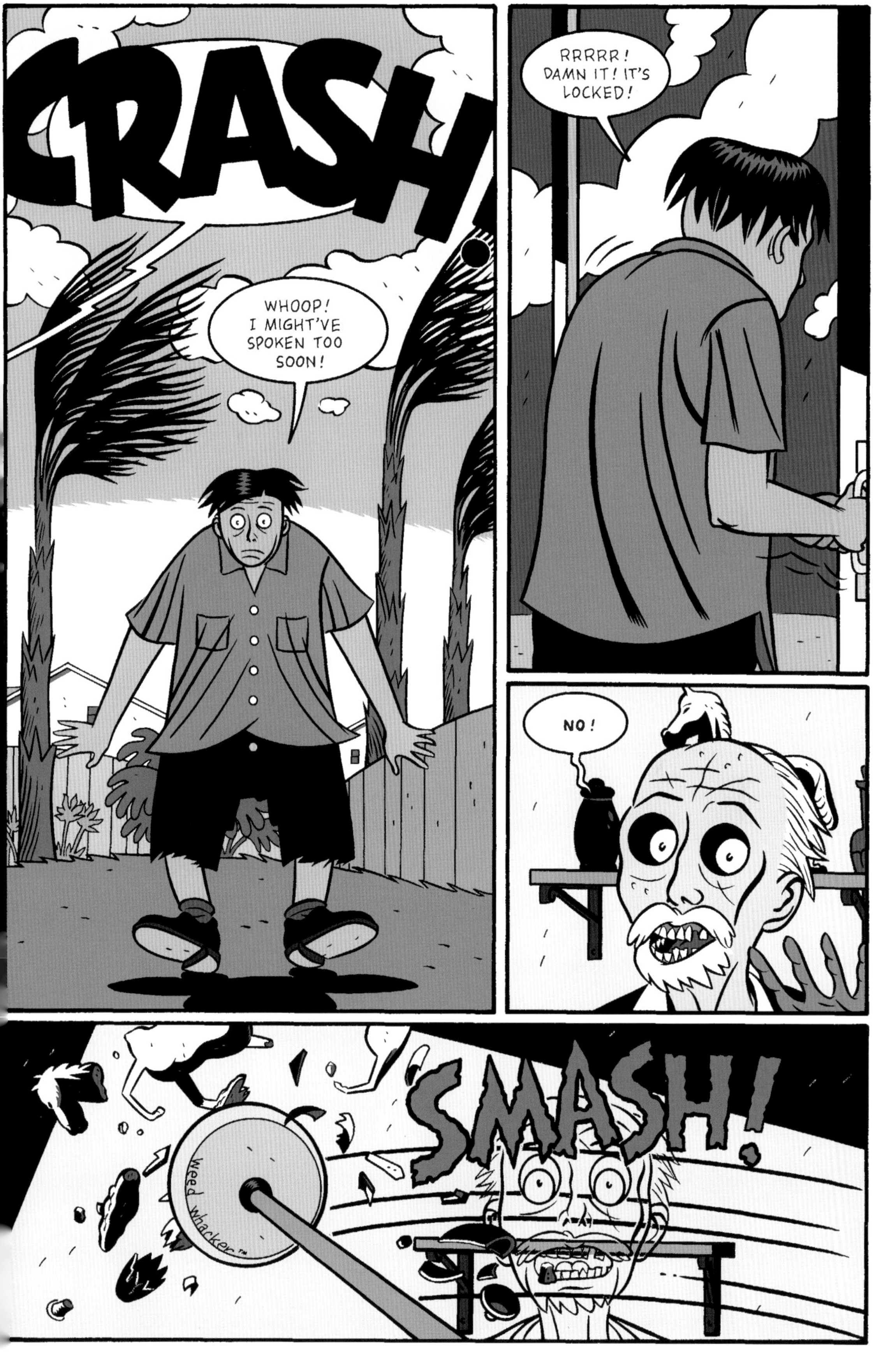
CRASH!
WHOOP! I MIGHT'VE SPOKEN TOO SOON!
RRRRR! DAMN IT! IT'S LOCKED!
NO!
SMASH!
weed wharker™

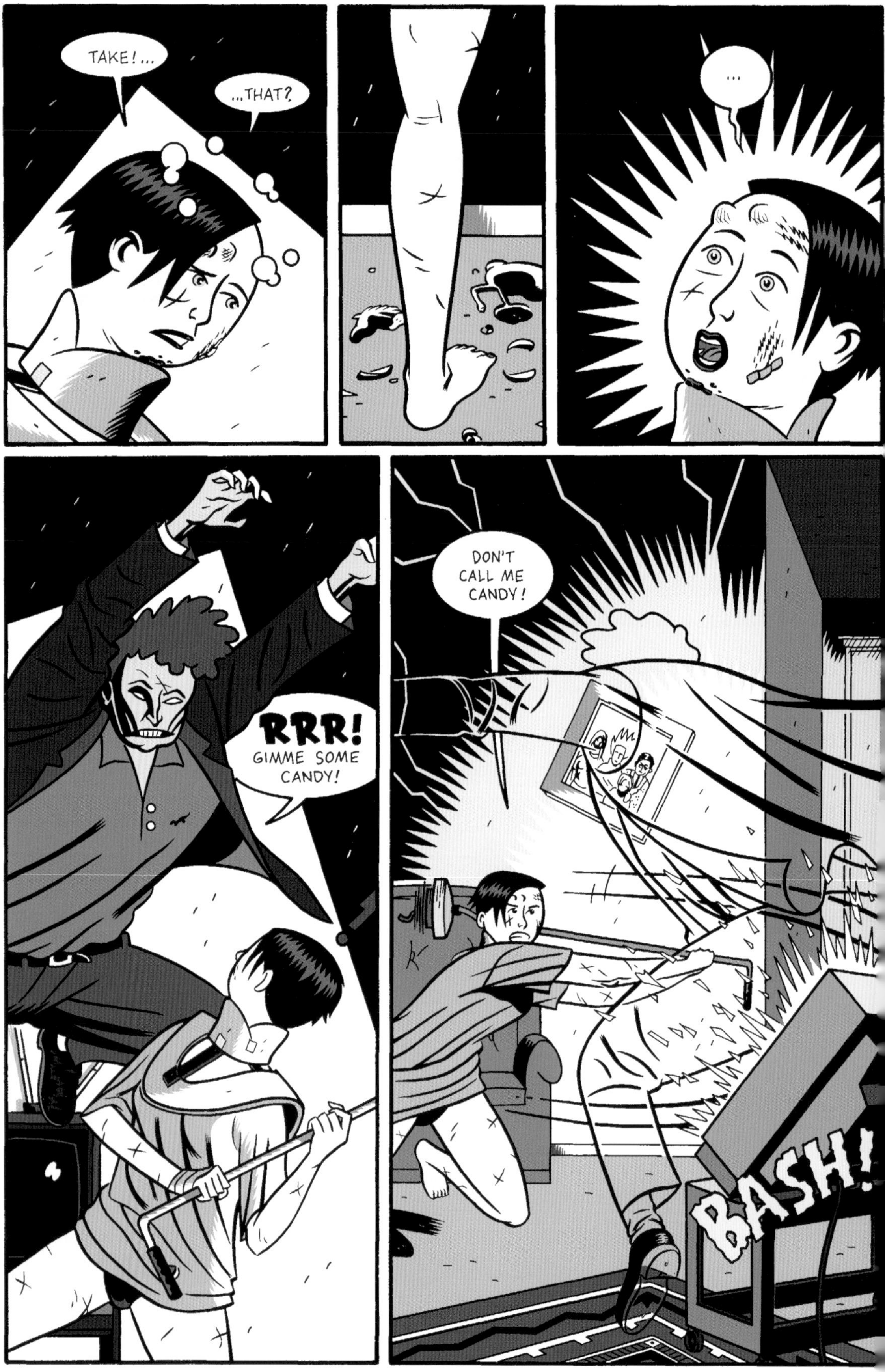
TAKE!...
...THAT?
...
RRR!
GIMME SOME CANDY!
DON'T CALL ME CANDY!
BASH!

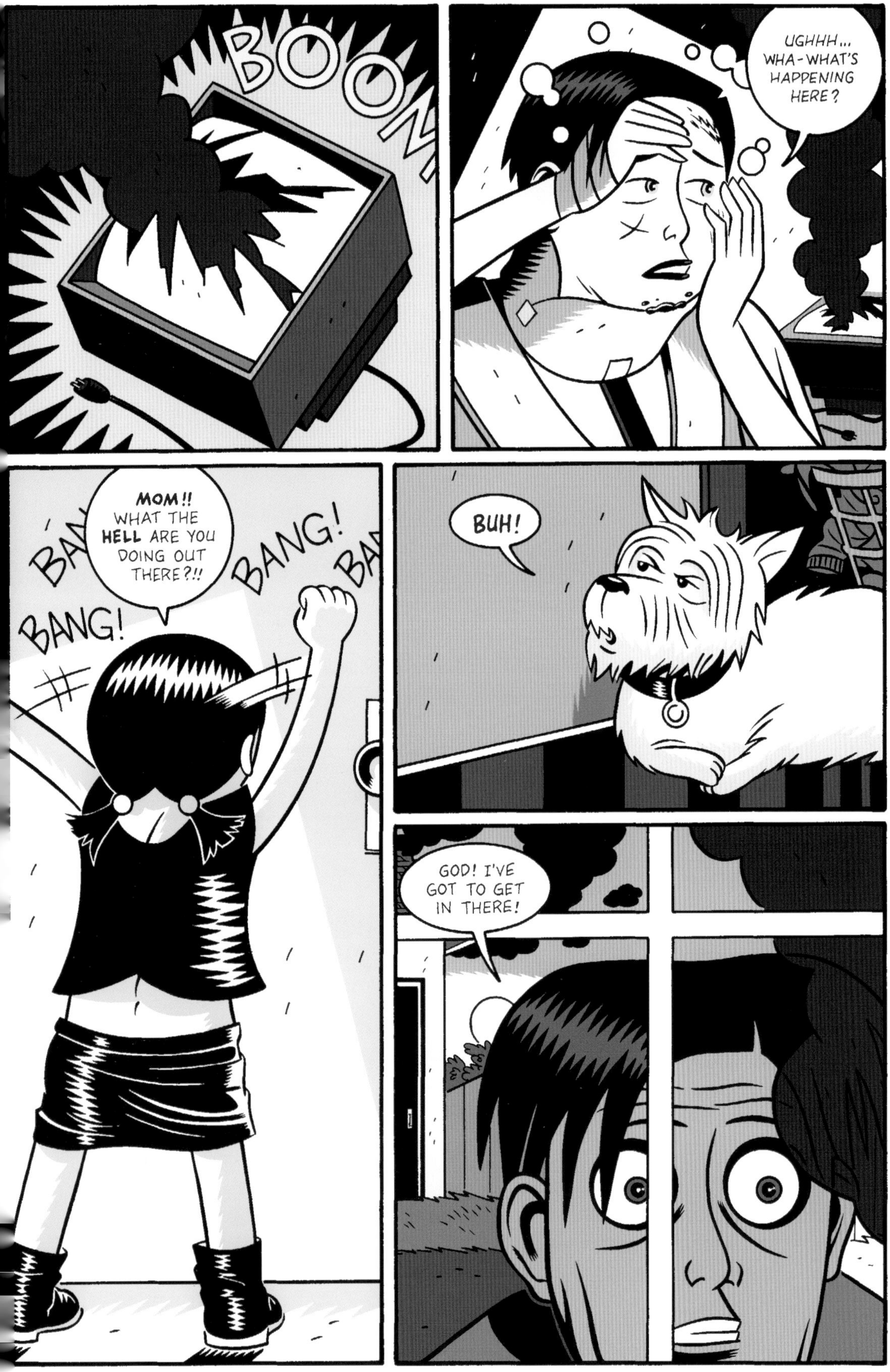
BOOM!
UGHHH... WHA-WHAT'S HAPPENING HERE?
BANG!
MOM!! WHAT THE **HELL** ARE YOU DOING OUT THERE?!!
BANG!
BANG!
BUH!
GOD! I'VE GOT TO GET IN THERE!

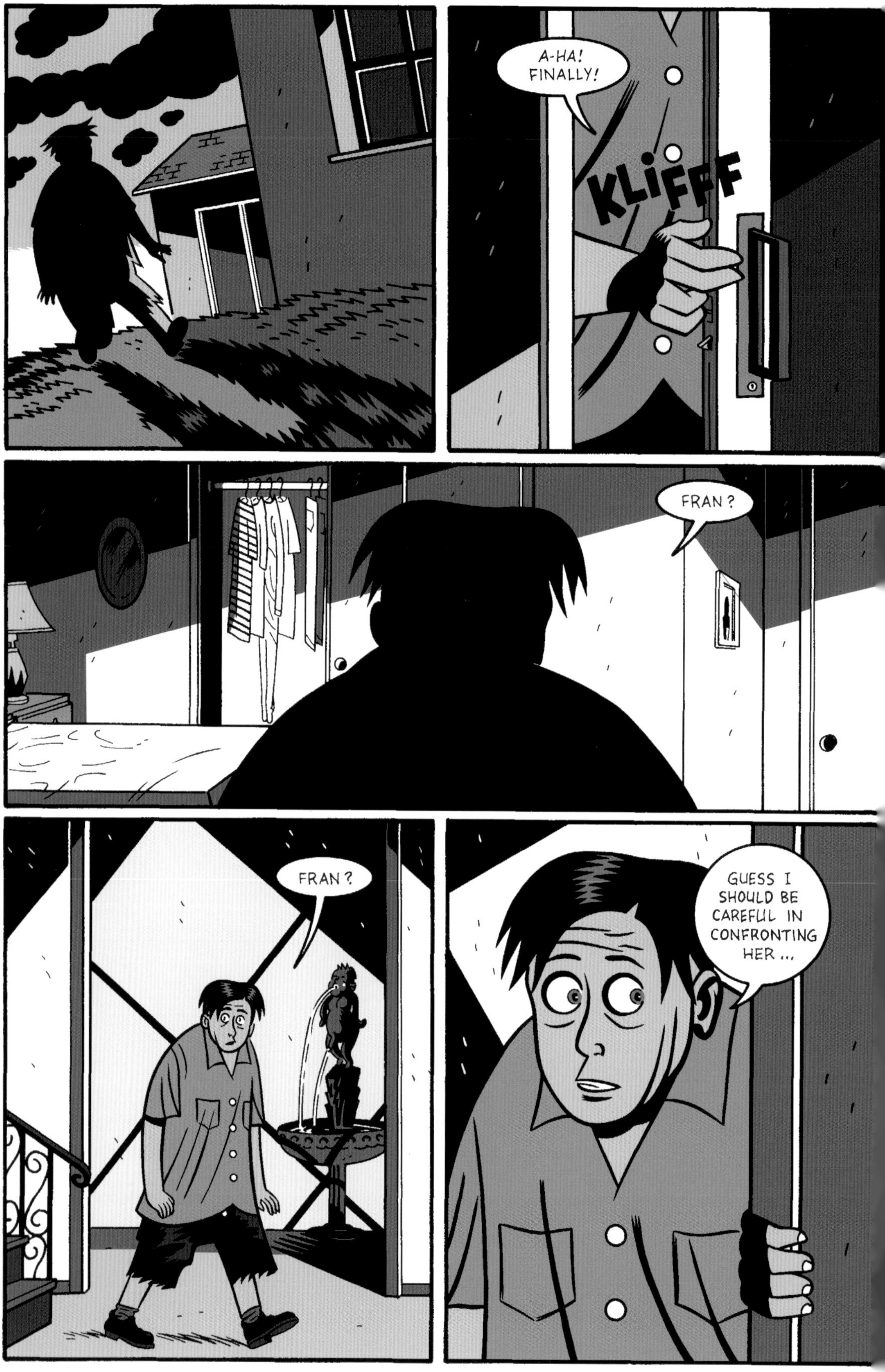

A-HA! FINALLY!
KLIFFF
FRAN?
FRAN?
GUESS I SHOULD BE CAREFUL IN CONFRONTING HER...

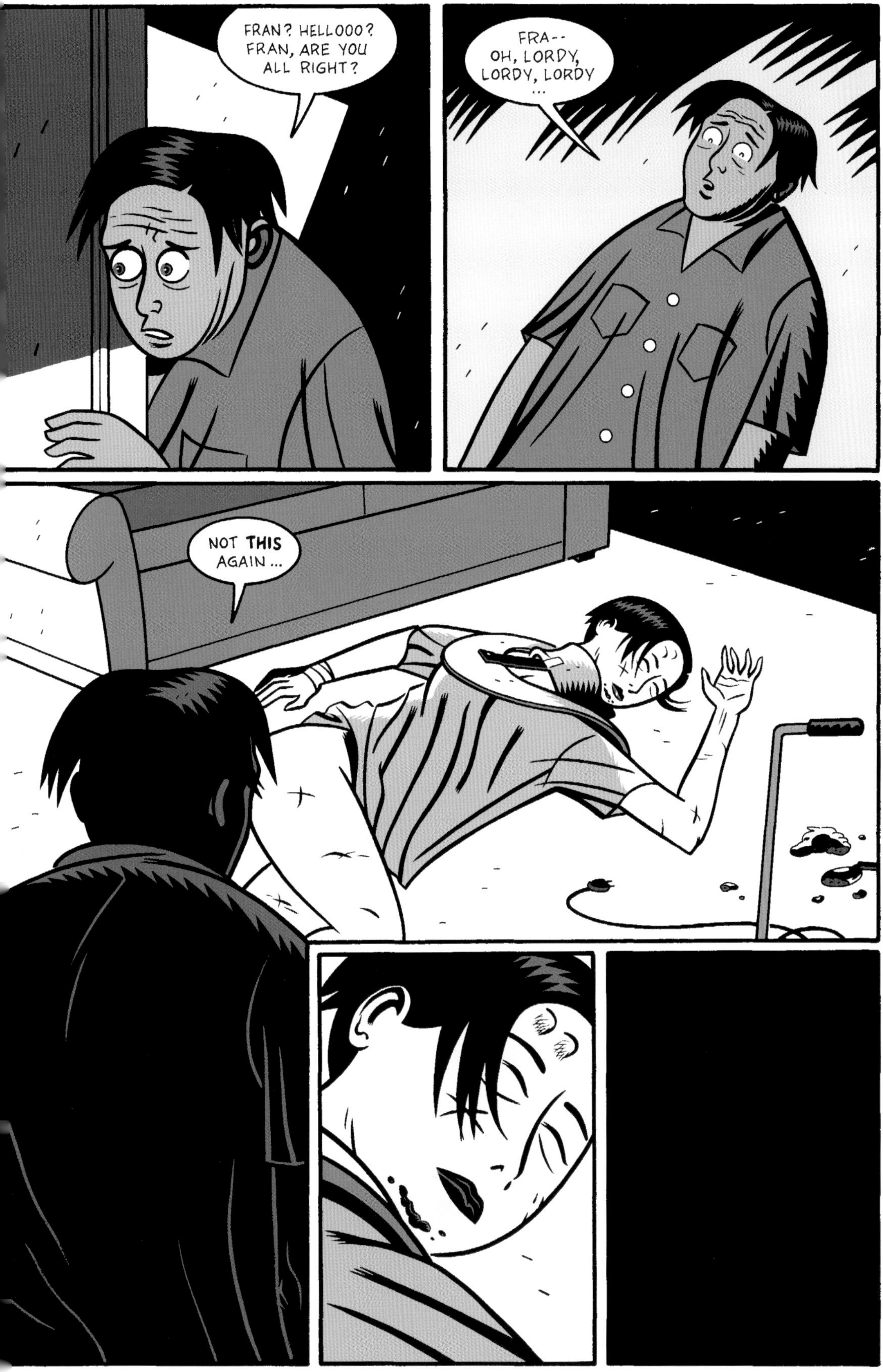
FRAN? HELLOOO? FRAN, ARE YOU ALL RIGHT?
FRA-- OH, LORDY, LORDY, LORDY ...
NOT THIS AGAIN ...

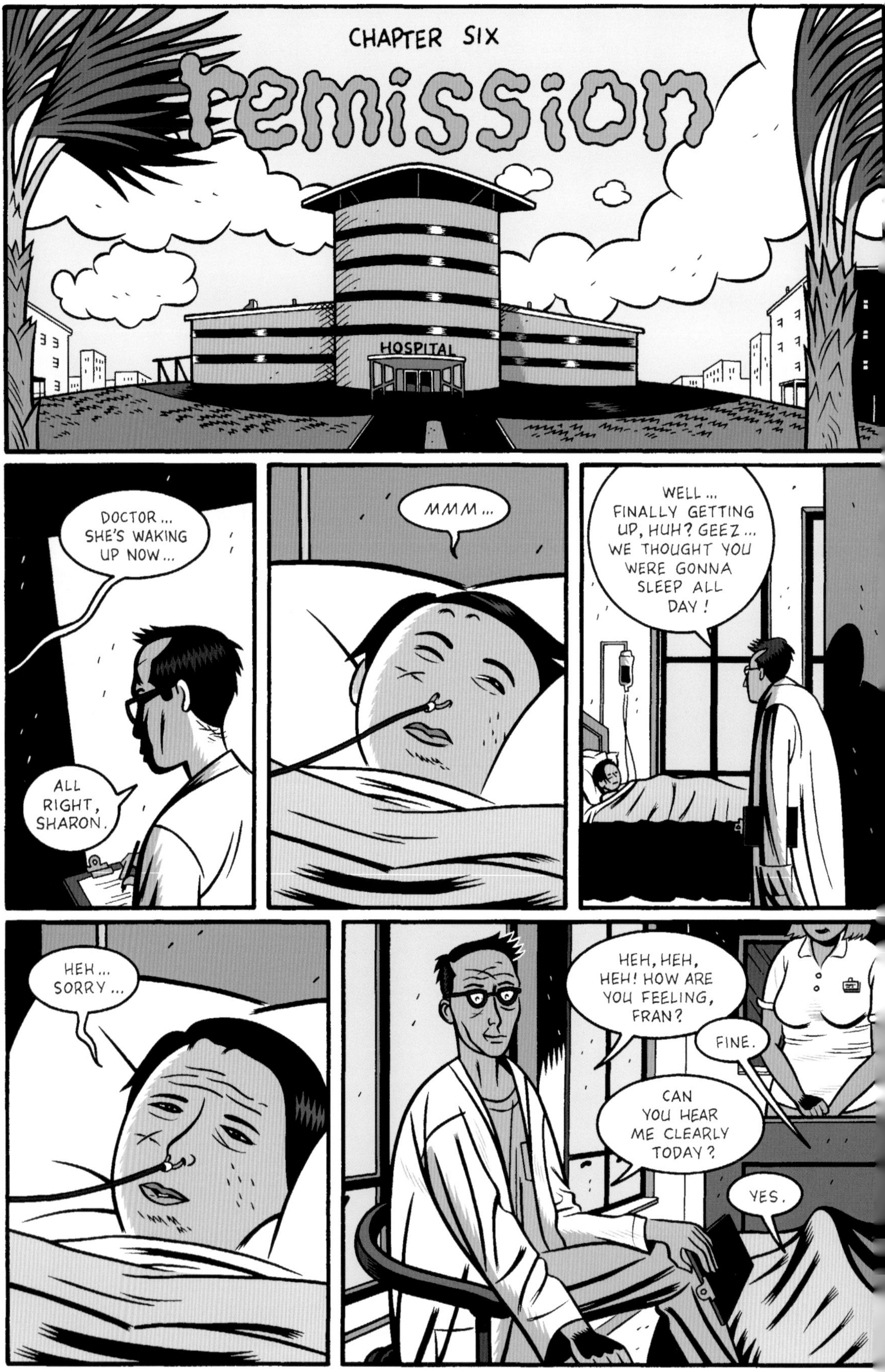
CHAPTER SIX
remission
HOSPITAL
DOCTOR... SHE'S WAKING UP NOW...
ALL RIGHT, SHARON.
MMM...
WELL... FINALLY GETTING UP, HUH? GEEZ... WE THOUGHT YOU WERE GONNA SLEEP ALL DAY!
HEH... SORRY...
HEH, HEH, HEH! HOW ARE YOU FEELING, FRAN?
FINE.
CAN YOU HEAR ME CLEARLY TODAY?
YES.

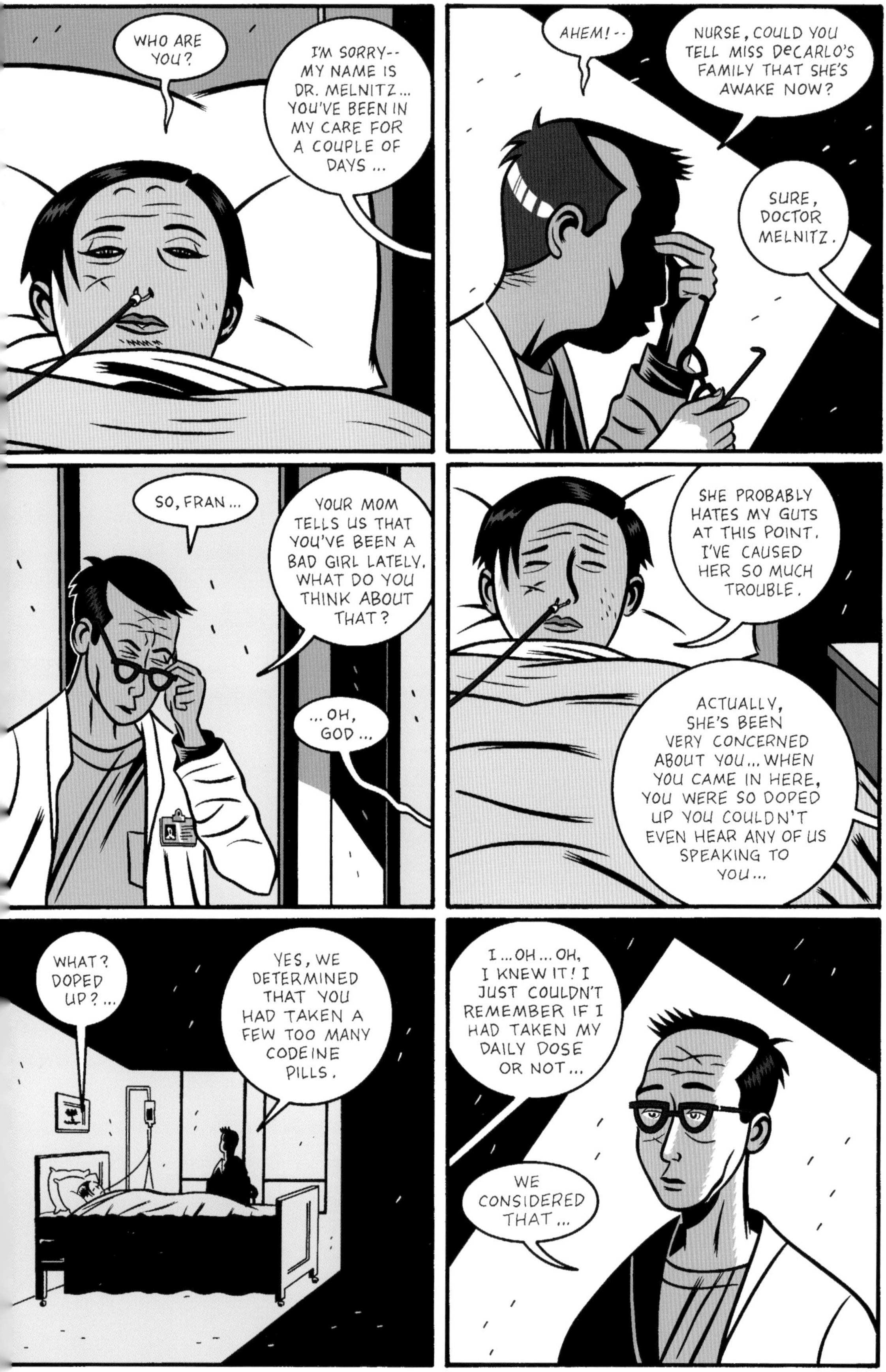
WHO ARE YOU?
I'M SORRY-- MY NAME IS DR. MELNITZ... YOU'VE BEEN IN MY CARE FOR A COUPLE OF DAYS...
AHEM!--
NURSE, COULD YOU TELL MISS DeCARLO'S FAMILY THAT SHE'S AWAKE NOW?
SURE, DOCTOR MELNITZ.
SO, FRAN...
YOUR MOM TELLS US THAT YOU'VE BEEN A BAD GIRL LATELY. WHAT DO YOU THINK ABOUT THAT?
...OH, GOD...
SHE PROBABLY HATES MY GUTS AT THIS POINT. I'VE CAUSED HER SO MUCH TROUBLE.
ACTUALLY, SHE'S BEEN VERY CONCERNED ABOUT YOU... WHEN YOU CAME IN HERE, YOU WERE SO DOPED UP YOU COULDN'T EVEN HEAR ANY OF US SPEAKING TO YOU...
WHAT? DOPED UP?...
YES, WE DETERMINED THAT YOU HAD TAKEN A FEW TOO MANY CODEINE PILLS.
I... OH... OH, I KNEW IT! I JUST COULDN'T REMEMBER IF I HAD TAKEN MY DAILY DOSE OR NOT...
WE CONSIDERED THAT...

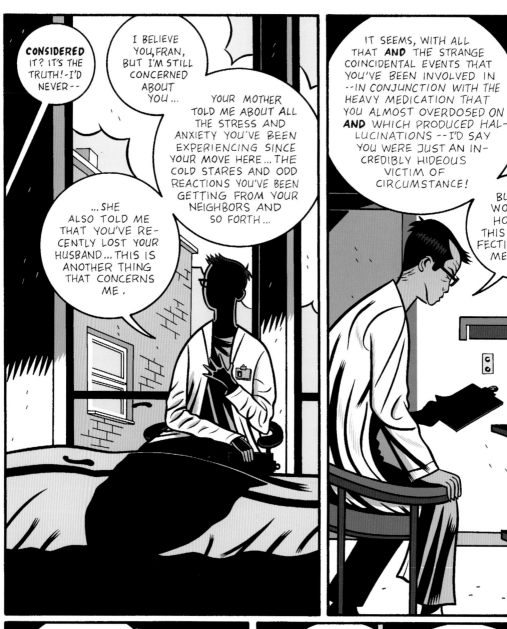

CONSIDERED IT? IT'S THE TRUTH!-I'D NEVER--

I BELIEVE YOU, FRAN, BUT I'M STILL CONCERNED ABOUT YOU...

YOUR MOTHER TOLD ME ABOUT ALL THE STRESS AND ANXIETY YOU'VE BEEN EXPERIENCING SINCE YOUR MOVE HERE... THE COLD STARES AND ODD REACTIONS YOU'VE BEEN GETTING FROM YOUR NEIGHBORS AND SO FORTH...

...SHE ALSO TOLD ME THAT YOU'VE RE-CENTLY LOST YOUR HUSBAND... THIS IS ANOTHER THING THAT CONCERNS ME.

IT SEEMS, WITH ALL THAT **AND** THE STRANGE COINCIDENTAL EVENTS THAT YOU'VE BEEN INVOLVED IN --IN CONJUNCTION WITH THE HEAVY MEDICATION THAT YOU ALMOST OVERDOSED ON **AND** WHICH PRODUCED HAL-LUCINATIONS --I'D SAY YOU WERE JUST AN IN-CREDIBLY HIDEOUS VICTIM OF CIRCUMSTANCE!

BUT I'M WORRIED HOW ALL THIS IS AF-FECTING YOU MENTALLY.

AND... FRAN, THERE'S ANOTHER MATTER...

DOCTOR!

SCREEE

DOCTOR, HOW IS SHE? CAN SHE--

I WAS JUST GETTING TO THAT, MRS. DeCARLO...

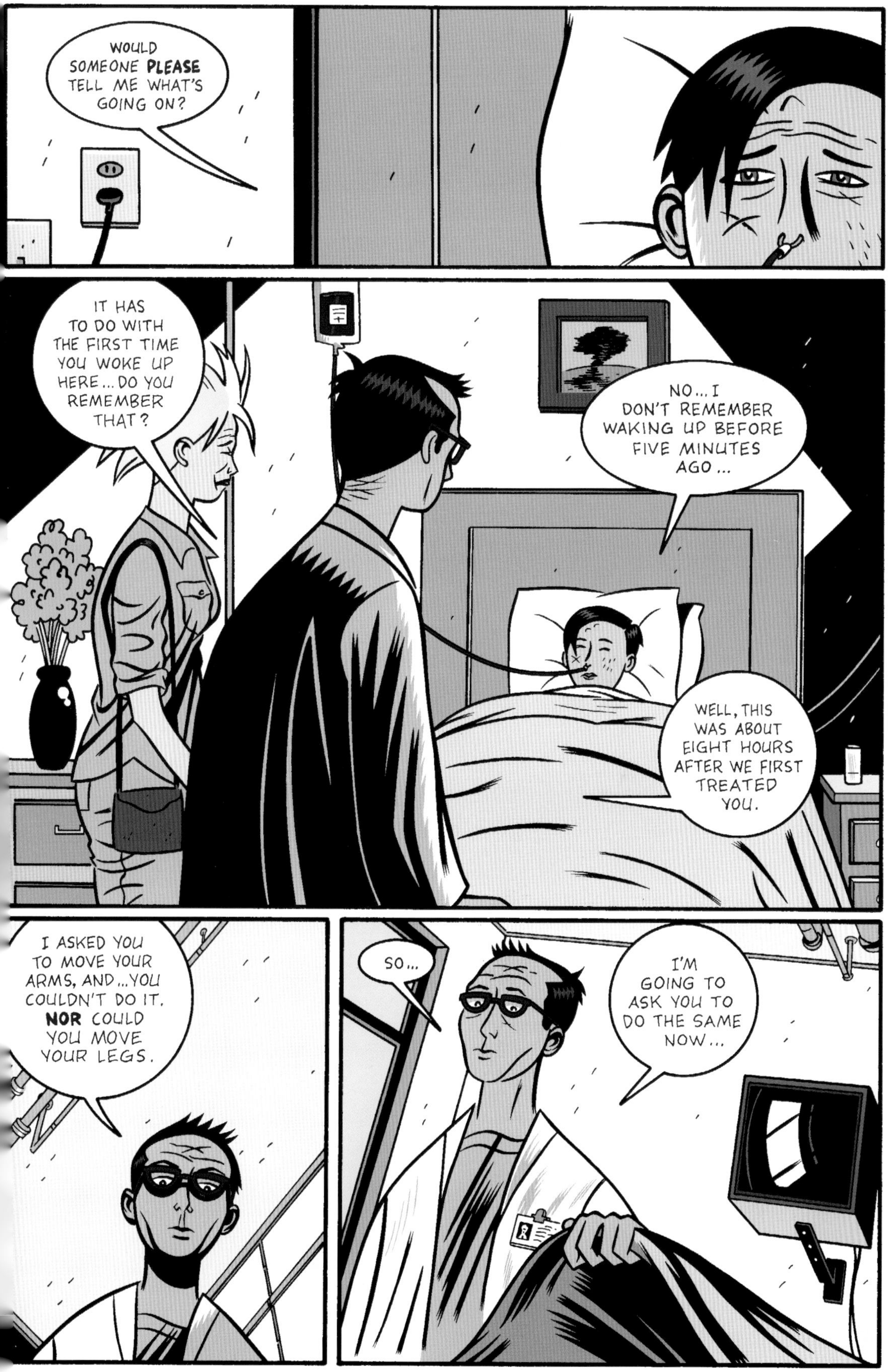
WOULD SOMEONE **PLEASE** TELL ME WHAT'S GOING ON?
IT HAS TO DO WITH THE FIRST TIME YOU WOKE UP HERE... DO YOU REMEMBER THAT?
NO... I DON'T REMEMBER WAKING UP BEFORE FIVE MINUTES AGO...
WELL, THIS WAS ABOUT EIGHT HOURS AFTER WE FIRST TREATED YOU.
I ASKED YOU TO MOVE YOUR ARMS, AND... YOU COULDN'T DO IT. **NOR** COULD YOU MOVE YOUR LEGS.
SO...
I'M GOING TO ASK YOU TO DO THE SAME NOW...

SHE'S IN ROOM 207... THIRD ROOM DOWN THE HALL, ON THE RIGHT.

THANK YOU.

YMENT DUE ON ARRIVAL ECKS OR ORDER!

207

WUP!

OH!

UH... MRS. DeCARLO?

YES... WHO -- OH! YOU'RE FRAN'S FRIEND... UH, MEL?

YES... HOW IS SHE?

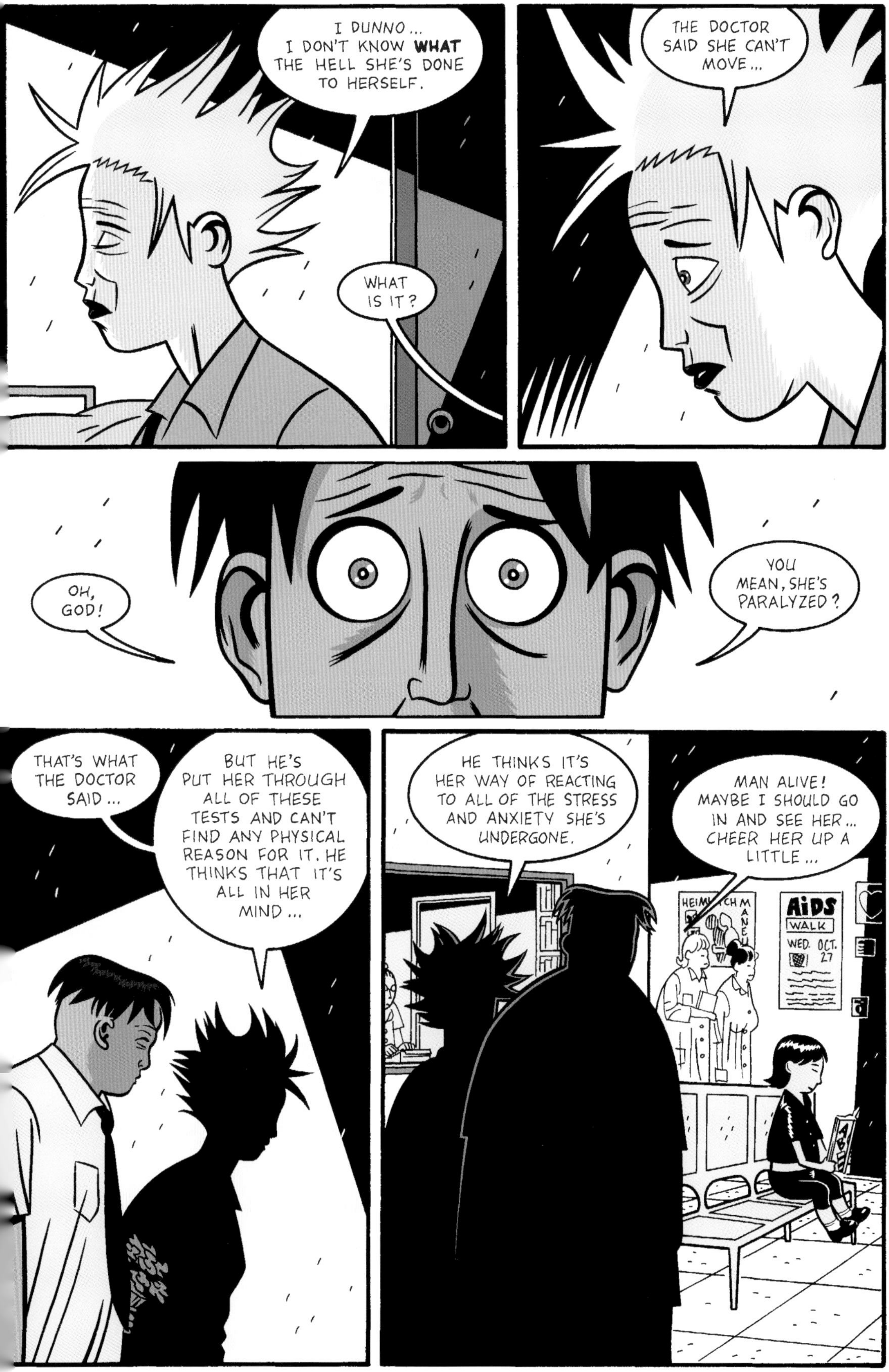
I DUNNO... I DON'T KNOW **WHAT** THE HELL SHE'S DONE TO HERSELF.
WHAT IS IT?
THE DOCTOR SAID SHE CAN'T MOVE...
OH, GOD!
YOU MEAN, SHE'S PARALYZED?
THAT'S WHAT THE DOCTOR SAID...
BUT HE'S PUT HER THROUGH ALL OF THESE TESTS AND CAN'T FIND ANY PHYSICAL REASON FOR IT. HE THINKS THAT IT'S ALL IN HER MIND...
HE THINKS IT'S HER WAY OF REACTING TO ALL OF THE STRESS AND ANXIETY SHE'S UNDERGONE.
MAN ALIVE! MAYBE I SHOULD GO IN AND SEE HER... CHEER HER UP A LITTLE...
AIDS WALK
WED. OCT. 27

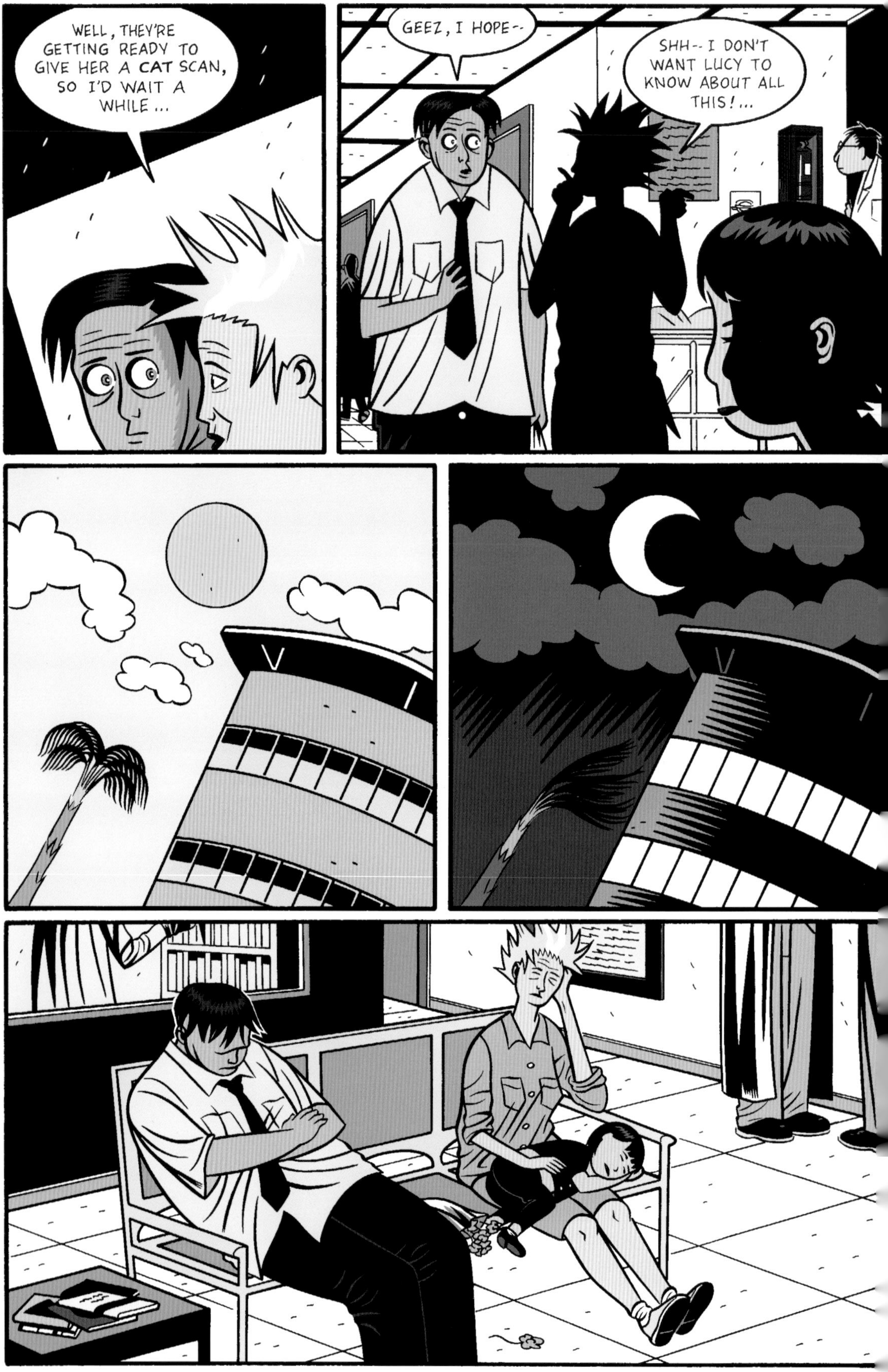
WELL, THEY'RE GETTING READY TO GIVE HER A CAT SCAN, SO I'D WAIT A WHILE...
GEEZ, I HOPE--
SHH-- I DON'T WANT LUCY TO KNOW ABOUT ALL THIS!...

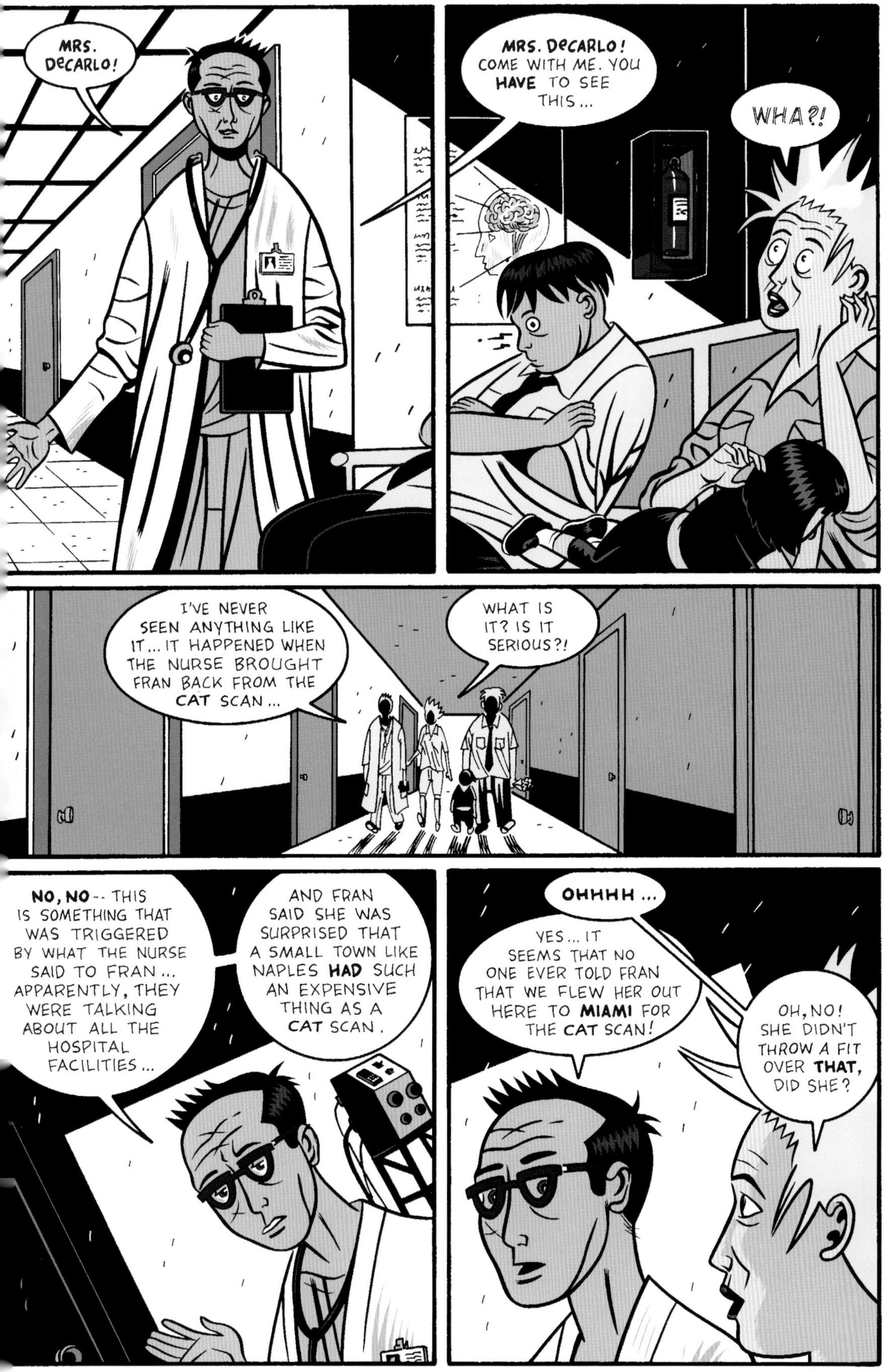
MRS. DeCARLO!
MRS. DeCARLO! COME WITH ME. YOU HAVE TO SEE THIS...
WHA?!
I'VE NEVER SEEN ANYTHING LIKE IT... IT HAPPENED WHEN THE NURSE BROUGHT FRAN BACK FROM THE CAT SCAN...
WHAT IS IT? IS IT SERIOUS?!
NO, NO -- THIS IS SOMETHING THAT WAS TRIGGERED BY WHAT THE NURSE SAID TO FRAN... APPARENTLY, THEY WERE TALKING ABOUT ALL THE HOSPITAL FACILITIES...
AND FRAN SAID SHE WAS SURPRISED THAT A SMALL TOWN LIKE NAPLES HAD SUCH AN EXPENSIVE THING AS A CAT SCAN.
OHHHH...
YES... IT SEEMS THAT NO ONE EVER TOLD FRAN THAT WE FLEW HER OUT HERE TO MIAMI FOR THE CAT SCAN!
OH, NO! SHE DIDN'T THROW A FIT OVER THAT, DID SHE?

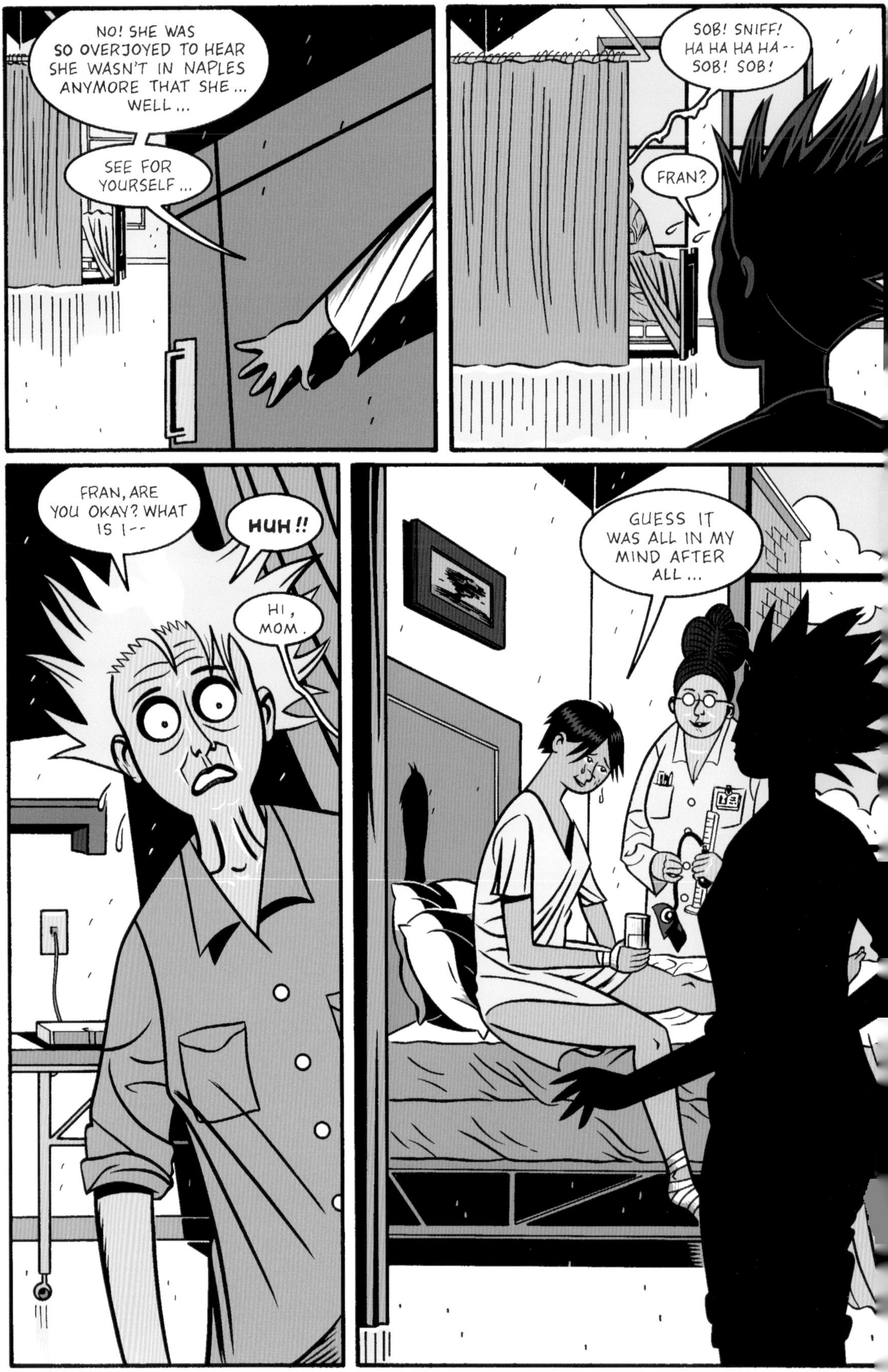
NO! SHE WAS SO OVERJOYED TO HEAR SHE WASN'T IN NAPLES ANYMORE THAT SHE... WELL...
SEE FOR YOURSELF...
SOB! SNIFF! HA HA HA HA-- SOB! SOB!
FRAN?
FRAN, ARE YOU OKAY? WHAT IS I--
HUH!!
HI, MOM.
GUESS IT WAS ALL IN MY MIND AFTER ALL...

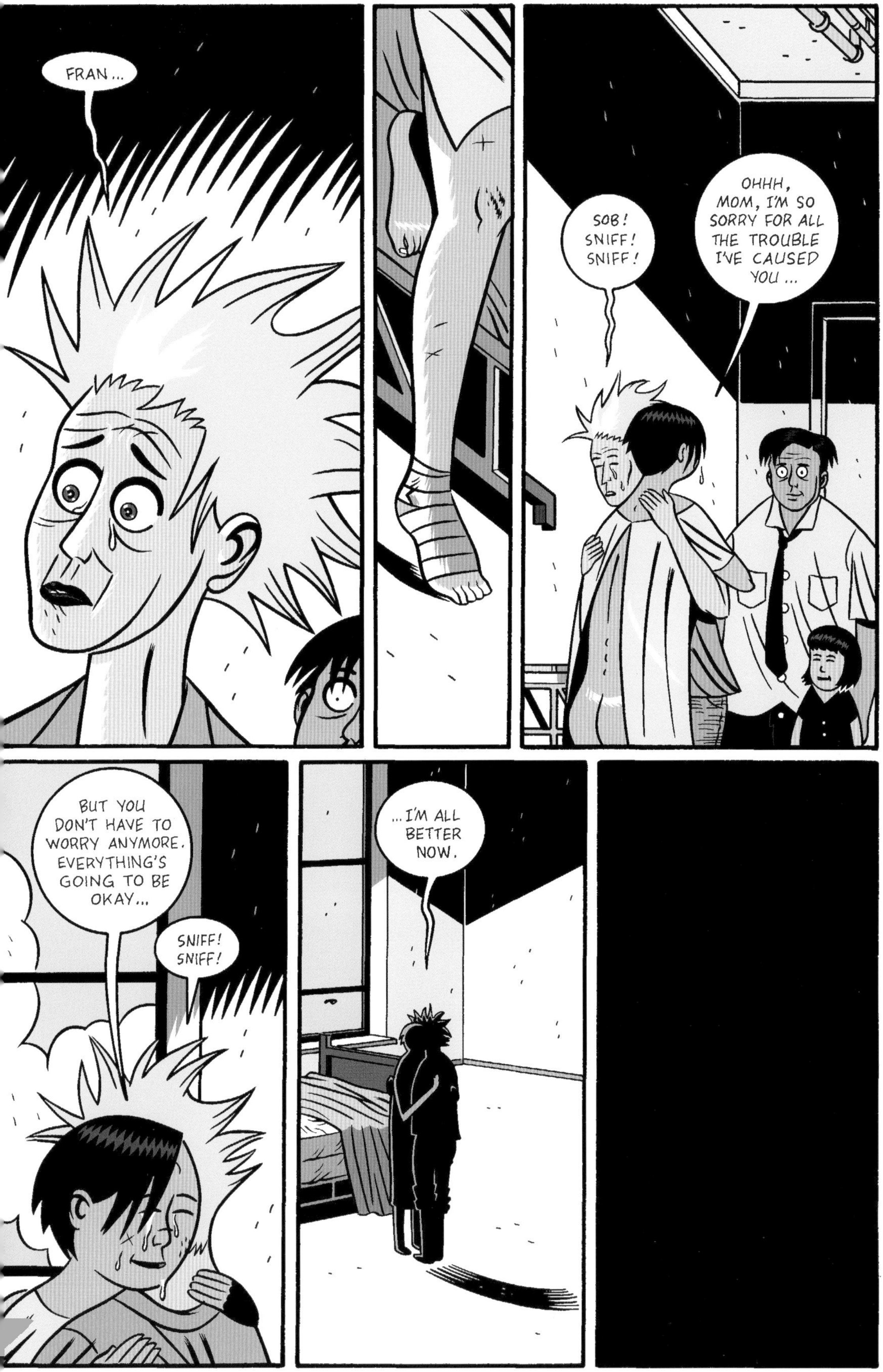
FRAN...
SOB! SNIFF! SNIFF!
OHHH, MOM, I'M SO SORRY FOR ALL THE TROUBLE I'VE CAUSED YOU...
BUT YOU DON'T HAVE TO WORRY ANYMORE. EVERYTHING'S GOING TO BE OKAY...
SNIFF! SNIFF!
...I'M ALL BETTER NOW.

epilogue

relapse

TWO MONTHS LATER

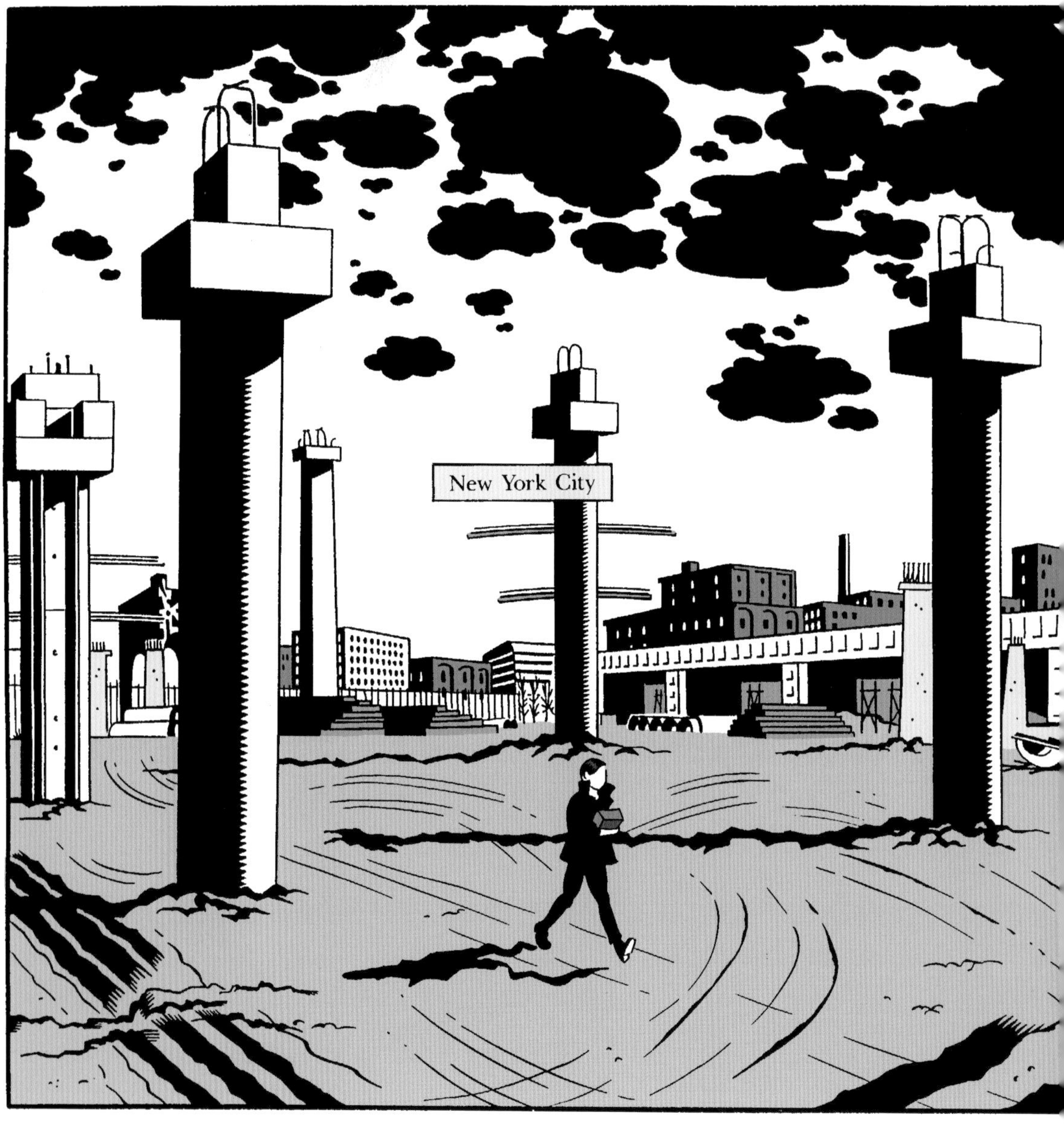
New York City

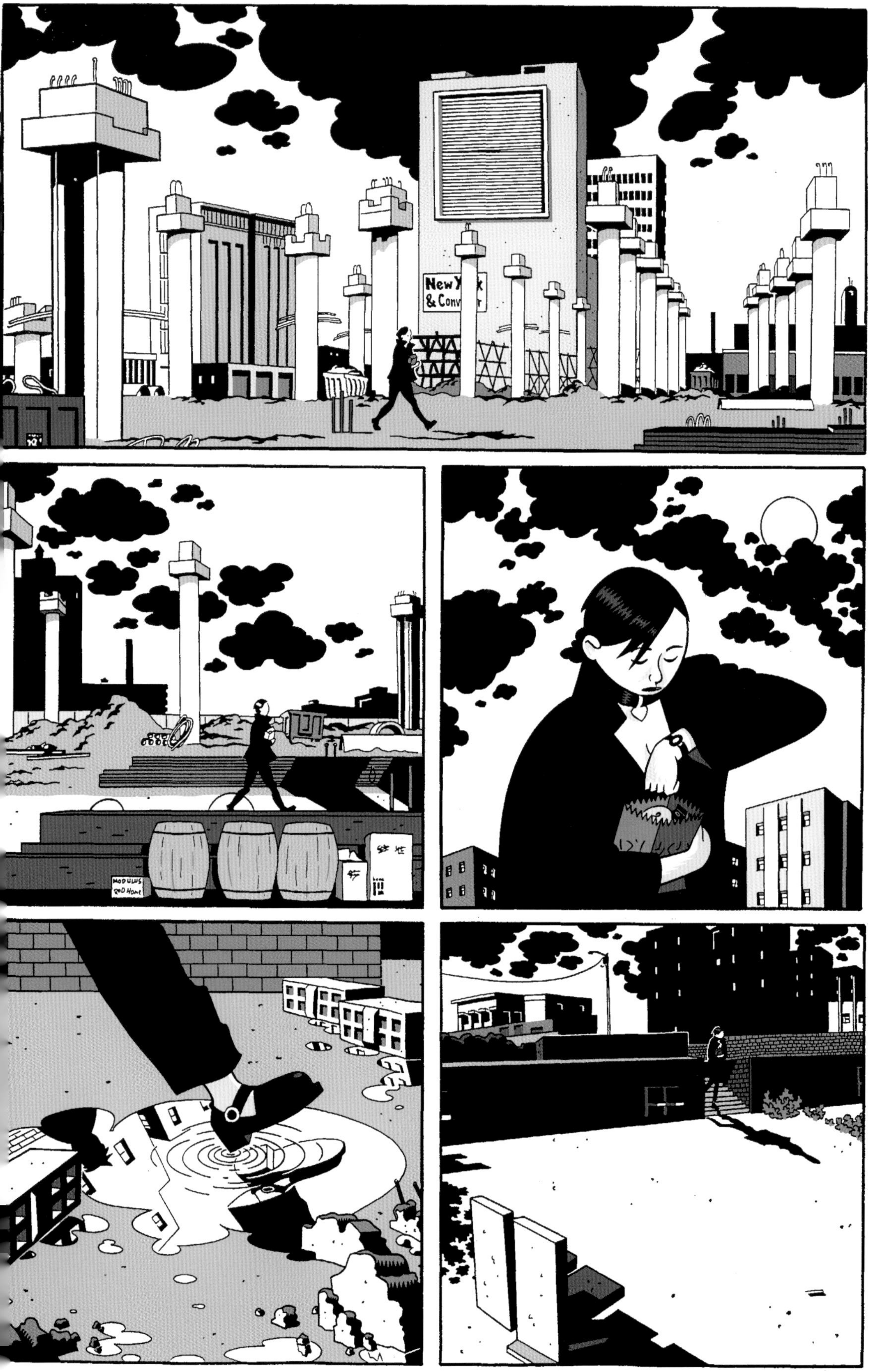

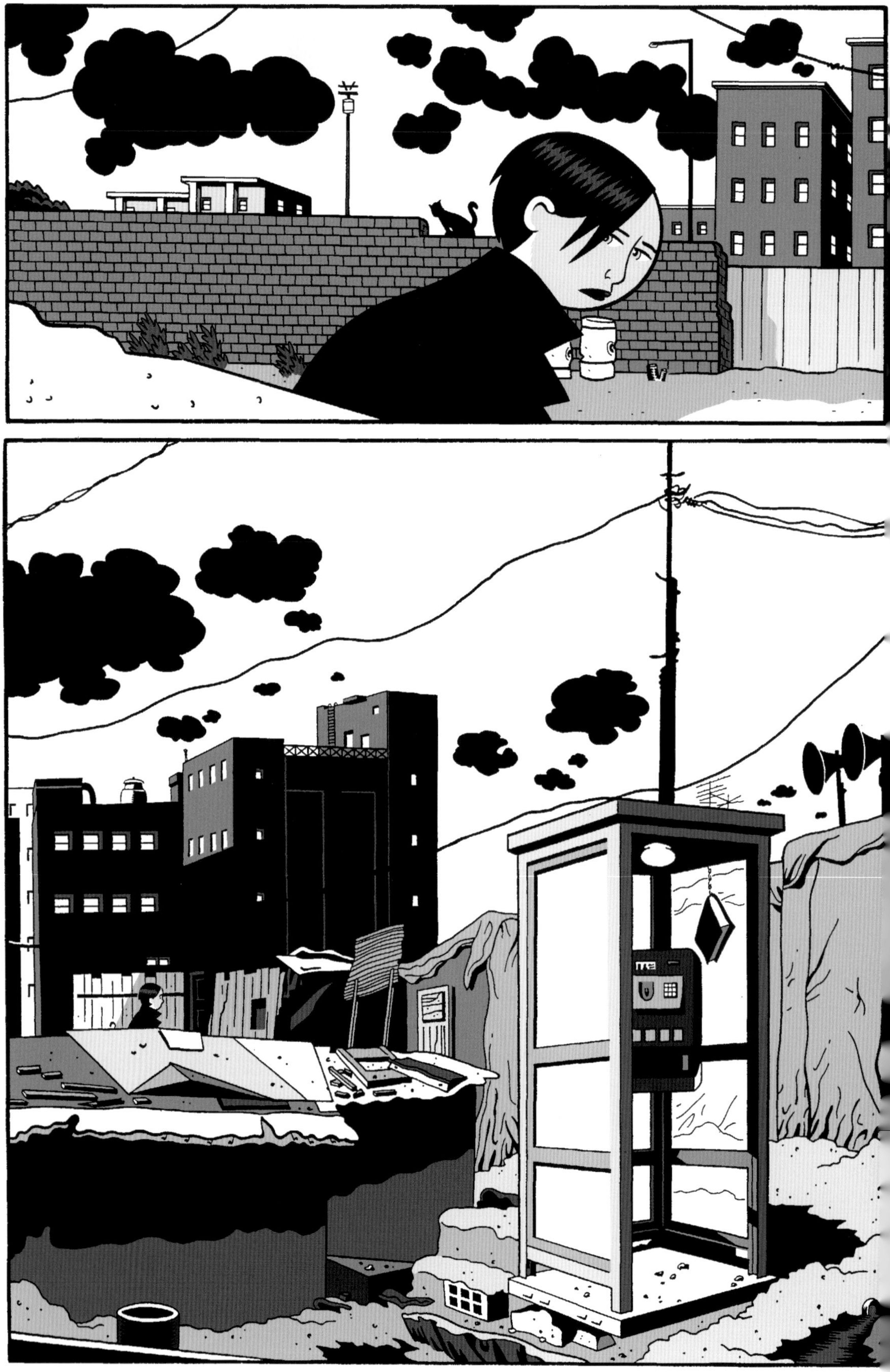

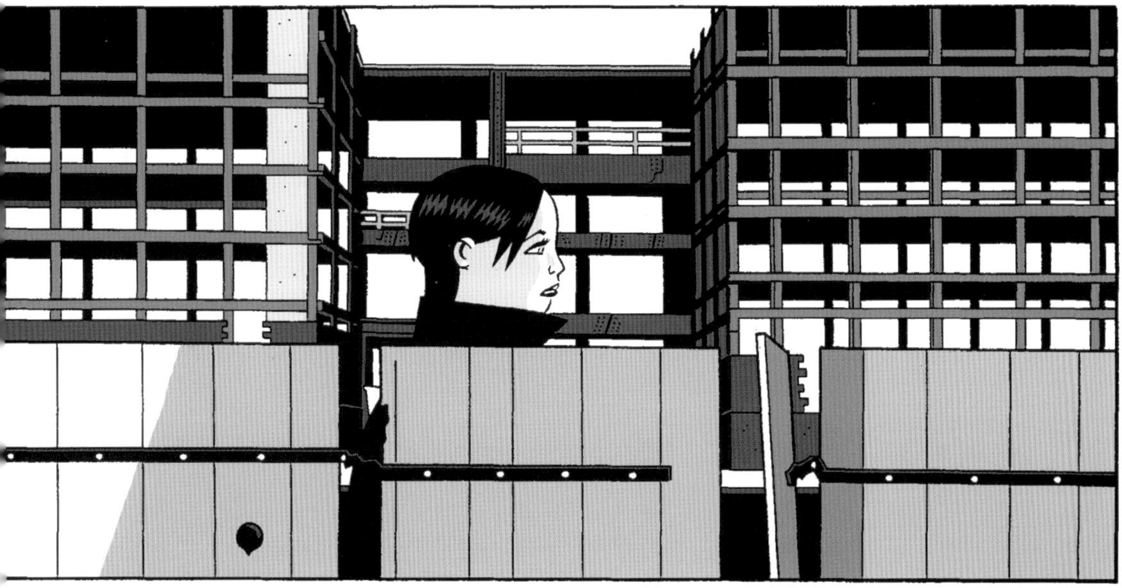

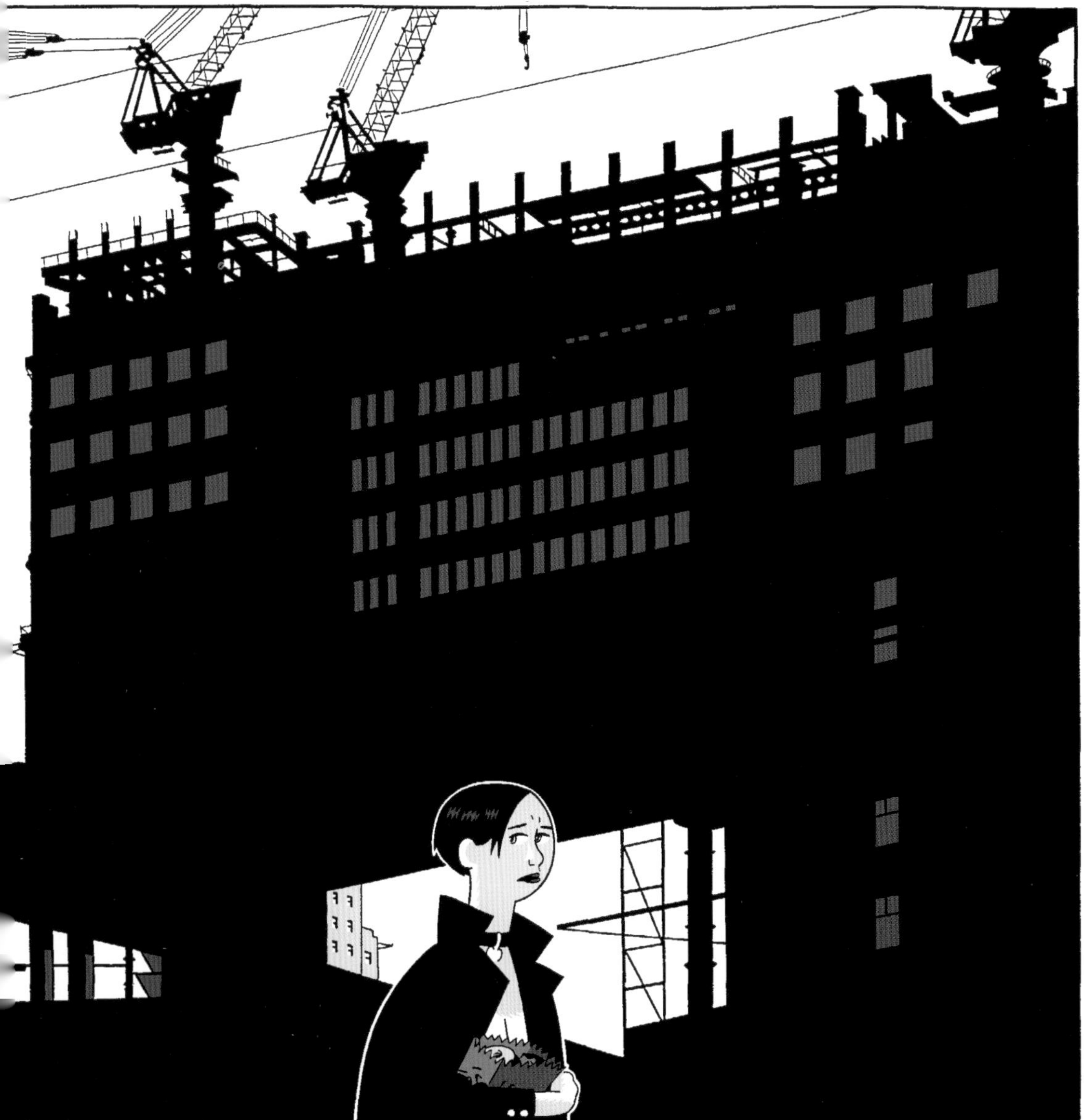

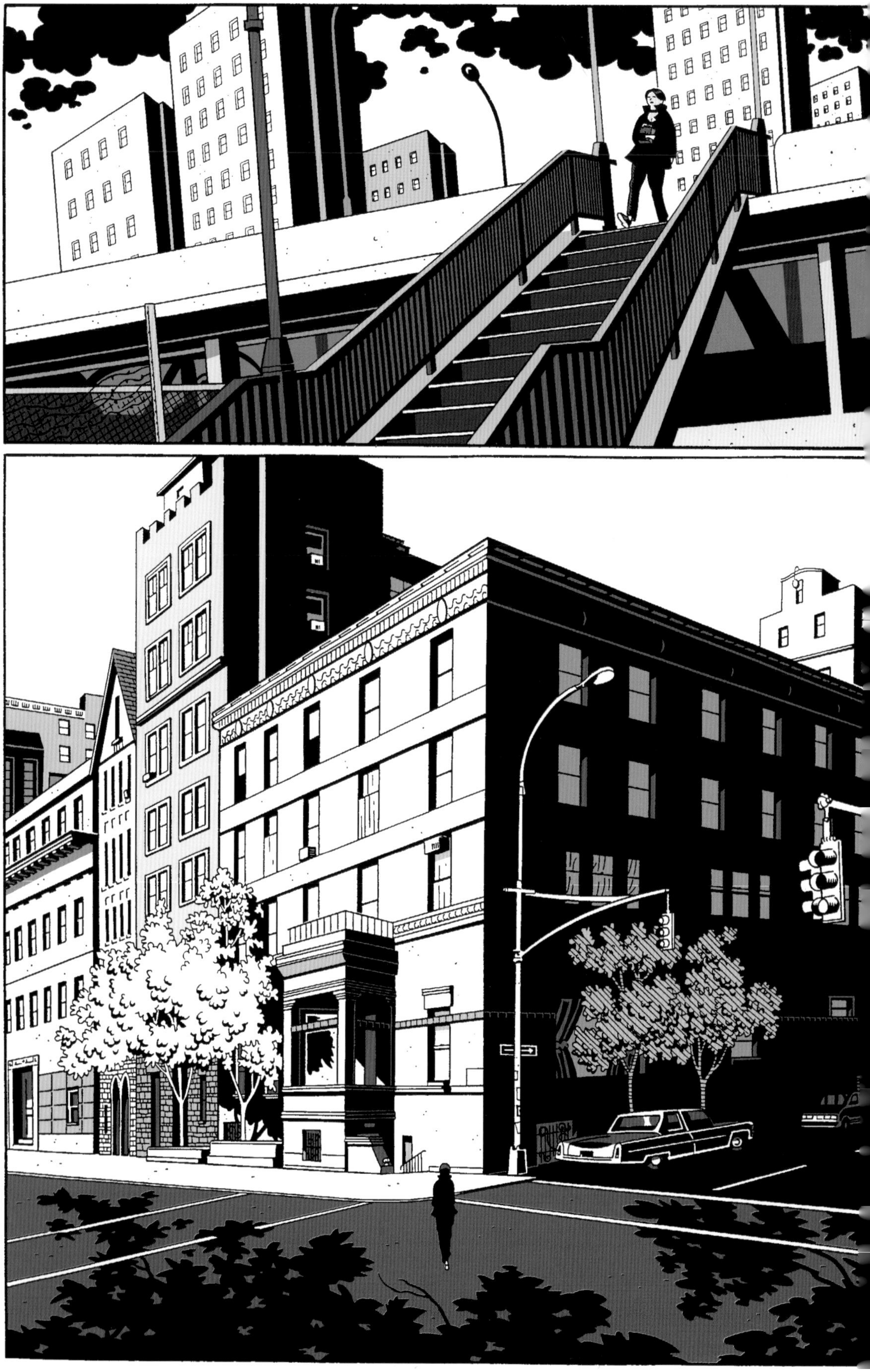

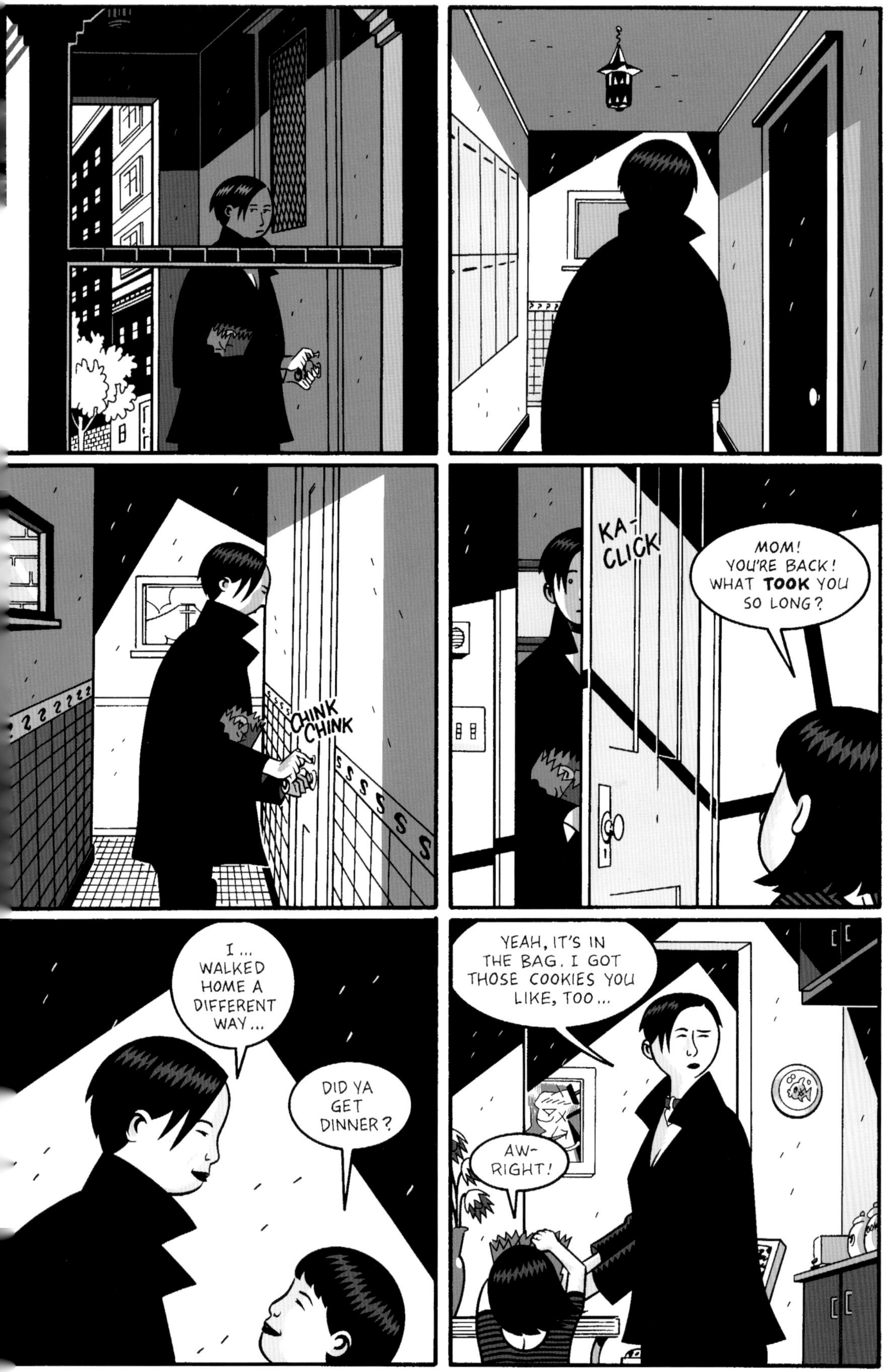
CHINK CHINK
KA-CLICK
MOM! YOU'RE BACK! WHAT **TOOK** YOU SO LONG?
I... WALKED HOME A DIFFERENT WAY...
DID YA GET DINNER?
YEAH, IT'S IN THE BAG. I GOT THOSE COOKIES YOU LIKE, TOO...
AW-RIGHT!

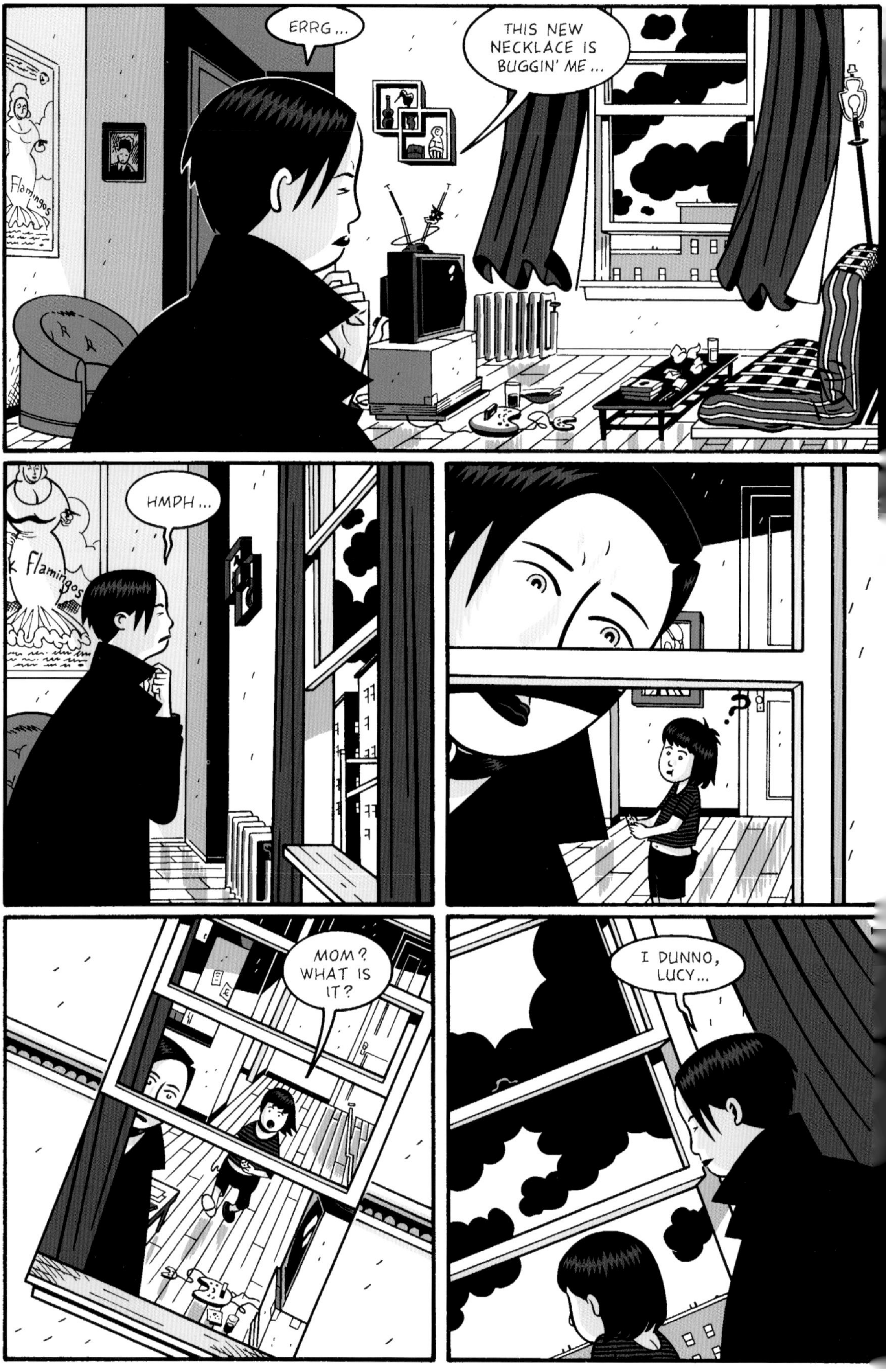
ERRG...
THIS NEW NECKLACE IS BUGGIN' ME...
Flamingos
HMPH...
Flamingos
MOM? WHAT IS IT?
I DUNNO, LUCY...

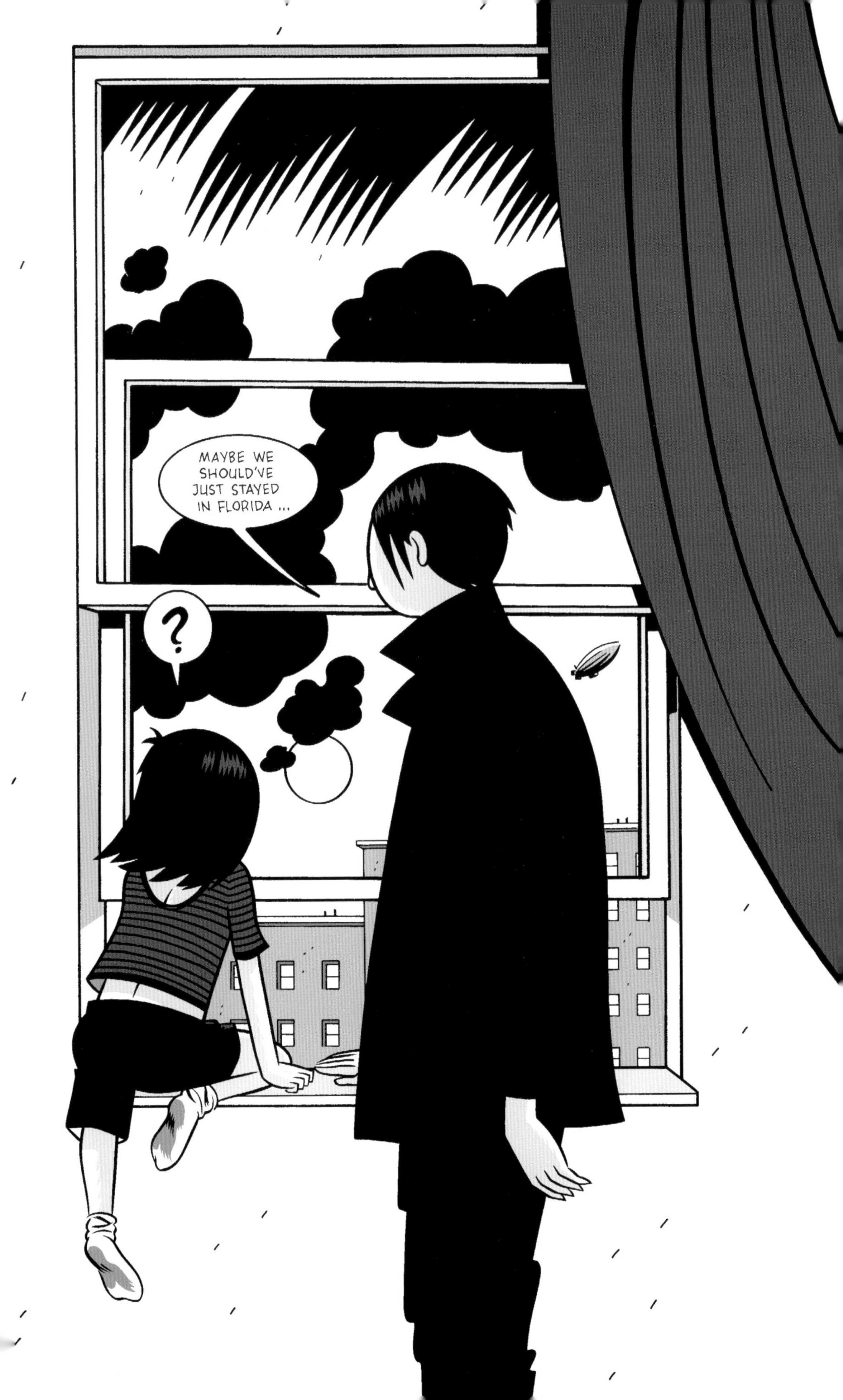
MAYBE WE SHOULD'VE JUST STAYED IN FLORIDA ...
?

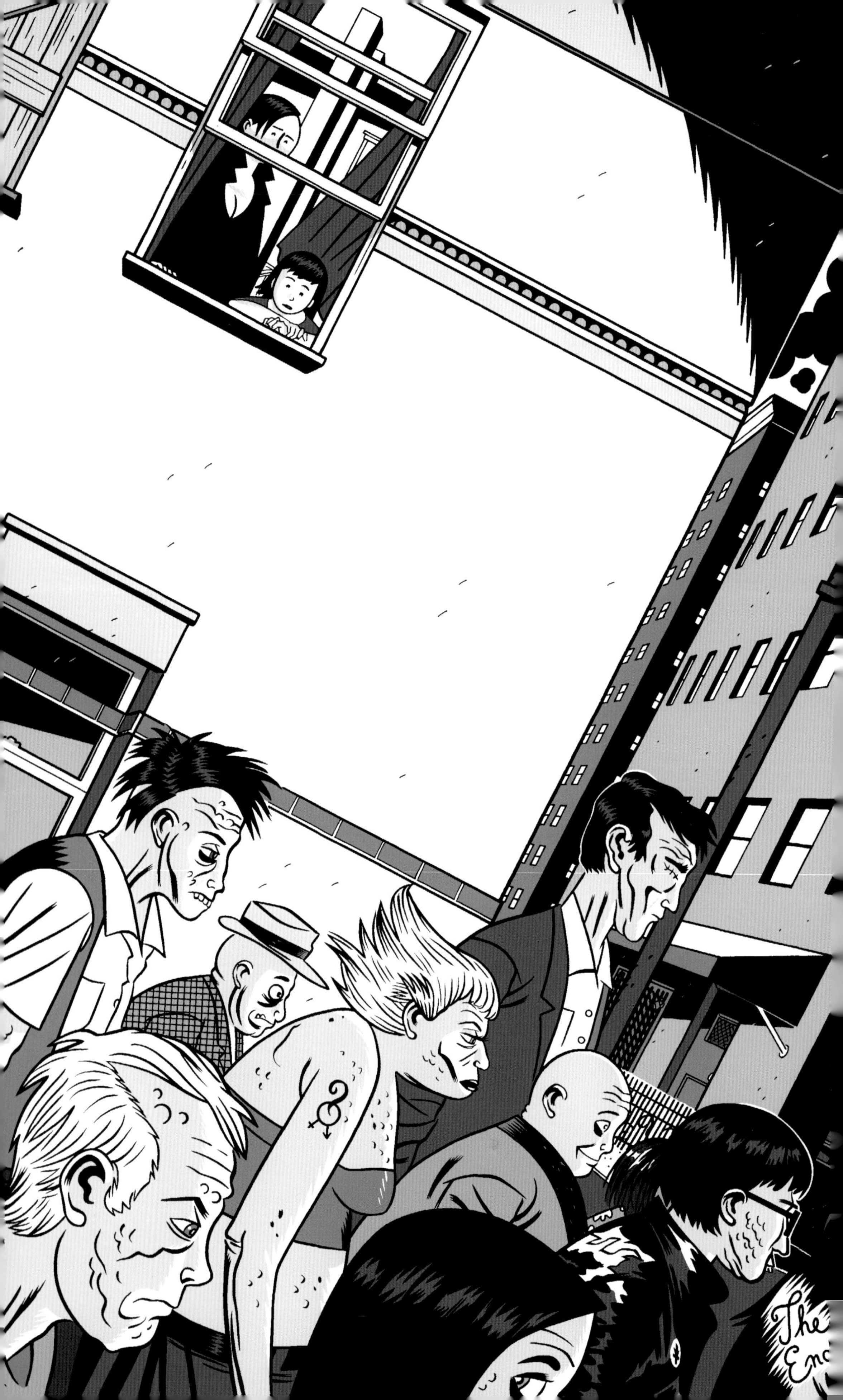
The

KING BLOOD

This is the story of Fran DeCarlo's long lost husband, Vlad Dracul...

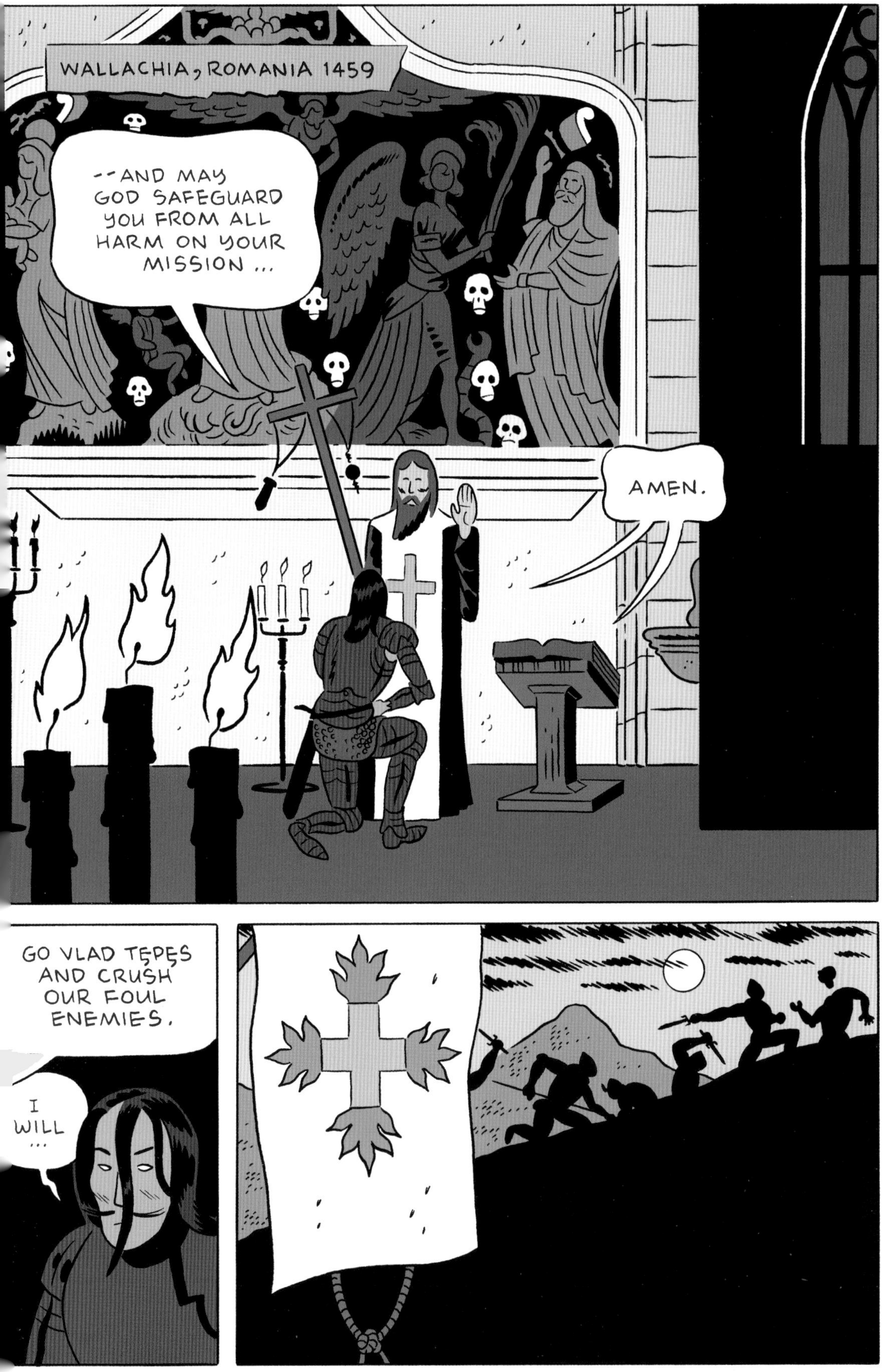
WALLACHIA, ROMANIA 1459
--AND MAY GOD SAFEGUARD YOU FROM ALL HARM ON YOUR MISSION ...
AMEN.
GO VLAD ȚEPEȘ AND CRUSH OUR FOUL ENEMIES.
I WILL ...

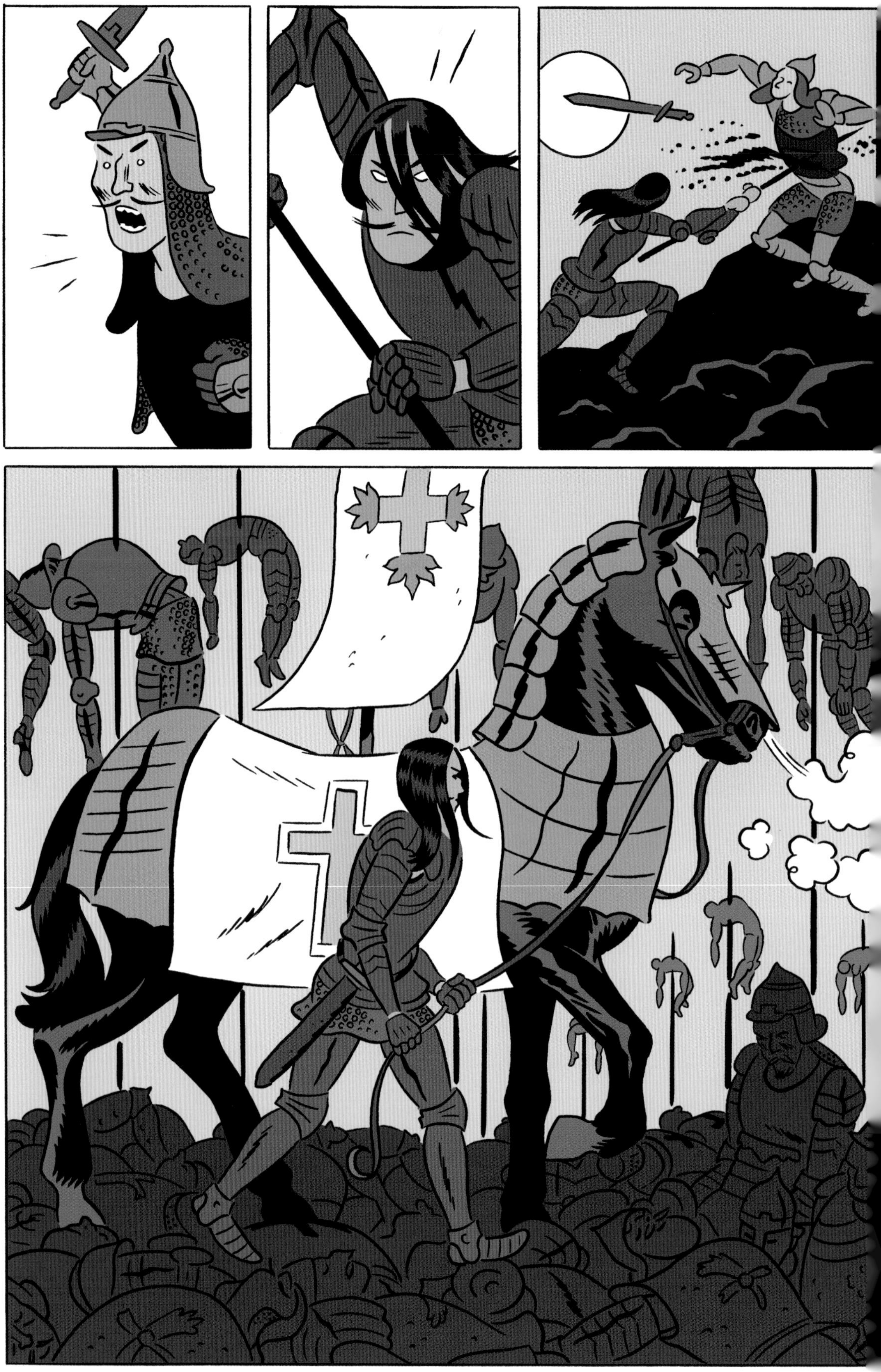

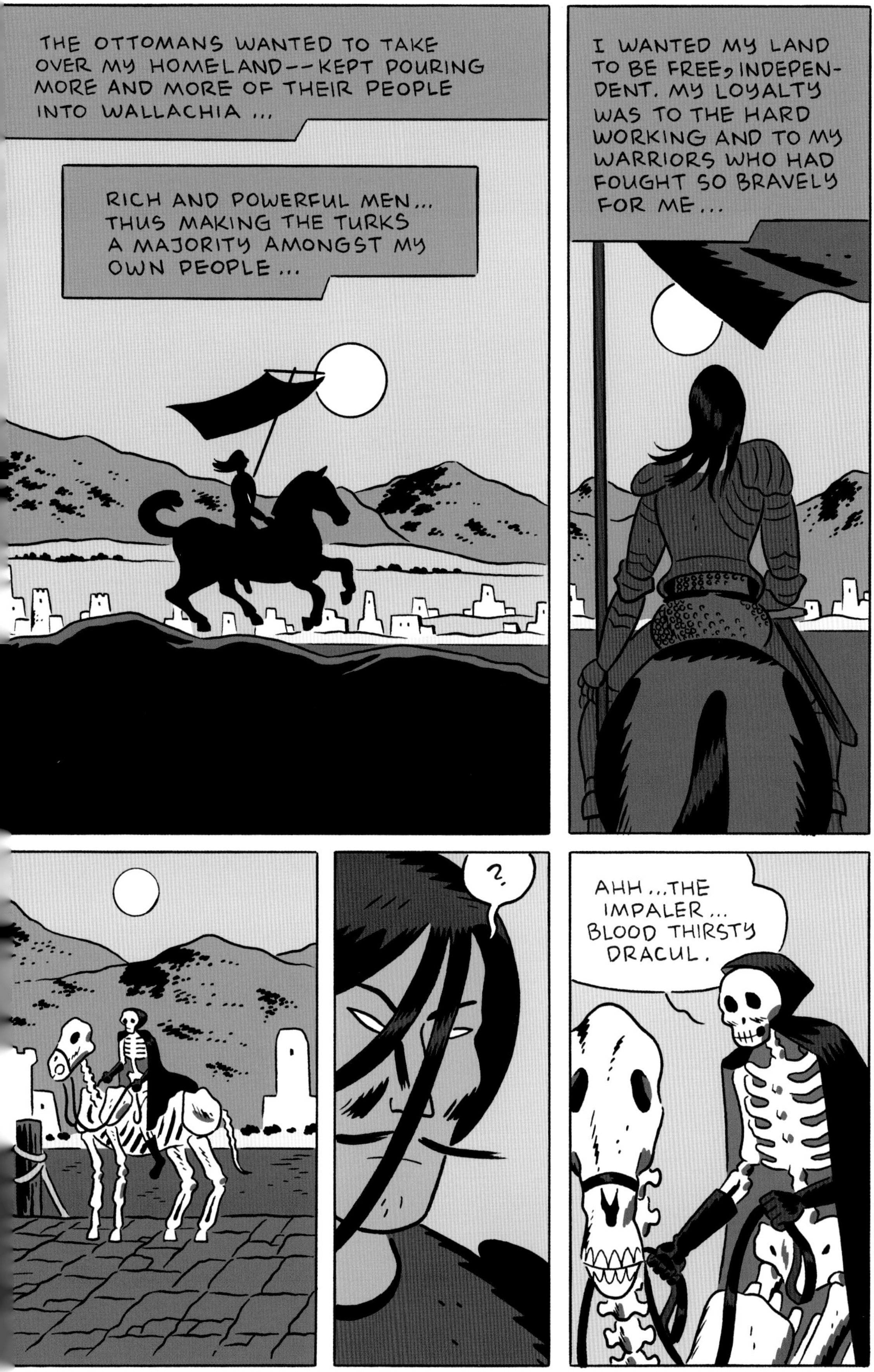
THE OTTOMANS WANTED TO TAKE OVER MY HOMELAND--KEPT POURING MORE AND MORE OF THEIR PEOPLE INTO WALLACHIA ...
RICH AND POWERFUL MEN... THUS MAKING THE TURKS A MAJORITY AMONGST MY OWN PEOPLE...
I WANTED MY LAND TO BE FREE, INDEPENDENT. MY LOYALTY WAS TO THE HARD WORKING AND TO MY WARRIORS WHO HAD FOUGHT SO BRAVELY FOR ME...
?
AHH...THE IMPALER... BLOOD THIRSTY DRACUL.

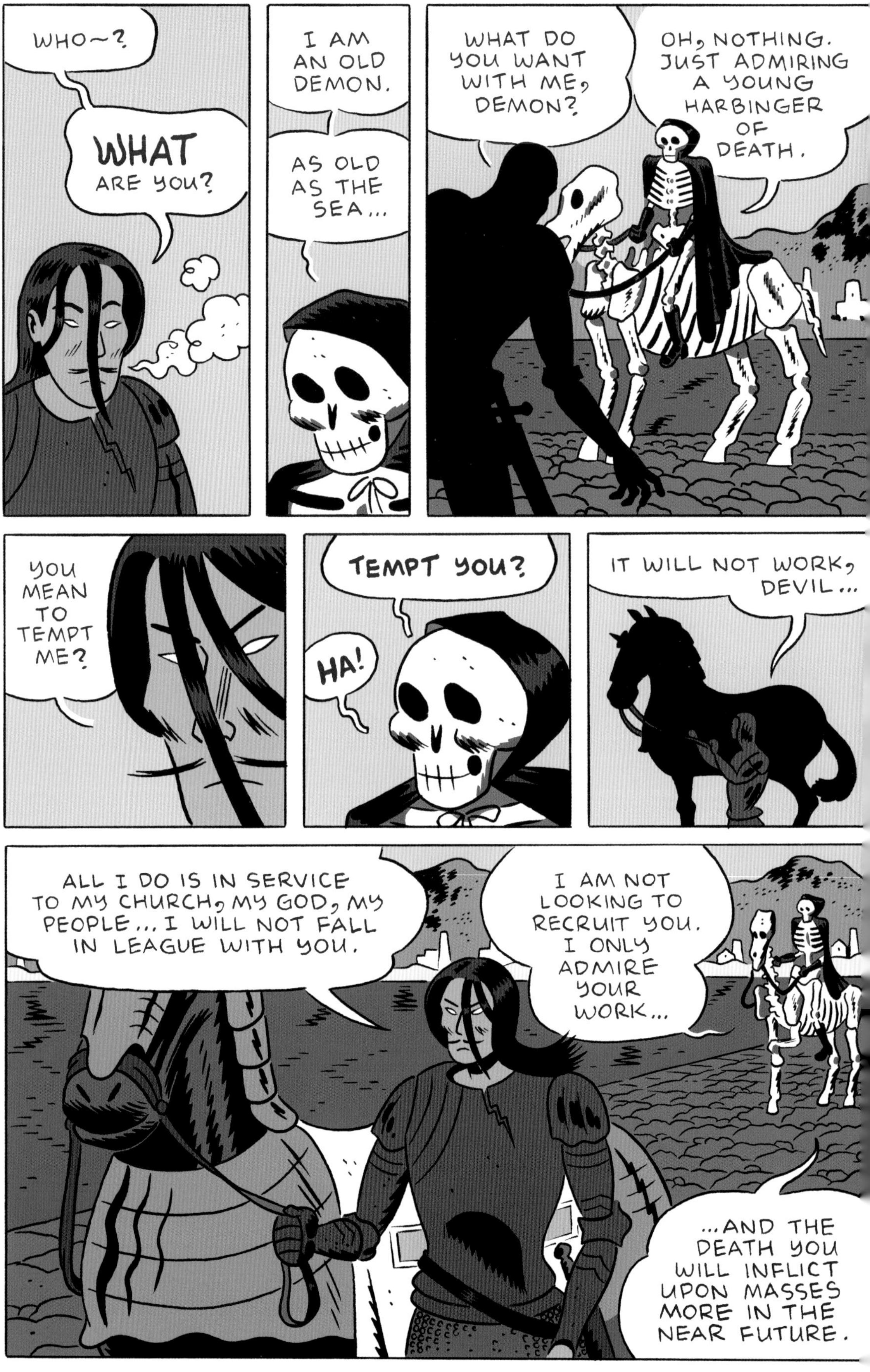
WHO~?
WHAT ARE YOU?
I AM AN OLD DEMON.
AS OLD AS THE SEA...
WHAT DO YOU WANT WITH ME, DEMON?
OH, NOTHING. JUST ADMIRING A YOUNG HARBINGER OF DEATH.
YOU MEAN TO TEMPT ME?
TEMPT YOU?
HA!
IT WILL NOT WORK, DEVIL...
ALL I DO IS IN SERVICE TO MY CHURCH, MY GOD, MY PEOPLE... I WILL NOT FALL IN LEAGUE WITH YOU.
I AM NOT LOOKING TO RECRUIT YOU. I ONLY ADMIRE YOUR WORK...
...AND THE DEATH YOU WILL INFLICT UPON MASSES MORE IN THE NEAR FUTURE.

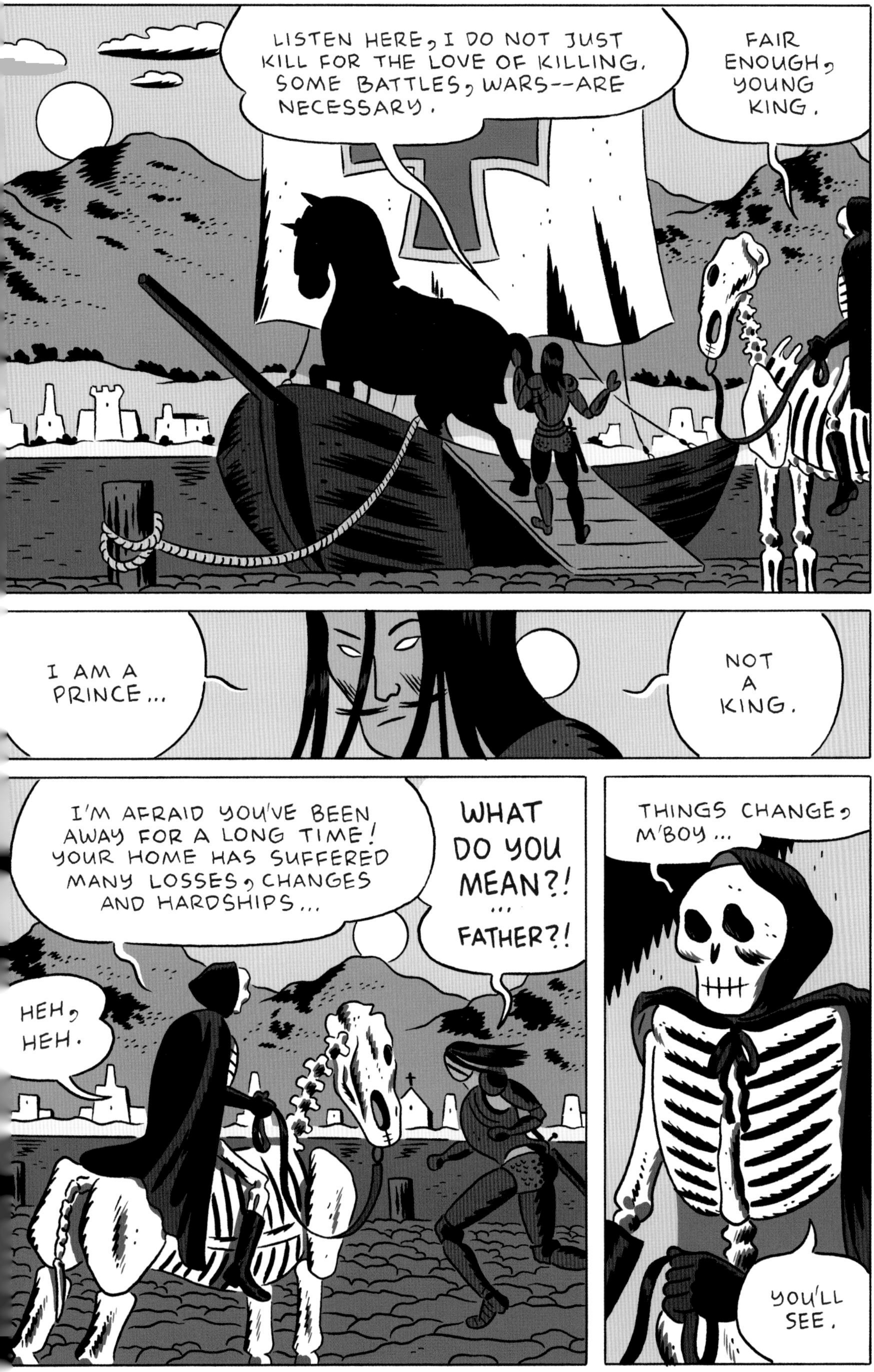
LISTEN HERE, I DO NOT JUST KILL FOR THE LOVE OF KILLING. SOME BATTLES, WARS--ARE NECESSARY.
FAIR ENOUGH, YOUNG KING.
I AM A PRINCE...
NOT A KING.
I'M AFRAID YOU'VE BEEN AWAY FOR A LONG TIME! YOUR HOME HAS SUFFERED MANY LOSSES, CHANGES AND HARDSHIPS...
WHAT DO YOU MEAN?! ... FATHER?!
HEH, HEH.
THINGS CHANGE, M'BOY...
YOU'LL SEE.

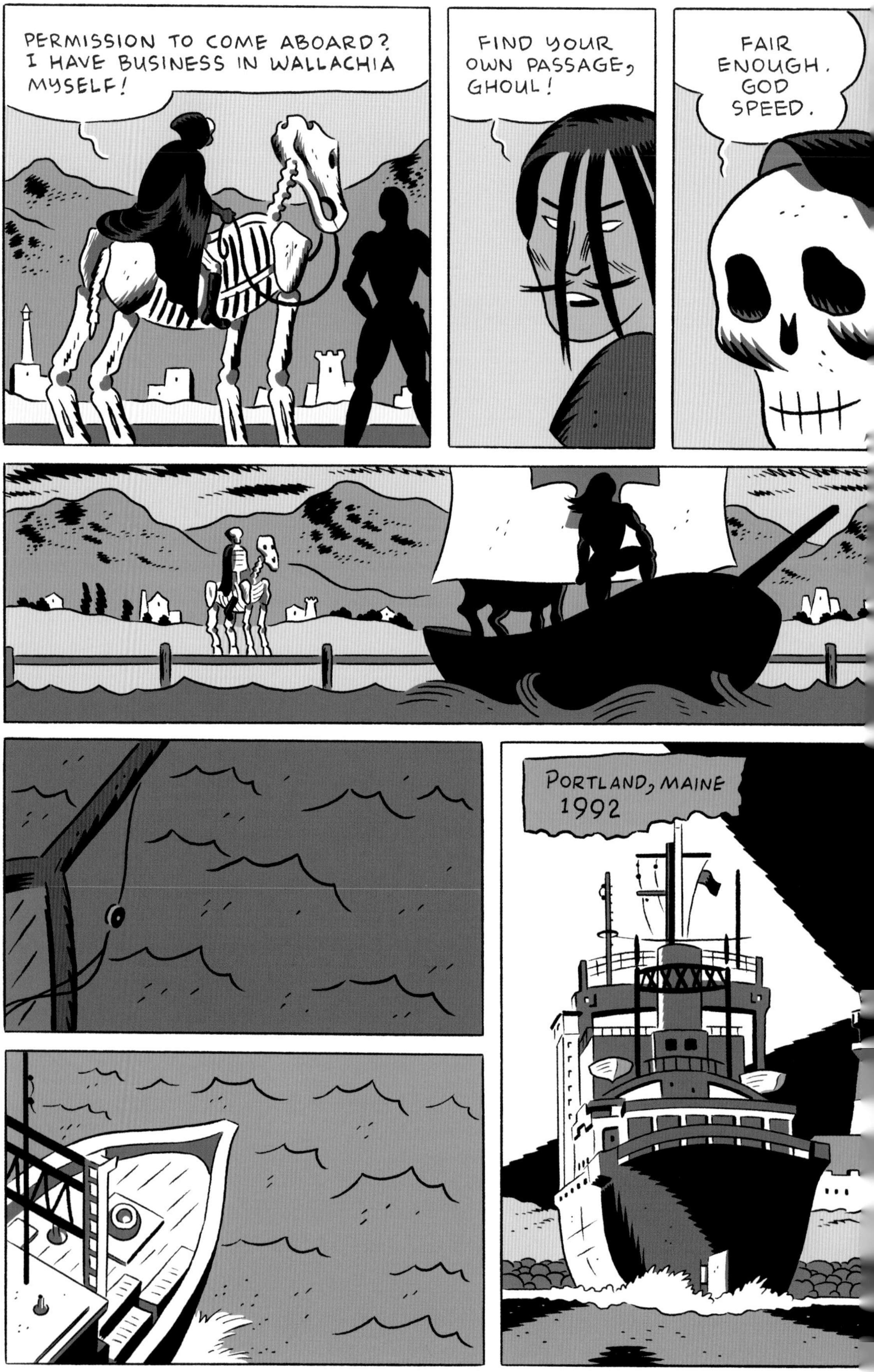
PERMISSION TO COME ABOARD? I HAVE BUSINESS IN WALLACHIA MYSELF!
FIND YOUR OWN PASSAGE, GHOUL!
FAIR ENOUGH. GOD SPEED.
PORTLAND, MAINE 1992

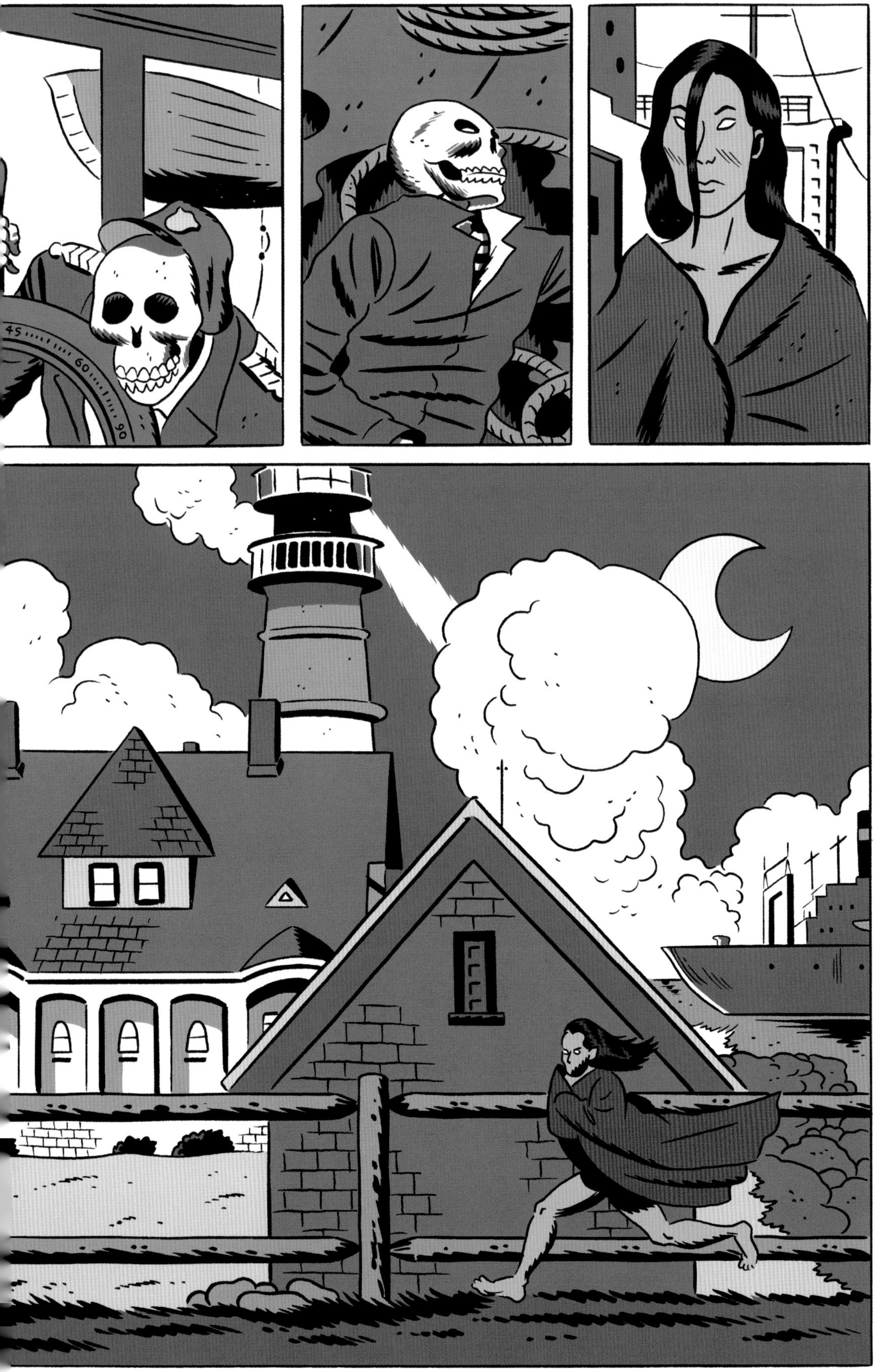
45
60
90

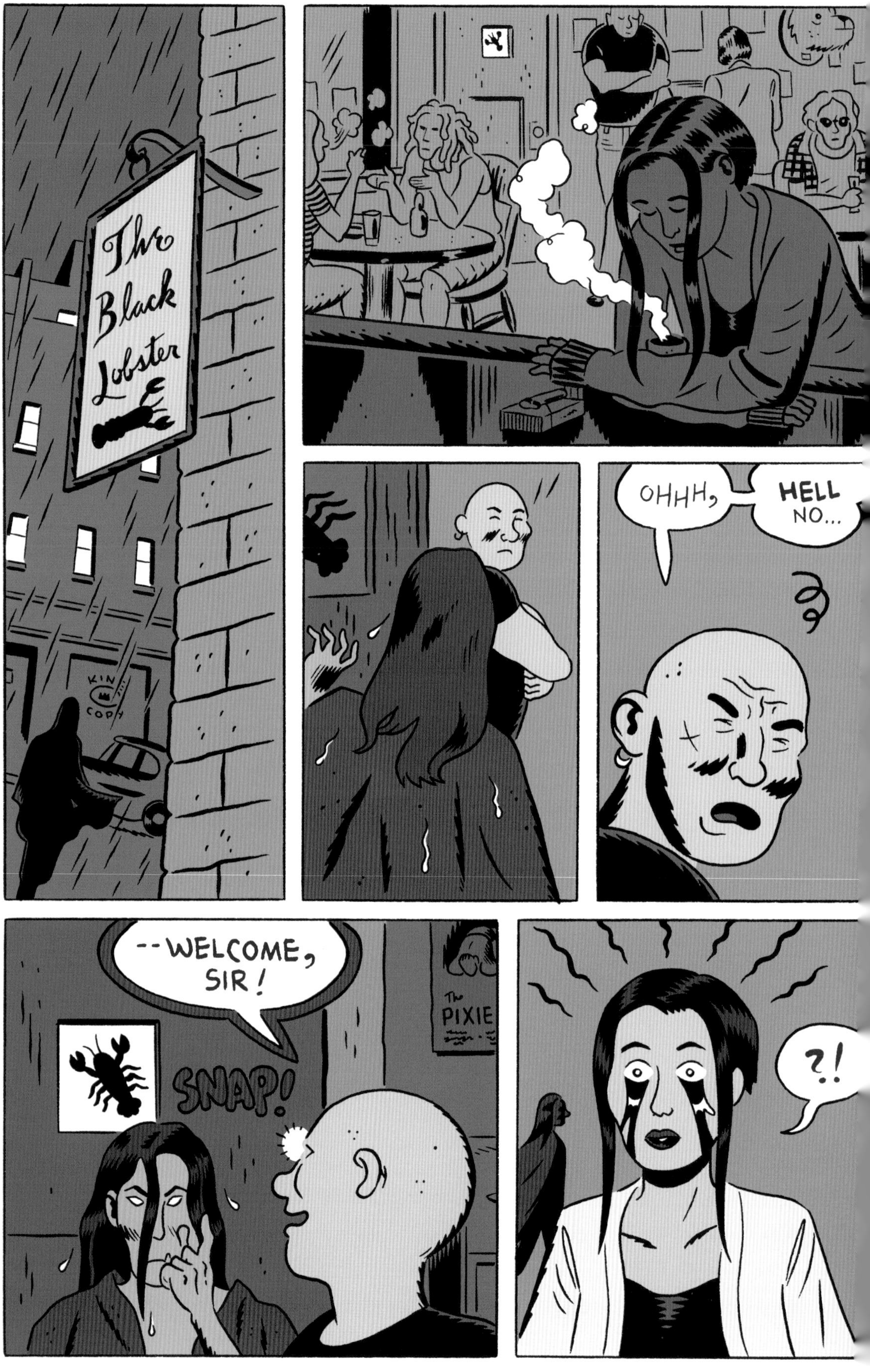
The Black Lobster
KIN COPY
OHHH, HELL NO...
--WELCOME, SIR!
SNAP!
The PIXIE
?!

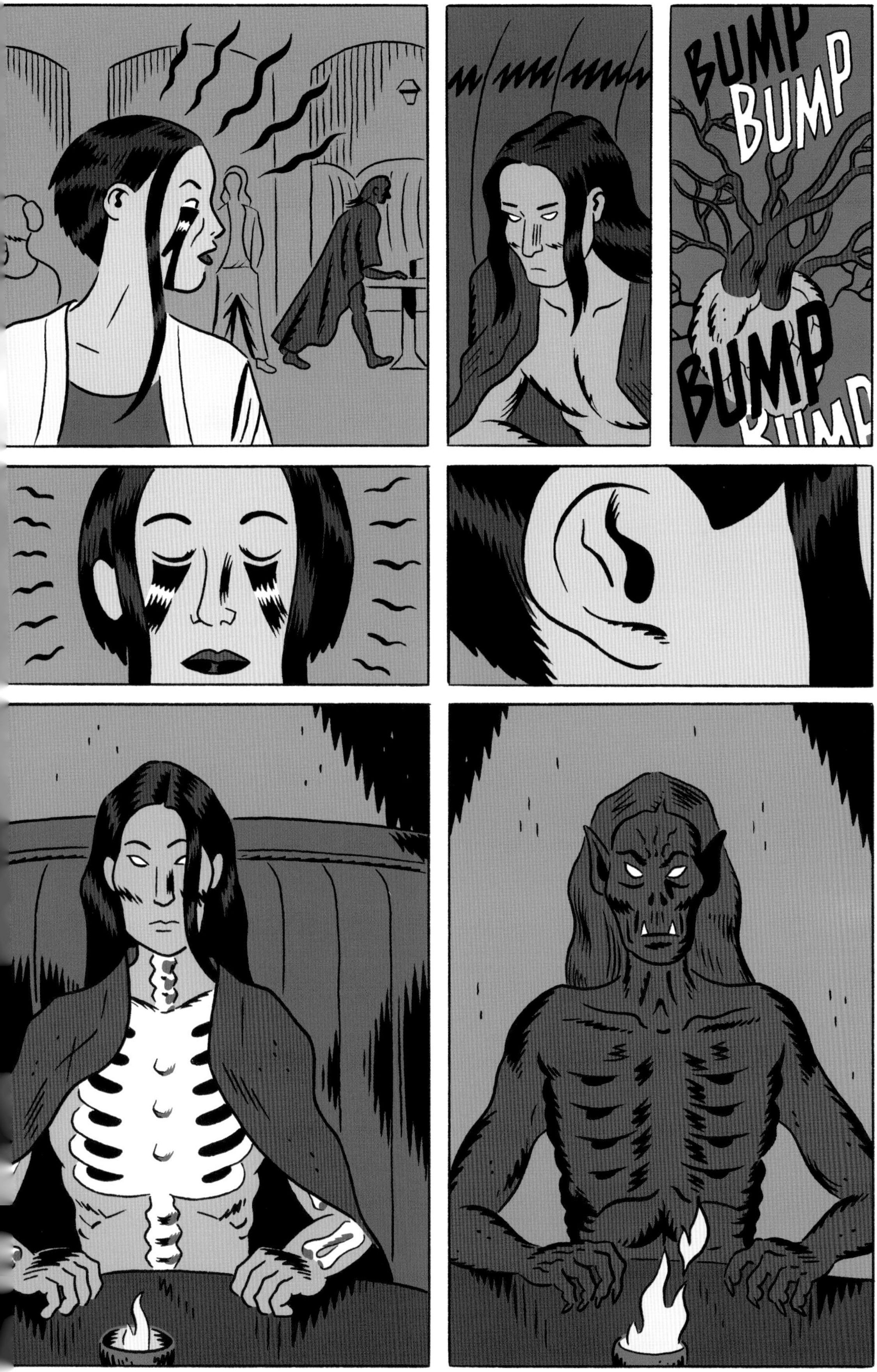
BUMP
BUMP
BUMP

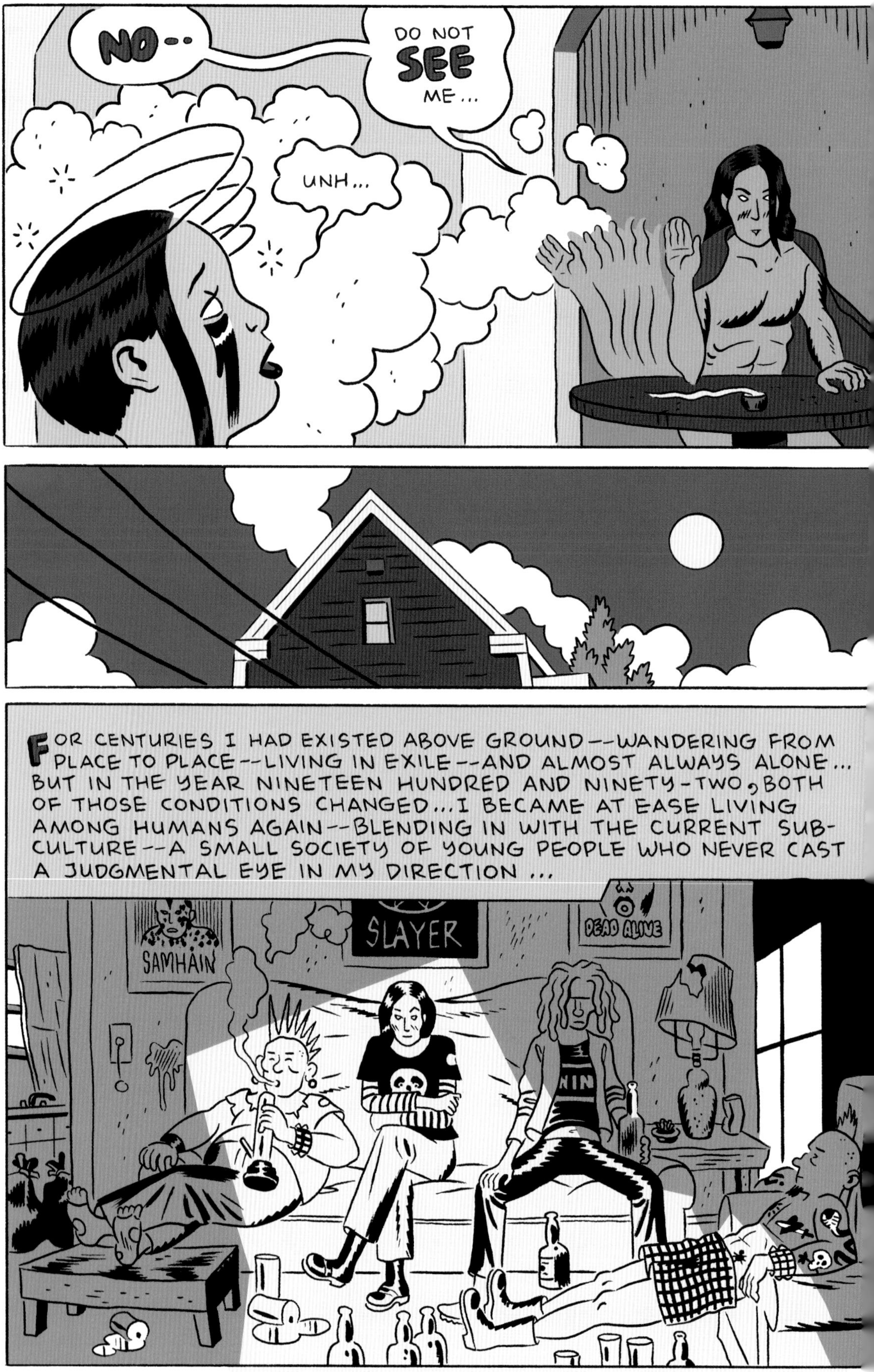
NO..
DO NOT SEE ME...
UNH...
FOR CENTURIES I HAD EXISTED ABOVE GROUND--WANDERING FROM PLACE TO PLACE--LIVING IN EXILE--AND ALMOST ALWAYS ALONE... BUT IN THE YEAR NINETEEN HUNDRED AND NINETY-TWO, BOTH OF THOSE CONDITIONS CHANGED...I BECAME AT EASE LIVING AMONG HUMANS AGAIN--BLENDING IN WITH THE CURRENT SUB-CULTURE--A SMALL SOCIETY OF YOUNG PEOPLE WHO NEVER CAST A JUDGMENTAL EYE IN MY DIRECTION...
SLAYER
SAMHAIN
DEAD ALIVE
NIN

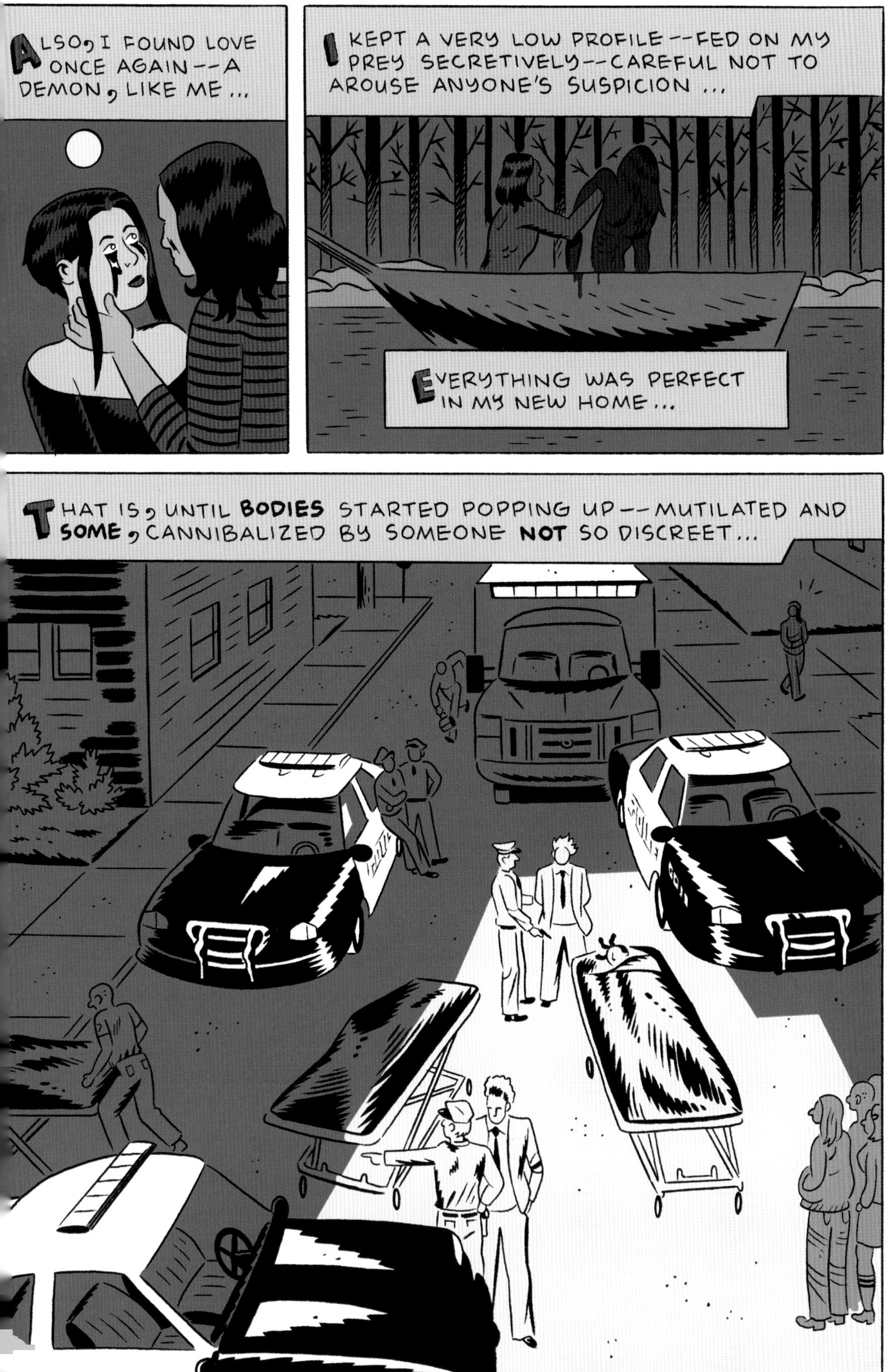
ALSO, I FOUND LOVE ONCE AGAIN--A DEMON, LIKE ME...
I KEPT A VERY LOW PROFILE--FED ON MY PREY SECRETIVELY--CAREFUL NOT TO AROUSE ANYONE'S SUSPICION...
EVERYTHING WAS PERFECT IN MY NEW HOME...
THAT IS, UNTIL **BODIES** STARTED POPPING UP--MUTILATED AND **SOME**, CANNIBALIZED BY SOMEONE **NOT** SO DISCREET...

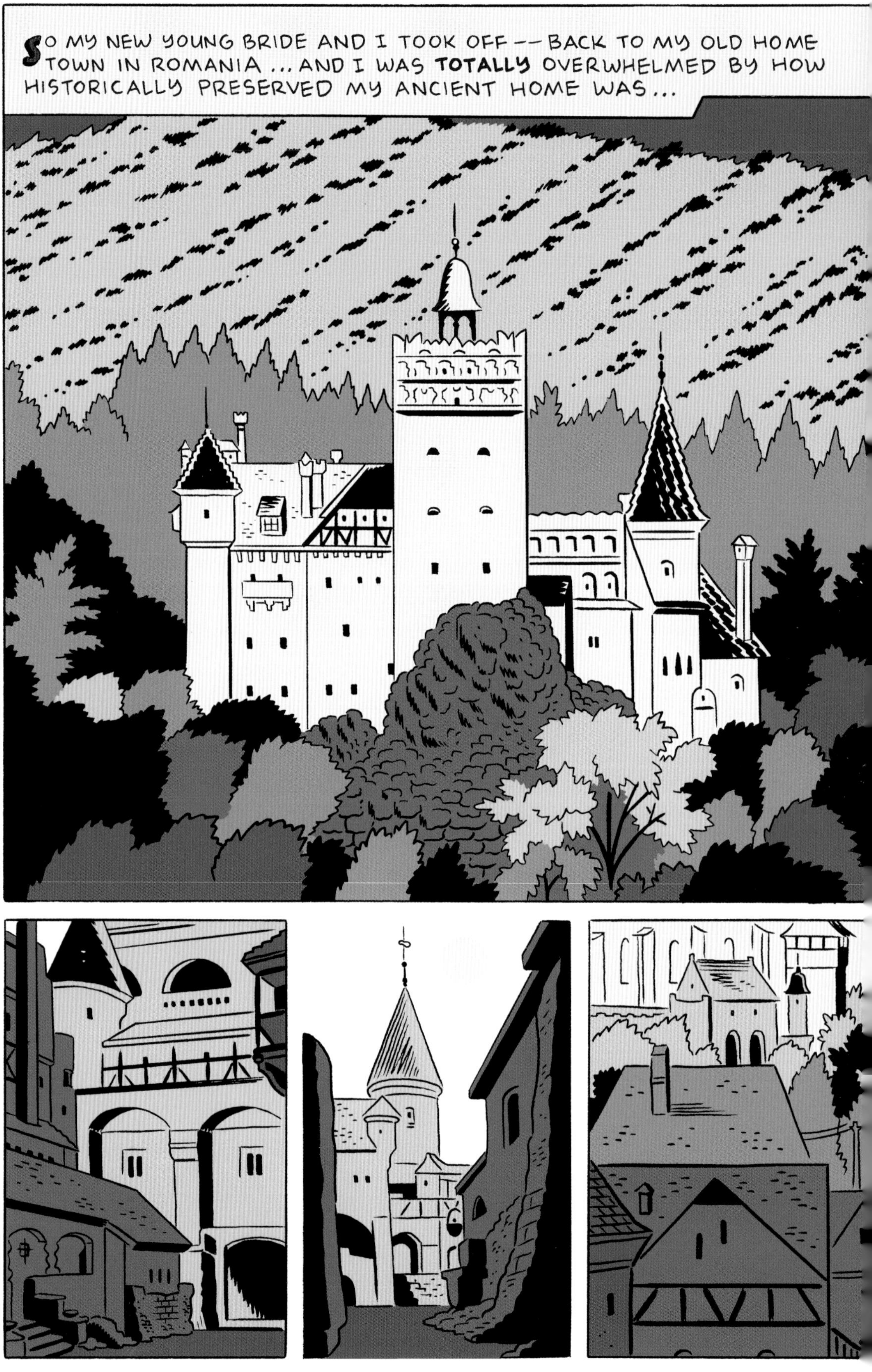
SO MY NEW YOUNG BRIDE AND I TOOK OFF -- BACK TO MY OLD HOME TOWN IN ROMANIA ... AND I WAS **TOTALLY** OVERWHELMED BY HOW HISTORICALLY PRESERVED MY ANCIENT HOME WAS ...

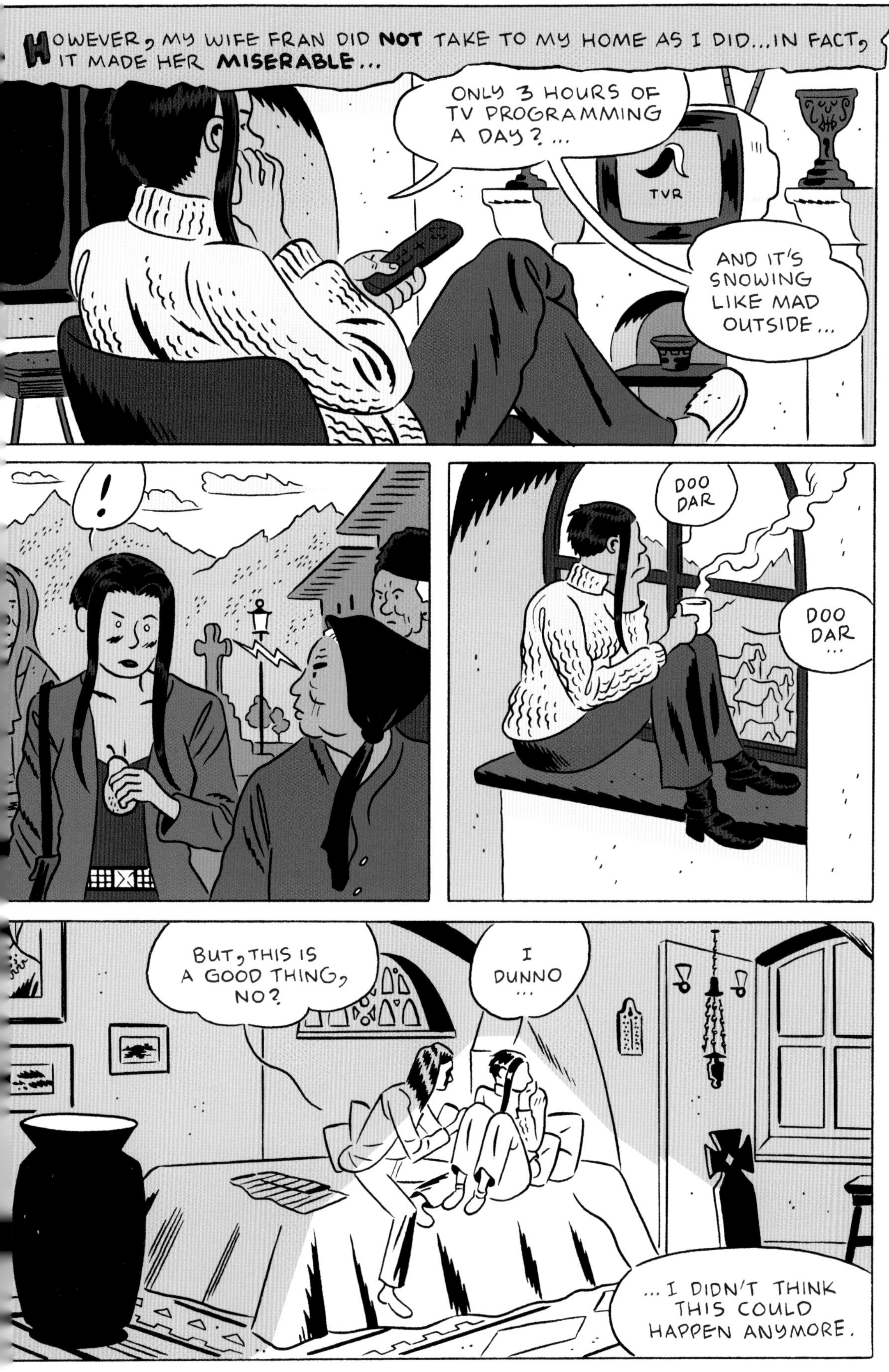
HOWEVER, MY WIFE FRAN DID NOT TAKE TO MY HOME AS I DID... IN FACT, IT MADE HER MISERABLE...
ONLY 3 HOURS OF TV PROGRAMMING A DAY?...
TVR
AND IT'S SNOWING LIKE MAD OUTSIDE...
!
DOO DAR
DOO DAR...
BUT, THIS IS A GOOD THING, NO?
I DUNNO...
...I DIDN'T THINK THIS COULD HAPPEN ANYMORE.

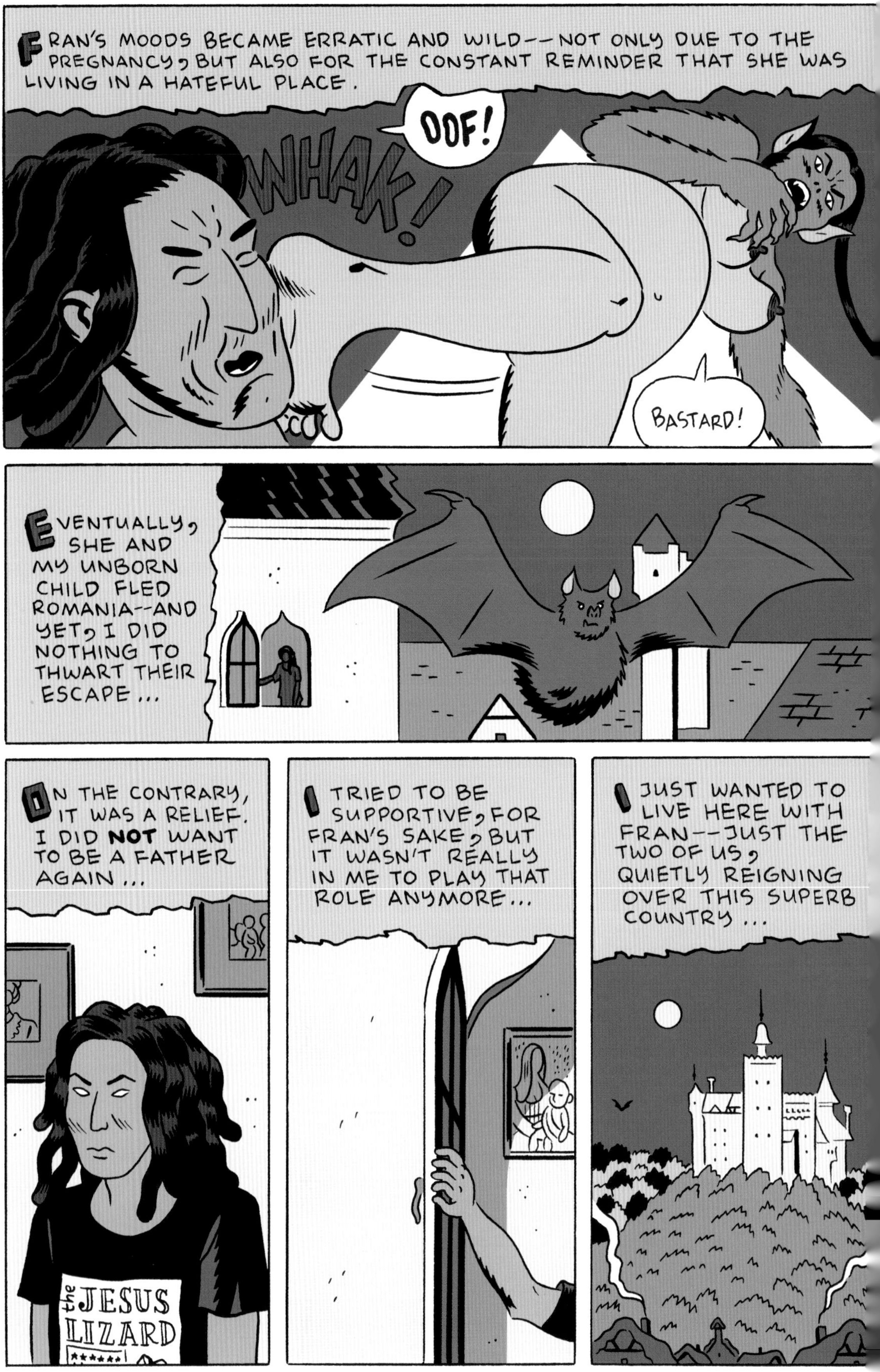
FRAN'S MOODS BECAME ERRATIC AND WILD--NOT ONLY DUE TO THE PREGNANCY, BUT ALSO FOR THE CONSTANT REMINDER THAT SHE WAS LIVING IN A HATEFUL PLACE.
OOF!
WHAK!
BASTARD!
EVENTUALLY, SHE AND MY UNBORN CHILD FLED ROMANIA--AND YET, I DID NOTHING TO THWART THEIR ESCAPE...
ON THE CONTRARY, IT WAS A RELIEF. I DID NOT WANT TO BE A FATHER AGAIN...
the JESUS LIZARD
I TRIED TO BE SUPPORTIVE, FOR FRAN'S SAKE, BUT IT WASN'T REALLY IN ME TO PLAY THAT ROLE ANYMORE...
I JUST WANTED TO LIVE HERE WITH FRAN--JUST THE TWO OF US, QUIETLY REIGNING OVER THIS SUPERB COUNTRY...

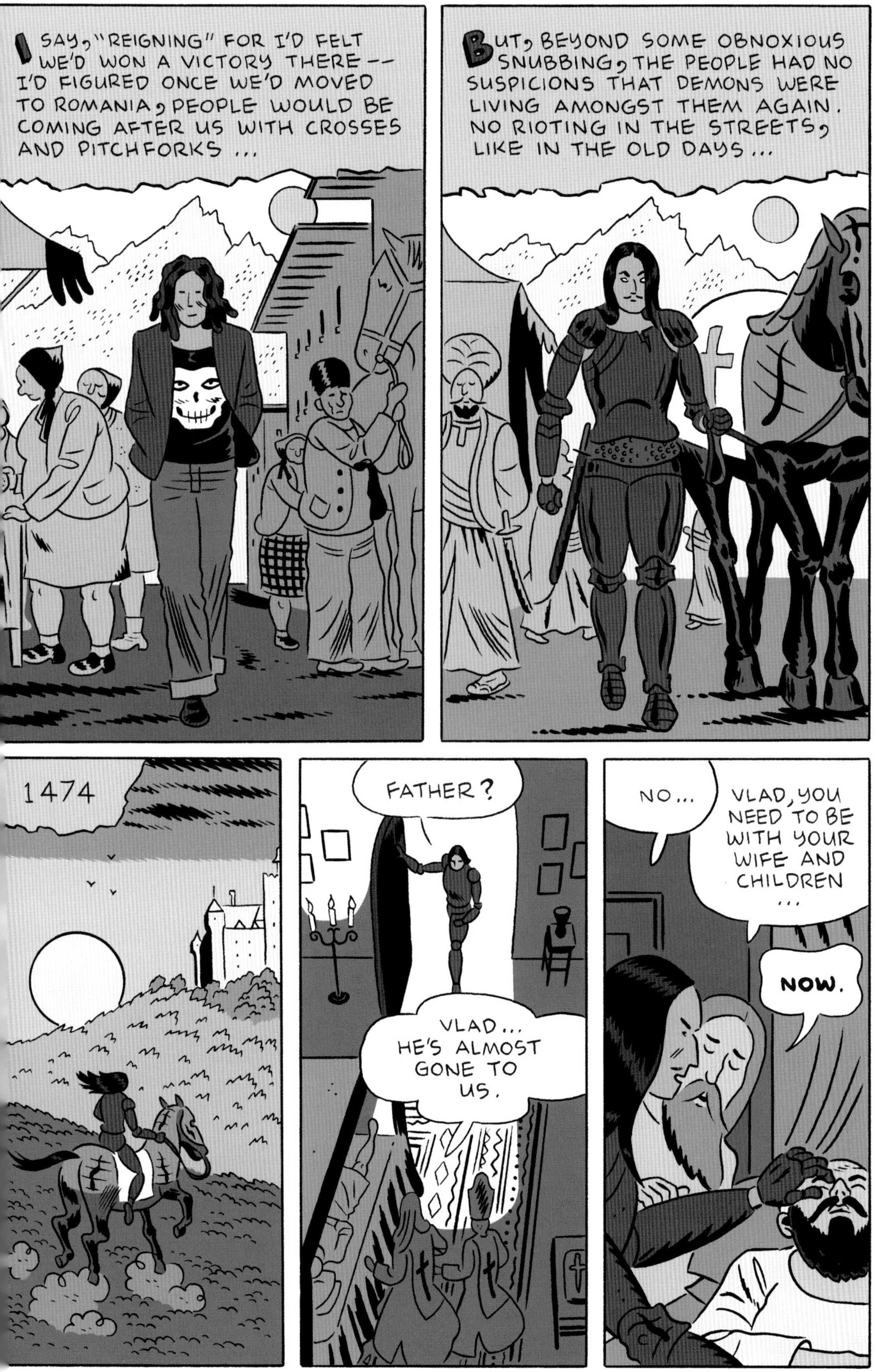
I SAY, "REIGNING" FOR I'D FELT WE'D WON A VICTORY THERE -- I'D FIGURED ONCE WE'D MOVED TO ROMANIA, PEOPLE WOULD BE COMING AFTER US WITH CROSSES AND PITCHFORKS ...
BUT, BEYOND SOME OBNOXIOUS SNUBBING, THE PEOPLE HAD NO SUSPICIONS THAT DEMONS WERE LIVING AMONGST THEM AGAIN. NO RIOTING IN THE STREETS, LIKE IN THE OLD DAYS ...
1474
FATHER?
VLAD... HE'S ALMOST GONE TO US.
NO...
VLAD, YOU NEED TO BE WITH YOUR WIFE AND CHILDREN ...
NOW.

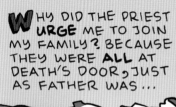

WHY DID THE PRIEST **URGE** ME TO JOIN MY FAMILY? BECAUSE THEY WERE **ALL** AT DEATH'S DOOR, JUST AS FATHER WAS...

DEAR GOD, NO!

PA~~PA?

THERE WERE WHISPERS THAT OTTOMAN NOBLES HAD SOMEHOW POISONED THEM TO DESTROY MY ENTIRE ROYAL LINEAGE ...

BY THIS TIME, YOU SEE, OTTOMAN POLITICIANS NEARLY RAN MY **ENTIRE** COUNTRY ...

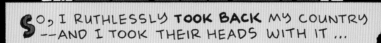

SO, I RUTHLESSLY **TOOK BACK** MY COUNTRY --AND I TOOK THEIR HEADS WITH IT ...

AND THUS BECAME THE **DEMON** THAT EVERYONE HAD ALREADY BRANDED ME AS...

AFTER ALL OF THAT LOSS ... I NEVER WANTED A CHILD AGAIN ... OR A FAMILY OF ANY KIND.

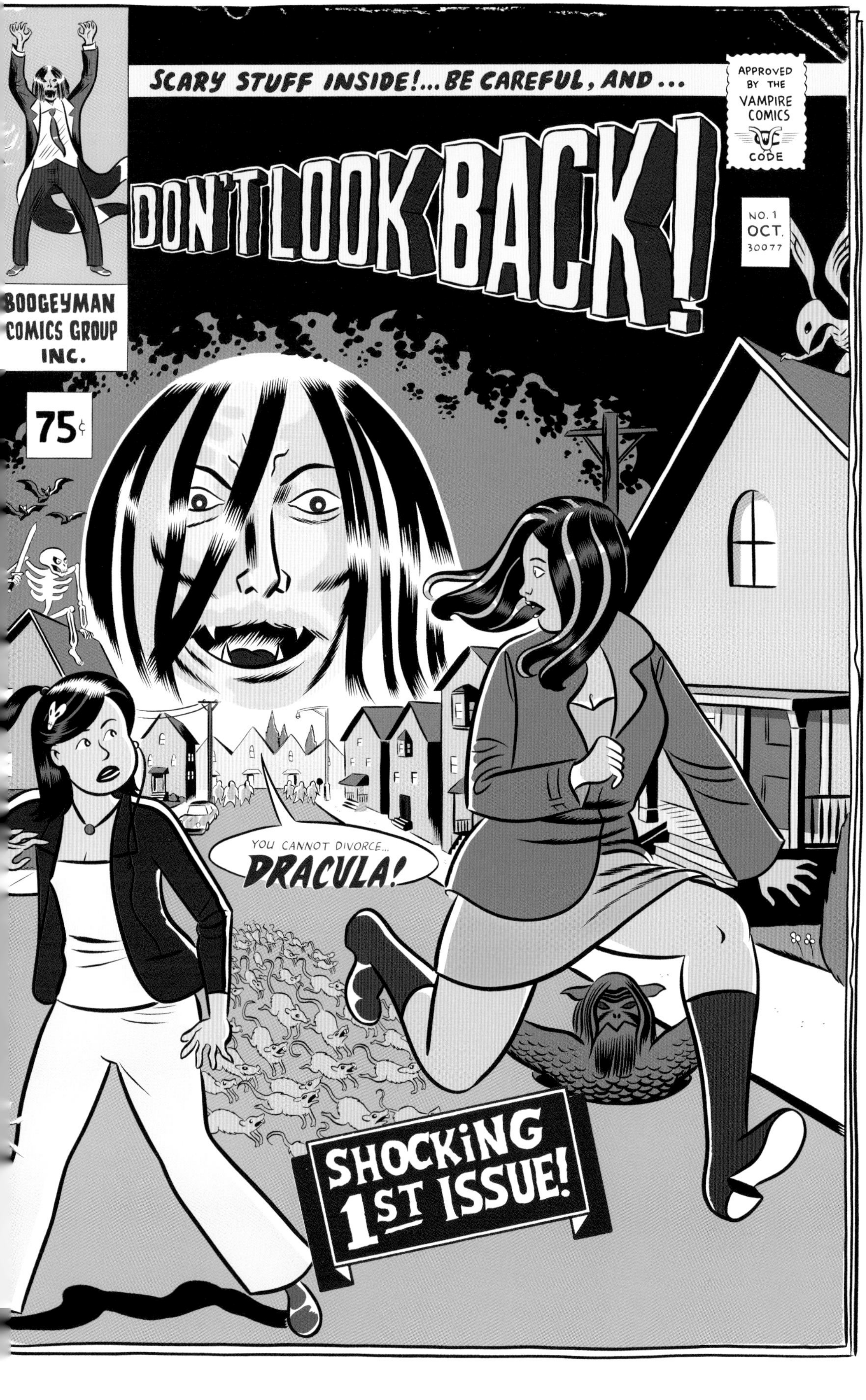

BOOGEYMAN COMICS GROUP INC.
SCARY STUFF INSIDE!... BE CAREFUL, AND ...
APPROVED BY THE VAMPIRE COMICS CODE
DON'T LOOK BACK!
NO. 1
OCT.
30077
75¢
YOU CANNOT DIVORCE...
DRACULA!
SHOCKING 1ST ISSUE!

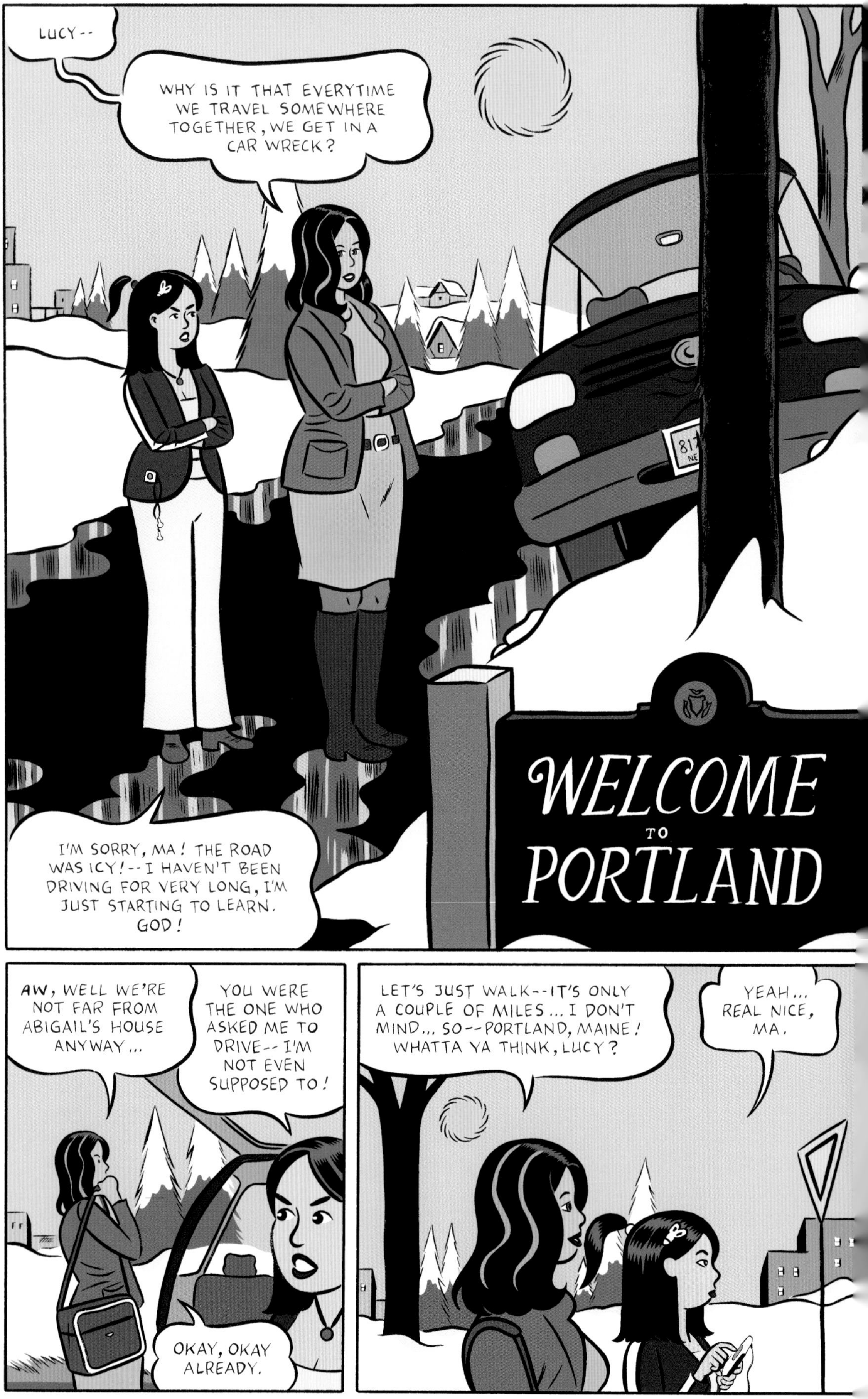
LUCY--
WHY IS IT THAT EVERYTIME WE TRAVEL SOMEWHERE TOGETHER, WE GET IN A CAR WRECK?
WELCOME TO PORTLAND
I'M SORRY, MA! THE ROAD WAS ICY!--I HAVEN'T BEEN DRIVING FOR VERY LONG, I'M JUST STARTING TO LEARN. GOD!
AW, WELL WE'RE NOT FAR FROM ABIGAIL'S HOUSE ANYWAY...
YOU WERE THE ONE WHO ASKED ME TO DRIVE--I'M NOT EVEN SUPPOSED TO!
OKAY, OKAY ALREADY.
LET'S JUST WALK--IT'S ONLY A COUPLE OF MILES... I DON'T MIND... SO--PORTLAND, MAINE! WHATTA YA THINK, LUCY?
YEAH... REAL NICE, MA.

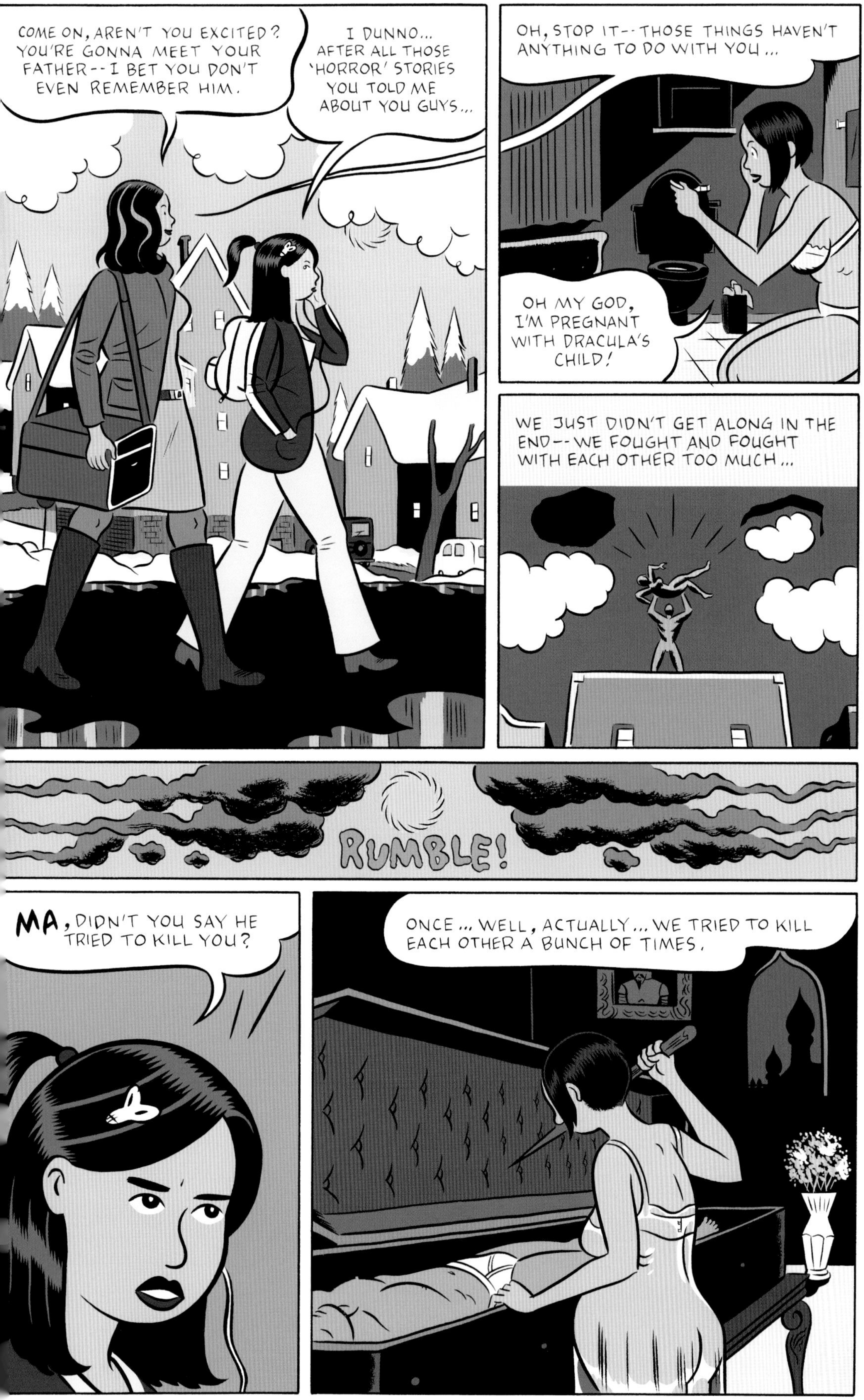
COME ON, AREN'T YOU EXCITED? YOU'RE GONNA MEET YOUR FATHER-- I BET YOU DON'T EVEN REMEMBER HIM.
I DUNNO... AFTER ALL THOSE 'HORROR' STORIES YOU TOLD ME ABOUT YOU GUYS...
OH, STOP IT-- THOSE THINGS HAVEN'T ANYTHING TO DO WITH YOU...
OH MY GOD, I'M PREGNANT WITH DRACULA'S CHILD!
WE JUST DIDN'T GET ALONG IN THE END-- WE FOUGHT AND FOUGHT WITH EACH OTHER TOO MUCH...
RUMBLE!
MA, DIDN'T YOU SAY HE TRIED TO KILL YOU?
ONCE... WELL, ACTUALLY... WE TRIED TO KILL EACH OTHER A BUNCH OF TIMES.

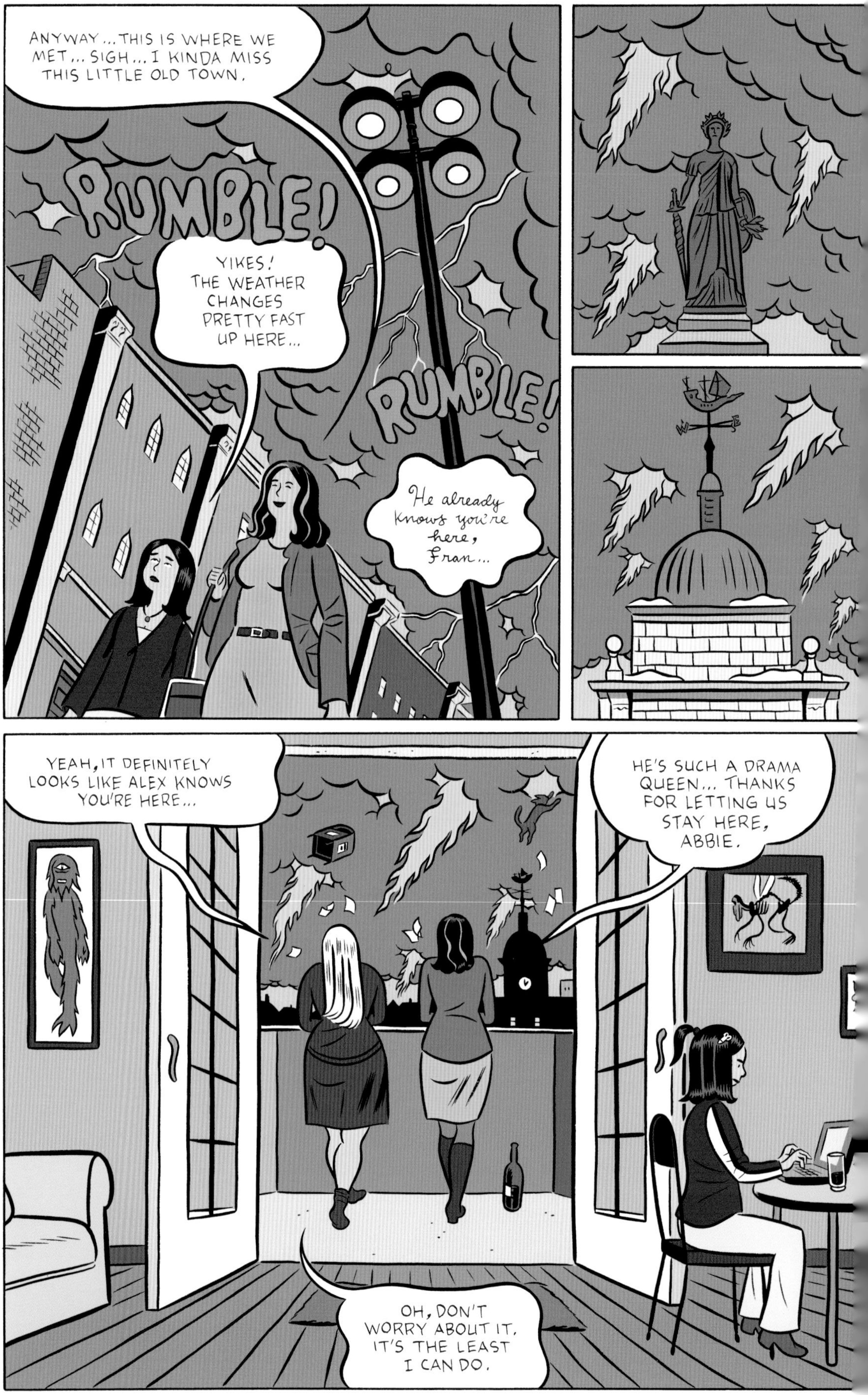
ANYWAY... THIS IS WHERE WE MET... SIGH... I KINDA MISS THIS LITTLE OLD TOWN.
RUMBLE!
YIKES! THE WEATHER CHANGES PRETTY FAST UP HERE...
RUMBLE!
He already knows you're here, Fran...
YEAH, IT DEFINITELY LOOKS LIKE ALEX KNOWS YOU'RE HERE...
HE'S SUCH A DRAMA QUEEN... THANKS FOR LETTING US STAY HERE, ABBIE.
OH, DON'T WORRY ABOUT IT. IT'S THE LEAST I CAN DO.

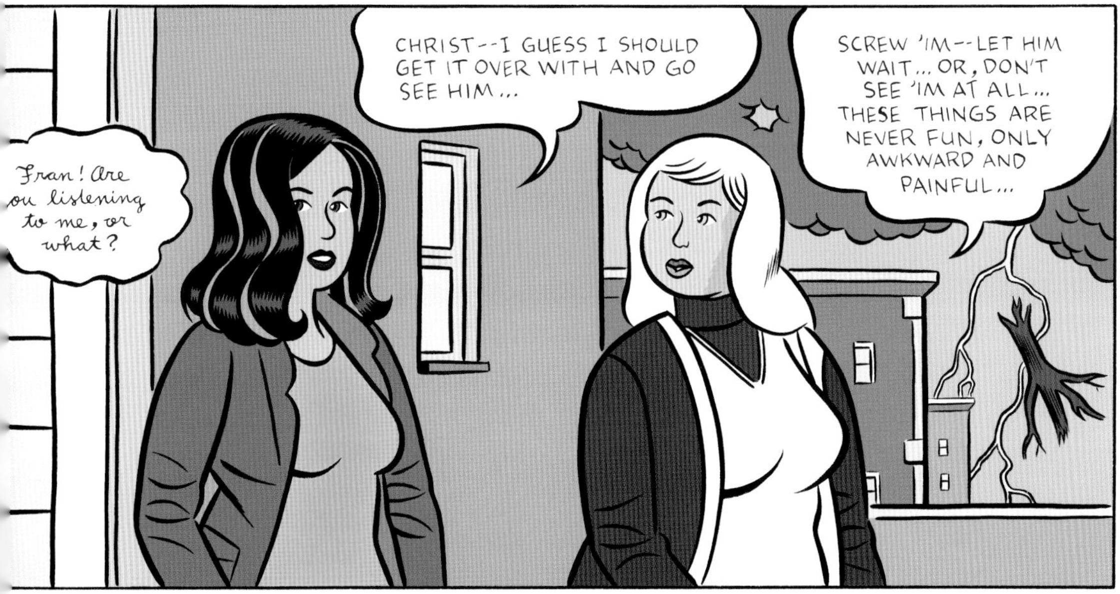
Fran! Are ou listening to me, or what?
CHRIST--I GUESS I SHOULD GET IT OVER WITH AND GO SEE HIM...
SCREW 'IM--LET HIM WAIT... OR, DON'T SEE 'IM AT ALL... THESE THINGS ARE NEVER FUN, ONLY AWKWARD AND PAINFUL...

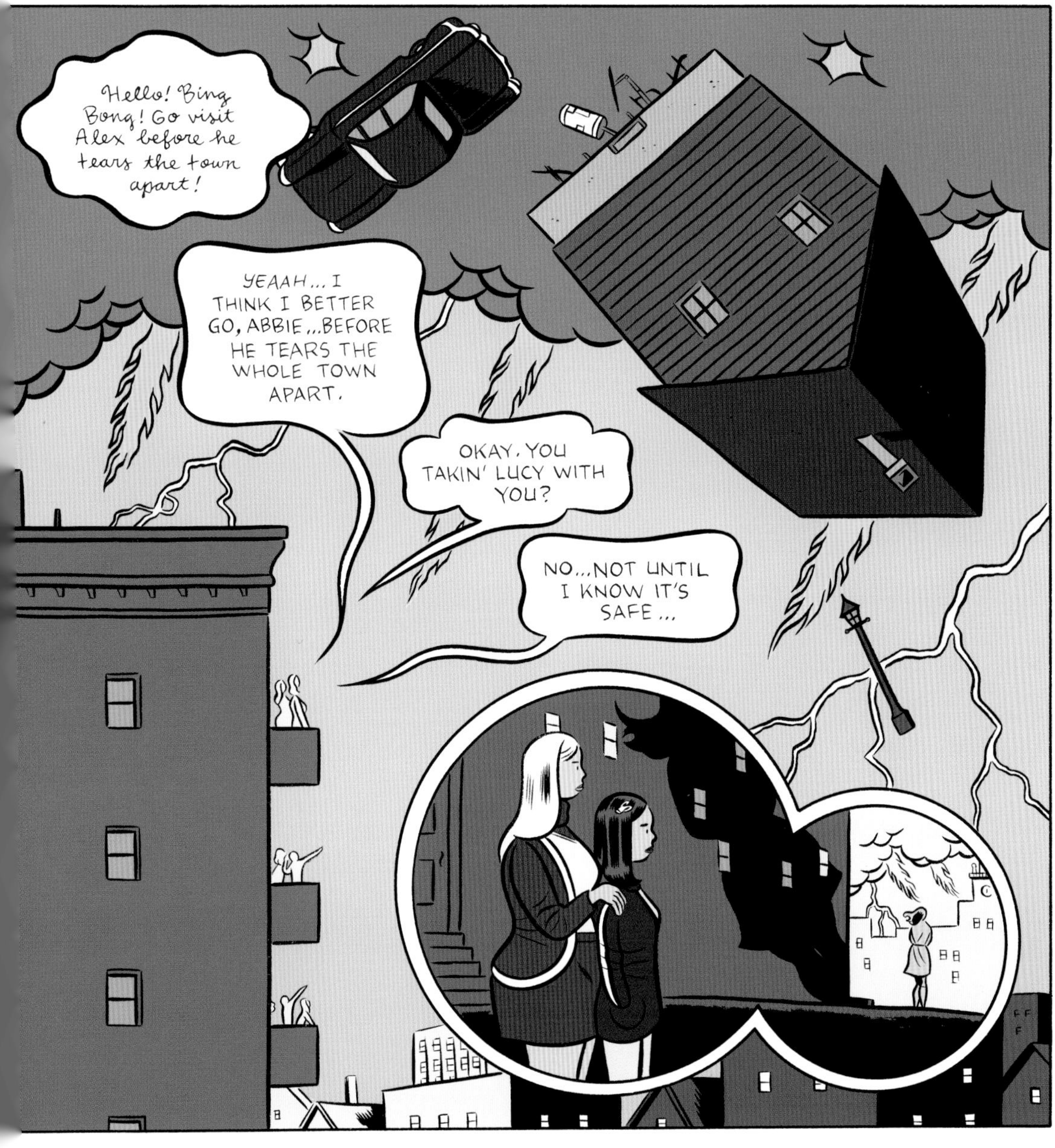
Hello! Bing Bong! Go visit Alex before he tears the town apart!
YEAAH... I THINK I BETTER GO, ABBIE...BEFORE HE TEARS THE WHOLE TOWN APART.
OKAY. YOU TAKIN' LUCY WITH YOU?
NO...NOT UNTIL I KNOW IT'S SAFE...

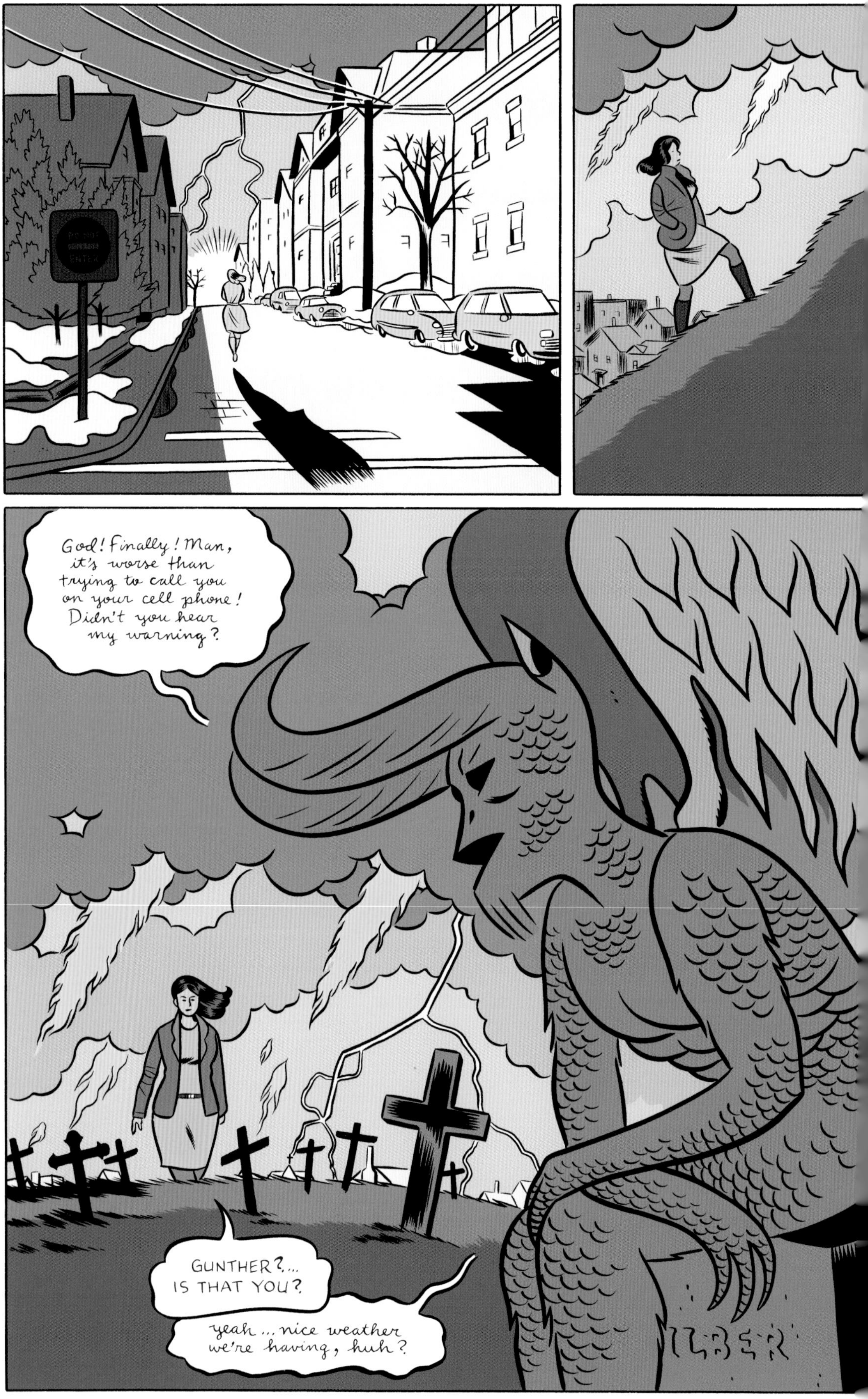
God! Finally! Man, it's worse than trying to call you on your cell phone! Didn't you hear my warning?
GUNTHER?... IS THAT YOU?
yeah ... nice weather we're having, huh?

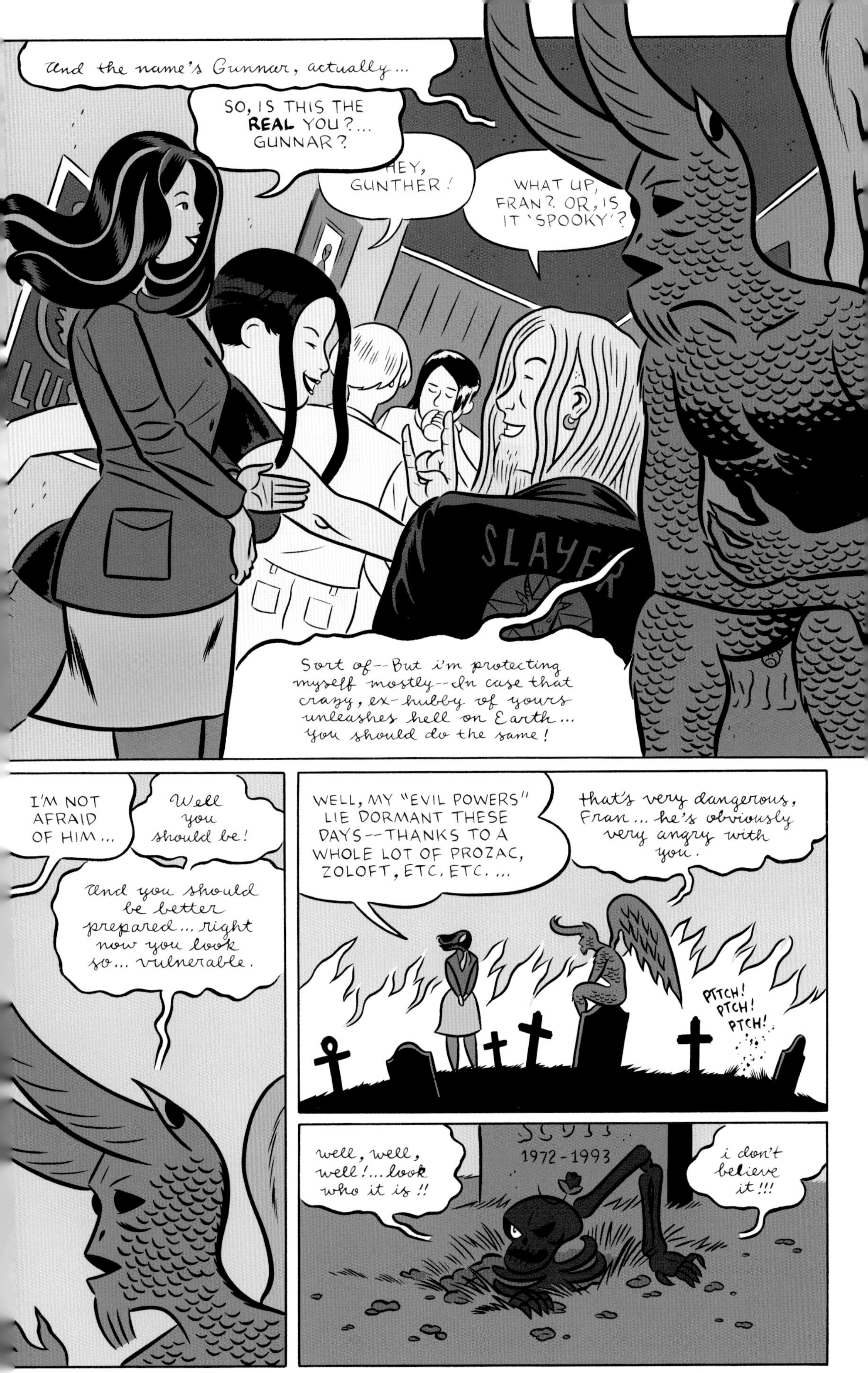

And the name's Gunnar, actually...
SO, IS THIS THE REAL YOU?... GUNNAR?
HEY, GUNTHER!
WHAT UP, FRAN? OR, IS IT 'SPOOKY'?
SLAYER
Sort of--But i'm protecting myself mostly--In case that crazy, ex-hubby of yours unleashes hell on Earth... You should do the same!
I'M NOT AFRAID OF HIM...
Well you should be!
And you should be better prepared... right now you look so... vulnerable.
WELL, MY "EVIL POWERS" LIE DORMANT THESE DAYS--THANKS TO A WHOLE LOT OF PROZAC, ZOLOFT, ETC. ETC. ...
that's very dangerous, Fran... he's obviously very angry with you.
PTCH! PTCH! PTCH!
well, well, well!... look who it is!!
1972-1993
i don't believe it!!!

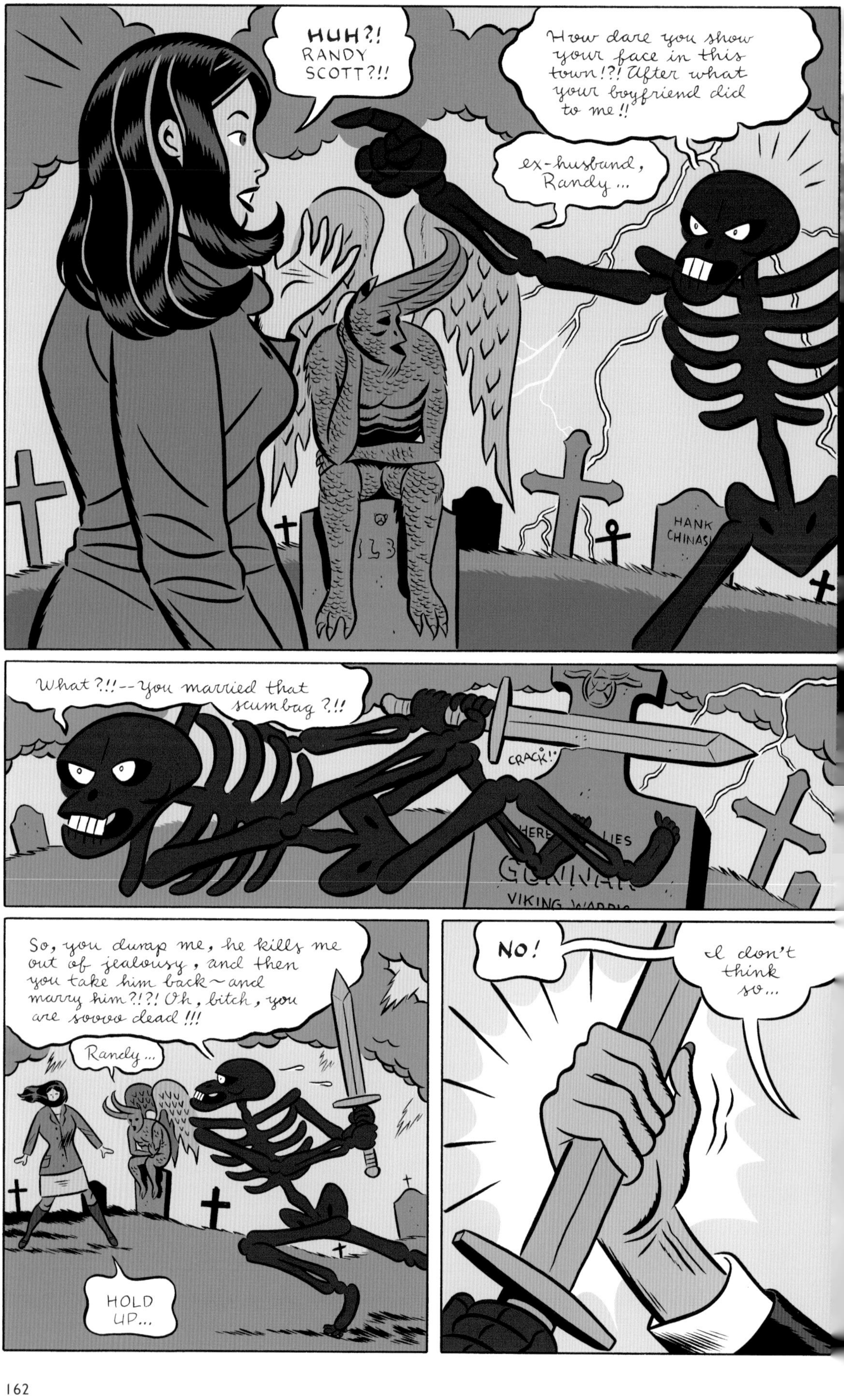
HUH?! RANDY SCOTT?!!
How dare you show your face in this town!?! After what your boyfriend did to me!!
ex-husband, Randy...
HANK CHINAS
What?!!--You married that scumbag?!!
CRACK!
HERE LIES
VIKING
So, you dump me, he kills me out of jealousy, and then you take him back~and marry him?!?! Oh, bitch, you are soooo dead!!!
Randy...
HOLD UP...
NO!
I don't think so...

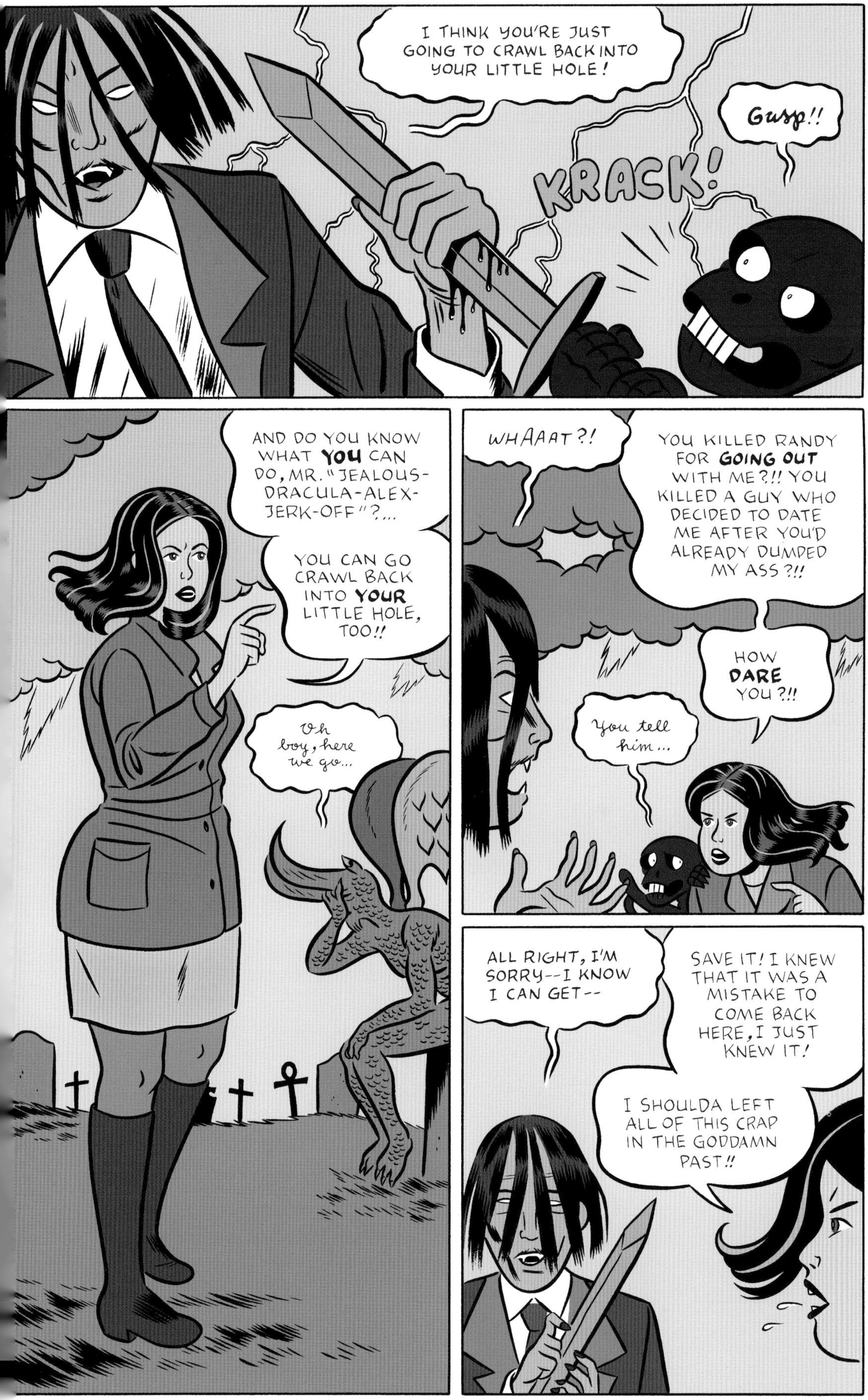

I THINK YOU'RE JUST GOING TO CRAWL BACK INTO YOUR LITTLE HOLE!
KRACK!
Gusp!!
AND DO YOU KNOW WHAT YOU CAN DO, MR. "JEALOUS-DRACULA-ALEX-JERK-OFF"?...
YOU CAN GO CRAWL BACK INTO YOUR LITTLE HOLE, TOO!!
Oh boy, here we go...
WHAAAT?!
YOU KILLED RANDY FOR GOING OUT WITH ME?!! YOU KILLED A GUY WHO DECIDED TO DATE ME AFTER YOU'D ALREADY DUMPED MY ASS?!!
HOW DARE YOU?!!
You tell him...
ALL RIGHT, I'M SORRY--I KNOW I CAN GET--
SAVE IT! I KNEW THAT IT WAS A MISTAKE TO COME BACK HERE, I JUST KNEW IT!
I SHOULDA LEFT ALL OF THIS CRAP IN THE GODDAMN PAST!!

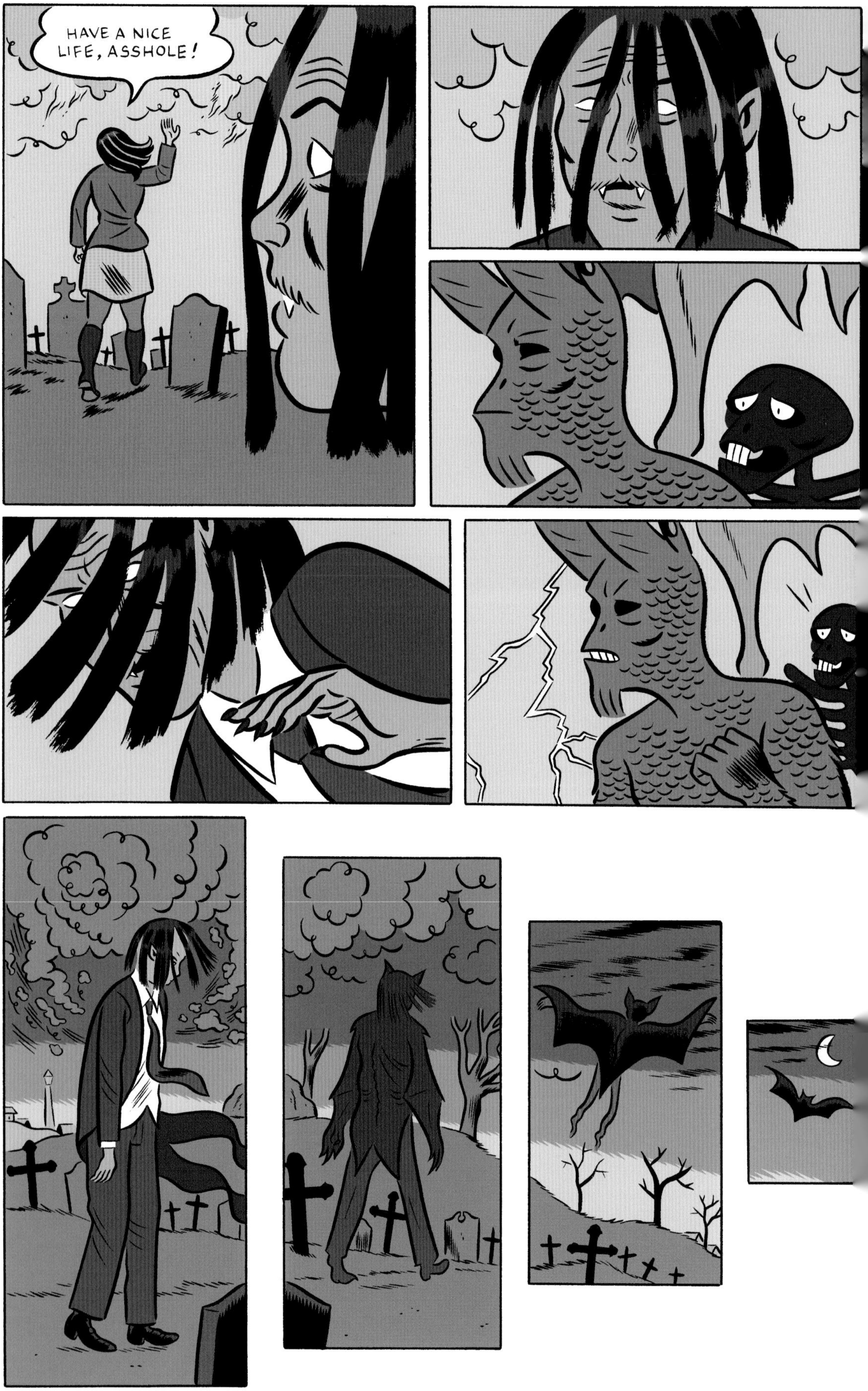
HAVE A NICE LIFE, ASSHOLE!

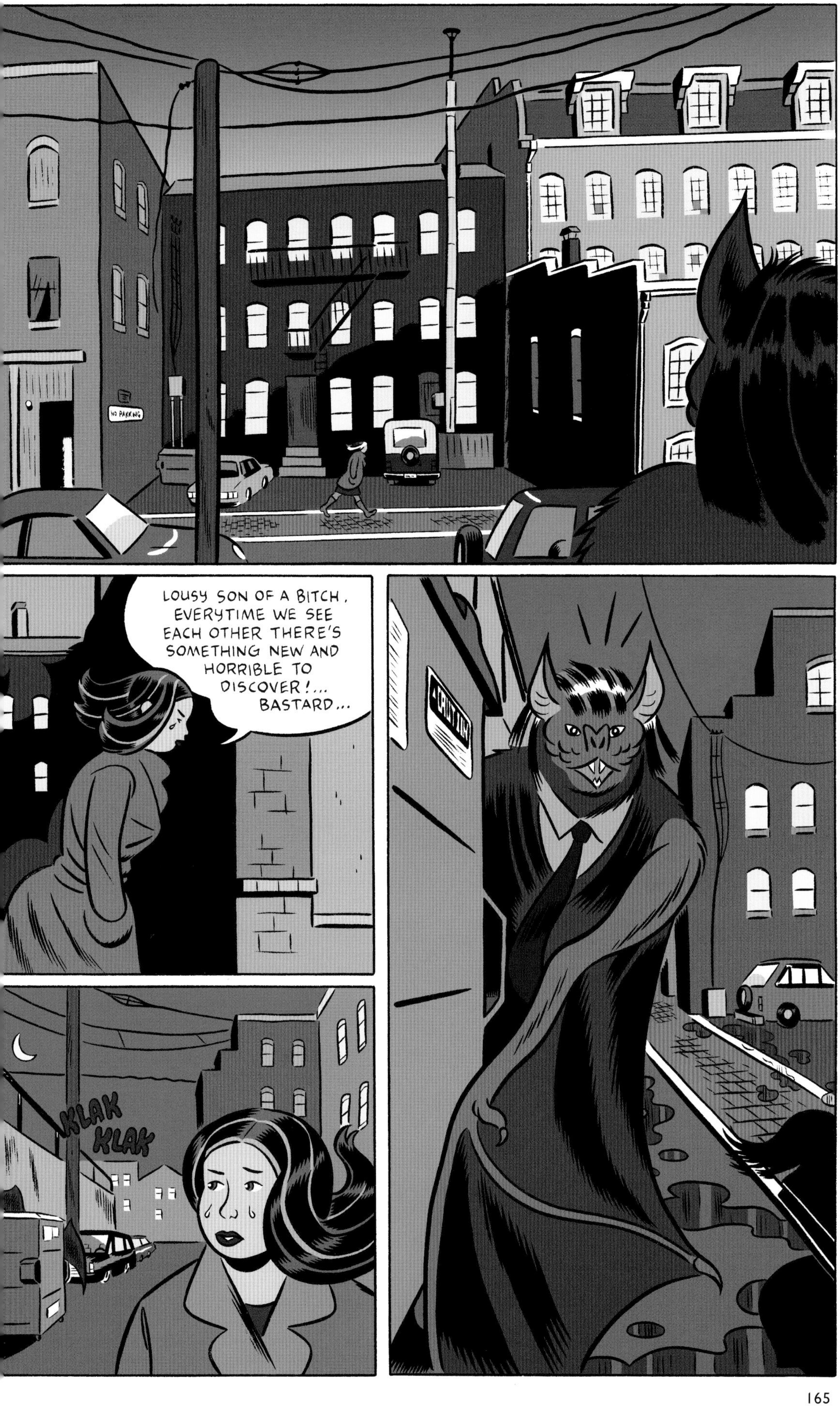
NO PARKING
LOUSY SON OF A BITCH, EVERYTIME WE SEE EACH OTHER THERE'S SOMETHING NEW AND HORRIBLE TO DISCOVER!... BASTARD...
KLAK KLAK

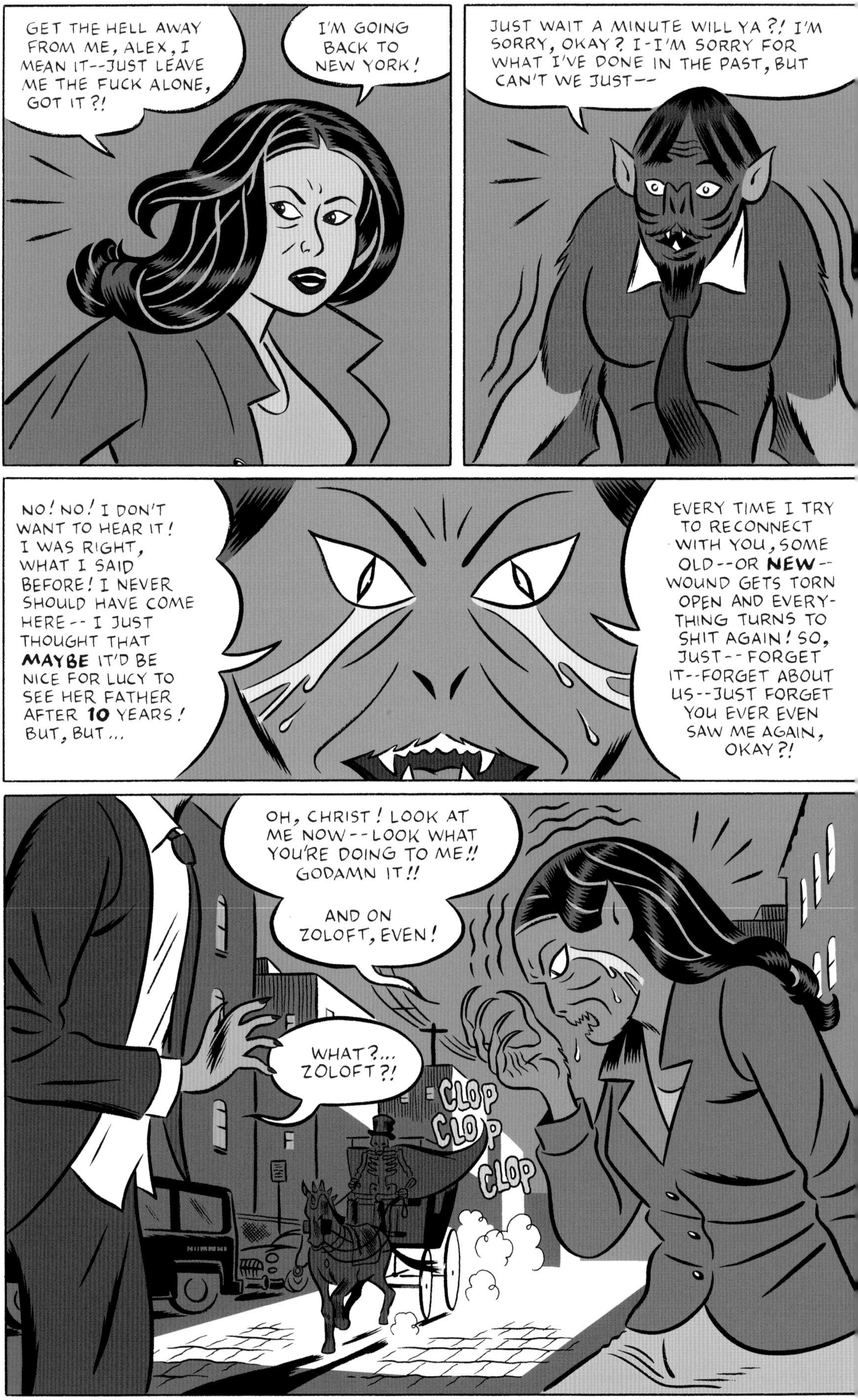
GET THE HELL AWAY FROM ME, ALEX, I MEAN IT--JUST LEAVE ME THE FUCK ALONE, GOT IT?!
I'M GOING BACK TO NEW YORK!
JUST WAIT A MINUTE WILL YA?! I'M SORRY, OKAY? I-I'M SORRY FOR WHAT I'VE DONE IN THE PAST, BUT CAN'T WE JUST--
NO! NO! I DON'T WANT TO HEAR IT! I WAS RIGHT, WHAT I SAID BEFORE! I NEVER SHOULD HAVE COME HERE-- I JUST THOUGHT THAT **MAYBE** IT'D BE NICE FOR LUCY TO SEE HER FATHER AFTER **10** YEARS! BUT, BUT...
EVERY TIME I TRY TO RECONNECT WITH YOU, SOME OLD--OR **NEW**--WOUND GETS TORN OPEN AND EVERY-THING TURNS TO SHIT AGAIN! SO, JUST--FORGET IT--FORGET ABOUT US--JUST FORGET YOU EVER EVEN SAW ME AGAIN, OKAY?!
OH, CHRIST! LOOK AT ME NOW--LOOK WHAT YOU'RE DOING TO ME!! GODAMN IT!!
AND ON ZOLOFT, EVEN!
WHAT?... ZOLOFT?!
CLOP
CLOP
CLOP

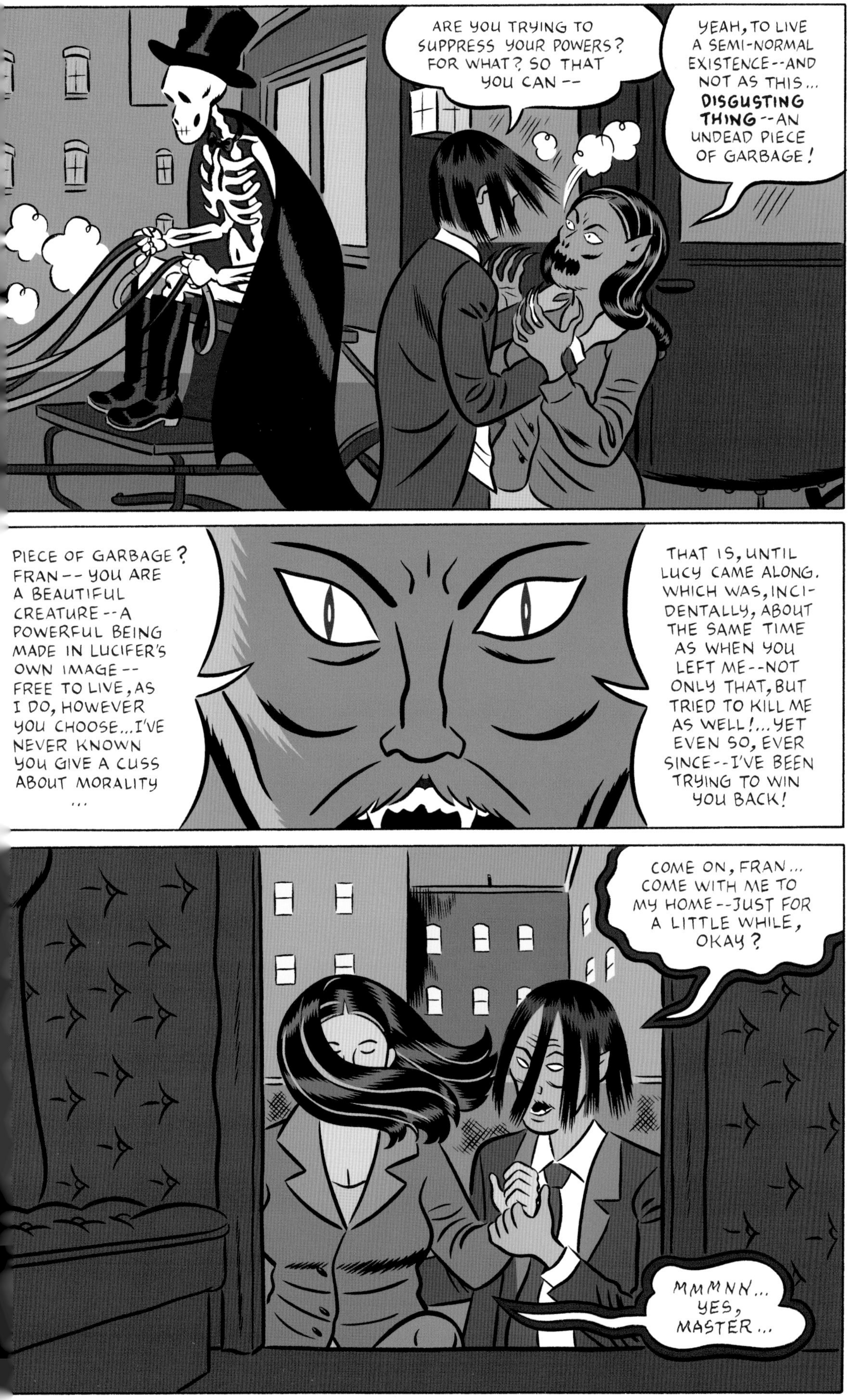

ARE YOU TRYING TO SUPPRESS YOUR POWERS? FOR WHAT? SO THAT YOU CAN --
YEAH, TO LIVE A SEMI-NORMAL EXISTENCE--AND NOT AS THIS... DISGUSTING THING--AN UNDEAD PIECE OF GARBAGE!
PIECE OF GARBAGE? FRAN-- YOU ARE A BEAUTIFUL CREATURE--A POWERFUL BEING MADE IN LUCIFER'S OWN IMAGE-- FREE TO LIVE, AS I DO, HOWEVER YOU CHOOSE...I'VE NEVER KNOWN YOU GIVE A CUSS ABOUT MORALITY ...
THAT IS, UNTIL LUCY CAME ALONG. WHICH WAS, INCIDENTALLY, ABOUT THE SAME TIME AS WHEN YOU LEFT ME--NOT ONLY THAT, BUT TRIED TO KILL ME AS WELL!...YET EVEN SO, EVER SINCE--I'VE BEEN TRYING TO WIN YOU BACK!
COME ON, FRAN... COME WITH ME TO MY HOME--JUST FOR A LITTLE WHILE, OKAY?
MMMNN... YES, MASTER...

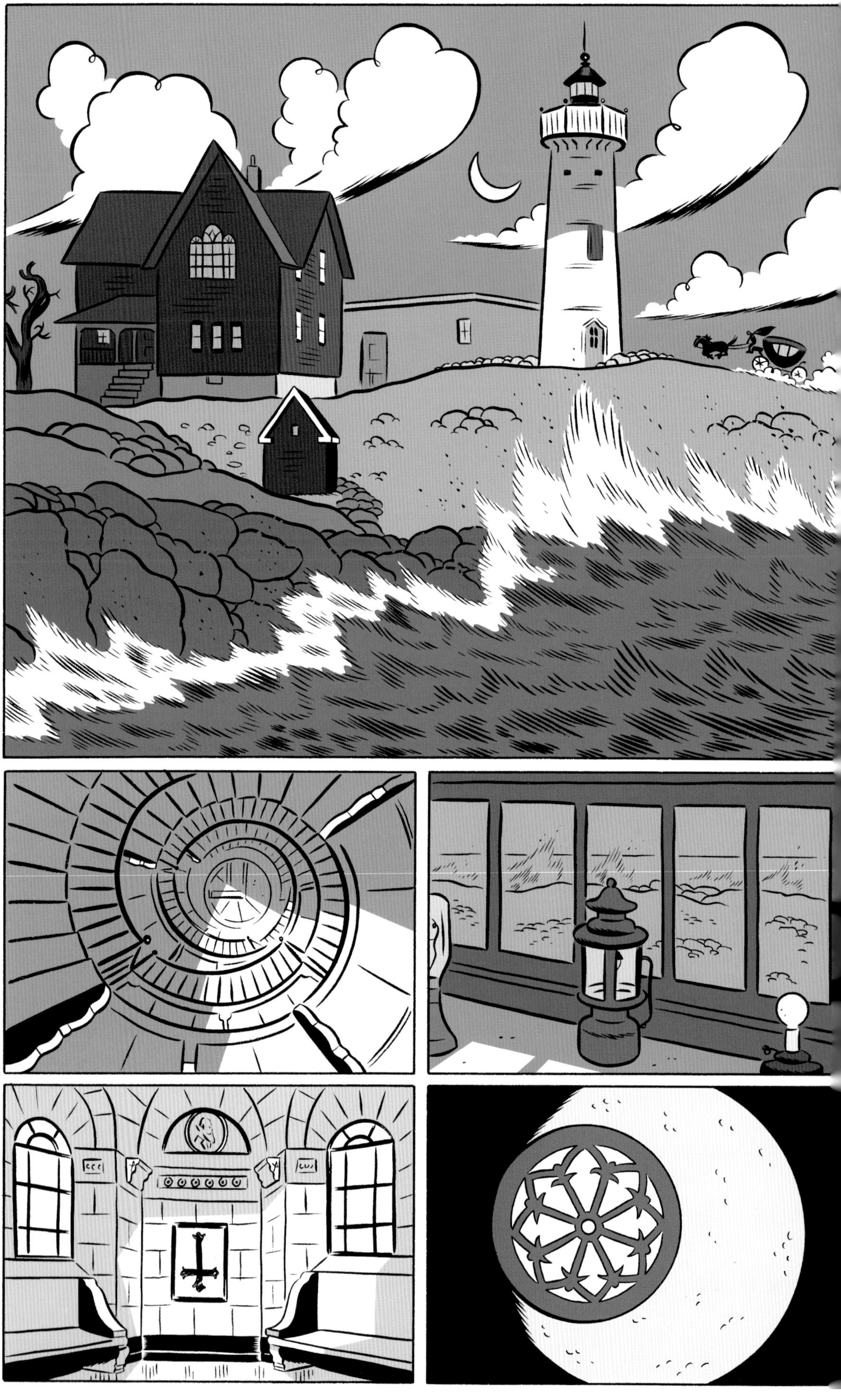

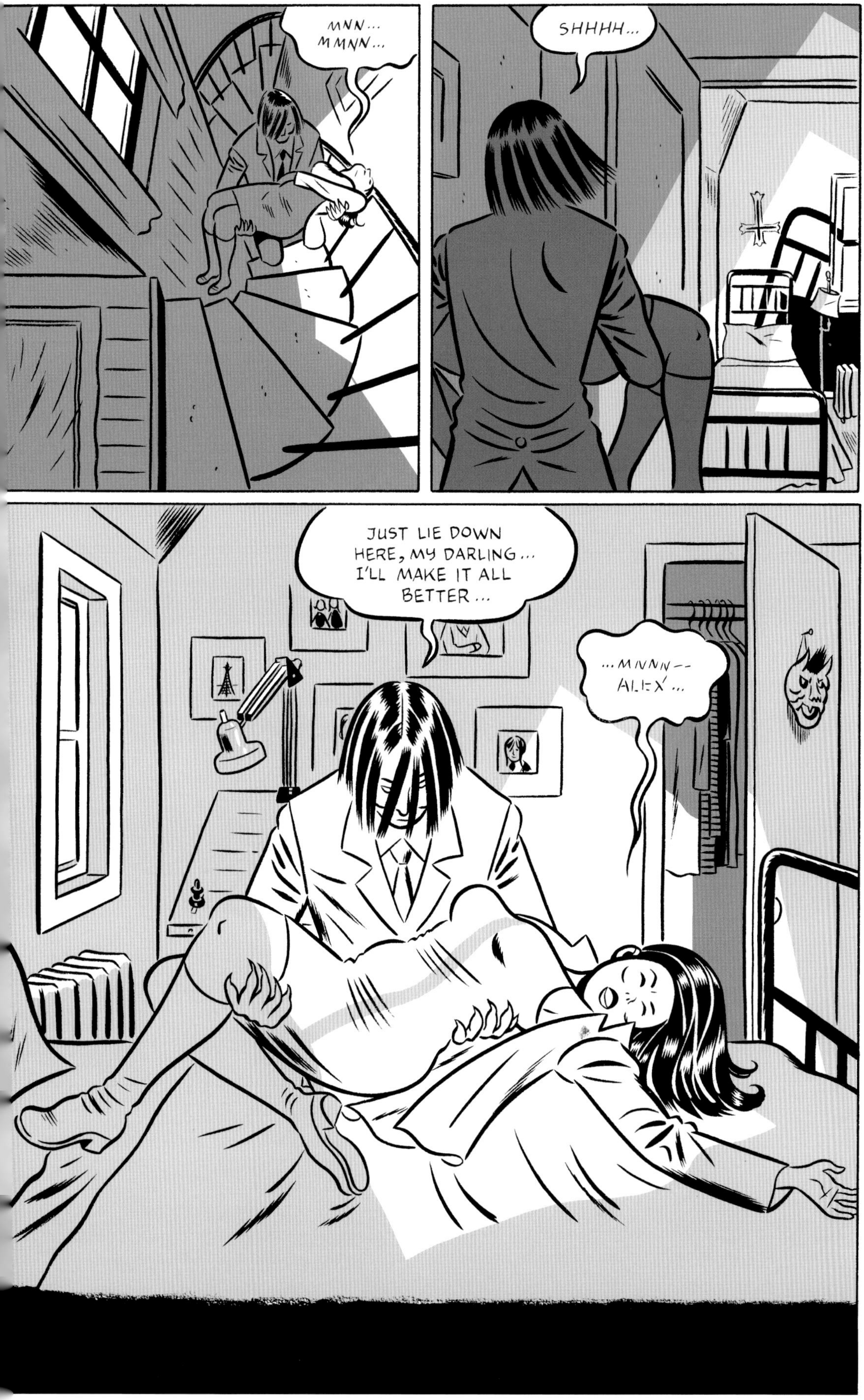
MNN...
MMNN...
SHHHH...
JUST LIE DOWN HERE, MY DARLING... I'LL MAKE IT ALL BETTER...
...MNNN--
ALEX...

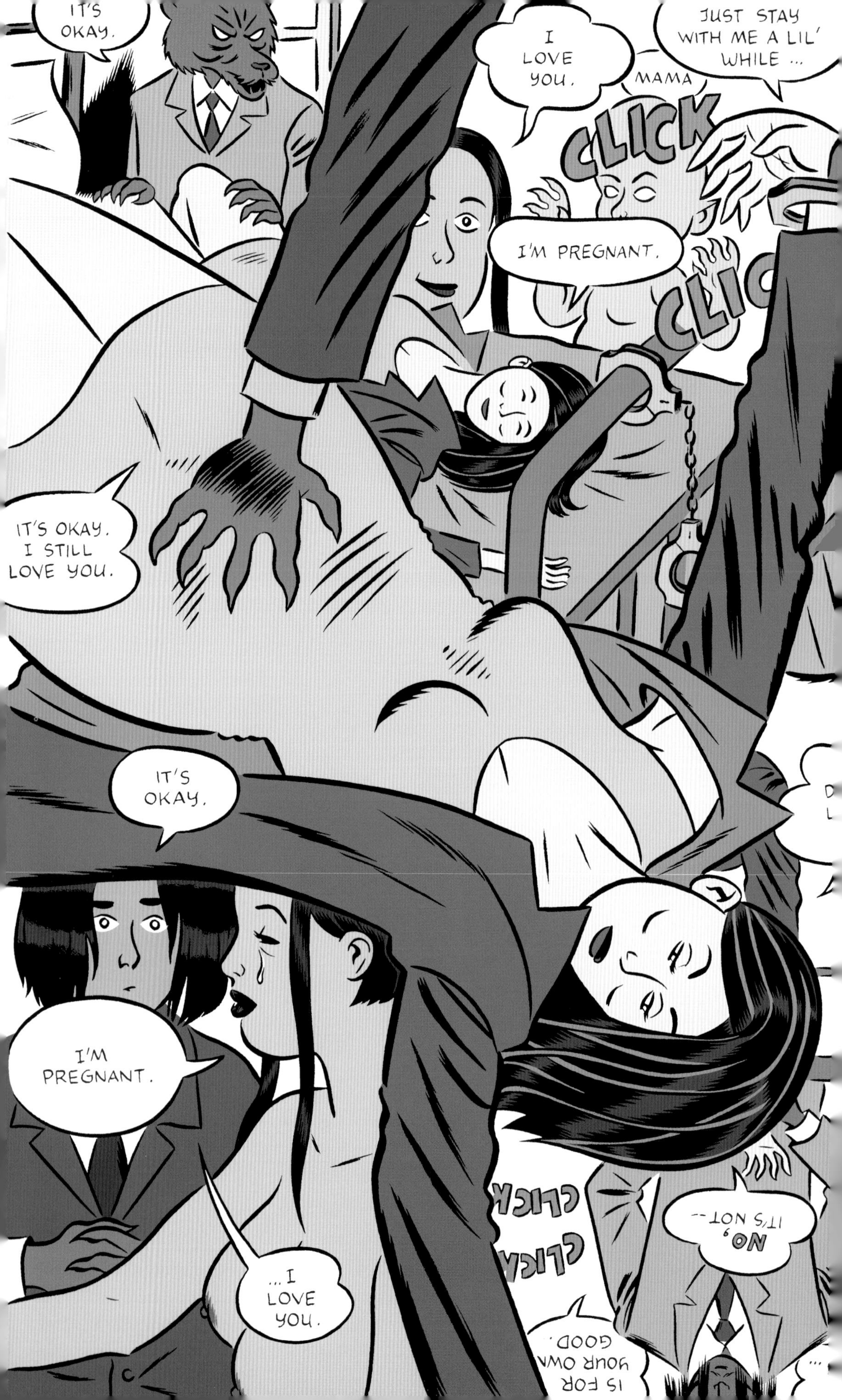
IT'S OKAY.
I LOVE YOU.
MAMA
JUST STAY WITH ME A LIL' WHILE ...
CLICK
I'M PREGNANT.
CLIC
IT'S OKAY. I STILL LOVE YOU.
IT'S OKAY.
I'M PREGNANT.
... I LOVE YOU.
CLICK
CLICK
NO, IT'S NOT--
IS FOR YOUR OWN GOOD.
...

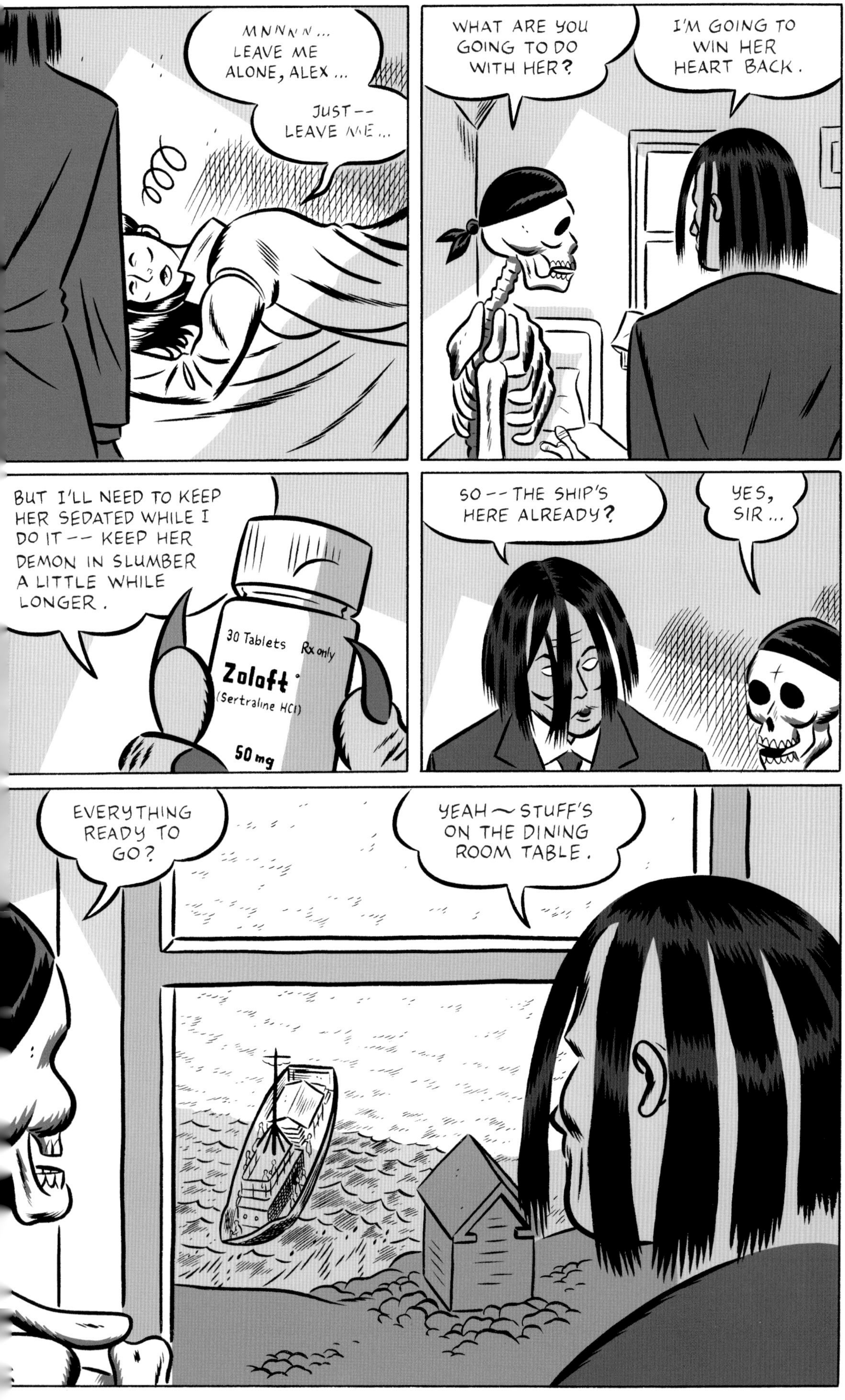
MNNNN... LEAVE ME ALONE, ALEX...
JUST-- LEAVE ME...
WHAT ARE YOU GOING TO DO WITH HER?
I'M GOING TO WIN HER HEART BACK.
BUT I'LL NEED TO KEEP HER SEDATED WHILE I DO IT -- KEEP HER DEMON IN SLUMBER A LITTLE WHILE LONGER.
30 Tablets
Rx only
Zoloft
(Sertraline HCl)
50 mg
SO -- THE SHIP'S HERE ALREADY?
YES, SIR...
EVERYTHING READY TO GO?
YEAH ~ STUFF'S ON THE DINING ROOM TABLE.

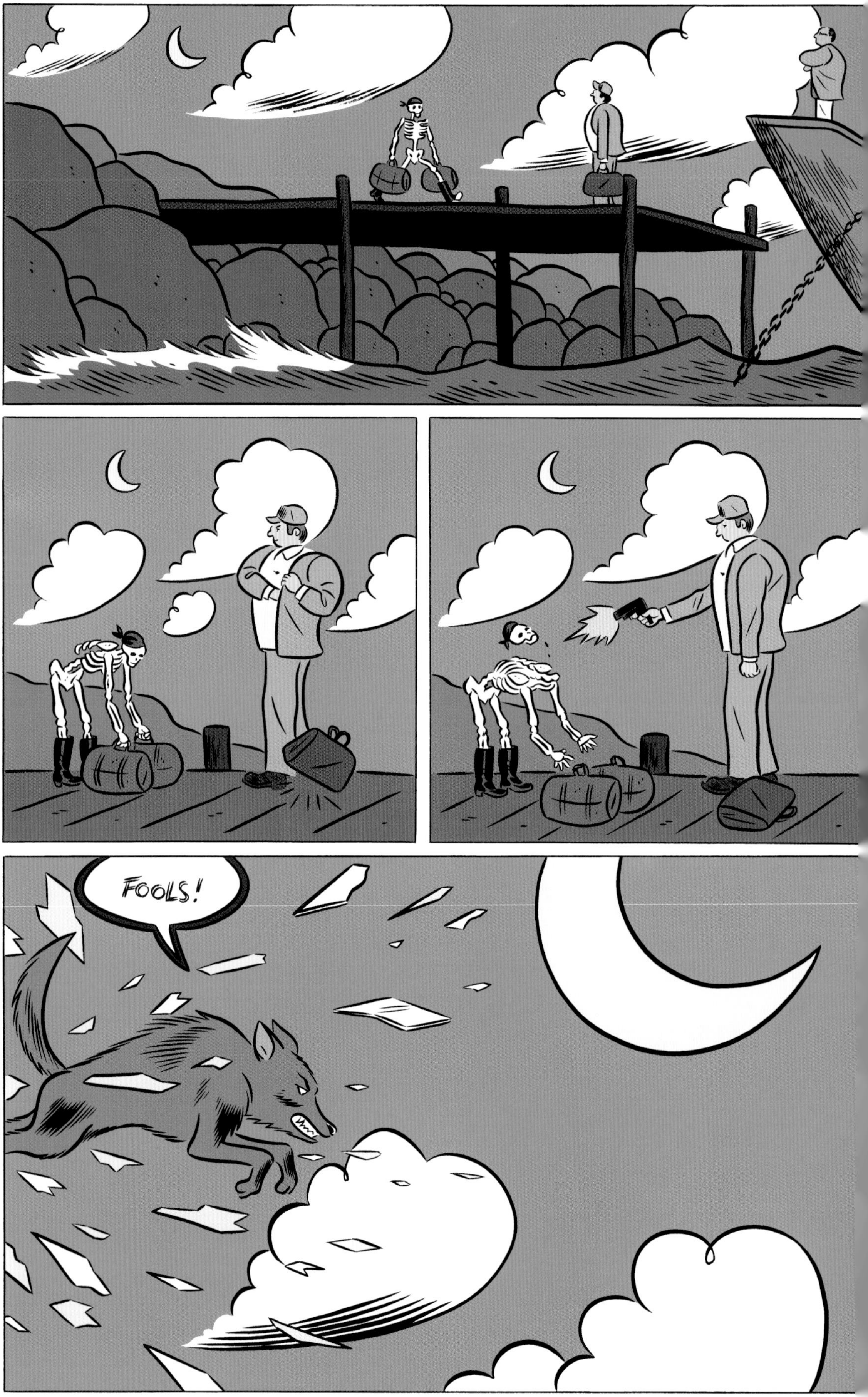
FOOLS!

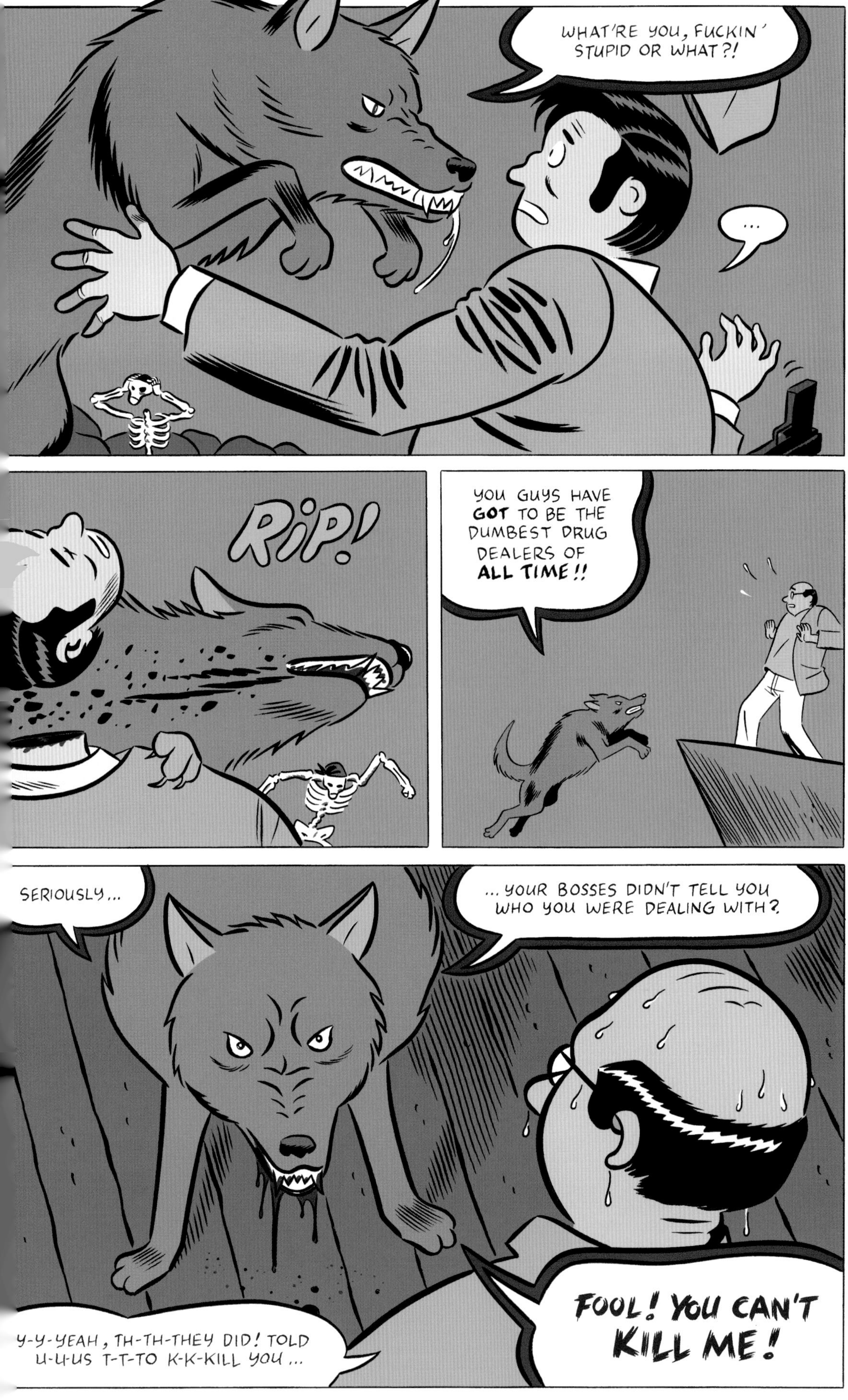
WHAT'RE YOU, FUCKIN' STUPID OR WHAT?!
...
RIP!
YOU GUYS HAVE GOT TO BE THE DUMBEST DRUG DEALERS OF ALL TIME!!
SERIOUSLY...
...YOUR BOSSES DIDN'T TELL YOU WHO YOU WERE DEALING WITH?
Y-Y-YEAH, TH-TH-THEY DID! TOLD U-U-US T-T-TO K-K-KILL YOU...
FOOL! YOU CAN'T KILL ME!

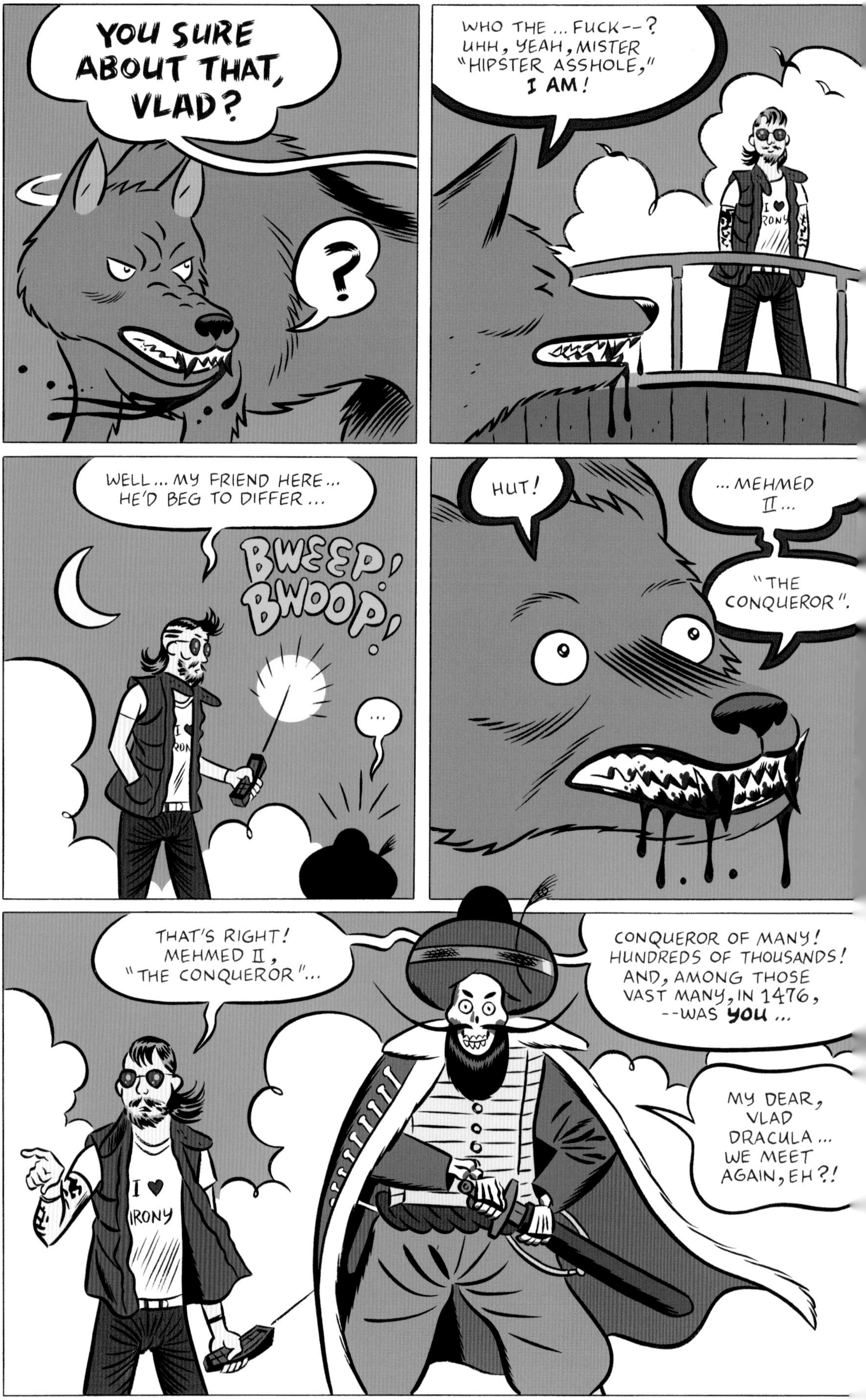
YOU SURE ABOUT THAT, VLAD?
?
WHO THE ... FUCK--? UHH, YEAH, MISTER "HIPSTER ASSHOLE," I AM!
I ♥ IRONY
WELL... MY FRIEND HERE... HE'D BEG TO DIFFER...
BWEEP! BWOOP!
...
HUT!
...MEHMED II...
"THE CONQUEROR".
THAT'S RIGHT! MEHMED II, "THE CONQUEROR"...
CONQUEROR OF MANY! HUNDREDS OF THOUSANDS! AND, AMONG THOSE VAST MANY, IN 1476, --WAS YOU...
MY DEAR, VLAD DRACULA... WE MEET AGAIN, EH?!
I ♥ IRONY

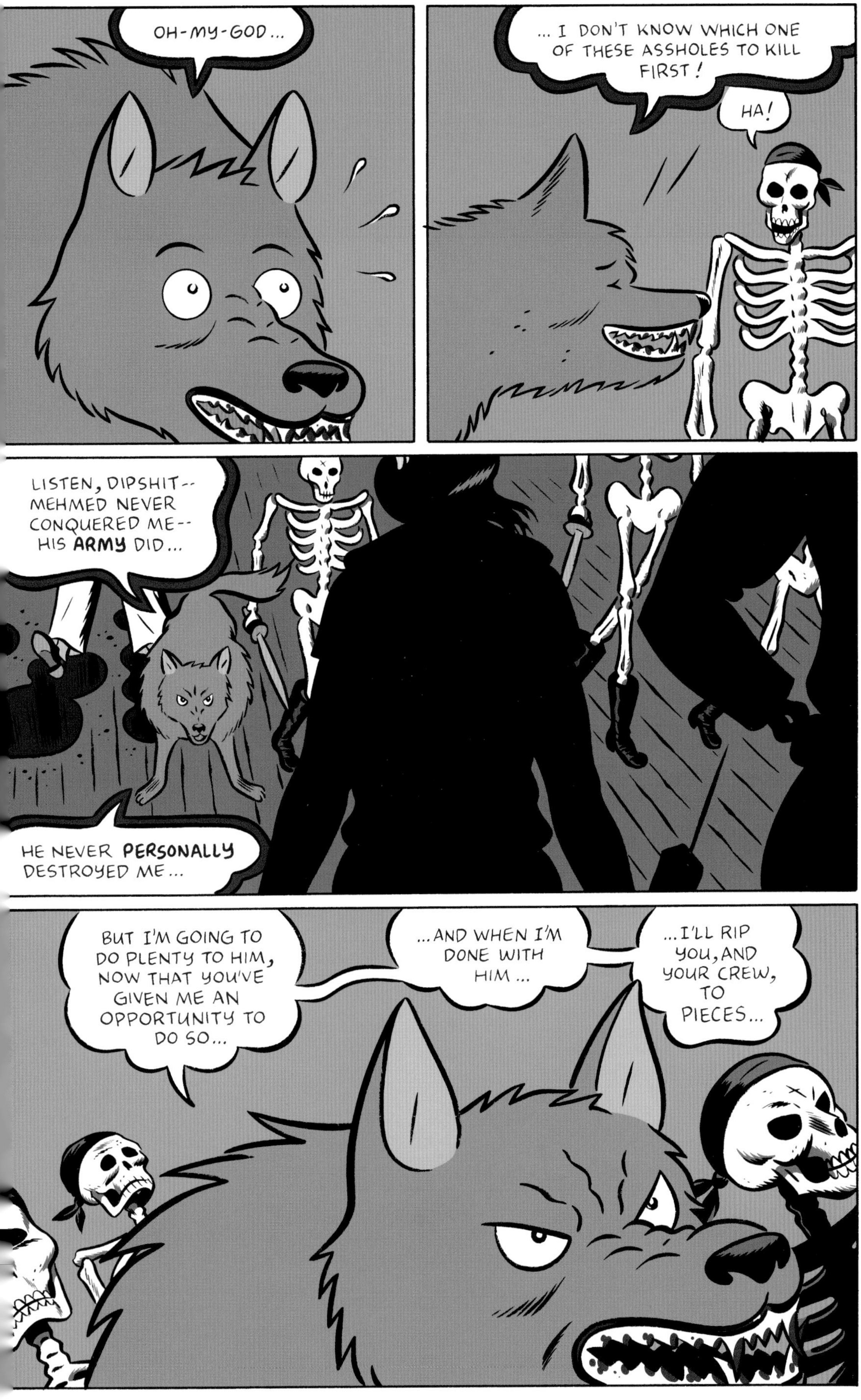
OH-MY-GOD...
...I DON'T KNOW WHICH ONE OF THESE ASSHOLES TO KILL FIRST!
HA!
LISTEN, DIPSHIT-- MEHMED NEVER CONQUERED ME-- HIS **ARMY** DID...
HE NEVER **PERSONALLY** DESTROYED ME...
BUT I'M GOING TO DO PLENTY TO HIM, NOW THAT YOU'VE GIVEN ME AN OPPORTUNITY TO DO SO...
...AND WHEN I'M DONE WITH HIM...
...I'LL RIP YOU, AND YOUR CREW, TO PIECES...

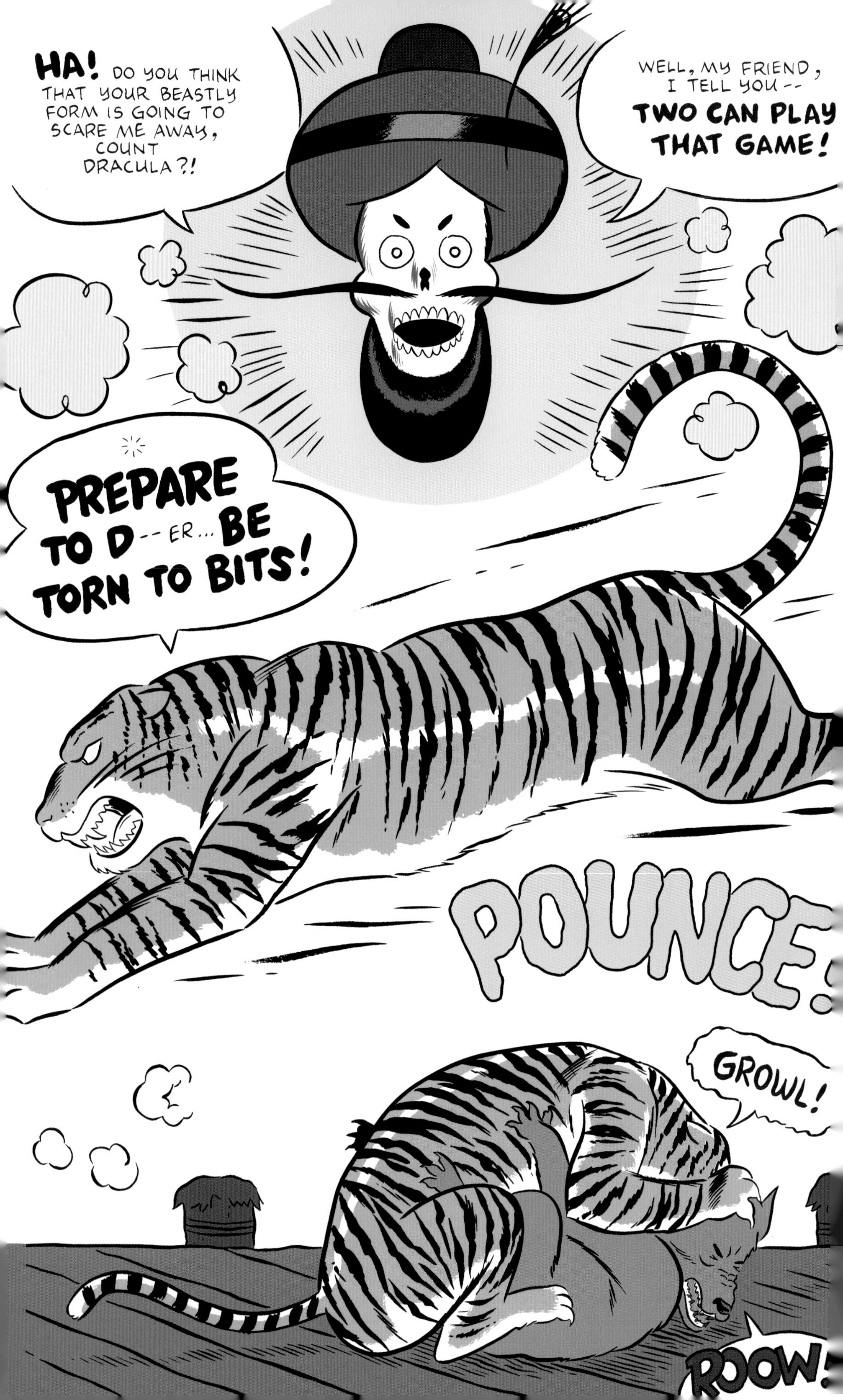
HA! DO YOU THINK THAT YOUR BEASTLY FORM IS GOING TO SCARE ME AWAY, COUNT DRACULA?!
WELL, MY FRIEND, I TELL YOU -- TWO CAN PLAY THAT GAME!
PREPARE TO D-- ER... BE TORN TO BITS!
POUNCE!
GROWL!
ROOW!

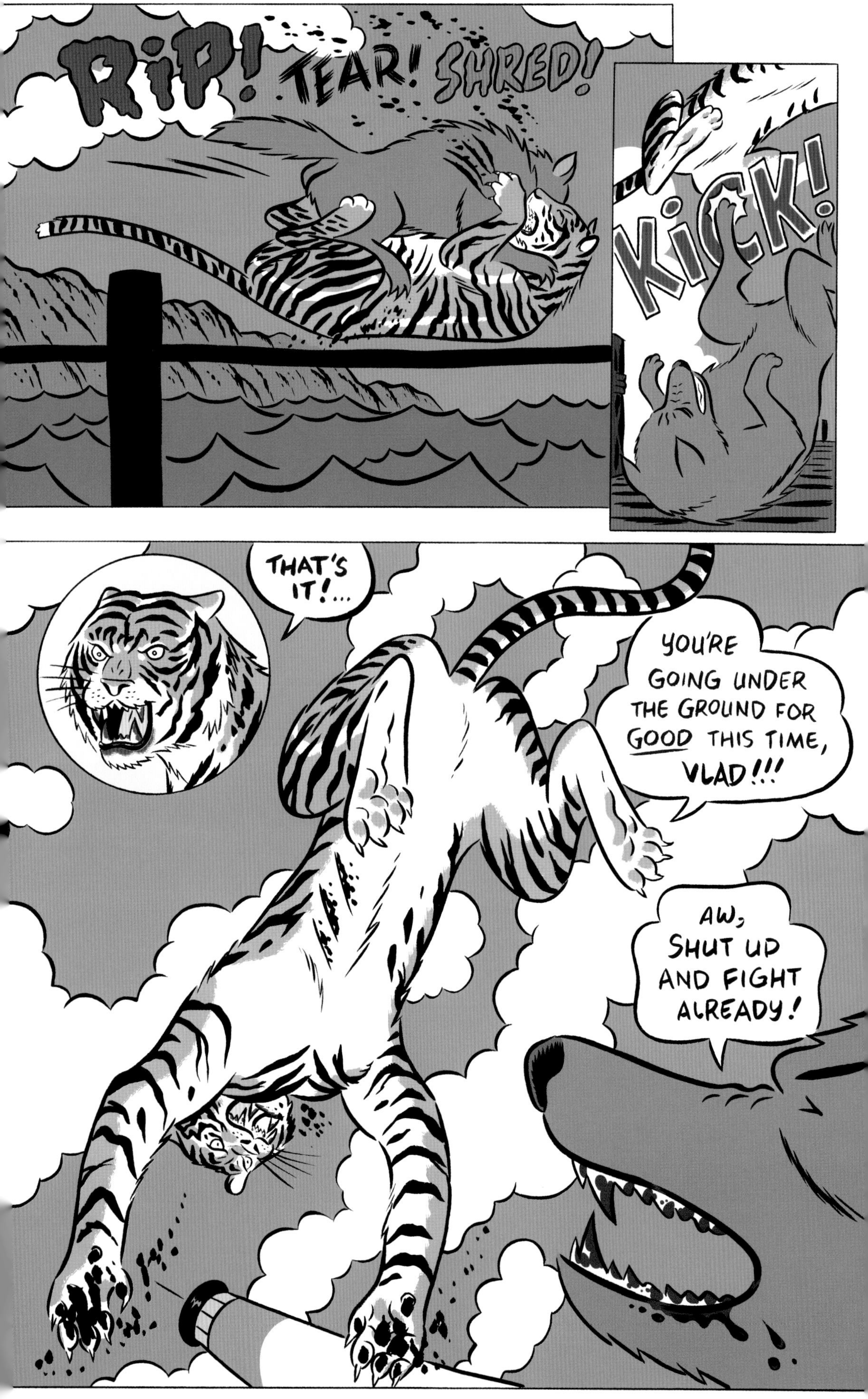
RIP! TEAR! SHRED!
KICK!
THAT'S IT!...
YOU'RE GOING UNDER THE GROUND FOR GOOD THIS TIME, VLAD!!!
AW, SHUT UP AND FIGHT ALREADY!

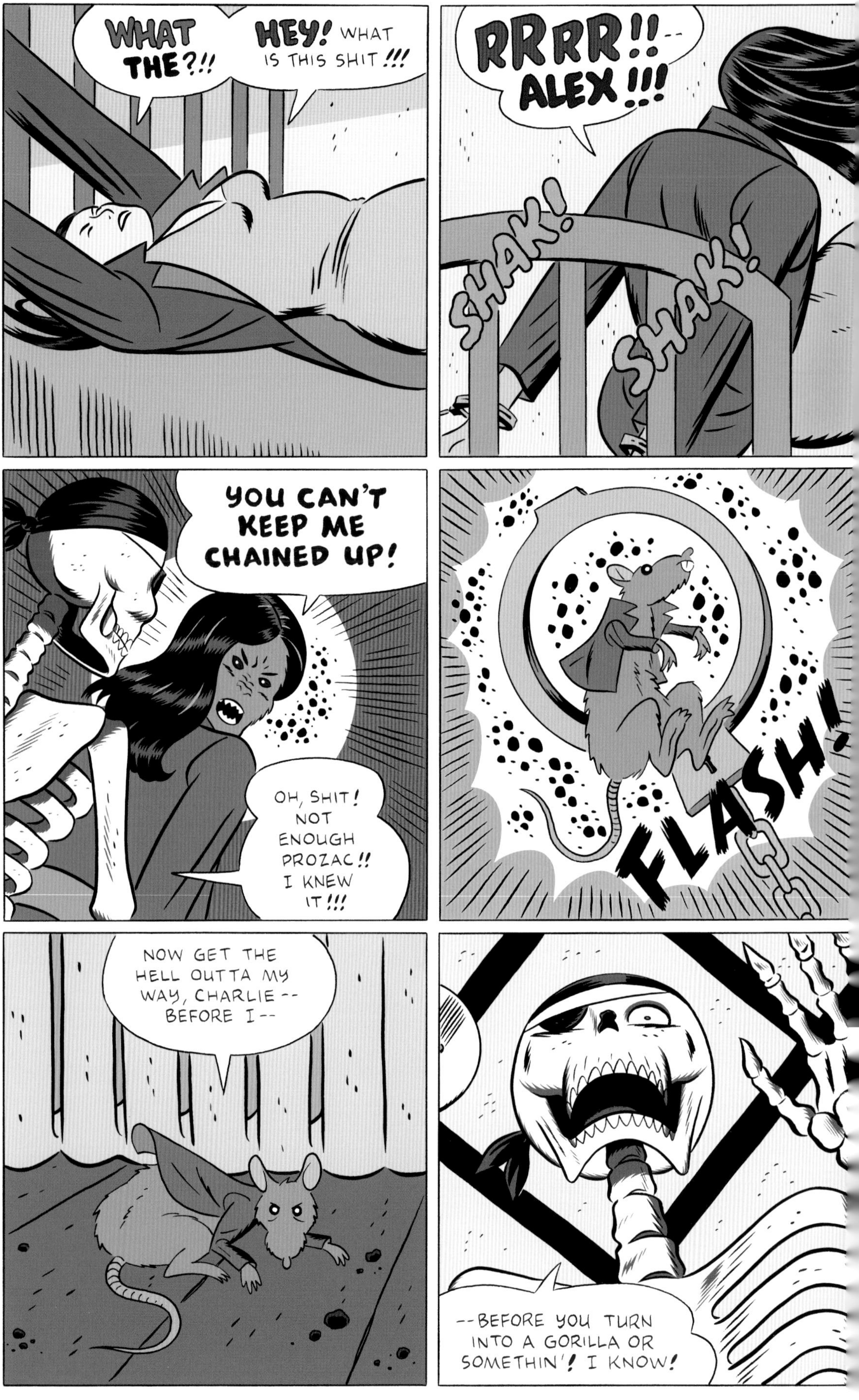
WHAT THE?!!
HEY! WHAT IS THIS SHIT!!!
RRRR!!-- ALEX!!!
SHAK!
SHAK!
YOU CAN'T KEEP ME CHAINED UP!
OH, SHIT! NOT ENOUGH PROZAC!! I KNEW IT!!!
FLASH!
NOW GET THE HELL OUTTA MY WAY, CHARLIE-- BEFORE I--
--BEFORE YOU TURN INTO A GORILLA OR SOMETHIN'! I KNOW!

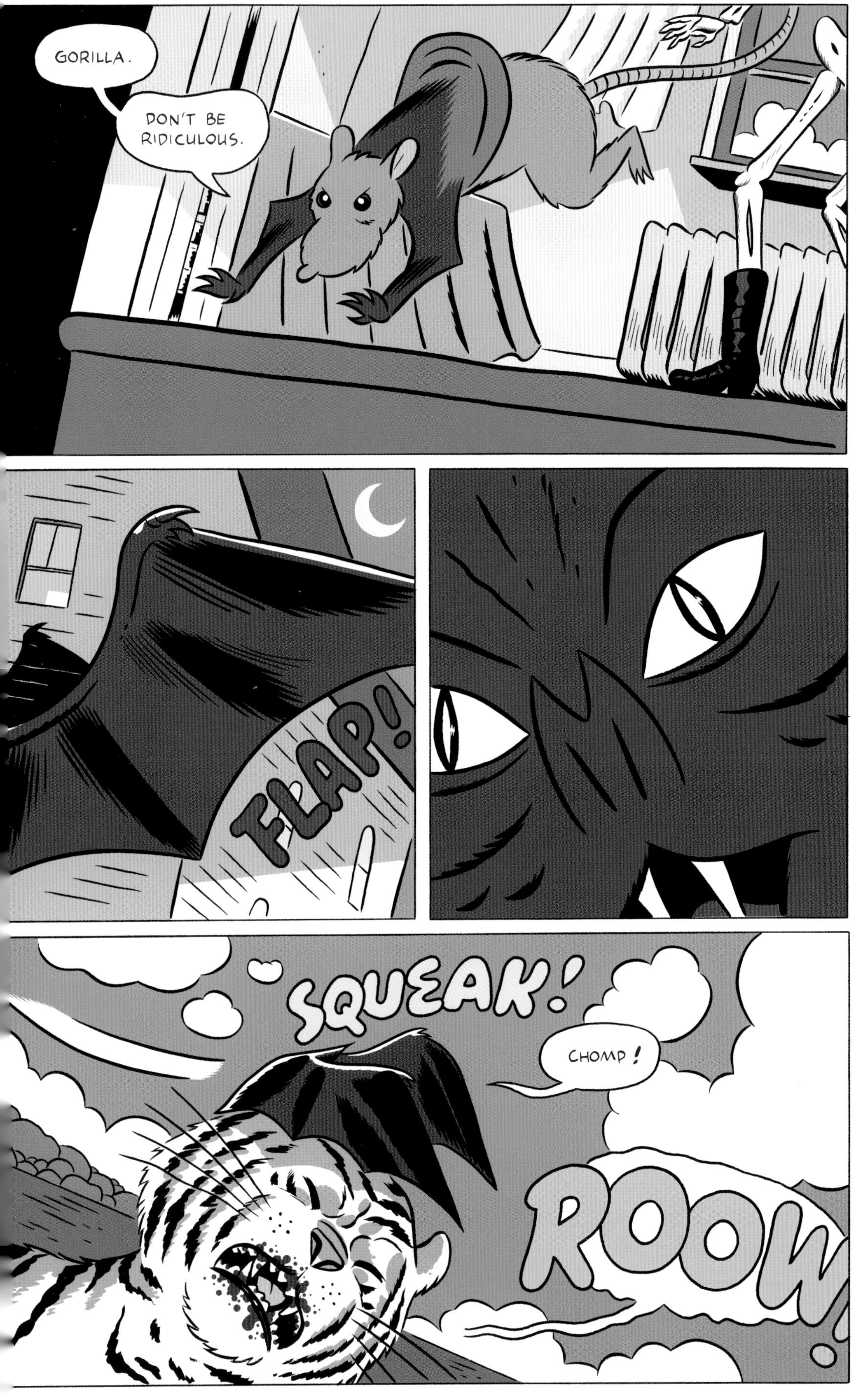
GORILLA.
DON'T BE RIDICULOUS.
FLAP!
SQUEAK!
CHOMP!
ROOW!

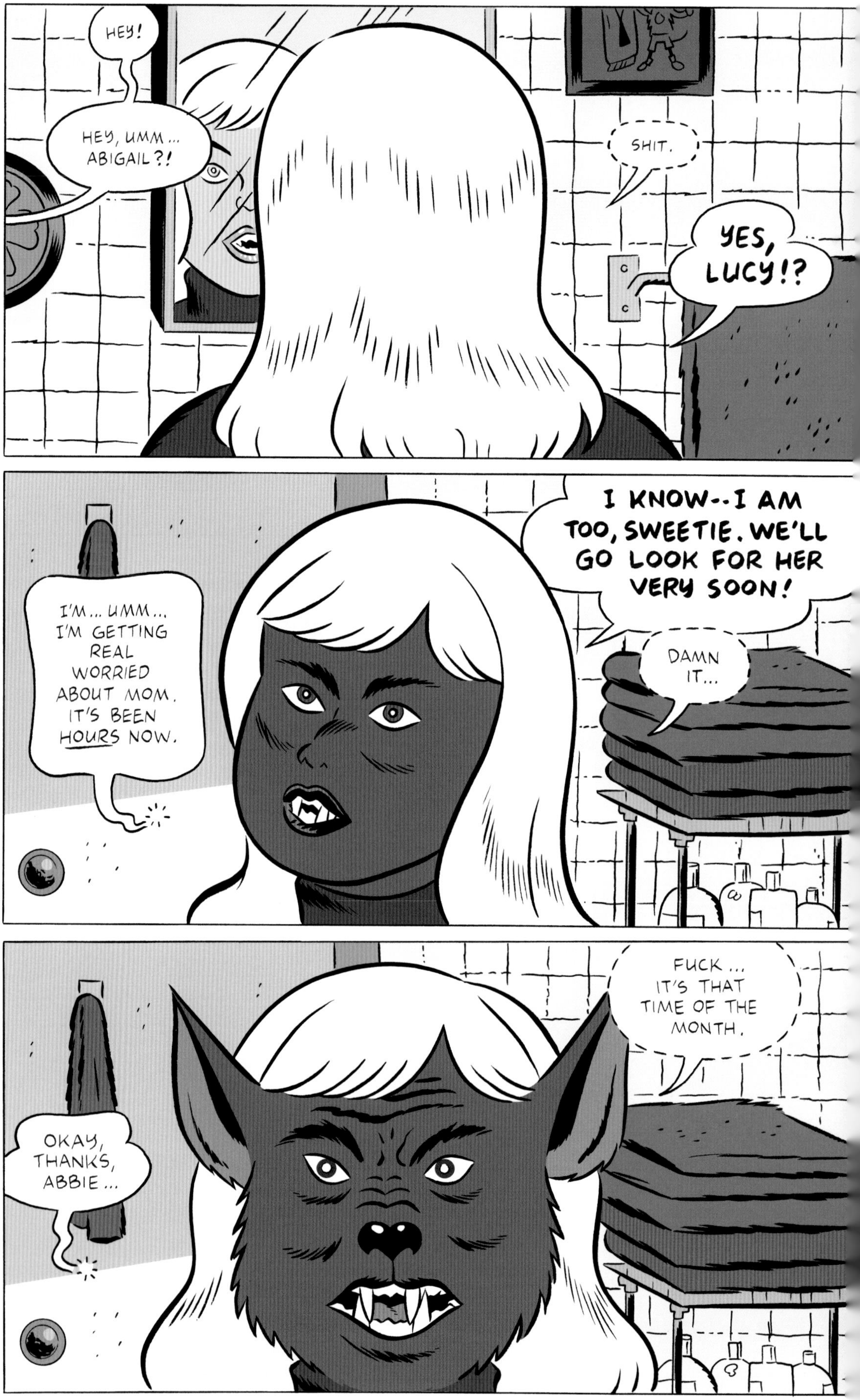

HEY!
HEY, UMM... ABIGAIL?!
SHIT.
YES, LUCY!?
I'M... UMM... I'M GETTING REAL WORRIED ABOUT MOM. IT'S BEEN HOURS NOW.
I KNOW--I AM TOO, SWEETIE. WE'LL GO LOOK FOR HER VERY SOON!
DAMN IT...
OKAY, THANKS, ABBIE...
FUCK... IT'S THAT TIME OF THE MONTH.

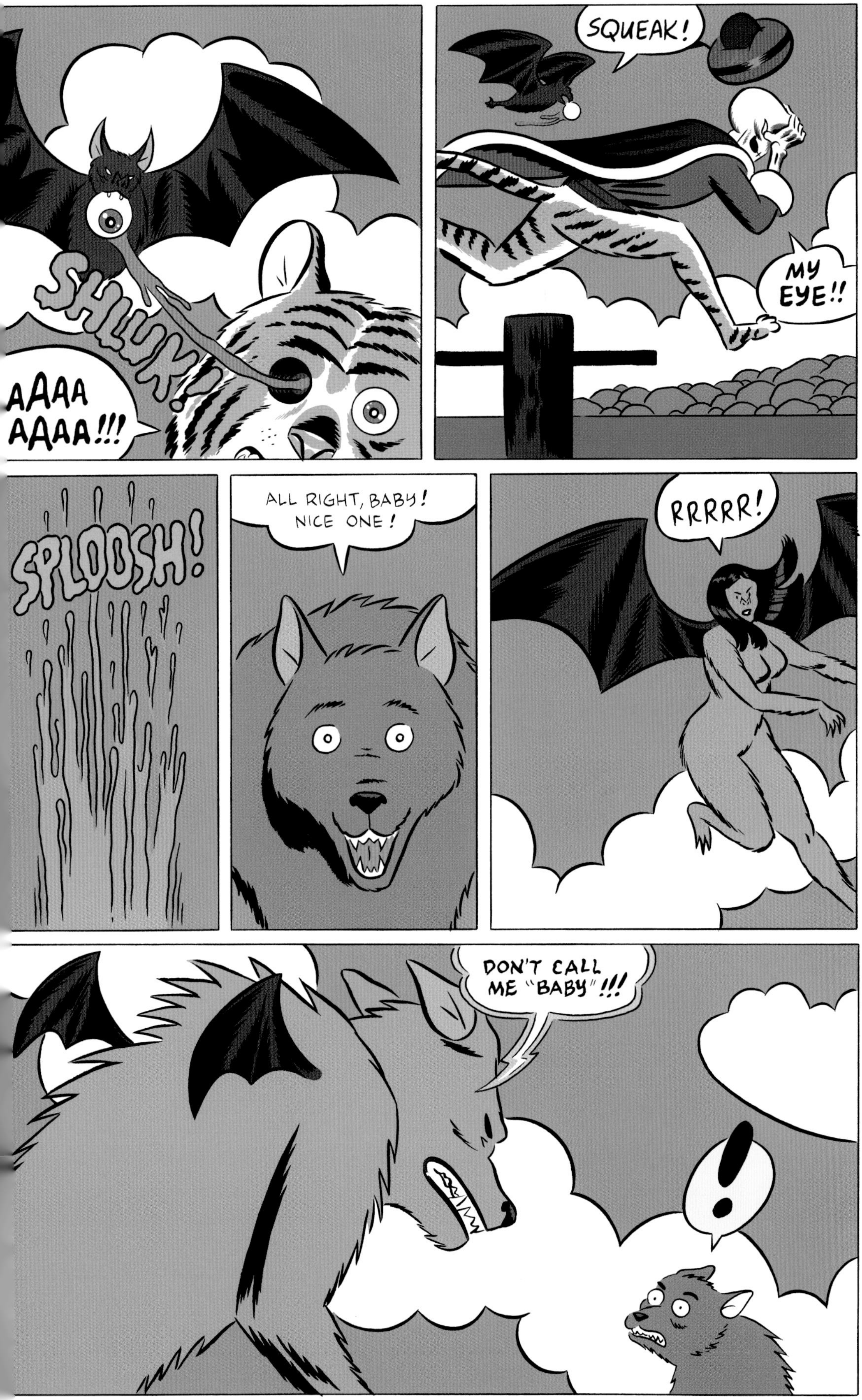
SHLUK!
AAAA AAAA!!!
SQUEAK!
MY EYE!!
SPLOOSH!
ALL RIGHT, BABY! NICE ONE!
RRRRR!
DON'T CALL ME "BABY"!!!
!

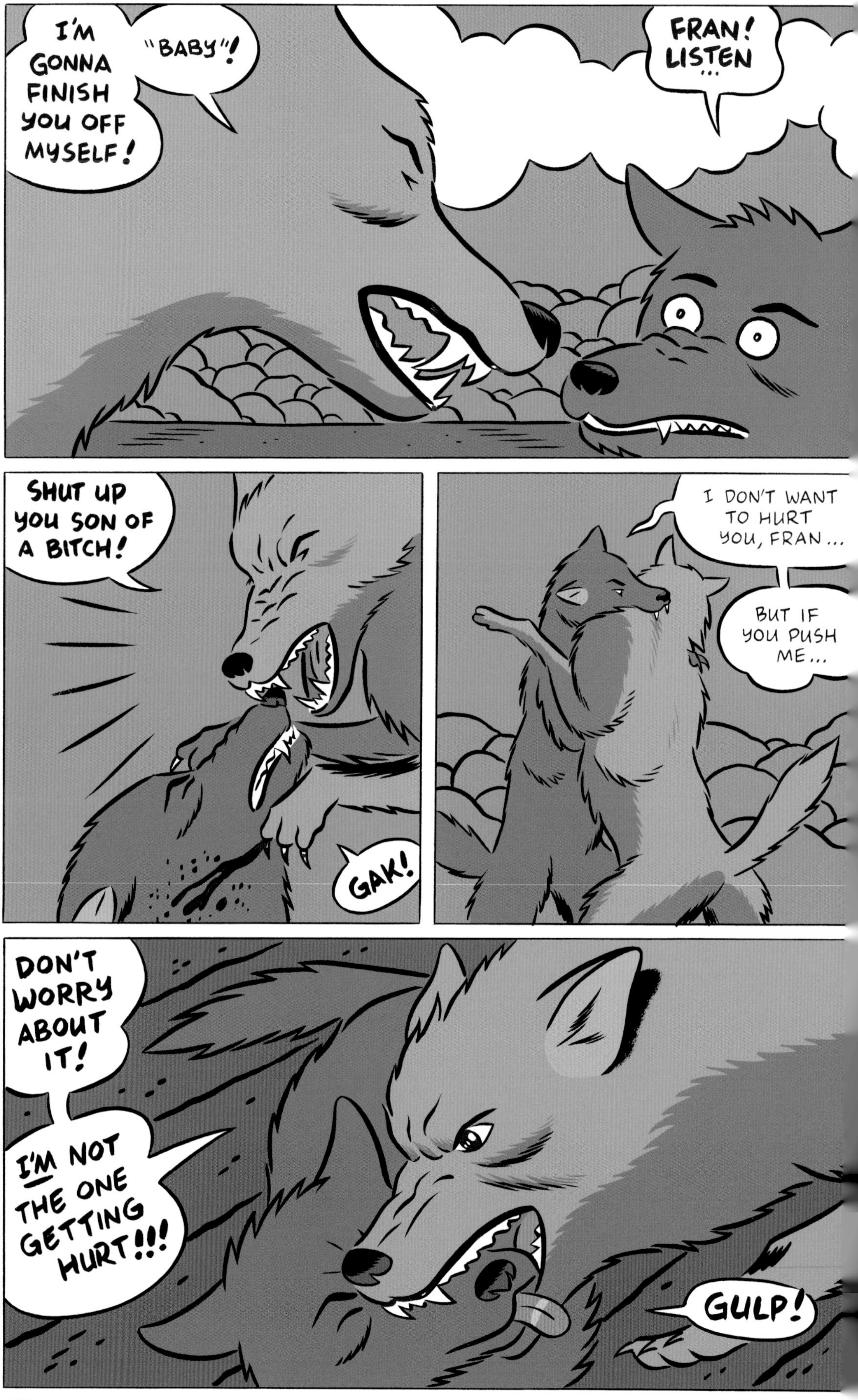

I'M GONNA FINISH YOU OFF MYSELF!
"BABY"!
FRAN! LISTEN...
SHUT UP YOU SON OF A BITCH!
GAK!
I DON'T WANT TO HURT YOU, FRAN...
BUT IF YOU PUSH ME...
DON'T WORRY ABOUT IT!
I'M NOT THE ONE GETTING HURT!!!
GULP!

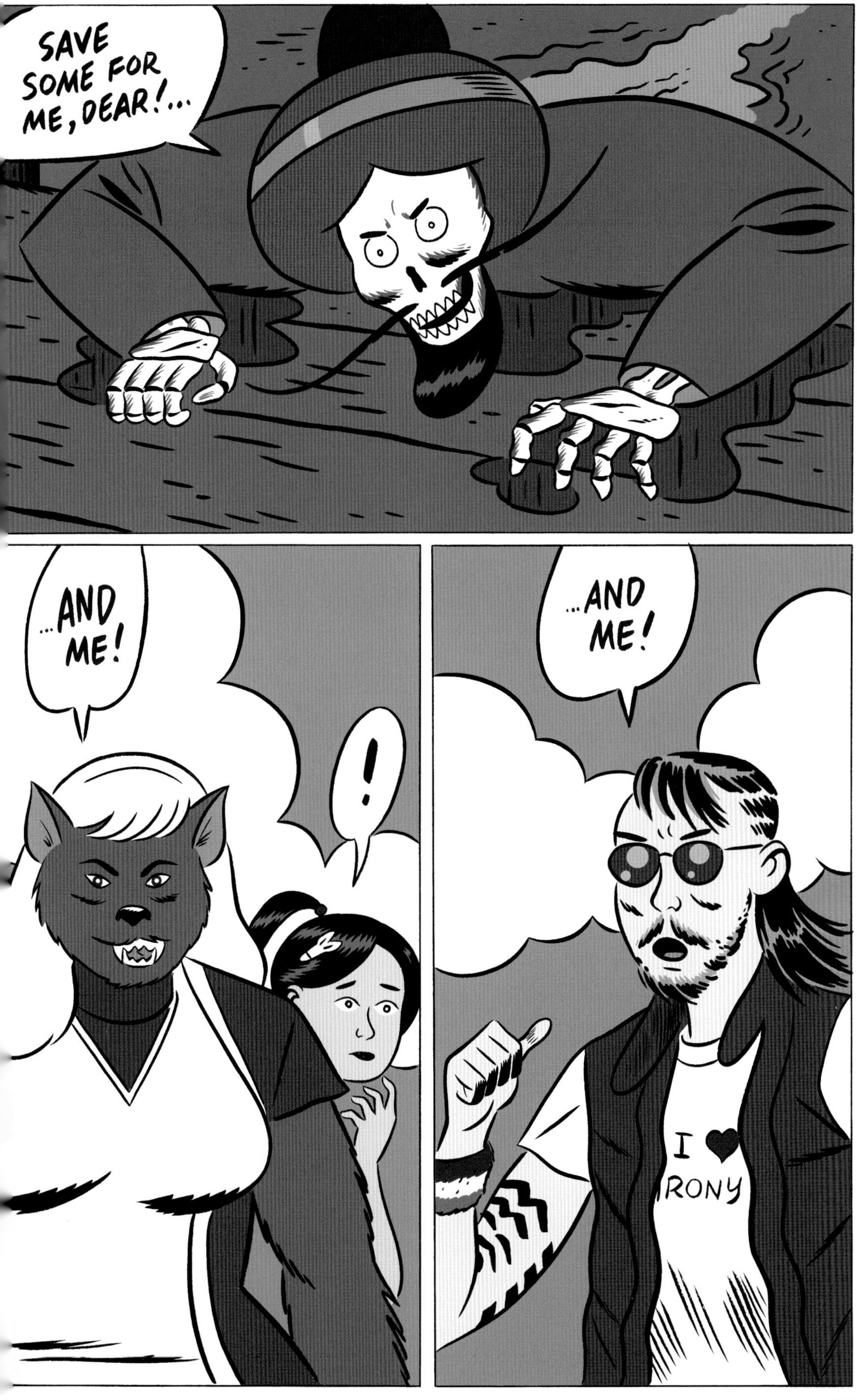
SAVE SOME FOR ME, DEAR!...
...AND ME!
!
...AND ME!
I ♥ RONY

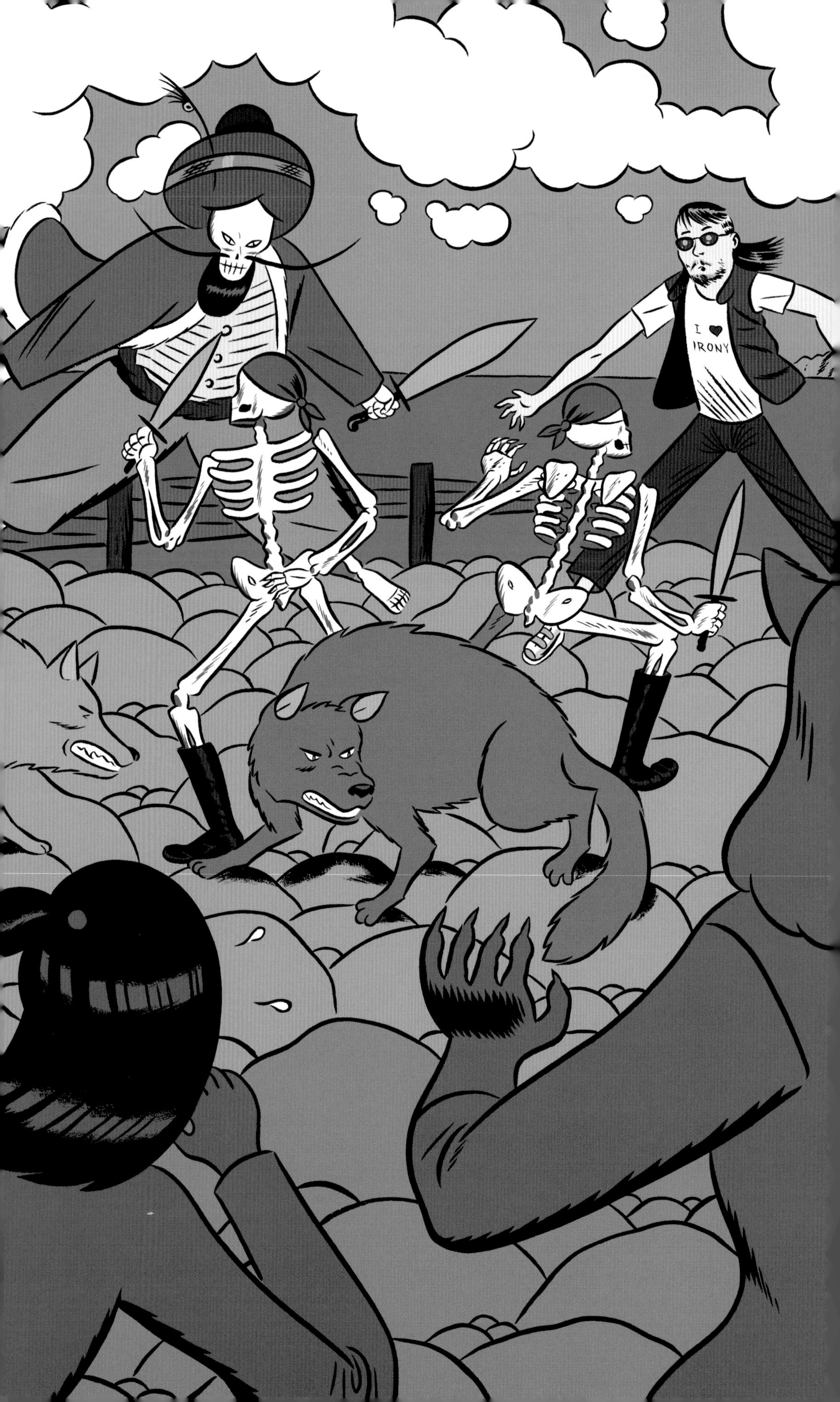
I ♥ IRONY

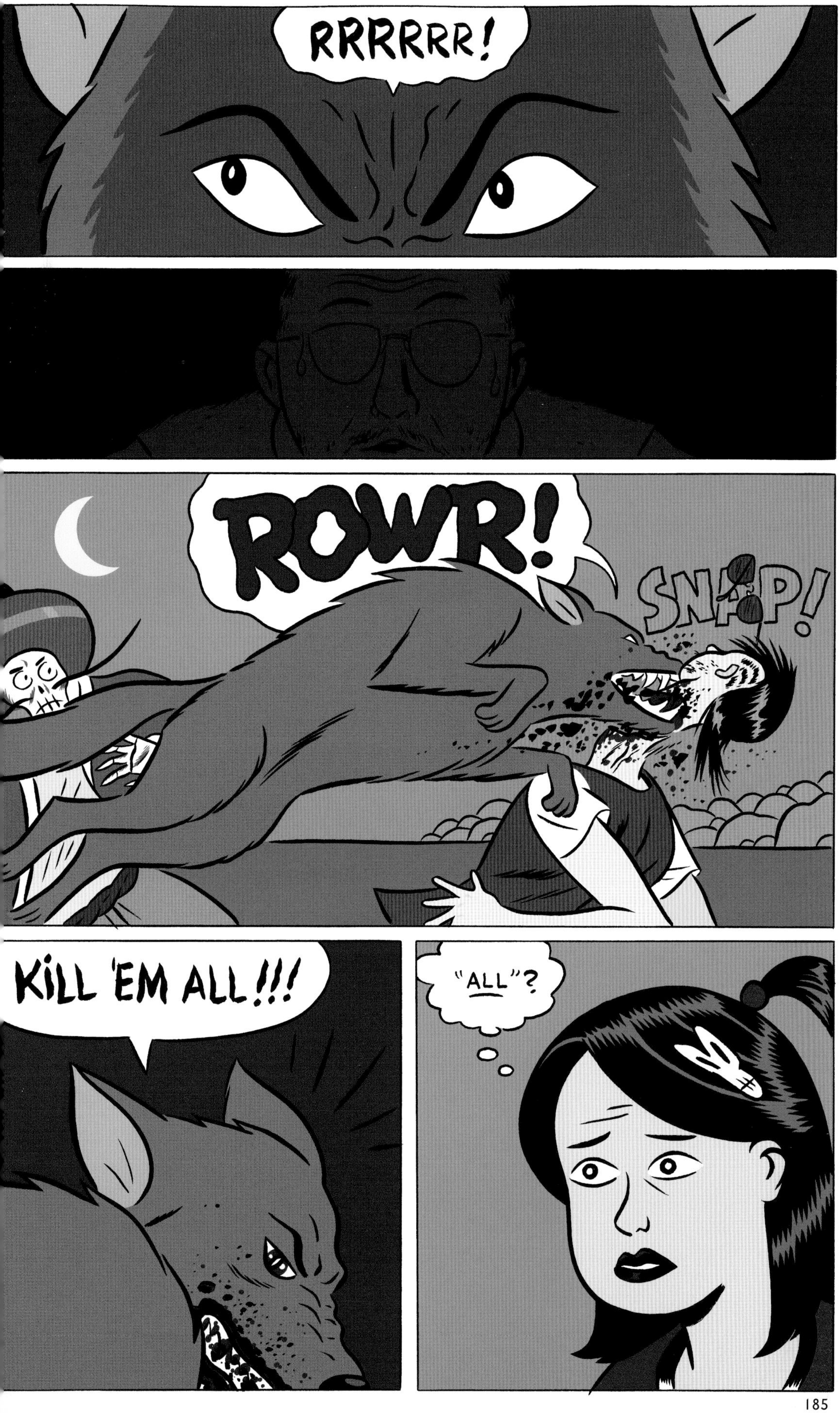
RRRRRR!
ROWR!
SNAP!
KILL 'EM ALL!!!
"ALL"?

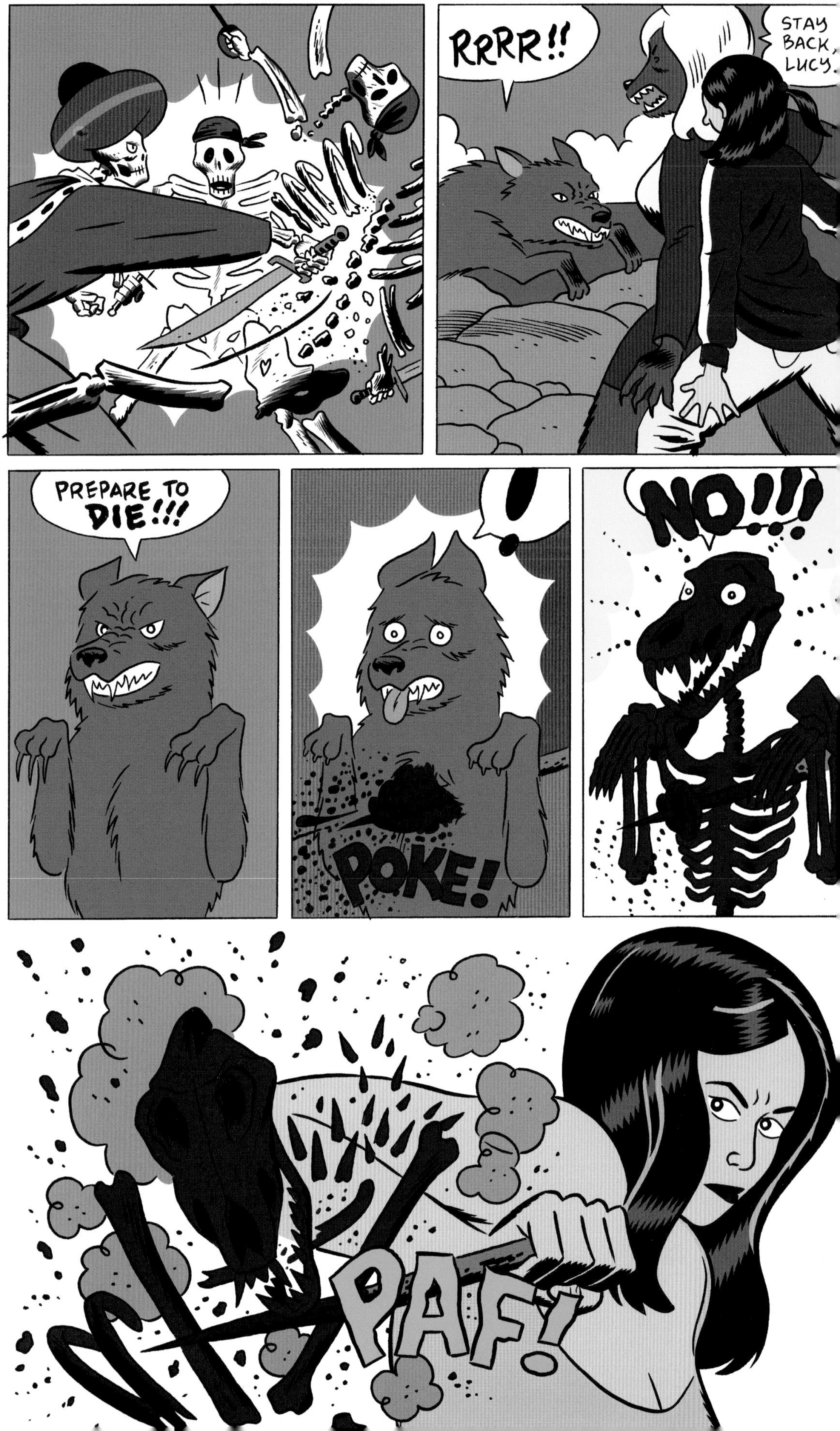
RRRR!!
STAY BACK, LUCY.
PREPARE TO DIE!!!
!
POKE!
NO!!!
PAF!

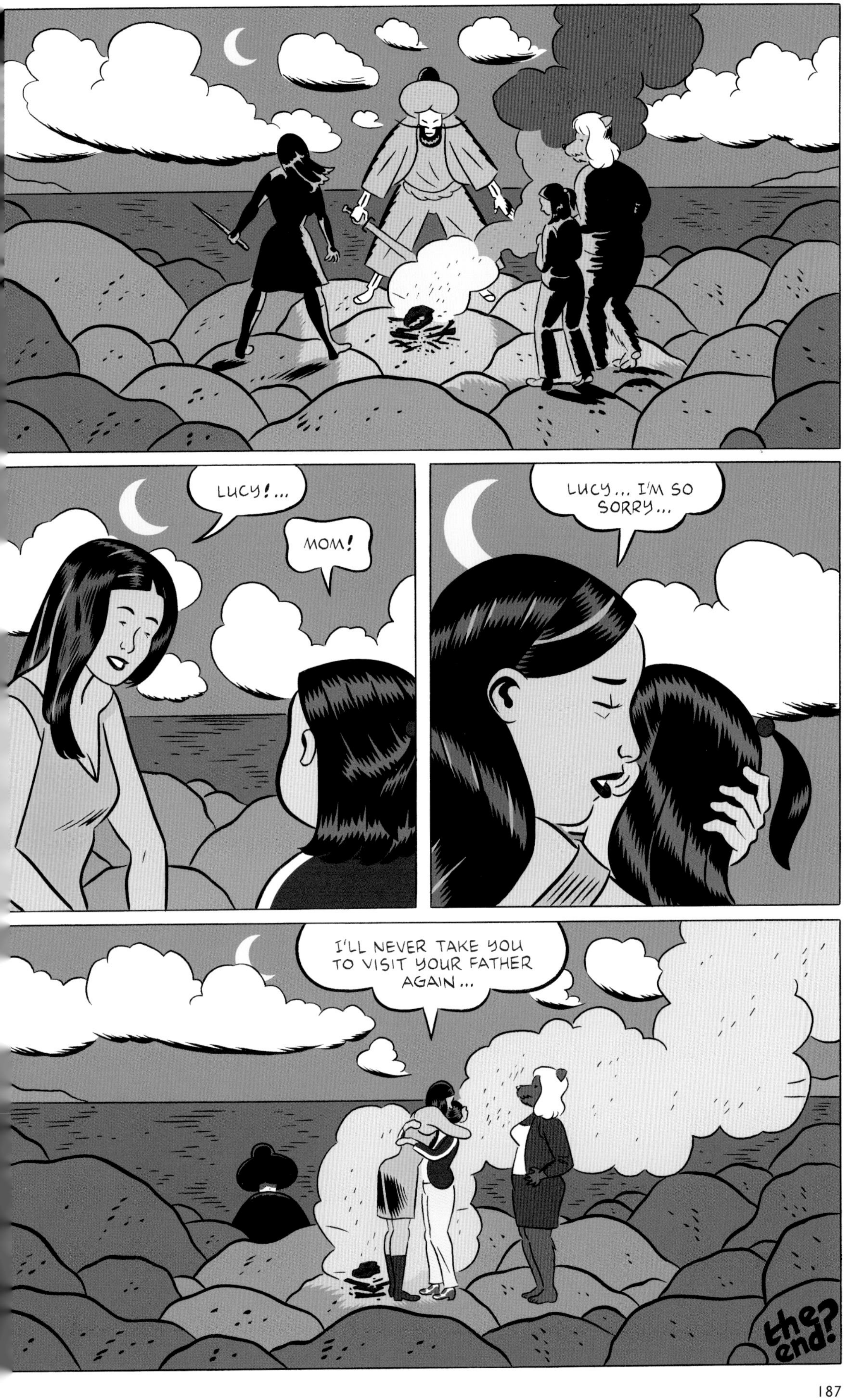
LUCY!...
MOM!
LUCY... I'M SO SORRY...
I'LL NEVER TAKE YOU TO VISIT YOUR FATHER AGAIN...
the end?

SPECIAL FEATURES

FRAN and VLAD DRACUL (or ALEX) in their debut comic book series from 1993:

CANNIBAL PORN

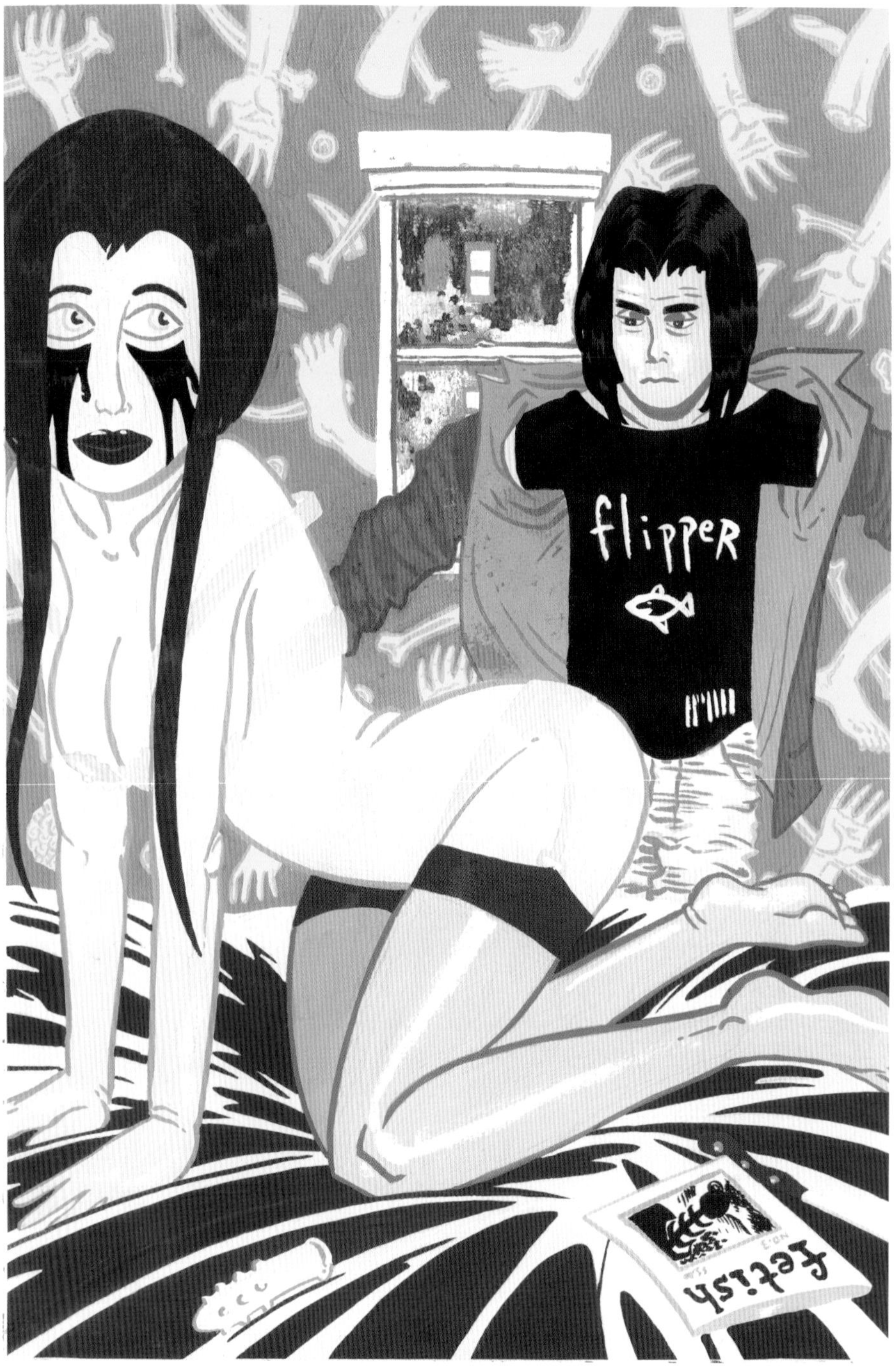
flipper
fetish

Published by Eros Comix as a three issue mini-series.

DELETED SCENE :

This man vs. beast scene was just too silly, so I cut it.

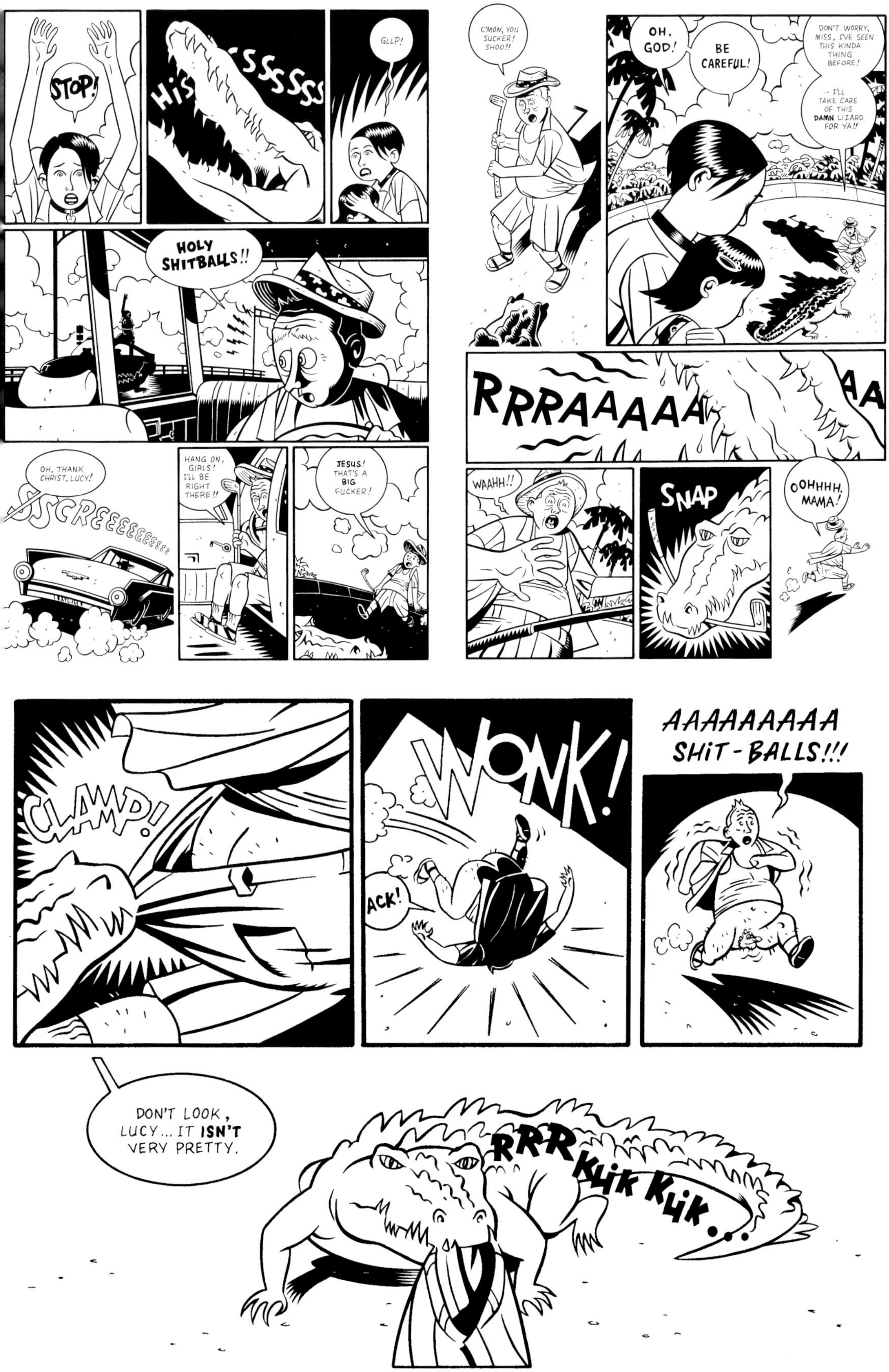
STOP!
HISSSSSSSS
GLLP!
HOLY SHITBALLS!!
OH, THANK CHRIST, LUCY!
SSCREEEEEEEEEEE
HANG ON, GIRLS! I'LL BE RIGHT THERE!!
JESUS! THAT'S A BIG FUCKER!
C'MON, YOU SUCKER! SHOO!!
OH, GOD!
BE CAREFUL!
DON'T WORRY, MISS, I'VE SEEN THIS KINDA THING BEFORE!
-- I'LL TAKE CARE OF THIS DAMN LIZARD FOR YA!!
RRRAAAAAA
AA
WAAHH!!
SNAP
OOHHHH, MAMA!
CLAMP!
WONK!
ACK!
AAAAAAAAA SHIT-BALLS!!!
DON'T LOOK, LUCY... IT ISN'T VERY PRETTY.
RRRKLIK KLIK...

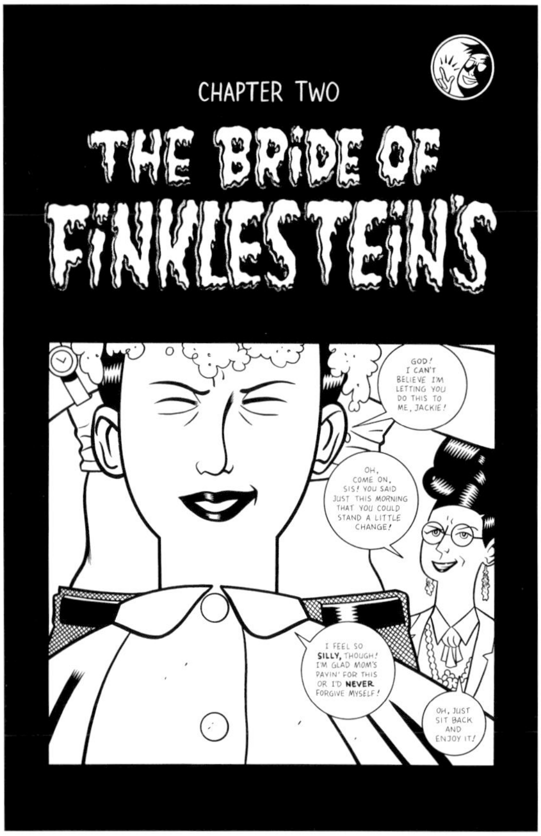
CHAPTER TWO
THE BRIDE OF FINKLESTEIN'S
GOD! I CAN'T BELIEVE I'M LETTING YOU DO THIS TO ME, JACKIE!
OH, COME ON, SIS! YOU SAID JUST THIS MORNING THAT YOU COULD STAND A LITTLE CHANGE!
I FEEL SO SILLY, THOUGH! I'M GLAD MOM'S PAYIN' FOR THIS OR I'D NEVER FORGIVE MYSELF!
OH, JUST SIT BACK AND ENJOY IT!

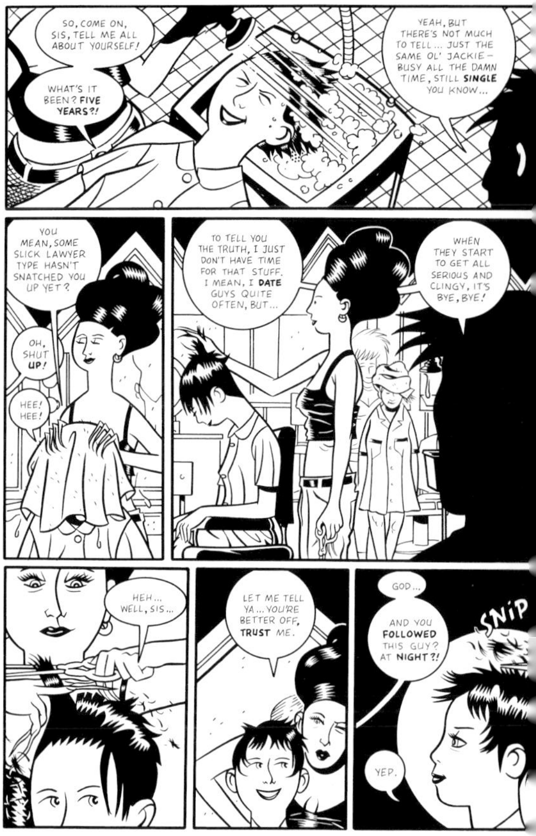
SO, COME ON, SIS, TELL ME ALL ABOUT YOURSELF!
WHAT'S IT BEEN? FIVE YEARS?!
YEAH, BUT THERE'S NOT MUCH TO TELL... JUST THE SAME OL' JACKIE — BUSY ALL THE DAMN TIME, STILL SINGLE YOU KNOW...
YOU MEAN, SOME SLICK LAWYER TYPE HASN'T SNATCHED YOU UP YET?
OH, SHUT UP!
HEE! HEE!
TO TELL YOU THE TRUTH, I JUST DON'T HAVE TIME FOR THAT STUFF. I MEAN, I DATE GUYS QUITE OFTEN, BUT...
WHEN THEY START TO GET ALL SERIOUS AND CLINGY, IT'S BYE, BYE!
HEH... WELL, SIS...
LET ME TELL YA... YOU'RE BETTER OFF, TRUST ME.
GOD...
AND YOU FOLLOWED THIS GUY? AT NIGHT?!
SNIP
YEP.

DELETED ISSUE : The story was heading in a ridiculous direction by the time I started on this early version of issue two. After seventeen pages, I chose a better path than this.

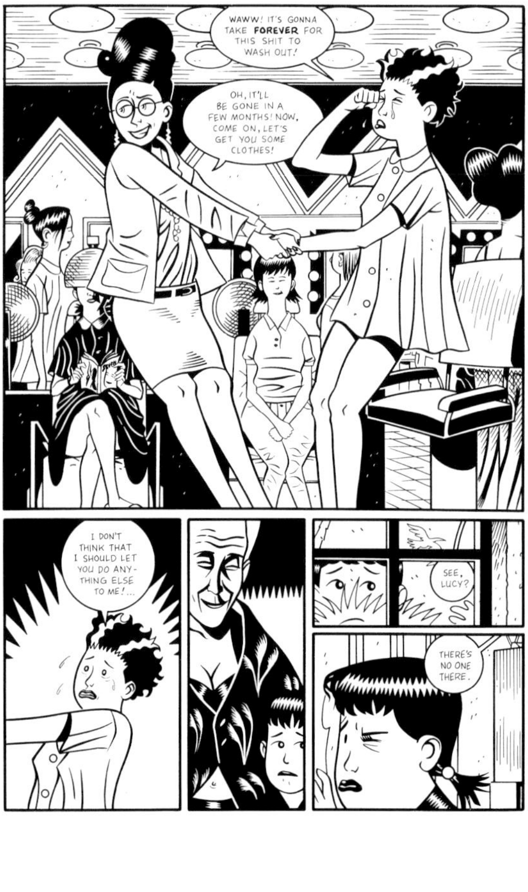
WAWW! IT'S GONNA TAKE FOREVER FOR THIS SHIT TO WASH OUT!
OH, IT'LL BE GONE IN A FEW MONTHS! NOW, COME ON, LET'S GET YOU SOME CLOTHES!
I DON'T THINK THAT I SHOULD LET YOU DO ANY-THING ELSE TO ME!...
SEE, LUCY?
THERE'S NO ONE THERE.

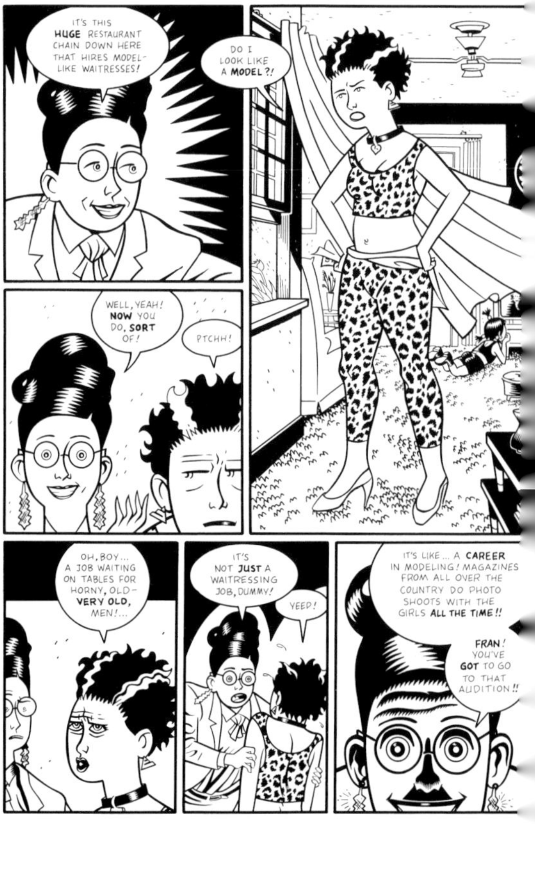
IT'S THIS HUGE RESTAURANT CHAIN DOWN HERE THAT HIRES MODEL-LIKE WAITRESSES!
DO I LOOK LIKE A MODEL?!
WELL, YEAH! NOW YOU DO, SORT OF!
PTCHH!
OH, BOY... A JOB WAITING ON TABLES FOR HORNY, OLD — VERY OLD, MEN!...
IT'S NOT JUST A WAITRESSING JOB, DUMMY!
YEEP!
IT'S LIKE... A CAREER IN MODELING! MAGAZINES FROM ALL OVER THE COUNTRY DO PHOTO SHOOTS WITH THE GIRLS ALL THE TIME!!
FRAN! YOU'VE GOT TO GO TO THAT AUDITION!!

COVER ART

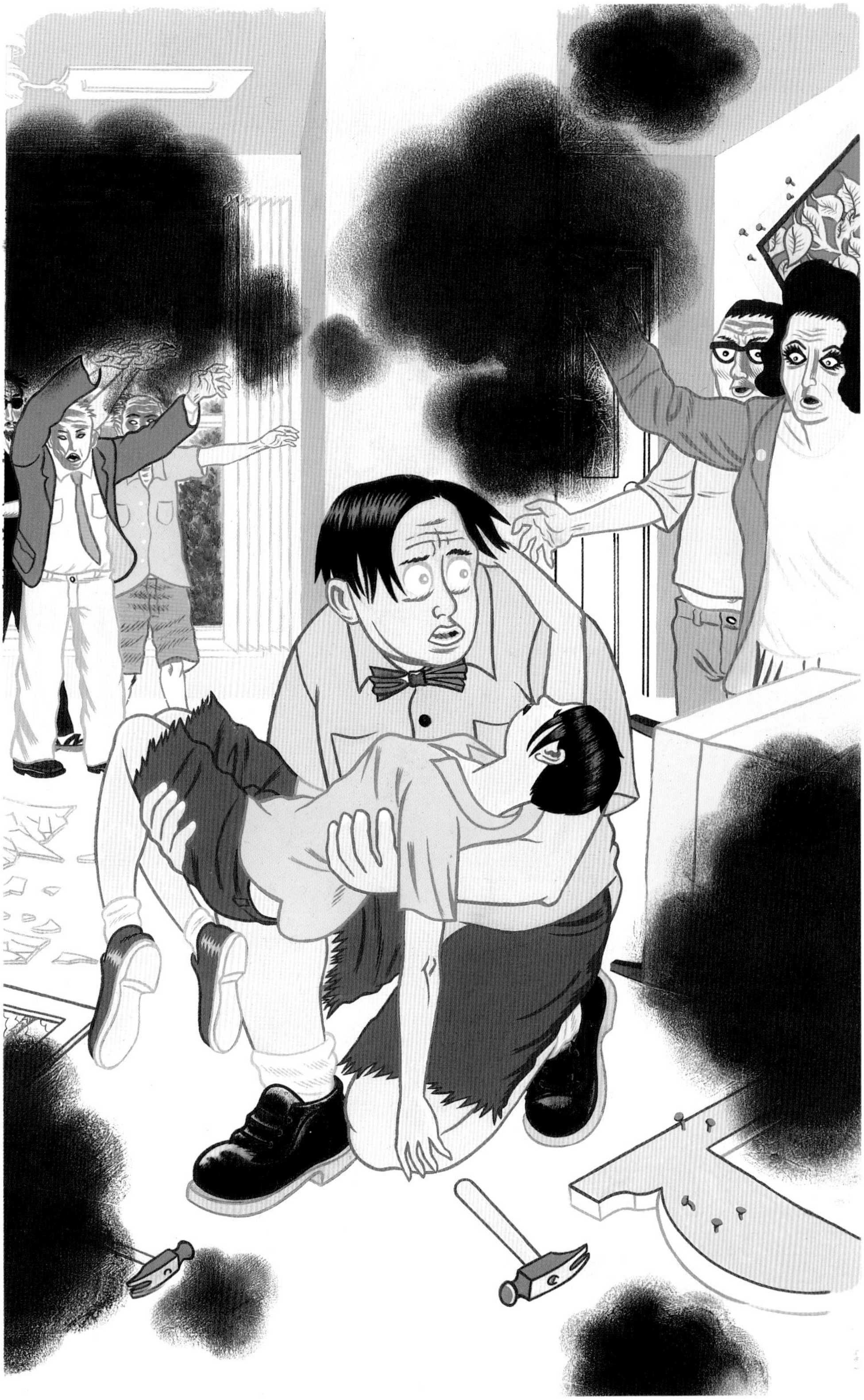

ORIGINAL TP COVER : A many layered acrylic painting from the 2001 collection.

The HORROR Of Collier County

ORIGINAL TITLE LOGO ART : I spent a whole day hand lettering the above logo.

ORIGINAL TP BACK COVER : A quick (and messy) watercolor from the 2001 collection.

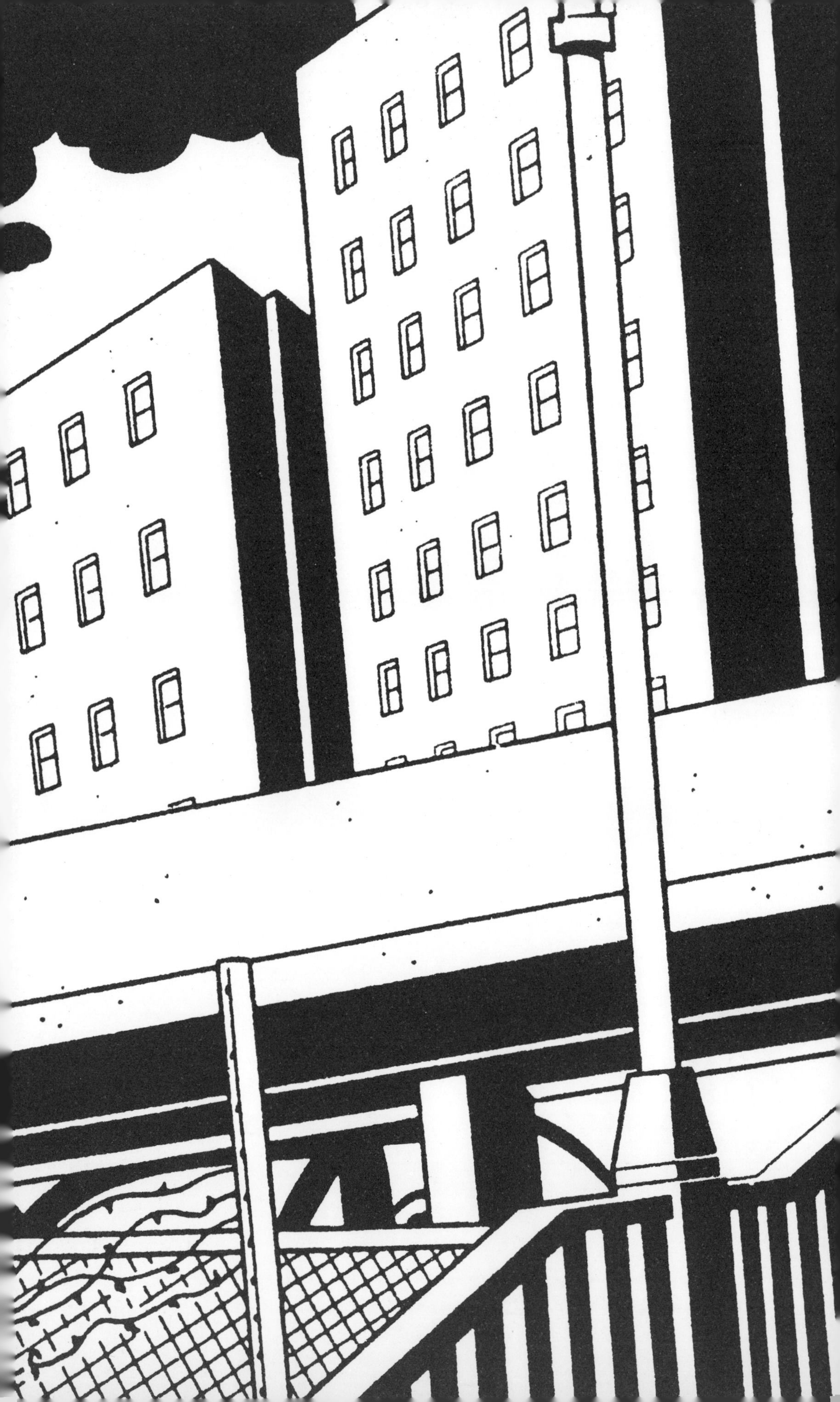

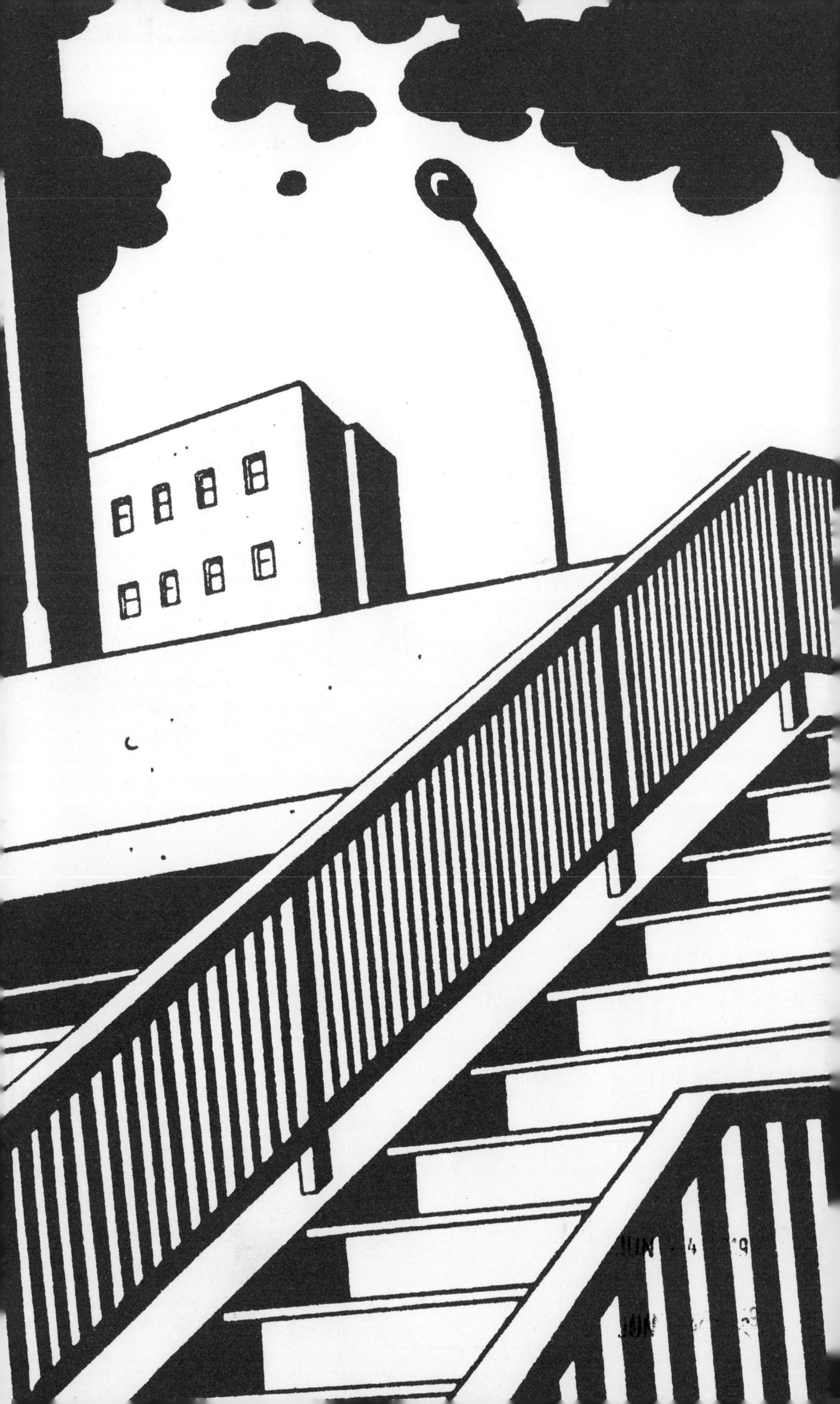